VISUAL QUICKPRO GUIDE

MAC OS X SERVER 10.3 PANTHER

Schoun Regan with Kevin White

⊙ Peachpit Press

Visual QuickPro Guide
Mac OS X Server 10.3 Panther
Schoun Regan with Kevin White

Peachpit Press

1249 Eighth Street
Berkeley, CA 94710
510/524-2178
800/283-9444
510/524-2221 (fax)
Find us on the Web at www.peachpit.com.
To report errors, please send a note to errata@peachpit.com.
Peachpit Press is a division of Pearson Education.

Copyright © 2005 by Schoun Regan

Editor: Rebecca Gulick
Project Editor: Tiffany Taylor
Production Editor: Lisa Brazieal
Technical Editor: LeRoy Dennison
Compositor: Jerry Ballew
Indexer: Karin Arrigoni
Cover Design: The Visual Group
Cover Production: George Mattingly / GMD

ISBN 0-321-24252-1

9 8 7 6 5 4 3 2 1

Printed and bound in the United States of America

Dedication

This book is dedicated to the memory of Sally Regan. It was by her strength and love that I became who I am.

Acknowledgments

From Schoun:

I'd like to thank the following people: Sally Regan, for her guidance, patience, and love. She taught me how to teach others, and I will never ever be able to repay her enough for what she brought into my life. It is to her memory that I dedicate this work. To my wife Susan, daughter Amie, and son Dakota, who all tolerate me quite well (I am often surprised at *how* well). To my editors Tiffany, Rebecca, and LeRoy, who cornered the market on stress-management books while dealing with me. To my loyal sidekick Kevin White; a better Tonto hath no one. I could not have written this book without him. It was a true dual effort. I'd also like to thank for their help and assistance Mike Hoffhines; Michael Bartosh; Joel Rennich; Juan Fernandez; Jeff Hoover; Paul Kent; Kyle Harmon; Todd Harper; Perry Marteny; the MMR listserv; the fine folks at MacTown in Louisville, Kentucky; and Randy Lavy, for allowing me to play with those things called computers a long time ago. And a special thank you to the folks at the Howard Stern show. Finally, I'd like to thank the employees of the World Wide Customer Training group within Apple Computer. There are many ways to learn about Mac OS X and Mac OS X Server, but the courses created and managed by this group are by far the best out there: http://train.apple.com. Come visit us at MacTown in Louisville, Kentucky, and take an Apple Certified course from us.

From Kevin:

To my parents who raised me, to my friends who motivated me, to my mentors who taught me, and to all the people who gave me a chance, I dedicate my work in this book to you.

CONTENTS AT A GLANCE

TABLE OF CONTENTS

INTRODUCTION

Congratulations! You're about to enter the world of Mac OS X Server.

Mac OS X Server is a robust, scalable, and secure operating system that permits the administrator of the server to share files; run various service; protect networks; and store user, group, and computer data. Mac OS X Server is also an integral part of many multiplatform networks, connecting to PCs and Linux boxes without a care in the world. You can achieve all this using a few major applications built right into Mac OS X Server—and, of course, this book!

Why use Mac OS X Server?

Why not just share files from another Mac OS X Client machine or a Windows Server? You'll want to use Mac OS X Server because it was built to help you manage very difficult tasks easily. It works well with other operating systems and can be a file server for older Mac operating systems, such as Mac 8.6 and Mac 9.2, Mac OS X, all versions of Windows, Linux, and Unix systems—which makes it very versatile.

You can also use Mac OS X Server as a Web server. Since it runs Apache, you'll be running one of the most secure and widely used Web servers on the Internet! You'll want to store all your users and groups on your Mac OS X Server so those users can take advantage of the single sign-on features afforded by being a Kerberos KDC. Mostly, you'll want to use Mac OS X Server because it was built to be secure: This, above all else, is the reason to switch from other, less secure server operating systems.

This book is your first step when you're deciding how to use Mac OS X Server.

How Mac OS X Server works

Now that you've decided Mac OS X Server will take its place in your network, you'll be happy to know that it's based on Mac OS X Client. Mac OS X Server works well because Mac OS X is based on Unix. This allows Apple to leverage all the power behind Unix and harness that power for you.

Mac OS X Server works by allocating various processes to do the work. These processes know how to act because they read from their configuration files before they start. You can manage the processes by using Apple's GUI server administration tools to make changes to their configuration files.

When I contemplate all the things Mac OS X Server can do, it becomes almost formidable to attempt to contain it all in one book. After all, Apple has generously sprinkled open-source software throughout Mac OS X and Mac OS X Server. Consider Apache for Web services, Samba for Windows file sharing, CUPS for printing, FreeBSD for some of the underlying substructure, BIND for DNS, Postfix and Cyrus for email, and so on. These applications are versatile and expandable; and when a GUI interface is placed on top of them, they become easier for those attempting to harness the power within them to understand. If nothing else, Mac OS X Server is a well-balanced collection of open-source software controlled primarily by buttons, frames, pop-up menus, and check boxes.

Not only is Mac OS X Server peppered with open-source software, the computer acronym game also is alive and well. LDAP, DNS, KDC, ipfw, var, QTSS, IMAP, SSL.... Each requires an explanation, and if you're purchasing Mac OS X Server for the first time, you may feel a little overwhelmed.

Added to the mix are the Xserve and the Xserve RAID, Apple's foray into the enterprise market. With the Xserve, we have the first Apple computer designed to be administered without the administrator sitting directly in front of the server itself—something totally foreign to most long-time Mac users. In fact, the Xserve doesn't even come with a video card! (If you want one, you must add it as an option.)

The remote administration aspect of the Xserve often leads to your first introduction to Unix. Powerful, expandable, customizable, dangerous, wonderful, old school—take your pick. If you want to really learn about Mac OS X Server, you should know a little about Unix.

Who should read this book?

Knowing what Mac OS X Server is about, what it can do, and how it works is what this book is all about. Buyers of this book will learn the basics of installing, setting up, and managing various services of Mac OS X Server. Novice users of Mac OS X Server will get the most out of this book, but veterans of Mac OS X Server will pick up valuable tips and tricks. No matter what your experience with Mac OS X Server, this book will provide solutions to questions you may have.

I've made every attempt to cover the most common uses of Mac OS X Server, but there was no way to include every possible service and every possible permutation, or to anticipate every possible use of Mac OS X Server. What you have before you is an attempt to get you up and running as quickly and correctly as possible. A good foundation goes a long way.

Before you begin...

Before you start your experience with Mac OS X Server, you should install the Mac OS X Server Administration tools on your Mac OS X Client computer so you can manage your server remotely (you can find these tools by searching Apple's support Web site). You should also have the Terminal application handy, possibly by placing it in your Dock; and you'll want to know a little about the network on which you're installing Mac OS X Server, such as what IP addresses are used on that network and whether that network is totally off—or connected to—the Internet.

About this book

When you're ready to go, you can use this book in a variety of ways. You can leaf through the chapters and tasks, locating just the tasks you want to do and following them from beginning to end. You can also read the book from start to finish, following the tasks along the way.

Since Mac OS X Server uses many services, several of them are interrelated. Be sure you read the DNS section of Chapter 6, "Network Configuration Options," and all of Chapter 3, "Open Directory," to understand what you want to do with your server before you start clicking buttons. Then, head to the sections of the book that are most relevant for your needs. If all you want to do is make your Mac OS X Server a QTSS, you can skim over the DNS section of Chapter 6 and head directly to Chapter 12, "QuickTime Streaming Server." Users of Mac OS X Server in the educational field will appreciate the user, group, and computer management discussion in Chapter 13, "Client Management." Use the book the way it was intended: as a guide to the basic setup and management of Mac OS X Server.

Resources

While you're using Mac OS X Server, you should keep track of current updates and other tips and tricks that pop up as Apple updates the software. Following are some resources to keep handy:

◆ http://train.apple.com/—Information about Apple's Training courses.

◆ http://www.apple.com/support/macosxserver/—Apple's support site for Mac OS X Server.

◆ http://www.openldap.org/—The place to learn more about LDAP, which is a must when you're dealing with Mac OS X Server and many users and groups.

◆ http://web.mit.edu/kerberos/www/krb5-1.3/krb5-1.3.1/doc/krb5-admin.html—MIT's site about Kerberos.

- http://alienraid.org/—A site devoted to using Apple's Xserve RAID in non-Apple environments.

- http://www.itinstruction.com/—Training and education for Mac OS X and Mac OS X Server.

- http://www.afp548.com/—An excellent resource to find all sorts of advanced tips and tricks for dealing with various aspects of Mac OS X Server.

- http://www.mac-mgrs.org/—A site devoted to a listserve that focuses on managing and troubleshooting Mac OS X and Mac OS X Server. If you can't find the answer anywhere else in the world, do your homework, read the list rules, and get your answers here. This is Mac-based community support at its finest.

- http://www.macenterprise.org/—The Mac OS X enterprise deployment project.

Software updates

Once a major version of server software is installed and working, the next major version generally isn't implemented immediately upon release, because issues may arise that make the server unusable—something not acceptable in an environment where the server must be running smoothly 24-7-365. Apple has plans to release its next major update to Mac OS X (Tiger) sometime in mid-2005. When Tiger Server comes out, careful evaluation of the initial release will reveal incredible additions as well as minor annoyances that will be attended to in updates to come. This is the game we play with software updates; but in the server market, careful evaluation and prudence should rule the day. While writing this book, I took careful notice of updates, and this book is as correct as it can be up to 10.3.6.

PLANNING AND INSTALLATION

One of the biggest decisions you're likely to make about Mac OS X Server is how to use it within your particular environment. Servers generally hold and distribute the crux of the information that flows throughout the organization. How many client machines will there be? What platforms must you support: Mac OS X? Windows? Mac OS 9? What services will you run? On what type of machine will you install Mac OS X Server? If you use an Xserve (Apple's rack-mountable server), will you be adding an Xserve RAID? Will you be adding two or three servers to your mix? How should you divide the workload? Will this be an upgrade instead of an install?

These questions and others are part of proper planning before you install Mac OS X Server. Knowing exactly what your requirements are will assist you in making the correct decisions. Once the planning is complete, it's time to decide how to partition your disks, if necessary, and then format them using the style of your choice. After the formatting is finished, you can install the server software.

Installation of Mac OS X Server is easy—almost too easy. You'd think that a server system this powerful would require all day to install. Not so. As long as you meet Apple's hardware requirements, the installation should take place without a hitch, in about 20 minutes, depending on the hardware configuration. One of the decisions you'll make is where to install Mac OS X Server. Another is whether you wish to install the server software while sitting in front of the Macintosh or from a remote location. Apple's Xserve server hardware mounts in a rack and can be purchased without a video card (meaning you can't connect a monitor to it), thus making remote installation, configuration, and management a necessity. You can also attach a RAID system to the Xserve. Apple's foray into the RAID array is called Xserve RAID, a hardware RAID array that can be used with Apple's Xserve and other platforms as well. Regardless of the hardware, there are a few things you'll need prior to installation.

Planning Your Deployment

Think about what Mac OS X Server can do—
offer various services such as file sharing,
storing user data, and running a Web server—and then think about what you want it
to do. **Table 1.1** lists the possible services
that Mac OS X Server offers, to help you
choose the ones you wish to implement.

Table 1.1

Major Mac OS X Server Services

SERVICE	DESCRIPTION	YOU MIGHT IMPLEMENT THIS SERVICE WHEN…
Application Server	Runs Java servlet or Tomcat applications directly from the server	You have qualified applications that must run from the server
AFP File Sharing	Shares files over the Apple Filing Protocol to other Macintosh computers	Users need to share files with both older and newer Macintosh operating systems
DHCP Server	Offers IP addresses and associated information to other computers and devices	Mac OS X Server is needed to offer addresses to all other devices, regardless of operating system
Domain Name Server	Directs requests for listed fully qualified domain names to be directed to given IP addresses	You want the server to have a fully qualified domain name, such as applecore.com
Firewall	Protects the server and network from possible attacks	Protection of the server is paramount
FTP File Sharing	Allows access to the server via the ubiquitous File Transfer Protocol	Users must transfer files to your server from a variety of operating systems and you aren't too concerned about security
Kerberos Key Distribution Services	Allows authorization of services without sending the password across the network	The services you wish to offer allow Kerberized connections, thus increasing security
LDAP Directory Server	Holds user information such as long name, short name, user ID, and preference settings	You want greater management capabilities over all your users
Mail Server	Used to send and/or receive mail	Users need to send and receive mail
NetBoot Server	Allows qualified Macintosh computers on the network to boot from a disk image on the server	You have a lab setting and want to boot and/or reconfigure disks on several Macintosh computers at once
Network Address Translation Service	Acts as a router, sending information from one network to another	You have two network cards pointing to two different networks
NFS File Sharing	Facilitates sharing with Unix machines	You need to share files with Linux or other Unix machines
Printer Server	Creates and manages printer queues and quotas	Control over printers is required
QuickTime Streaming Server	Streams live or prerecorded audio and video content	Video/Audio files need to be seen by others locally and over the Internet
SMB File Sharing	Shares files with Windows computers	Users need to share files with Windows computers
Virtual Private Network Server	Permits the secure connection of remote clients	Remote clients need to log in to your server in a secure fashion
Web Server	Serves up Web sites	There is at least one Web site you want others to have access to

With all these services available to you, keep in mind that they tax your RAM, CPU, and hard disk(s). If you have a newer computer, you could run several of these services on one machine, but with older computers you're more limited. Your budget may only allow for a single Mac OS X Server, or you may have been asked to install Mac OS X Server on a much older Macintosh with just the bare system requirements. In later chapters, we discuss which services tax server hardware the most and which are likely to work fine on older Macintosh computers.

As you saw in Table 1.1, a variety of services can be run on Mac OS X Server. Some of the more popular implementations of Mac OS X Server are as a Lightweight Directory Access Protocol (LDAP) directory server; as an Apple Filing Protocol (AFP), a Server Message Block (SMB), and/or a File Transfer Protocol (FTP) file server; or possibly as a print server. Other, older, more entrenched servers handle the duties of Domain Name Server (DNS), Dynamic Host Configuration Protocol (DHCP), Web, and email services. It's also likely that a separate server or other network device, such as a dedicated device designed just to protect your network, is providing security services, such as a firewall, network address translation, and/or a proxy service. Other servers probably provide secure remote logins and run as application servers.

Decide carefully what you want to run on your server. Overloading a new server with several services at once makes troubleshooting difficult. Don't misunderstand: Mac OS X Server on a multiprocessor G5 Xserve with 2 GB of RAM can handle just about anything thrown at it. But turning on services without proper planning can lead to an insecure server and possible conflicts later.

continues on next page

PLANNING YOUR DEPLOYMENT

Throughout, this book will discuss which services demand more of the server than others. Should this server be elevated in the hierarchy of computers in your organization, you might want to utilize a second network card so you can connect your server to another network, something that is standard on the G5 Xserve and was optional on the G4 Xserve. If you choose to have Mac OS X Server become your domain name server, take great pains to understand the ramifications involved: Incorrectly implementing the domain name server can cause many services not to function properly, as you'll see in Chapters 3 ("Open Directory") and 6 ("Network Configuration Options"). Often an existing domain name server is present, so making the Mac OS X Server a secondary domain name server is an excellent idea in case the first one fails. Allowing your Mac OS X Server to be the path between your local area network inside and the brutally insecure and hostile world of the outside Internet requires some education about the firewall rules, discussed in Chapter 10 ("Security").

For some, this will be the first time you've installed a server of any kind. Others may be adding Mac OS X Server to a network with existing servers that run a variety of software. Let's look at some popular scenarios that exist today.

Secondary server scenario

Let's examine a common scenario where one server—in this case, an Active Directory server—is already in place (we'll discuss Active Directory in Chapter 3). The Active Directory server is the primary domain name server and the directory data store. It may also be the application server, the DHCP server, and the print server. Mac OS X Server can fit perfectly into this network by providing file-sharing services for both the Macintosh and Windows computers on the network. Mac OS X Server can also control how the

Mac OS X client computer's preferences are handled, hold the folders where users store their data, function as an internal Web server (possibly running WebDAV), and run as a NetBoot server to allow the lab Macintosh computers to boot off an identical system disk every time (see Table 1.1 for a brief explanation of the services in this paragraph).

AppleShareIP server upgrade scenario

Another common scenario involves upgrading an AppleShareIP server to or replacing it with Mac OS X Server. In this case, the Mac OS X Server is king of the hill, responsible for the directory data store, domain name service, file and print services, DHCP, mail, and more. The server will likely have more services running than the ASIP server it's replacing, and it will be busy handling requests for all sorts of data. In this case, a fast connection utilizing the Macintosh's Gigabit Ethernet network card(s) will serve you best, because if you have a G5 Xserve, both network interfaces are likely to be active. If you're doing the upgrade on a PowerMac, you'll probably have one network interface that will be utilized to its full potential.

Megabit and Gigabit

Newer Macintosh computers can communicate with other devices on the network much faster than older ones. Whereas older computers started transferring data at 10 megabits per second, 100 megabits per second soon became the standard. Now, any PowerMac or Xserve you purchase can transfer data at 1000 megabits per second! This transfer rate is called *1 Gigabit per second*; and since it's done over the Ethernet interface, it's commonly referred to Gigabit Ethernet.

A Bit about Unix and Mac OS X Server

Mac OS X and Mac OS X Server were built on top of Unix. This book isn't intended to teach you Unix; however, you should know some basics before you dive into Mac OS X Server. Planning your installation with a nod toward optional Unix administration makes good sense.

With that in mind, know that Mac OS X Server was designed to be administered either locally or remotely with a few main tools, as you'll see in the next chapter. It was also designed with the option to be administered almost totally from the command line. Understanding a few fundamentals of the command-line structure will help you better manage Mac OS X Server.

The structure of Unix lends itself to the path style of naming, such as /Applications/iTunes, where Applications is a folder and iTunes is the item within that folder. If the folder begins with a slash (/), then you can assume the folder is sitting on the top level of the hard disk or volume. In this book, we'll use this method to describe the location of items.

The main application used to launch a command-line interface is the Terminal, which is located inside /Applications/

Utilities. After Mac OS X Server has been configured, the Terminal is automatically placed in the Dock for you.

If you can use a command-line interface while sitting in front of a computer, you can use that interface to manage any other Mac OS X and/or Mac OS X Server system by remotely accessing that computer. Mac OS X Server has a command-line process (a *process* is an application that, in this case, has no user interface) called the ssh daemon (sshd for short) running automatically. This process allows a user to log in to the server from a remote location.

It's easy to log in to your Mac OS X Server from a remote machine. Open the Terminal application, and type the following: ssh *server-administrator's-short-name@ip-address-of-the-server* and press Return. Answer yes to the next question about setting up a key, press Return again, and enter the server administrator's password.

You're now logged in to your Mac OS X Server from where you sit, and you can manage things remotely with several command-line tools at your disposal. These tools take a bit of getting used to, but they can often save you a trip to the location of the server to change a setting.

NetBoot server scenario

This scenario involves setting up a Mac OS X Server as a school NetBoot server. This server provides the initial startup image. It erases the internal hard disk on each machine in the school's various labs and copies customized, bootable images; each lab receives the appropriate image for its particular task that day. This server may also act as the directory data store, allowing students to log in from anywhere in the school and see their home folder.

QuickTime Streaming server scenario

In this scenario, a server has been set up as a QuickTime Streaming server and possibly a QuickTime Broadcaster server. This server's job is to take live input from a camera and stream it out to all employees, allowing them to watch the CEO's latest company announcement. When it isn't being used as a live streaming server, it streams audio and video content stored as movie files on the server to employees' desktops. These files consist of mandatory safety videos, human resource updates, and meetings recorded earlier so that attendees can gather information they missed in the initial meeting. All these audio and video streams are, of course, logged to a file so human resources can document who watched what safety video and when. The result is a reduction in the amount of time employees spend away from their desks engaging in such mandatory activities.

Each of these scenarios takes proper planning to set up, deploy, and install Mac OS X Server, and they are by no means the only uses of Mac OS X Server. Nor are you pigeonholed into a particular scenario, running only the configurations mentioned here. The bottom line is to carefully evaluate your needs, what role Mac OS X Server will play with respect to those needs, and how Mac OS X Server will grow and possibly take over the duties of some lesser, inferior servers.

System Requirements

Mac OS X Server 10.3's system requirements aren't much different than those of Mac OS X Client 10.3. The reason is that Mac OS X Server is Mac OS X Client, with three extra packages:

- QuickTimeStreamingServer.pkg
- ServerAdministrationSoftware.pkg
- ServerEssentials.pkg

You can download and install the QuickTime Streaming Server from Apple's Web site on your Mac OS X Client Macintosh. Called the Darwin Streaming Server, it's identical to QuickTime Streaming Server without the trademark name QuickTime.

You can also download and install the Server Administration Software package on your client machine. These are the server administration tools discussed in Chapter 2, "Server Tools."

That leaves one package. ServerEssentials.pkg is all that separates Mac OS X Client and Mac OS X Server. And inside that package, what really makes Mac OS X Server tick?

- Squirrel Mail (Web-based email interface)
- Mailman (mailing list manager)
- Cyrus (POP and IMAP mail server)
- FTP Server Directory
- Streaming directories for each user
- Extra print frameworks
- Apache 2.0 (in case you want to use it instead of Apache 1.x)
- Five Apple-specific Apache modules
- MySQL files

continues on next page

SYSTEM REQUIREMENTS

- A few migration files

- Eleven additional Startup items: NAT,
  IPFilter, IPFailover, IPAliases, Mailman,
  Watchdog, MySQL, Samba, Headless
  Startup, SerialTerminalSupport, and
  ServerManagerDaemon

- About 96 additional executables (processes that run in the background, or
  useful Unix utilities)

- Additional and edited configuration files
  for the new Startup items

As you can see, the only things absolutely
necessary to make a Mac OS X Client a Mac
OS X Server are the executables, the configuration files (almost all stored in the hidden
/private/etc directory), and the Startup
items. The other items are necessary to utilize some of the services that run on Mac
OS X Server, but there is little difference
between the two.

The hardware requirements for Mac OS X
Server are listed in **Table 1.2**. Keep in mind
that although Apple has a set of hardware
requirements, this table includes a column
of real-world requirements.

Apple doesn't support Mac OS X Server on
PowerBooks or iBooks, although it works on
those machines. If you just want to install
Mac OS X Server and poke around, looking
at and testing the services with one or two
client machines attached to a small network,
running the server software on a portable
Macintosh works fine.

✔ Tip

- Mac OS X Server works more reliably
  when it's plugged into an active Ethernet
  connection as opposed to an AirPort or
  FireWire connection.

Table 1.2

Hardware Requirements for Mac OS X Server 10.3		
	APPLE REQUIREMENTS	REAL-WORLD REQUIREMENTS
Macintosh type	eMac, iMac, PowerMac G3, PowerMac G4, PowerMac G5, Xserve	PowerMac G4, PowerMac G5, or Xserve
Hard Disk Size	4 GB	80 GB
RAM	128 minimum, 256 high demand	1 GB minimum
Other	Built-in USB	Built-in USB, Gigabit Ethernet

Partitioning Choices

You've planned the services to run on your Mac OS X Server and chosen the hardware on which the server will reside. It's now time to decide if you wish to partition the disk.

Partitioning your disk allows you to easily reformat one partition while keeping software or data on the other. However, partitioning may waste valuable disk space and be less secure, depending on the way the partitions are formatted. You might want to partition a disk to separate the data from the operating system. Or, you might wish to have three partitions: one containing the operating system, one containing the data, and one to back up the data or the operating system. There is no right or wrong way to proceed when you're dealing with partitions. However, with respect to Mac OS X Server, you undoubtedly know the value of backing up your data to another physical location; so, having a local partition for backup isn't likely to be useful.

You have the option of partitioning the disk whether you're installing Mac OS X Server on a Mac with a single disk or multiple disks, such as a RAID array. For example, you may have an Xserve RAID or an Xserve that supports hardware RAID (the G5 Xserve has an option to support hardware RAID via an optional internal hardware RAID card).

✔ Tips

■ Remember, partitioning a disk erases all the data on that disk!

■ It isn't necessary to create several partitions from your disk. Many people run their server software on a nonpartitioned disk.

Clarifying Some Terms

Now is a good time to look at some terminology to ensure that you understand this book's geek-speak (**Table 1.3**).

Table 1.3

Computer Terminology Regarding Disks

Term	Meaning	Examples
Storage device	Any item connected to your Macintosh that can store information. Storage devices may have the ability to be partitioned.	FireWire hard disk, iPod, USB hard disk, Flash cards, USB storage device, PC storage cards.
Drive	A storage device that's physically connected to the computer and that has or can read from spinning platters or disks.	Hard disk drive, CD-ROM drive, SuperDrive.
Disk	A storage device or the part of a storage device that actually stores data. Sometimes used to describe a partition.	CD-ROM disk, hard disk, or external disk, such as a Zip disk.
Volume	A logical section of a disk that can store files. Volumes are always partitions, even if a disk contains only one partition.	If a hard disk is partitioned into three volumes, each volume appears as a separate icon on the desktop.
Media	Items that store information and that generally are disposable and plentiful.	CD-Rs, CD-RWs, DVD-Rs, DVD-RAMs, floppy disks, Zip disks.
RAID	Redundant Array of Independent Disks. Makes several drives act and look like a single drive. Levels of RAID exist.	Since RAID arrays are multiple disks, examples generally involve additional internal hard disks or preconfigured external RAID systems such as Xserve RAID from Apple.

RAID Review

RAID stands for Redundant Array of Independent Disks. The concept is easy to understand: Take two disks, make the operating system think they're one disk, and you can perform digital magic.

For example, if the operating system thinks it has one big disk, you can have the RAID software write the same information to both disks. The reason to do this is clear: redundancy of data (fault tolerance). If disk one fails, disk two has the identical data. This is known as RAID level 1. **Table 1.4** describes the RAID levels.

RAID systems must have at least two disks but can have several, based on the configuration and your budget. RAID can be software based or hardware based; hardware-based RAID is more versatile.

Apple's support for RAID involves both software and hardware RAID. The Disk Utility application can do software RAID on disks, and hardware RAID is supported by Apple's Xserve and Xserve RAID. The G5 Xserve can hold 3 disks, the G4 Xserve can hold 4; the Xserve RAID can hold up to 14 disks over two controllers and is managed by an application called RAID Admin.

Table 1.4

RAID Levels and Their Uses

RAID NUMBER	RAID NAME	IMPLEMENTATION	ADVANTAGES	DISADVANTAGES
0	Striping	Writes small amounts of data to each drive, switching back and forth	Speed	No gain in disk space / If one disk dies, all data is lost (no fault tolerance)
1	Mirroring	Writes identical data to both drives	Fault tolerance / Hot swapping of disks, if supported	No gain in disk space
3	Striping with parity	Writes to each disk, and writes a parity check to a separate disk	Speed	Usually involves a move to hardware RAID
0+1	Mirrored striping	Two sets of striped arrays	Speed / Fault tolerance	Somewhat expensive
5	Distributed parity	Writes data to each disk; parity is written across the disks	Extremely fast read rates / Fault tolerance	Somewhat slower writes / Three-disk minimum to implement
10	Mirroring	Mirrored array is striped across two RAID controllers	RAID level 1 advantages over two controllers	Four-disk minimum to implement
30	Striping with parity	Parity and striping across two controllers	RAID level 3 advantages over two controllers	Six-disk minimum to implement
50	Distributed parity with striping	Writes data to each disk; parity is written across disks across two controllers	RAID level 5 advantages over two controllers	Six-disk minimum to implement

When you're setting up Mac OS X Server for the first time, you'll boot from Install CD 1. Once you've booted off a Mac OS X Server CD, you have access to the disk(s) via Disk Utility on the CD and remotely via ssh (the ssh daemon doesn't run when you boot from a Mac OS X Client CD). You'll likely run Disk Utility and partition the disk(s) in this manner.

To partition a disk:

1. Boot from the Mac OS X Server Install CD 1.

2. Choose Installer > Open Disk Utility.

   The Disk Utility window appears, showing all mounted volumes in the left pane's disk and volume list.

3. Select your disk from the disk list menu.

4. Click the Partition tab (**Figure 1.1**).

5. Choose the number of partitions you wish to create from the Volume Scheme pop-up menu.

6. Click each partition in the map below the pop-up menu, and give it a name, format, and size.

   Recall that the minimum size for a Mac OS X Server 10.3 hard disk is 4 GB.

7. Click the Partition button, and wait for the confirmation dialog. Then click the Partition button in the confirmation dialog (**Figure 1.2**).

8. Choose Disk Utility > Quit Disk Utility.

   You have now partitioned your disk into individual volumes.

Command-Line Partitioning

diskutil is a useful command that lets you partition a disk when a Mac OS X Server is booted from a CD and is on the same subnet as another machine running a Unix shell (see the later sidebar "Subnetting" for more information about subnets). When Mac OS X Server boots from a CD, the ssh daemon is running, meaning you can see it and connect to it via the command line. Once you've connected, diskutil can be used to partition, format, and name disks and volumes. To learn more about diskutil, type diskutil from the command line.

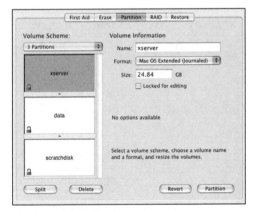

Figure 1.1 Click the Partition tab.

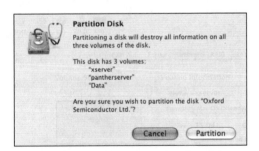

Figure 1.2 Click Partition in the confirmation dialog.

Disk Formatting Options

Disks and partitions can be formatted in a variety of ways depending on how you wish to utilize them. Mac OS X Server 10.3 prefers to format a disk as Mac OS X Extended (Journaled). This is a departure from previous versions of Mac OS X Server. Let's look at the various formatting options (**Table 1.5**).

Formatting as Mac OS X Extended (Journaled) is your best bet, because adding case sensitivity may cause problems with Classic and SMB mounts. Mac OS Extended (Journaled) adds built-in protection for the directory; the journaling process stores any related changes made in a journal and then writes them to their normal locations on the disk all at once. In the case of an unexpected shutdown or hard crash, the state of the journal dictates whether the changes are written to disk or ignored.

✔ Tip

- For more information on journaling, please refer to http://developer.apple.com/technotes/tn/tn1150.html#Journal.

If you aren't partitioning the disk, you have the option of wiping, or *zeroing*, the disk. Doing so erases the disk so that any data previously on the disk is now essentially unrecoverable (although companies such as Drive Savers can attempt the recovery of data, albeit for a price). Zeroing a large disk will increase the amount of time before an installation can take place.

Another important choice to make is how you name your disk(s). In days of old, Macintosh users named their disks whatever they wished. Since multiplatform functionality is paramount with Mac OS X Server, you may wish to use all small letters, no spaces, and no other characters in the name of the

continues on next page

Table 1.5

Disk Formatting Options	
FORMAT	USE
DOS	Compatible with FAT (Windows) file systems
Mac OS X Extended	Hierarchical File System Extended Format (HFS+)
Mac OS X Extended (Journaled)	HFS+ with constant directory backup (journaling)
Mac OS X Extended (Journaled + Case Sensitive)	HFS+ with constant directory backup (journaling) plus added case sensitivity
Unix file system	Case sensitive but can't be a boot volume for Mac OS X Server; no support for resource forks
Free space	Unformatted space used for Linux or some other operating system

DISK FORMATTING OPTIONS

disk. Although naming your disk "My Mac OS X Server 10.3" is fine, you may find that "osxserver" works better in the long run. Minimizing the length of the name will offer an advantage in certain areas, as you'll see later.

To wipe a disk:

1. Boot from the Mac OS X Server Install CD 1.

2. Choose Installer > Open Disk Utility.

3. Select your disk from the disk list menu.

4. Select the Erase tab.

5. Select a disk formatting structure from the Volume Format pop-up menu.

6. Choose a name for the disk.

7. Click the Options button near the bottom of the window.

   The Erase Options dialog opens (**Figure 1.3**).

8. Choose the erase options you wish to invoke, and click the OK button.

9. Click the Erase button, and wait for the confirmation dialog. Then, click the Erase button in the confirmation dialog (**Figure 1.4**).

10. When the erase and format are finished, you may wish to run Verify Disk `Verify Disk` from the First Aid tab `First Aid` on your newly formatted disk or volumes.

    Doing so ensures the integrity of the newly formatted disk or volumes.

11. Choose Disk Utility > Quit Disk Utility.

    Your disk has now been erased and formatted and is ready for the installation of Mac OS X Server.

✔ Tip

■ Using the `diskutil` command-line utility to format your disk(s) is perfectly acceptable and is an excellent way to format disks from a remote location on an Xserve booted from a Mac OS X Server CD 1.

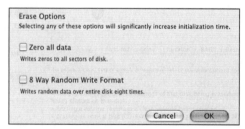

Figure 1.3 In the Erase Options dialog, choose the erase options you wish to invoke.

Figure 1.4 Click Erase in the Erase Disk confirmation dialog.

System Installation

Once the disk has been partitioned (if necessary) and properly formatted, you can turn to the installation of software.

The Mac OS X Server software ships on two CDs, with a third CD containing the Admin Tools (covered in Chapter 2). This means that someone must physically be at the server location to swap CDs. This is somewhat different than the restore DVDs included with most Macintosh computers sold today, because those require only one DVD to restore the Macintosh. The install can be performed a few ways: You can install the software using the Installer GUI while sitting at the machine or remotely, or you can install it remotely via the command line. Unless the machine has been supplied with a real-world IP address, automatic discovery of servers is done via Rendezvous, as you'll see later. Since most installs are on cleanly formatted disks, let's begin there.

After booting the machine off the first installer CD, you're presented with Server Assistant's initial setup screen. However, much more is going on behind the scenes.

First, if there is a DHCP server on the network, your Macintosh has likely picked up an address from it. If the server is doling out real-world IP addresses, the installation and configuration can start from halfway around the world. If the address is private, installation and configuration can take place from your network. If a DHCP server is absent, the Macintosh will assign itself an IP address in the 169.254.x.x range; this self-assigned address is a function of Rendezvous, Apple's term for its implementation of ZeroConf. If this is the case, remote installation can take place from any Macintosh on the local subnet.

continues on next page

Second, the ssh daemon is running, meaning you can access the machine remotely via the command line. This will only work via the built-in Ethernet (serial on Xserve) interface on the Macintosh that is to become the server. If you wish to install the server software while sitting in front of the Macintosh that's booted from the CD, you're set; you won't need the information required next (except the server software serial number), although you should be aware of the remote install procedures.

Before you run away from your soon-to-be-server to do the remote installation, you'll need three things:

◆ *Server software serial number*—The 29-digit array that allows you to configure and use Mac OS X Server software.

◆ *Ethernet addresses*—A unique, 12-digit address that is used, in this case, to identify the server when installing remotely. It can be found in several places, depending on the model of Macintosh involved. For example, on PowerMacs, it will be on the back of the computer.

◆ *Hardware serial number*—The first eight digits of the hardware serial number are the root password used to authenticate your access to remotely install and configure that server. On older Macintosh computers, root's password is 12345678 (yes, it's typed correctly). This serial number can also be found in several locations, depending on the Macintosh model.

You should also take Install CD 2 or download the Server Admin tools from Apple's Web site and install them on the remote administration machine. Remote GUI installation and administration can't take place without the Server Admin tools package being installed. Let's examine three installation methods: local, remote GUI, and remote command line.

IP Address Review

The Internet is made up of millions of devices, communicating with each other in a flurry of activity, all so you can send and receive email, chat with others, visit the Peachpit Web site, and so on. In order for this communication to take place, computers must all be talking the same basic language: Internet Protocol (IP). The protocol most associated with this is Transmission Control Protocol (TCP). The combination is often expressed as TCP/IP.

Let's review the addresses, because a good understanding of IP addressing will help you understand how to implement Mac OS X Server in your environment. IP addressing comes in three main ranges—A, B, and C (there are more, but this book will stick to the first three)—and two types—routable and non-routable. The three primary IP address ranges are

◆ A 0–127

◆ B 128–191

◆ C 192–253

Each range includes a set of IP addresses that the Internet doesn't care about. (There is much more to the story here. This discussion is only concerned with the basics.) These are often referred to as *non-routable, or Private address ranges.* They are

◆ In the A range 10.x.x.x

◆ In the B range 172.16.x.x

◆ In the C range 192.168.x.x

continues on next page

IP Address Review *(continued)*

If a computer or device has any address in these ranges, it can't (without the help of another device) communicate directly with another computer or device on the Internet. You should know whether your Mac OS X Server will have an IP address the rest of the world can see, commonly known as Public IP addresses, or if it will only be used inside your organization, possibly with a non-routable address-commonly known as Private IP addresses. This will make a difference when you attempt to communicate with other devices on the Internet.

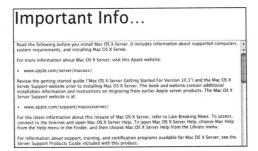

Figure 1.5 Initial Welcome screen of Server Assistant running from a remote Macintosh.

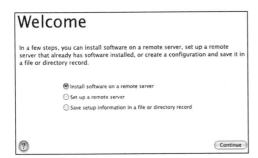

Figure 1.6 Important Information window.

To install Mac OS X Server locally:

1. Boot the Macintosh from the Mac OS X Server CD 1.

2. Click the Continue button ⟨ Continue ⟩ on the Welcome window (**Figure 1.5**).

3. Scroll through and read the Important Information window for any additional information (**Figure 1.6**).

4. Scroll through and accept the license agreement (**Figure 1.7**).

5. Choose the destination disk or volume, and click the Continue button.

6. Click the Customize button to remove or change components to be installed. You may wish to remove print drivers and additional languages here.

7. Click the Install button to begin the installation.

8. After the server reboots, insert Mac OS X Server CD 2 to finish the installation process.
   After the second CD is finished, Mac OS X Server is ready for the configuration stage.

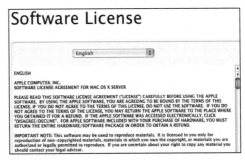

Figure 1.7 License Agreement window.

To install Mac OS X Server from a remote Macintosh using Server Assistant:

1. Boot the Macintosh from the Mac OS X Server CD 1.

2. On your remote machine, navigate to and launch /Applications/Server/Server Assistant.

   You'll see the Welcome screen with three options:

   ▲ Install software on a remote server

   ▲ Set up a remote server

   ▲ Save setup information in a file or directory record

3. Choose "Install software on a remote server".

   The Destination window opens (**Figure 1.8**).

   Provided you're on the same subnet, you'll see your Mac OS X Server(s) listed with an IP address, hostname, Ethernet hardware address (commonly known as the MAC address [Media Access Control], the layer of the standard OSI model that deals with network hardware identification), and status. If there are more servers on your network, you may need to locate your server by identifying and matching its MAC or Ethernet address. The Status column indicates whether server software can be set up on that machine.

4. Clicking the Continue button initiates the authentication drop-down dialog asking for the server's password (**Figure 1.9**).

   Enter the password, click the OK button, and wait for authentication to take place (**Figure 1.10**).

Subnetting

A *subnet* is a set of computers and other devices that, by default, only see each other and are separated from other devices. A large organization may subnet its network using a logical divisor, such as one network for finance, one for manufacturing, and one for sales. Or it may choose to subnet based on location: Cleveland, Akron, and Canton. A subnet is often referred to as a *local network*.

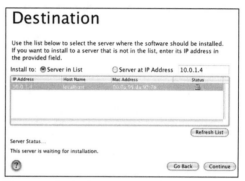

Figure 1.8 The destination screen shows a server in the list.

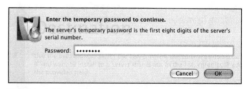

Figure 1.9 Enter the server's password in the authentication drop-down dialog.

Figure 1.10 Authentication indicator.

Rendezvous

Apple wisely added ZeroConf (Zero Configuration) support to Mac OS X and Mac OS X Server back in version 10.2. It called the implementation *Rendezvous*. Rendezvous does three main things:

◆ Assigns an IP address automatically if no DHCP server is present to provide an address. The IP address assigned is in the 169.254.x.x range.

◆ Shows the name you gave your computer instead of the IP address when others browse the local network for your computer.

◆ Provides the discovery of other Rendezvous services on the local network.

Although Rendezvous isn't configurable (remember, it's nothing more than ZeroConf), it will be important in later chapters, especially those dealing with file sharing.

5. Click through the following screens:

   ▲ The Language preference window.

   ▲ The Important Information window. It's a good idea to read all the information here before proceeding.

   ▲ The License Agreement and Agree windows.

6. In the Volumes window, decide which volume to install the server software on (**Figure 1.11**).

   This window shows the name of the volume, the format of the volume (including space available), and the current system, if any.

7. A system check is initiated automatically. Should incompatible software already exist on the disk or partition, a drop-down dialog appears, giving you three options (**Figure 1.12**):

   ▲ Don't Erase

   ▲ Erase and format as Mac OS Extended (Journaled)

   ▲ Erase and format as Unix File system

   Choose the option most suitable for your needs, and click the OK button.

   continues on next page

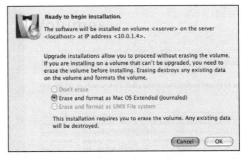

Figure 1.11 Volume format drop-down dialog.

Figure 1.12 The Installation window gives you several options.

SYSTEM INSTALLATION

8. The following Installation window has but one button: Install (**Figure 1.13**). Click this button to install the software on the Macintosh.

9. After a short period and an automatic reboot of the server, you'll be asked to insert the second install CD into the server (**Figure 1.14**).

You may need a second person physically located near the server to swap CDs for you. Doing so completes the installation of Mac OS X Server.

✔ Tips

- Keep the server disks in a safe place. If you're managing a server remotely, it may be a good idea to keep the Install CD 1 in the CD/DVD tray and/or affix the server serial number stickers to the CD itself.

- Apple has provided almost every GUI tool with a command-line equivalent. If you wish to install via the command line, you can do so. Booting from the Install CD 1 runs the ssh daemon, so you can discover and connect to the Macintosh with a command-line interface. To do so, you should install the Server Admin tools on the Macintosh from which you wish to issue commands.

Finding Your Server

The IP address in the Destination window can be the 169.254.x.x Rendezvous style with a host name of *localhost*; or, if a DHCP server is present, it may have an IP address and subsequent host name designated by the DHCP and DNS servers on your network. If you're in New York and you're setting up a server in Los Angeles, you can choose the Server at IP Address option in the Destination window and type in the real-world IP address of the machine booted off the CD in Los Angeles.

Installing...

Click Install to start installing Mac OS X Server software on volume <xserver>.

(Install)

Figure 1.13 Click Install to install the software on the Macintosh.

Installation Status

Software from Mac OS X Server Install Disc 1 has been installed on <xserver> on server <localhost> at IP address <10.0.1.4>.

You need to place Mac OS X Server Install Disc 2 into the drive on <localhost> at IP address <10.0.1.4> before installation can be completed.

Figure 1.14 You're asked to insert the second disk.

Packages and the Installer Command

Packages are collections of files that are placed on a disk. A package can contain all the files necessary for a certain application to run. Packages can also contain other packages. For example, the OSInstall package is a metapackage, which means it has instructions to install other packages.

The `installer` command is used to install packages via the command line. Some of the Unix flags include:

◆ Setting the language.

◆ Listing all packages inside a meta-package.

◆ Allowing older versions of packages to be installed over newer ones. This option is useful when you need to install an older update because the latest update caused issues with your computer.

◆ Showing installation progress via verbose output.

To install Mac OS X Server from a remote Macintosh using the command line:

1. Boot the Macintosh from the Mac OS X Server CD 1.

2. Open the Terminal application on your remote Macintosh.

3. Run the command-line tool `sa_srchr` by typing in

   `cd /System/Library/ServerSetup/`
   `sa_srchr 224.0.0.1`.

   This command searches out your local subnet and returns information about any Macintosh booted from a Mac OS X Server Install CD 1.

4. Locate the IP address in the returned information.

5. Type in `ssh root@`*the-IP-address-you-saw-in-step-four*, and authenticate using the Mac OS X Server's hardware serial number or 12345678 as the password.

6. Run the installer command by typing in

   `installer –pkg /System/Installation/`
   `Packages/OSInstall.mpkg –target/`
   `Volumes/`*name-of-your-volume*

   The computer on which you're installing Mac OS X Server will reboot after a successful installation.

✔ Tip

■ Always write down the Ethernet address, hardware serial number, and server software serial number and keep them handy in case you need to reinstall Mac OS X Server.

Viewing the Installation Log and Installed Files

Log files are a critical piece of the computer administration architecture. Mac OS X and Mac OS X Server keep log files in various locations:

- ◆ /var/log/
- ◆ /Library/Logs/
- ◆ *your-username*/Library/Logs/

You can view these log files locally with the Console application located in /Applications/Utilities/. Currently, the Console application doesn't allow remote viewing of log files, so if you wish to view the log files on your server from a remote location, you must ssh into the server and read the files via the command line.

Log files are especially useful during the installation process. When you're installing locally, you have the option of viewing errors during installation or viewing everything taking place during the installation, from the mounting of disks to the cleaning up of temporary files, which takes place after all packages have been installed. To view the install log remotely, run the `tail -f` command on the system log. Doing so will show the installation's progress and any errors that may crop up during the process.

To run the tail command on the system log during remote installation:

1. Open the Terminal application on the remote Macintosh.

2. ssh into your server prior to clicking the Install button in the Server Assistant:

   `ssh root@your-server's-current-ip-address`

3. Type `tail -f /var/log/system.log`.

4. Open a new Terminal window, and perform steps 5 and 6 of the previous task, "To install Mac OS X Server from a remote Macintosh using the command line."

5. View the system log in the first Terminal window as the software is being installed on your server.

2

SERVER TOOLS

When you install Mac OS X Server, the installer automatically installs a package called ServerAdministrationSoftware.pkg. Within this package are all the tools needed to manage Mac OS X Server. This package can be installed later on any Mac OS X client machine, allowing remote management of your server. Some of these tools can only be run from the command line. Some only work with the Xserve and the Xserve RAID. Some are only important if you're moving from an older server version, such as AppleShare IP or Mac OS X Server 1.2. Of all the tools, two of them—Server Admin and Workgroup Manager—are used to manage almost all aspects of Mac OS X Server. Additional applications found on both Mac OS X and Mac OS X Server fall under the category of server management, and this chapter will briefly look at these applications as well. This chapter also covers a variety of ways to update the software on your server.

Running Server Assistant

Once Mac OS X Server software is installed, it must be initially configured. This is the job of the Server Assistant tool, one of the server tools installed with Mac OS X Server.

Before you proceed with the configuration, have a few things handy:

◆ Your server's software serial number.

◆ Your server's hardware serial number (needed for remote installations).

◆ Your server's Ethernet (MAC) address (needed for remote installations).

◆ If you didn't receive a separate Administration Tools CD (**Figure 2.1**), use your server's second CD, which contains the Server Administration Software package; or download it from Apple's Web site.

If you're setting up the server remotely, install the Administration Tools on any Mac OS X Client from which you wish to administer the setup and management of Mac OS X Server.

Now that you have the appropriate information, consider what information is required for initial setup:

◆ Server language and keyboard layout options.

◆ The initial administrator's account.

◆ Name of the computer, in three variations:

  ▲ Host name

  ▲ Computer name

  ▲ Rendezvous name

◆ Network information such as primary interface, IP address, subnet mask, router, DNS server, and search domain.

Figure 2.1 The Administration Tools CD window.

Figure 2.2 Server Assistant allows you to choose the language...

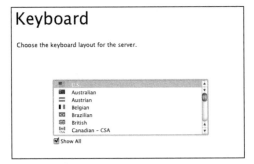

Figure 2.3 ...and keyboard layout of your Mac OS X Server.

◆ Server type and subsequent information:

  ▲ Stand-alone server

  ▲ Open Directory master

  ▲ Connected to a directory system

◆ Services you wish to start.

◆ Date, time, and time zone information.

◆ Whether to save server settings and, if so, how.

◆ Optional entries for the server you are about to set up, entered into the DNS zone files of your organization's existing DNS server (these may be out of your control; consult your network administrator about adding zone entries for your server). Although this information has no window or dialog associated with it, DNS is a critical piece of Mac OS X Server. See Chapter 6, "Network Configuration Options."

Let's examine each of these items in detail. Understanding what is asked of you in the Server Assistant can affect the future operation and performance of your Mac OS X Server. The screen snapshots you will see in the subsequent sections are from the Server Assistant.

Server language and keyboard layout options

Server Assistant allows you to choose the language (**Figure 2.2**) and keyboard layout (**Figure 2.3**) of your Mac OS X Server. You have several languages to choose from; multiple keyboard layouts are available for some languages.

Initial administrator's account

Any time you install software on an empty disk, you're required to create an initial user account. On a Mac OS X client, the initial user account, called the *local account*, is also an administrator, meaning it can manage files that others can't (nonadministrators, aka regular users). Mac OS X Server works the same way (**Figure 2.4**). One difference is that Mac OS X Server initially enables root and gives root the same password as the initial administrator (see the sidebar "Who Is Root?").

The short name of your initial user should be four to eight characters. (Don't use the short name admin.) Mac OS X and Mac OS X Server create a group for every user, and the group name for each user is the user's short name. Since you're dealing with Unix, there is already a group called admin.

✔ Tip

■ Never use mixed case when setting Mac OS X Server's initial administrator's short name. Doing so can prevent the Kerberos KDC from running.

Password Practices

You should *pick a password that's difficult to guess*. (Having an easy password on Mac OS X Server is like dangling your data out there for anyone to grab.) You can choose a password that's extremely long, but doing so may cause problems when you log in (you're likely to forget a 48-character password). You might want to choose an 8- to 12-character password that includes letters (both lowercase and uppercase), numbers, and possibly additional characters like an exclamation point or ampersand.

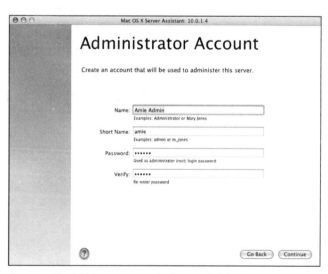

Figure 2.4 The initial user account is also an administrator.

Who Is Root?

Whereas regular administrators have read and write access to most areas of the file system, root (the short name for System Administrator) has full read and write access anywhere on the disk. Root can see all files, change any files, and delete anything, regardless of the owner. Root can also change ownership of any folder or file from anyone to anyone else. Obviously, root privileges are very powerful and, in the hands of a novice, very dangerous.

Many a Mac OS X administrator has logged in as root and inadvertently deleted folders; or created files for others to use, only to find out later that because they created the files and folders as root, others couldn't use them. To be on the safe side, use your root login sparingly.

Logged in as a regular administrator, you can generally place files and remove files from locations other users can't access, by *authenticating* (entering your user name and password) via a dialog that appears

when you attempt such a change. Similarly, when you launch the Terminal application while logged in as a regular administrator, you can temporarily get root powers by preceding any command with the word sudo (Super User Do). You have this power for a period of five minutes, after which you're required to enter your password again for another five minutes.

You can disable root at any time after the initial setup by opening /Applications/ Utilities/NetInfo Manager and choosing Disable Root User from the Security menu (**Figure 2.5**), although doing so may prevent the LDAP database and the Kerberos KDC from being created later.

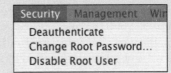

Figure 2.5 Disabling the root user with NetInfo Manager.

RUNNING SERVER ASSISTANT

Computer naming

Naming your computer involves three names: the host name, the computer name, and the rendezvous name (**Figure 2.6**). Each name is used differently. They can all be different, but this can lead to confusion, especially for first-time administrators of Mac OS X Server.

First is the host name. By default, this name is *localhost*. Setting this field properly is critical when Mac OS X Server is utilized as an LDAP Master, a DNS server, or a Kerberos Key Distribution Center, among others. You can change the host name via a command-line tool after initial setup, but take care to pick the right name now.

For example, say your Mac OS X Server will have a public IP address and be connected live to the Internet. You may want this computer to be a Web server with the name www.example.com. DNS records from your ISP and DNS records on your server must point to the server. The machine could have the host name xserver, in which case you would type in `xserver.example.com` for the host name and get this machine to respond with an IP address (this is called a *name lookup*, and you can do it by opening /Applications/Utility/Network Utility and using the Lookup tab). DNS records mask the name so that www.example.com also resolves to this server. This is a standard setup, so pick your host name carefully: If you aren't sure what the name should be, use a name like xserver or myfileserver or something that you'll remember. You'll need the *whatevername*.com or .edu or .gov now, too. (In the book's figures, it was necessary to know in advance that the server is either part of example.com or will *be* example.com; hence the name xserver.example.com.) Don't use any characters except letters, numbers, and dashes (–).

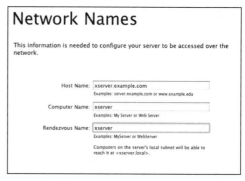

Figure 2.6 Naming your computer involves configuring three names.

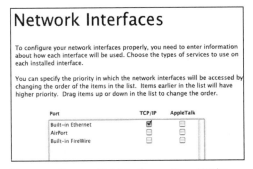

Network Interfaces

To configure your network interfaces properly, you need to enter information about how each interface will be used. Choose the types of services to use on each installed interface.

You can specify the priority in which the network interfaces will be accessed by changing the order of the items in the list. Items earlier in the list will have higher priority. Drag items up or down in the list to change the order.

Port	TCP/IP	AppleTalk
Built-in Ethernet	☑	☐
AirPort	☐	☐
Built-in FireWire	☐	☐

Figure 2.7 Choose which interfaces will run TCP/IP and which interface will run AppleTalk.

TCP/IP Connection

Enter the interface's configuration. This information identifies the interface on the local network and the internet.

Interface: Built-in Ethernet

Configure: Manually

IP Address: 10.0.1.4

Subnet Mask: 255.255.255.0

Router: 10.0.1.1

Ethernet Address: 00:0a:95:da:92:78

DNS Servers
10.0.1.1

Search Domains   (Optional)
example.com

Example: apple.com

Figure 2.8 Provide the required information for each interface that will run TCP/IP.

The second name is the computer name, which others will see when they browse the network for your server from Macintosh operating systems. The name can include letters, numbers, spaces, and special characters.

Last is the rendezvous name. Mac OS X clients and servers see this name when they browse the network using the Network icon 🌐 with a protocol other than AFP. You can use letters, numbers, and dashes.

✔ Tips

- It's a good idea to spell all three names exactly the same, especially if you aren't sure how you wish to implement Mac OS X Server at this time.

- By convention, the computer and rendezvous names should only be the host name.

Network interfaces and information

Depending on the hardware on which you're installing Mac OS X Server, you may have more than one network interface with which to connect to other networks. Xserves come with one or two Ethernet cards, depending on the revision and options chosen; FireWire interfaces can be used for networking; and, of course, some computers have AirPort cards.

On initial setup, you can choose which interfaces will run the TCP/IP protocol and which interface (only one) will run the older AppleTalk protocol (**Figure 2.7**). Mac OS X Server's interface won't let you enable AppleTalk on more than one interface at a time. Should you decide to run TCP/IP on more than one interface, the subsequent dialogs require you to set up each interface with TCP/IP information (**Figure 2.8**) such as the IP address, subnet mask, router, DNS addresses, and search domains. Having more than one interface active is called *multihoming*.

continues on next page

RUNNING SERVER ASSISTANT

You can assign more than one static IP address to your Mac OS X Server. You might do this because you have one IP address that connects to the Internet, and that IP address is on one Ethernet interface. You might use a second IP address for your internal network, and that IP address is associated with a second Ethernet interface (as would be the case with an Xserve). If you don't know which IP address you'll need, or you have a Dynamic Host Configuration Protocol (DHCP) server present, set your Mac OS X Server to use DHCP for the time being. (This is a last resort. The initial IP address should never be an address that may change frequently, like one obtained from a DHCP server.) You should understand that under almost all circumstances, Mac OS X Server should have a static IP address. A server that has the opportunity to change IP addresses would, for the most part, be useless.

✔ Tip

- Mac OS X Server won't cooperate if you lack a physical Ethernet cable connection from an active hub or switch to your server. Be sure, at the bare minimum, that you have an active connection via an Ethernet interface.

Initial directory usage setup options

Setting up Mac OS X Server's directory service options can seem daunting, because some of the options require an in-depth knowledge of the existing directory service infrastructure on your network. However, the options aren't difficult to understand, and this section explains the basics. Your options for initial directory usage are as follows (**Figures 2.9** and **2.10**):

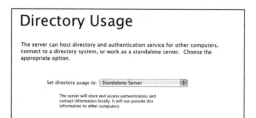

Figure 2.9 Choose your options for initial directory setup.

```
   Standalone Server
 ✔ Connected to a Directory System
   Open Directory Master
```

Figure 2.10 The options when installing Mac OS X Server on an empty disk.

Jaguar Upgrades

If you're upgrading from Mac OS X Server 10.2 (Jaguar), you'll see one additional option: "Set Directory Usage to no change." This option keeps the NetInfo shared directory domain intact.

Network Interfaces

A *network interface* is a way that your computer connects to other devices and computers on the network. It's often the built-in Ethernet interface, but it can be FireWire, AirPort, or a third-party interface card. In System Preferences, these interfaces are called Network Ports. This naming can lead to confusion, since the word *ports* has a different technical meaning when speaking about computers.

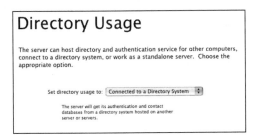

Figure 2.11 When you choose the Connected to a Directory System option...

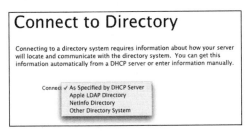

Figure 2.12 ...you have four choices for connecting to the directory system.

Connect to Directory

Connecting to a directory system requires information about how your server will locate and communicate with the directory system. You can get this information automatically from a DHCP server or enter information manually.

Connect: [As Specified by DHCP Server ⬍]

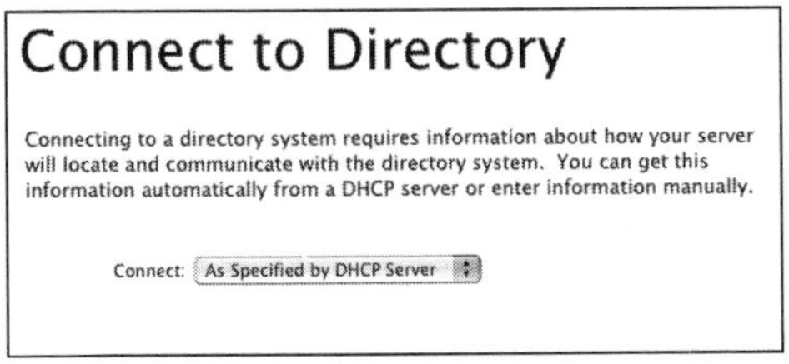

Figure 2.13 Choosing the As Specified by DHCP Server option.

Standalone Server—The best option for first-time administrators. It doesn't create a secondary database. If you aren't sure what your needs are with respect to adding users and groups, choose this option; you can always change it later.

Connected to a Directory System—Places your Mac OS X Server as a secondary server to another, generally larger, directory server. When you choose this option, you have four options for connecting to the directory system (**Figures 2.11** and **2.12**):

▲ **As Specified by DHCP Server** means your Mac OS X Server's directory information will be passed down from a DHCP server on your network, provided the DHCP server is configured to send down that information (**Figure 2.13**). In Chapter 6, "Network Configuration Options," this book discusses how to set this option if you happen to *be* that DHCP server. This option is rarely used, because your server still gets an IP address from another server; therefore it's possible that this IP address could change, rendering your server inaccessible to others outside your local network.

continues on next page

DHCP Options

DHCP servers need to forward the LDAP information to the clients. They do so via an option in the DHCP specifications. If you're working with a non–Mac OS X Server DHCP server, you should tell the administrator of that server to use Option 95 to pass the LDAP information down to the clients.

RUNNING SERVER ASSISTANT

▲ **Apple LDAP Directory** tells your Mac OS X Server to obtain its directory information from another Apple LDAP Server (**Figure 2.14**). Again, you must configure that server at the top of the food chain, so to speak, before you can tell your server to get information from another server.

▲ **NetInfo Directory** tells your Mac OS X Server to receive its directory information from an older Mac OS X Server running a NetInfo shared/parent database (**Figure 2.15**).

▲ **Other Directory System** enables your Mac OS X Server to retrieve directory information from another directory service, such as OpenLDAP on another Unix computer (**Figure 2.16**).

Keep in mind that these four options under the Connected to a Directory System option aren't used by a single Mac OS X Server on a small network that has no other directory servers.

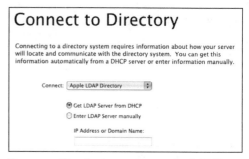

Figure 2.14 Choosing to connect to an Apple LDAP directory and the resulting options.

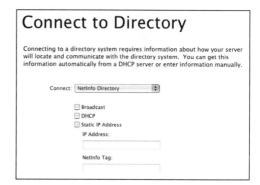

Figure 2.15 Choosing to connect to a NetInfo parent database and the three options for connecting to such a database.

Figure 2.16 Selecting Other Directory System to connect your Mac OS X Server to another directory service.

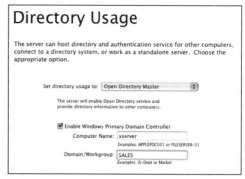

Figure 2.17 Choosing an Open Directory Master as your directory type isn't recommended at startup.

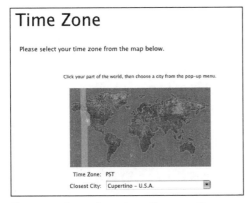

Figure 2.18 Choosing a service will result in that service always being started when Mac OS X Server starts up or restarts.

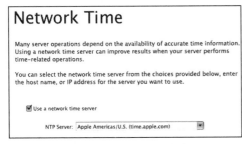

Figure 2.19 Choose from among the server time zone options.

Network Time

Many server operations depend on the availability of accurate time information. Using a network time server can improve results when your server performs time-related operations.

You can select the network time server from the choices provided below, enter the host name, or IP address for the server you want to use.

☑ Use a network time server

NTP Server: Apple Americas/U.S. (time.apple.com)

Figure 2.20 Choosing a network time server ensures that Mac OS X Server always has the correct time.

Open Directory Master—Should *not* be chosen during the initial setup of your server (**Figure 2.17**). You can promote your Mac OS X Server from a stand-alone server to a master any time after setup is completed. You should delay this promotion, because you want to make sure your Mac OS X Server can do both forward and reverse lookups on itself to ensure that the DNS structure on your network functions properly. This topic is discussed in Chapter 3, "Open Directory."

✔ **Tip**

■ When you go through the initial setup, unless you're connecting your Mac OS X Server to another, larger directory server, the best option is to make it a stand-alone server.

Service startup options

Mac OS X Server can run many services: file sharing, Web, QuickTime streaming, NetBoot, and so on. You can decide on initial setup which services you want to start immediately upon the completion of the Server Assistant. Choosing to start any service will result in that service always being started when Mac OS X Server starts up or restarts (**Figure 2.18**). If you don't select any services, you can start them later with the Server Admin tool.

Time setup

Standard settings for time zone and whether to choose a network time server round out the initial setup. Choosing a network time server is an excellent way to ensure that Mac OS X Server always has the correct time. Of course, you must be connected to the Internet to take advantage of using Apple's time server. You can use other time servers if you don't want to use Apple's (**Figures 2.19** and **2.20**).

To configure Mac OS X Server using Server Assistant:

1. If you're installing from a remote Mac OS X client, launch Server Assistant, located in /Applications/Server/Server Assistant.

   If you're in front of the Mac OS X Server, you'll see the Welcome screen (**Figure 2.21**). Skip to step 5.

2. Select the "Set up a remote server" option (**Figure 2.22**), and click the Continue button [Continue].

   The Continue button appears at the bottom of all the Server Assistant windows. Clicking Continue in each window forwards you to the next window.

3. Choose your server from the list of available servers in the Destination window by clicking the check box.

   The name *localhost* appears in the Name column (**Figure 2.23**).

   If you have a server with another IP address and that server is not on your local network, click the Add button and add that server to the Destination list.

4. Enter either the first eight digits of your server's hardware serial number (newer Macintosh computers) or 12345678 (older Macintosh hardware).

   Click the Continue button to authenticate your setup (**Figure 2.24**).

Figure 2.21 The initial welcome screen for remote installations.

Figure 2.22 Select the "Set up a remote server" option.

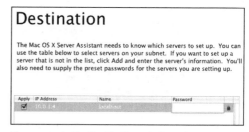

Figure 2.23 In the Destination window, choose your server by clicking the check box.

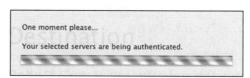

Figure 2.24 Clicking Continue in the Destination window authenticates your setup.

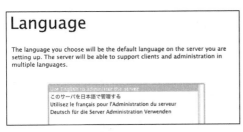

Figure 2.25 Select the language for setting up your server.

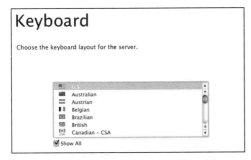

Figure 2.26 Select the keyboard layout for setting up your server.

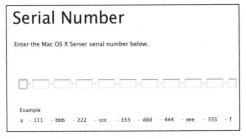

Figure 2.27 Enter your server's serial number.

Figure 2.28 Enter your administrator account information.

5. Choose your optional language setup preference (local setup only) and the keyboard layout in their respective windows (**Figures 2.25** and **2.26**).

6. Enter your Mac OS X Server's software serial number (**Figure 2.27**).

7. Enter the initial administrator information in the Administrator Account window (**Figure 2.28**). You'll need to enter the

▲ Name

▲ Short name

▲ Password and password verification

Keep in mind that the initial administrator's password is also root's password.

8. Enter the three computer names in the Network Names window (**Figure 2.29**):

▲ Host Name

▲ Computer Name

▲ Rendezvous Name

Take care to not make any spelling errors in the host name, because changing it later involves command-line work. The other names can be changed later by using the Server Admin tool.

continues on next page

Network Names

This information is needed to configure your server to be accessed over the network.

Host Name: xserver.example.com
Examples: server.example.com or www.example.edu

Computer Name: xserver
Examples: My Server or Web Server

Rendezvous Name: xserver
Examples: MyServer or WebServer

Computers on the server's local subnet will be able to reach it at <xserver.local>.

Figure 2.29 Naming your computer involves configuring three names.

RUNNING SERVER ASSISTANT

9. Decide which interfaces you'll activate: TCP/IP and/or AppleTalk (**Figure 2.30**).

10. Choose a method for TCP/IP connectivity (**Figures 2.31** and **2.32**). Your choices are

   ▲ Manually

   ▲ Using DHCP with manual IP address

   ▲ Using DHCP

   ▲ Using BootP

   You'll choose a TCP/IP connection method for each selected interface.

11. Choose a way to implement directory services in the Directory Usage window (**Figure 2.33**).

   If you're starting from scratch, you'll likely choose Standalone Server.

   If you choose Connected to a Directory System and click Continue, a few options will be available in the Connect to Directory window. Refer to the Initial Directory usage and setup options section for an explanation of these options.

   Don't choose Open Directory Master at this point, because it may not set up properly.

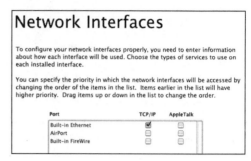

Figure 2.30 Choose which interfaces will run TCP/IP and which interface will run AppleTalk.

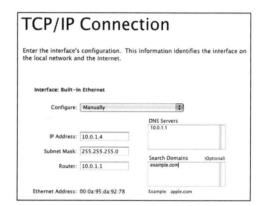

Figure 2.31 Choose a method for TCP/IP connectivity.

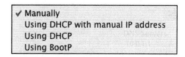

Figure 2.32 TCP/IP connection options.

Figure 2.33 In the Directory Usage window, choose a way to implement directory services.

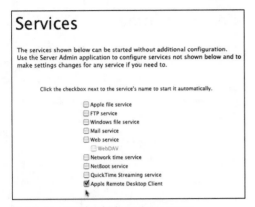

Figure 2.34 Decide which services to start.

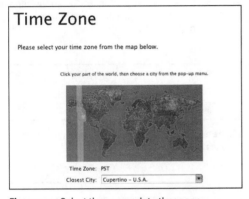

Figure 2.35 Select the appropriate time zone.

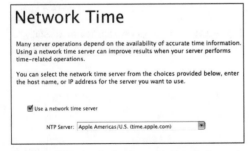

Figure 2.36 Choose whether to connect to a time server.

12. Select the services you wish to start immediately after the Server Assistant finishes (**Figure 2.34**).

13. Set the appropriate time zone from the Time Zone window (**Figure 2.35**).

14. Choose to enable a network time server from which to obtain time data (**Figure 2.36**).

If you have a local time server, select it from the NTP Server list.

Before you complete the next step, you may wish to save your settings to a file (see the next section, "Saving Configuration Settings").

continues on next page

15. Confirm your settings (**Figure 2.37**). When you're satisfied, click the Apply button.

You'll see a configuration window as the settings are applied (**Figure 2.38**).

16. A window opens, indicating that the settings were applied successfully. Click the Continue Now button to reboot Mac OS X Server (**Figure 2.39**).

You can now log in and begin exploring Mac OS X Server. If you completed this process from a remote Mac OS X machine, you can begin trying the other server tools.

✔ Tips

- Starting unnecessary services can slow down your server and present security risks. Only turn on the services you absolutely need.

- Mac OS X Server comes in two flavors: a 10-user license and an unlimited user license (defined as the number of simultaneous users that can connect to the server). The serial number controls this license. You can change the serial number any time on Mac OS X Server if you choose to upgrade your server from the 10-user license to the unlimited license.

- To change the IP address and host name of a stand-alone Mac OS X Server, you can use the changeip command from the Terminal. Log in and type sudo changeip - old-ip new-ip old-hostname new-hostname. Check and change your Network Preference pane as well. Reboot your server in order for the changes to propagate.

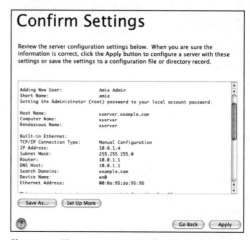

Figure 2.37 The server setup Confirm Settings window displays all the options and parameters you've chosen during the initial setup.

Figure 2.38 You'll see a configuration window as the settings are applied.

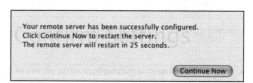

Figure 2.39 The settings were applied successfully. Click Continue Now to reboot Mac OS X Server.

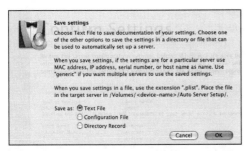

Figure 2.40 You can save your configuration settings as a text file for possible printing and saving.

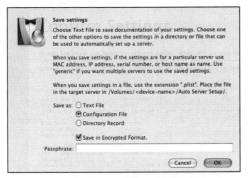

Figure 2.41 Saving the configuration settings as a property list file offers a Passphrase option.

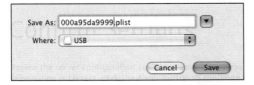

Figure 2.42 If you save the configuration settings as a configuration property list file, the Ethernet address is used as the filename.

Table 2.1

Saving Directory Data Options

SAVING OPTION	SAVE LOCATION	ENCRYPTION?
Text file	Any connected device	No
Configuration file	Any connected device	Optional
Directory record	Other directory server	Optional

Saving Configuration Settings

The Server Assistant's Confirm Settings window gives you the option of saving your configuration settings (**Figure 2.40**). Doing so has several benefits. You can save a small test file to a local USB storage device or iPod and transfer these settings to a clean installation of Server, thus saving you from typing in the information again. You may also wish to create a clone of your server or quickly reformat and reinstall your server software after a severe disk failure. In addition, you can save the file to a directory record; doing so lets you save the configuration to another directory server on your network, in case a server needs reformatting. You can reformat the server and pull down the initial settings again, saving you from running through the Server Assistant repeatedly. **Table 2.1** lists the possible ways to save your configuration settings.

When you're saving configuration settings, choose the method that best fits your infrastructure. Saving to a text file doesn't allow encryption, so anyone can open the file and see your configuration settings. You can save the file anywhere, but the best idea is to save it on a USB, an iPod, or another storage device.

Another method is to save the configuration settings as a configuration property list file. Doing so allows for encryption of the file, and the Ethernet address is automatically used as the name of the file (**Figures 2.41** and **2.42**). To allow for automatic setup, place the file inside a folder called Auto Server Setup on a removable storage device.

continues on next page

✔ Tip

■ You can change the name of the configuration property list file to generic.plist. When you do this, any server can use the file to configure itself with the parameters contained in that particular property list file (**Figure 2.43**).

The third option is to save the file in a directory record. Doing so creates the file inside another Mac OS X Client or Mac OS X Server. When a freshly installed (and not configured) copy of Mac OS X Server reboots, depending on how the *other* Mac OS X Server on the network is configured, it will discover the plist directory record on the local network and automatically configure itself (**Figure 2.44**).

To save initial server settings:

1. In the Confirm Settings window, click the Save As button in the lower-left corner.

2. Choose Configuration File from the list of options.

3. If you want to associate a passphrase with the file, enter one now (**Figure 2.45**).

   There is no confirmation of the passphrase, so make sure you type it correctly.

4. Insert a USB, a FireWire, or another storage device, if you have one.

   If you don't have one, you can save the file elsewhere on the local or remote volume for later use.

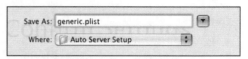

Figure 2.43 Changing the name of the configuration property list file to generic.plist lets any server use the file to configure itself.

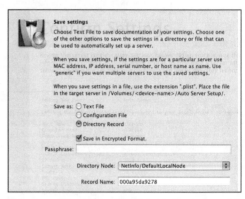

Figure 2.44 You can save the file as a directory record in another directory server.

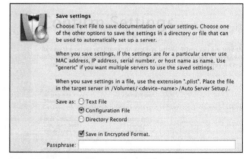

Figure 2.45 You can save the configuration with a passphrase.

Directory Records

When you save your server setup information to a directory record, all the server setup information is placed inside a NetInfo database on a Mac OS X Client or a stand-alone Mac OS X Server. If you have created an LDAP database on your server (as you will in the next chapter), you also have the option of saving it there.

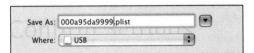

Figure 2.46 Saving the configuration file on a removable USB device allows for automatic configuration upon another installation.

Figure 2.47 Clicking the Apply button will apply all the settings.

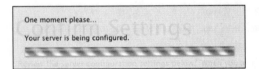

Figure 2.48 You'll see a configuration window as the settings are applied.

5. Decide whether you wish to keep the Ethernet address as the filename or change the name to `generic.plist`, an IP address, or a host name.

Keeping the Ethernet address ties that file to the server with that address (**Figure 2.46**).

6. Before you save the file to the storage device or local volume, expand the Save dialog, and create a folder at the base level of the device called Auto Server Setup.

Transfer the file to a remote storage device if you haven't done so.

7. Save the file inside the Auto Server Setup folder.

8. Apply the settings, and the server will reboot (**Figure 2.47**).

This configuration file may come in handy should you need to reformat and reinstall your server. It ensures all your settings are exactly as they were when you first installed Mac OS X Server.

To reapply saved server settings:

1. To reapply the server settings, the computer's disk(s) running the server software must have been reformatted and the server software installed.

2. After the first Mac OS X Server CD finishes its installation, the server will reboot itself and ask for the second Server CD.

Insert the CD and, any time after that, connect the remote storage device.

3. After the second CD is done installing, the server may take a few minutes to locate the configuration file. Then it will reboot itself, fully configured (**Figure 2.48**).

SAVING CONFIGURATION SETTINGS

Server Admin Overview

The Server Admin tool is where you start and stop, configure, and monitor most of the services Mac OS X Server has to offer. You can also change the serial number, computer name, and rendezvous name; run Software Update; set the date, time, and time zone; and enable a few advanced options (discussed later).

Since Server Admin is part of the Server Administration Software package, it can be installed on any Mac OS X Client (running version 10.3). As a result, multiple servers can be administered from virtually anywhere, provided the server has a public IP address (**Figure 2.49**).

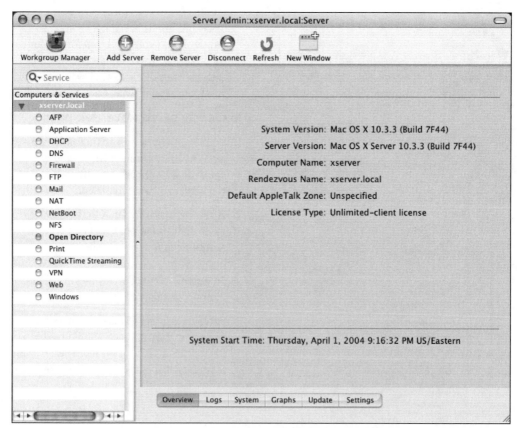

Figure 2.49 The Server Admin tool lets you administer multiple servers from virtually anywhere.

Figure 2.50 Enter your administrator name and password, choose whether you wish to add the password to your keychain, and click Connect.

Address Name Differences

In certain cases, you may see another name in the Address field. This may be due to the TCP/IP information you entered. If you entered a DNS address, you may have a domain name for your server assigned by another Domain Name Server. A *fully qualified domain name* is another name that is related to the IP address you have for your server. This name may be out of your control if you aren't the administrator of that Domain Name Server.

The basics of DNS and Domain Name Server are covered in Chapter 6.

Table 2.2

Advanced Server Admin Settings

SETTING	MEANING	USAGE
Enable SNMP	Simple Network Management Protocol	Allows remote queries of the server information via SNMP tools. These tools are often command-line or Web based and read data in a format that is likely to be unfamiliar to most users.
Enable NTP	Network Time Protocol	Allows a server to become a time server. Other computers can now enter the IP address or name of the server and receive their time synchronization from it.
Enable Macintosh Manager	Macintosh Manager	Starts the Macintosh Manager, which allows older Mac OS 8.1–9.2.2 clients to be managed.

The first time you launch Server Admin, you'll need to connect to your server. A Connect dialog will drop down from the Server Admin window. Depending on where you're physically located, you have three options in the drop-down dialog:

◆ A direct connection to the server.

If you're doing this on the server, the Address field contains the rendezvous name of the server and the logged-in administrator's name.

◆ A connection from another Mac OS X Server or Mac OS X Client running the Server Admin tool on your local network/subnet.

You can click the Browse button (Browse...) in the Server Admin Connect dialog and search for your server on your local network, or type in the known IP address or fully qualified domain name.

◆ A remote connection from anywhere around the globe, provided your server has a public IP address.

You'll need to have the IP address handy for entry into the Address field.

You'll enter your administrator name password, choose whether you wish to add the password to your keychain so you don't have to type it in later, and click the Connect button (Connect) (**Figure 2.50**).

Once you're connected, you'll see your server in the left frame of Server Admin. Clicking the disclosure triangle expands or contracts your server, showing or hiding all the services available on that server (**Table 2.2**). Clicking any service shows you that service's settings and options in the right frame of the window.

continues on next page

Across the top is the Toolbar, which lets you add, remove, disconnect from, and refresh your server information (**Figure 2.51**). You can also create a new Server Admin window from the Toolbar, as well as launch the other main server management tool, Workgroup Manager. If you've selected a service, you may also see a Start Service button in the Toolbar . If you wish to customize your Toolbar, you may do so by choosing View > Customize Toolbar.

Figure 2.51 The Server Admin Toolbar lets you add, remove, disconnect from, and refresh your server information.

✔ Tip

■ You have two additional view options. You can view all your services and their respective status by choosing View > Show Summary, and you can quickly see your users and groups by choosing View > Show User Records. The former option displays the services and their status horizontally (**Figure 2.52**, below), and the latter opens a drawer on the left or right of the Server Admin tool that lets you see all the users and groups (**Figure 2.53**).

Figure 2.53 Choosing View > Show User Records opens a drawer on the left or right of the Server Admin tool that lets you see all the users and groups.

Figure 2.52 Choosing View > Show Summary displays services and their status horizontally.

SERVER ADMIN OVERVIEW

Figure 2.54 Choose Favorites > Add To Favorites and select your server...

Figure 2.55 ...to be able to access your server from the Server Admin Favorites menu.

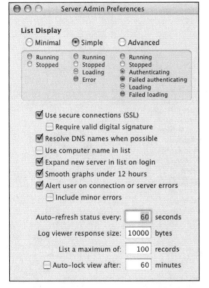

Figure 2.56 You can customize Server Admin in the Server Admin Preferences dialog.

Server Admin and Unix

Server Admin has a counterpart in the command line called `serveradmin`. You can run this tool from the server directly or, when you're connected to the server, from a remote machine via ssh. `serveradmin` has many options and can be used just like its GUI counterpart. Consult the man page for `serveradmin` to learn about all the features.

You'll probably access the Server Admin tool frequently; so, you may benefit from adding your server(s) to a Favorites list that gives you menu and keyboard shortcuts to the server(s). To do this, launch the Server Admin tool, choose Favorites > Add To Favorites, and select your server. You can now access your server when launching Server Admin by heading to the Favorites menu and choosing your server or using the Command key and the number associated with your server in the Favorites menu. If this is the first time you've done this, your server number will be 1 (**Figures 2.54** and **2.55**).

Setting Server Admin preferences

You can customize Server Admin to further suit your needs. To do so, choose Preferences from the Server Admin menu. Some of the major options available to you are as follows (**Figure 2.56**):

◆ You can change the list display from Simple to Advanced, which will provide you with more information about how services are operating.

◆ You can enable secure connections and, if you do so, also provide a digital signature to ensure encryption. The digital signature option is discussed in Chapter 10. This option is especially important when you're administering a server from halfway around the world.

◆ The "Resolve DNS names when possible" option is used when servers have a properly configured DNS (discussed in Chapter 6).

To increase your Server Admin refresh rate:

1. Launch the Server Admin tool, located in /Applications/Server (**Figure 2.57**).

   You don't need to authenticate, although you can.

2. Choose Preferences from the Server Admin menu.

   The Server Admin Preferences window opens.

3. Change the option in the "Auto-refresh status" box to 30 seconds (**Figure 2.58**).

4. Close the Preferences window.

   Your Server Admin tool will now update the status of all services much more quickly. It will also do this for all the servers in your Server Admin list.

✔ Tip

- If you're working directly on the server, you'll notice that the Server Admin tool is already in the Dock. If you're working remotely, you may wish to add the Server Admin tool to the Dock.

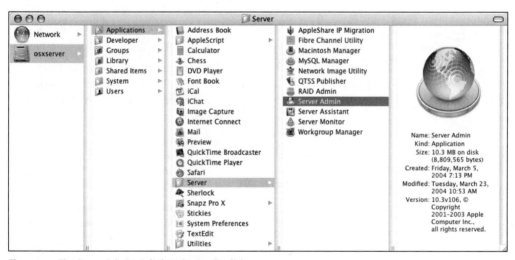

Figure 2.57 The Server Admin tool's location on the disk.

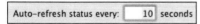

Figure 2.58 Change the Auto-refresh value in the Server Admin tool.

Using Workgroup Manager

Workgroup Manager is another too you'll use frequently when you're managing Mac OS X Server (**Figure 2.59**). The main job of Workgroup Manager is to manage users and groups; add share points such as folders and volumes; and edit preferences for users, groups, and computer accounts. You can access Workgroup Manager directly via Server Admin and vice versa, using the top-left icon in the Toolbar.

Like other tools in the Server folder, Workgroup Manager can be run locally and remotely; the authentication process is identical to that of Server Admin. The first time you launch Workgroup Manager, you'll need to connect to your server. A dialog will drop down from the Workgroup Manager window. Depending on where you're physically located, you have three options:

◆ A direct connection to the server.

   If you're doing this on the server, the Address field contains the rendezvous name of the server and the logged-in administrator's name.

◆ A connection from another Mac OS X Server or Mac OS X client running the Workgroup Manager tool on your local network/subnet.

   You can click the Browse button Browse... in the Workgroup Manager Connect dialog and search for your server on your local network.

◆ A remote connection from anywhere around the globe, provided your server has a public IP address.

   You'll need to have the IP address handy for entry into the Address field.

continues on next page

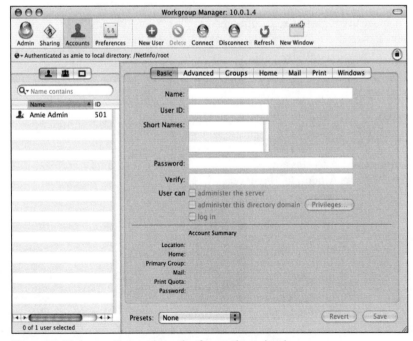

Figure 2.59 Workgroup Manager is another frequently used tool.

Enter your administrator name password, choose whether you wish to add the password to your keychain so you don't have to type it in later, and click the Connect button `Connect` (**Figure 2.60**).

✔ Tip

■ If you're working directly on the server, you'll notice that the Workgroup Manager tool is already in the Dock. If you're working remotely, you may wish to add the Workgroup Manager tool to the Dock.

The Workgroup Manager Toolbar gives you access to the following buttons (from left to right) (**Figure 2.61**):

◆ **Admin**, which launches the Server Admin tool

◆ Buttons that narrow the focus of Workgroup Manager to three specific areas:

  ▲ **Sharing** settings

  ▲ **Accounts** management, which lets you manage users, groups, and computers

  ▲ **Preferences** settings for user, groups, and/or computers

◆ **New User** and **Delete** for account management

◆ **Connect**, **Disconnect**, and **Refresh**

◆ **New Window**, which creates a new Workgroup Manager window for the server

  You might use this option to view users in one window and groups in another.

Managing Workgroup Manager

Workgroup Manager is used to enter or import user and group information. You can also use it to view and edit accounts not located on a Mac OS X Server. Although this topic is more advanced than this chapter can explore, it's useful to understand how important Workgroup Manager is in your daily dealings with Mac OS X Server.

Figure 2.60 In the Workgroup Manager Connect dialog, enter your administrator name password, choose whether you wish to add the password to your keychain, and click Connect.

Figure 2.61 The Workgroup Manager Toolbar gives you access to a variety of useful buttons.

Authenticated as amie to local directory: /NetInfo/root

Figure 2.62 The Workgroup Manager Directory drop-down menu lets you select directories you're authenticated to see.

In the drop-down menu directly beneath the Toolbar on the left, you can select various directories you're authenticated to see (directories are discussed in the next chapter) (**Figure 2.62**). Clicking on the globe or triangle allows you to see those directories.

Altering Workgroup Manager preferences

Workgroup Manager has preferences that affect how you'll use this tool, regardless of the server(s) you connect to. To see Workgroup Manager's preferences, choose Preferences from the Workgroup Manager menu. Some of the important options available to you are as follows (**Figure 2.66**):

Resolve DNS names when possible. This option is used when servers have properly configured DNS (discussed in later chapters).

Use secure transactions (SSL) for Sharing (secure connections are discussed in Chapter 10).

Show system users and groups, including root and those used by various services. These are hidden by default; you shouldn't change any parameters to the system users and groups unless you're absolutely sure of the result.

continues on next page

Account Types

To switch between user, group, and computer lists, click the Accounts button in the Toolbar and then select the icon 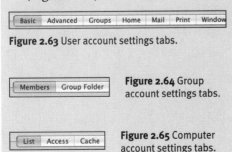 that corresponds to the account type.

When you choose each account type, you'll notice the settings (tabs) for those account types change (in the settings frame to the right in Workgroup Manager) based on the account type:

◆ User account settings tabs (**Figure 2.63**)

◆ Group account settings tabs (**Figure 2.64**)

◆ Computer account settings tabs (**Figure 2.65**)

| Basic | Advanced | Groups | Home | Mail | Print | Window |

Figure 2.63 User account settings tabs.

| Members | Group Folder |

Figure 2.64 Group account settings tabs.

| List | Access | Cache |

Figure 2.65 Computer account settings tabs.

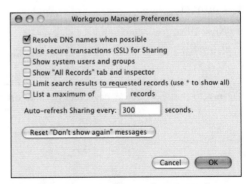

Figure 2.66 Choose Preferences from the Workgroup Manager menu to open the Workgroup Manager Preferences dialog.

USING WORKGROUP MANAGER

Show "All Records" tab and inspector.
You can show the Inspector tab (to be discussed in Chapter 4, "User and Group Management"), which lets you see and edit attributes for user, group, or computer accounts on both the local and LDAP databases. This tab becomes incredibly useful when you're doing such advanced editing as adding attributes to users (attributes are discussed in the next chapter).

Limit search results to requested records and **List a maximum of () records**. These options become important in large organizations where you have thousands of records. You may wish to show only 500 and do searches for the rest. Chapter 4 covers searching for account records.

Auto-refresh Sharing. You can auto-refresh this portion of Workgroup Manager more or less frequently.

✔ Tip

■ In both Workgroup Manager and Server Admin (as well as most other applications), you can use the combination of the Command and comma keys to open the Preferences window.

To add the All Records tab and Inspector to your view:

1. Launch the Workgroup Manager tool located in /Applications/Server (**Figure 2.67**).

   You don't need to authenticate, although you can.

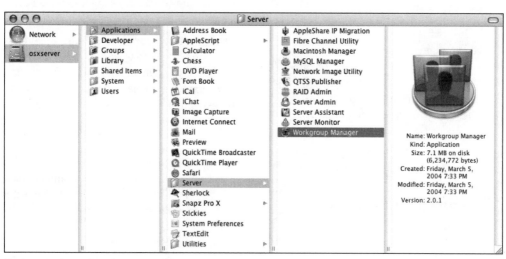

Figure 2.67 The Workgroup Manager tool's location on the disk.

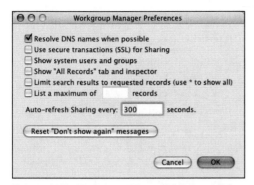

Figure 2.68 The Workgroup Manager Preferences dialog.

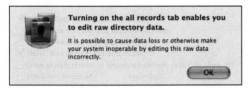

Figure 2.69 The Inspector tab check box in Workgroup Manager.

Figure 2.70 A warning dialog tells you that you can lose data or make your system inoperable by editing raw attributes.

2. Choose Preferences from the Workgroup Manager menu.

The Workgroup Manager Preferences window opens (**Figure 2.68**).

3. Select the "Show 'All Records' tab and inspector" check box (**Figure 2.69**).

4. Click OK to close the Preferences window.

5. A warning dialog tells you that you can possibly lose data or make your system inoperable by editing raw attributes.

Click OK to dismiss the dialog (**Figure 2.70**).

If you click the Accounts icon, regardless of account type (user, group, computer), you'll see an additional tab at the end of the account types and an additional tab at the end of the account configuration frame. This tab will be discussed in more detail in Chapter 4.

✔ Tips

■ The more you learn about your server and user attributes, the more you'll appreciate the Inspector tab. It's a good idea to leave it up so you can refer to it.

■ Add your server to the Favorites menu in Workgroup Manager by launching Workgroup Manager, entering your server information, authenticating, and choosing your server from the Add to Favorites selection from the Favorites menu.

Increasing the Workgroup Manager refresh rate

When you're setting up and managing shared folders or volumes, you may wish to get a faster response from Workgroup Manager when it updates the information in the window.

To increase the refresh rate:

1. Launch the Workgroup Manager tool located in /Applications/Server, and authenticate as the administrator.

2. Choose Preferences from the Workgroup Manager menu.

   The Preferences window opens (**Figure 2.71**).

3. Change the auto-refresh rate from the default 300 seconds to something shorter, such as 60 seconds (**Figure 2.72**).

4. Click OK to close the Preferences window.

   When you work with share points, you'll now see a faster response when the Workgroup Manager window refreshes.

✔ Tip

■ Should you wish to do this manually, you can always click the Refresh button in the toolbar ![Refresh].

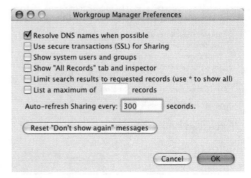

Figure 2.71 The Workgroup Manager Preferences dialog.

Figure 2.72 Change the Workgroup Manager auto-refresh option to 60 seconds.

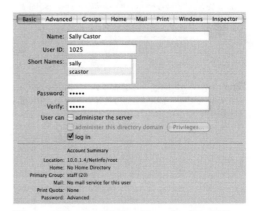

Figure 2.73 You can quickly add users to Mac OS X Server on the Workgroup Manager Basic tab.

USING WORKGROUP MANAGER

Adding users to your Mac OS X Server

Mac OS X Server can have more than one directory database (discussed in the next chapter). However, you can quickly add users to Mac OS X Server using Workgroup Manager. You'll add users to the local database at this point, but the process of adding them to another directory database is the same (**Figure 2.73**).

To add user accounts to Mac OS X Server:

1. Launch the Workgroup Manager tool located in /Applications/Server, and authenticate as the administrator.

2. Select the Accounts icon ![Accounts] in the Toolbar and the User icon ![icons] in the Account Types tab.

3. In the user settings frame on the right, select the Basic tab ![Basic].
   Click the New User icon ![New User] in the Toolbar.

4. *Enter the following information* in the appropriate fields:
   Name—The full name of the user, such as Sally Castor.

User ID—Already entered for you in this case. A unique ID that Mac OS X Server (and Client) uses to enforce folder and file permissions.

Short Names—The user's short name(s). For compatibility with older operating systems, this name should only use letters (usually lowercase) and numbers and be eight characters or less, such as sally or scastor. Additional short names can be longer if you wish.

Password and **Verify**—Passwords should include a variety of characters and both uppercase and lowercase letters. Passwords can be well over 64 characters long; however, this is impractical, and not all computer software that requires authentication can accept such a long character string.

5. Click the Save button ![Save] in the Workgroup Manager window.
   There are many other options when adding users, as you'll see in Chapter 4.

✔ Tip

- Both Server Admin and Workgroup Manager will be used to manage Mac OS X Server for the remainder of this book. You might want to take the time to click the various icons in the Toolbar and familiarize yourself with these tools.

Additional Administration Tools

In addition to the tools discussed here, you may wish to add the following items to the Dock on your server (some items, such as the Terminal, are already on the Dock):

Activity Monitor—Monitors processes

Console—Lets you view local log files easily

Directory Access—Allows the server to authenticate and connect to other directory types

Disk Utility—Lets you carry out permissions repair on your server

NetInfo Manager—Lets you edit data on local accounts

Network Utility—Checks the network status and connections

Printer Setup Utility—Lets you create printers on your server

Migration and Compatibility Tools Overview

Not every Mac OS X Server is born from an empty disk. Sometimes previous server versions can't be erased and upgrades must be performed. When you're upgrading a previous version of Mac OS X Server or AppleShare IP, you can take advantage of some tools that not only ease migration, but also allow for the management of older Macintosh operating systems, such as 8.6 and/or 9.2. You may also want to manage services not directly manageable by either Server Admin or Workgroup Manager. Apple provides tools to manage these services.

Using the AppleShare IP Migration tool

The AppleShare IP Migration tool is used to upgrade server settings from AppleShare IP (ASIP) to Mac OS X Server 10.3. Specifically, this tool updates users and groups, share points, permissions, and the mail database. It's important to understand, however, that using the ASIP Migration tool is only one step in the series of steps necessary to migrate and update the entirety of your server.

There are two methods for migrating from ASIP to Mac OS X Server: migrating to an entirely new server, or migrating in place by upgrading an existing server to Mac OS X Server. The path you choose will determine how you use the ASIP Migration tool. If you're migrating a server in place, then all the functions of the ASIP Migration tool work properly.

On the other hand, if you're migrating to a new server, you can't use the ASIP Migration tool to migrate share points and privileges: Your shared folders must be copied to the new server and configured manually. (Configuration of share points is covered in Chapter 5, "File Sharing.") Similarly, you shouldn't use the ASIP Migration tool to move user and group accounts to a new server. It's best to export a user and group settings file from ASIP and then import that file directly into Workgroup Manager. (The import and export tools are covered in Chapter 4.)

✔ Tips

■ It's strongly suggested that you back up your data and perform a clean installation on an empty, freshly formatted disk whenever possible.

■ Realistically, when you're moving to a new server, the only proper use for the ASIP Migration tool is to migrate the mail database. A clean installation is always better than an upgrade.

Privileges and Permissions

For most purposes (and the purposes of this book), *privileges* and *permissions* mean the same thing: what a user is authorized to do. That may be reading the contents of a folder or opening a file. Mac OS 9 and ASIP use the term *privileges*. Mac OS X and Mac OS X Server largely use the term *permissions*. Apple does use the word *privileges* when dealing with administration of users, groups, and computers, as you'll see in Chapter 4, but this has nothing to do with the ability to access disks, folders, and files.

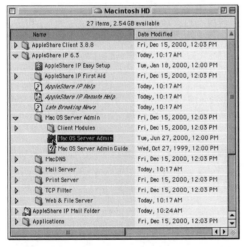

Figure 2.74 To open the Mac OS Server Admin tool, choose /AppleShare IP 6.3/Mac OS Server Admin/Mac OS Server Admin.

Figure 2.75 Connect and authenticate to your ASIP server.

To upgrade from ASIP to Mac OS X Server using ASIP Migration:

1. On your ASIP server, open the Mac OS Server Admin tool by choosing /AppleShare IP 6.3/Mac OS Server Admin/Mac OS Server Admin (**Figure 2.74**).

2. Connect and authenticate to your ASIP server (**Figure 2.75**).

   The Server Admin window opens.

3. Click the Users and Groups icon, and then select Show Users & Groups List from the drop-down menu (**Figure 2.76**).

   The Users & Groups list appears.

continues on next page

Figure 2.76 Click the Users and Groups icon, and then select Show Users & Groups List from the drop-down menu.

4. Double-click any user in the list to open an edit window for that user (**Figure 2.77**).

Assign an Internet alias name, and then click the Save button.

5. Install and configure Mac OS X Server. Please refer to Chapter 1 ("Planning and Installation") and the beginning of this chapter for installation and configuration information.

6. Open the ASIP Migration tool by choosing /Applications/Server/AppleShare IP Migration (**Figure 2.78**).

7. Select the migration options you want from the various check boxes (**Figure 2.79**).

Remember that you can only migrate share points and permissions if you're upgrading a server in place.

8. At the bottom of the AppleShare IP Migration window, *select either of the following options* to handle duplicate user names:

Do not migrate the AppleShare user—Ignores the duplicate accounts.

Migrate the AppleShare user's privileges and mail to the Mac OS X Server user—Only moves permissions and mail settings. You'll use this choice when you're moving to an entirely new server and you've already imported the users and groups into Workgroup Manager, but you now need to migrate the mail database.

9. Click the lock icon at the bottom of the dialog, and authenticate as an administrative user.

10. Click the Migrate button to begin the conversion process (**Figure 2.80**).

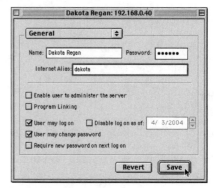

Figure 2.77 In the user edit dialog, assign an Internet alias name.

Figure 2.78 Open the ASIP Migration tool by choosing /Applications/Server/AppleShare IP Migration.

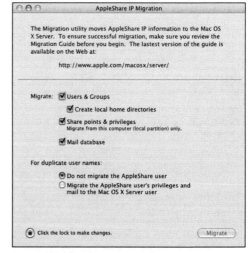

Figure 2.79 Select the migration options you want in the AppleShare IP Migration dialog.

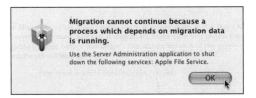

Figure 2.80 Click the lock icon to authenticate and the Migrate button to start the migration process.

Migration cannot continue because a process which depends on migration data is running.

Use the Server Administration application to shut down the following services: Apple File Service.

OK

Figure 2.81 A warning dialog may appear if a related service is running while you're using the migration tool.

Figure 2.82 Specify where the ASIP users and groups database file is located.

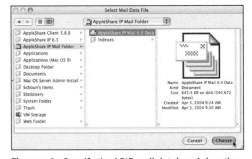

Figure 2.83 Specify the ASIP mail database's location.

11. You may have to temporarily disable certain services, such as the AFP service, to continue (**Figure 2.81**).

These services can be disabled with the Server Admin tool. You should disable services to reduce the chance of an error when performing an upgrade.

12. Specify where the ASIP users and groups database file is located, and click Choose (**Figure 2.82**).

Typically this file is located in the /System Folder/Preferences folder.

13. Specify the ASIP mail database's location, and click Choose (**Figure 2.83**).

Typically this file is located in the /AppleShare IP Mail Folder.

14. The ASIP Migration tool will show a progress bar while it migrates your settings.

When the migration is finished, you should verify the migration process by checking the imported settings from the Mac OS X Server tools. Additionally, a variety of migration log files are located in the /Library/Logs/Migration folder.

✔ Tips

■ The ASIP utility will only import users into the local directory. If you need to import users into a shared directory, use the Import function in Workgroup Manager.

■ Use the Macintosh Manager tool's built-in migration utility to migrate your Macintosh Manager account information, documents, and preferences.

■ Always make a complete backup of your ASIP server before migrating or installing a new system. It's also a good idea to set Internet aliases for your user accounts before migration.

■ The ASIP user Internet alias will be used as the short name on OS X Server.

Macintosh Manager Overview

Mac OS X Server can support user and group management on older versions of the Macintosh operating system, in case you need to support them. This is good, because Mac OS 9 and Mac OS X are clearly very different operating systems; thus they require different applications for user preference management.

The Workgroup Manager tool is used to manage Mac OS X user preferences, whereas the Macintosh Manager tool is used to manage Mac OS 9 user preferences. Furthermore, Workgroup Manager uses Open Directory to store all user information, whereas Macintosh Manager uses a proprietary database for managed user preferences. However, Macintosh Manager still uses Open Directory for user authentication. In other words, you use Workgroup Manager to create and manage all user accounts, but you must use Macintosh Manager to control any user's Mac OS 9 preferences.

To enable Macintosh Manager:

1. Open the Server Admin tool by choosing /Applications/Server/Server Admin.

2. Connect and authenticate to the server you intend to configure.

3. Select the server name or address from the service list, click the Settings button, and then click the Advanced tab (**Figure 2.84**).

4. Select the Enable Macintosh Manager check box in the Settings window (**Figure 2.85**).

5. Click the Save button.

    The Server Admin tool automatically configures the Macintosh Manager share points and database files. The Macintosh Manager service will start up automatically from this point forward whenever the server is restarted.

6. Open the Macintosh Manager tool by choosing /Applications/Server/ Macintosh Manager (**Figure 2.86**).

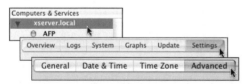

Figure 2.84 Select the server name or address from the service list, click the Settings button, and then click the Advanced tab.

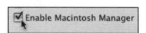

Figure 2.85 Select the Enable Macintosh Manager check box.

7. Double-click the Macintosh Manager tool; it will launch and search for the server. You can also manually type the server's name or address in the Select Macintosh Management Server dialog (**Figure 2.87**).

8. Authenticate with your administrator account (**Figure 2.88**).

Note that there is no keychain integration in Macintosh Manager, so you'll always have to authenticate when you want to manage this service.

9. You're presented with the Macintosh Manager interface.

From here, you can import user accounts into the Macintosh Manager database and manage their Mac OS 9 preferences.

✔ Tips

■ The Macintosh Manager tool is the only server tool that will run on both Mac OS 9 and Mac OS X Client or Server.

■ It's good practice to use Macintosh Manager from one of the clients, because it's easier to configure certain client-specific settings.

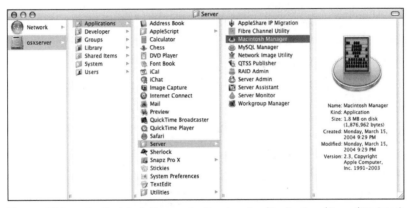

Figure 2.86 Open the Macintosh Manager tool by choosing /Applications/Server/Macintosh Manager.

Figure 2.87 You can manually type the server's name or address in the Select Macintosh Management Server dialog.

Figure 2.88 Macintosh Manager has no keychain integration, so you'll always have to authenticate.

MySQL Manager Overview

MySQL (Structured Query Language) is an open-source relational database management system that is primarily used on Mac OS X Server as part of a dynamic Web site. The MySQL Manager tool is designed to set up and enable the MySQL service with the default settings. MySQL is complicated and is typically managed using command-line tools and text configuration files. However, free detailed documentation is available at http://www.mysql.com/documentation/.

To enable MySQL:

1. On your server, open the MySQL Manager tool by choosing /Applications/ Server/MySQL Manager (**Figure 2.89**).

2. Click the lock, and authenticate as an administrative user (**Figure 2.90**).

3. Click the Install button to install the default files needed for the MySQL service (**Figure 2.91**).

   You must do this in order to enable the Start button.

4. Once the MySQL files are installed, click the Start button to start the MySQL service (**Figure 2.92**).

✔ Tip

- Although doing so isn't required to use MySQL, installing the Mac OS X Xcode development tools is highly recommended. Xcode includes many of the tools used to build Web-based applications.

Figure 2.89 Open the MySQL Manager tool by choosing /Applications/Server/MySQL Manager.

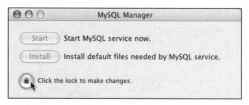

Figure 2.90 Click the lock, and authenticate as an administrative user.

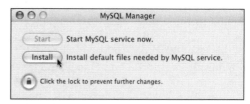

Figure 2.91 Click Install to install the default files needed for the MySQL service.

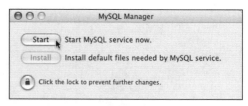

Figure 2.92 Click Start to start the MySQL service.

Using Server Monitor

The Apple Xserve hardware has a number of unique features, including a 1U rack mount form-factor, blower fans, and fast-swap hardware. Xserve also includes built-in real-time hardware monitoring and diagnostic tools. The Server Monitor tool is the user interface for this feature.

The Server Monitor tool can run on any Mac OS X Client or Server and monitor hundreds of different Xserves simultaneously. Server Monitor also has the ability to automatically notify you, via electronic mail and/or paging services, when there is a potential problem. Initially, there are no Xserves in the Server Monitor list; you must add any computer you want to monitor.

Xserve

Apple introduced the Xserve as a solution for enterprise customers who wanted a rack-mounted solution while still using Apple hardware. The G4 Xserve came with four hot-swappable disk bays and the ability to use Gigabit and/or fibre connections. The G5 Xserve has three available hot-swappable disk bays and similar options for networking. Each Xserve comes with a CD drive for installing the software.

The main difference between the Xserve and running Mac OS X Server on another Apple product is that the Xserve was designed to be managed remotely. You don't generally sit in front of an Xserve to install software or configure Mac OS X Server. While you can purchase a video card for either Xserve (allowing you to plug in a video monitor), you can just as easily manage your Xserve remotely from another room or another state.

If you choose to manage your Xserve remotely, you'll need to know how to use a few command-line tools. Installing and initial configuration can easily be done remotely, but you'll use such command-line tools to make changes to the networking structure and base system configuration. If the command line interface (CLI) isn't your cup of tea, you can purchase an Apple product called Apple Remote Desktop. This software allows you to take control of the mouse and keyboard of another Macintosh. Using this software from a remote Macintosh lets you see the desktop of the Xserve as if you were sitting in front of it.

Another option available to each Xserve (G4 and G5) is the ability to configure the hot-swappable disks in various RAID configurations (see the RAID table on RAID configurations). Not only can you configure the disks, but you can also add the optional Xserve RAID hardware to your Xserve.

Figure 2.93 Open the Server Monitor tool by choosing /Applications/Server/Server Monitor.

Figure 2.94 Click the Add Server button.

Figure 2.95 Enter the IP address or name of the server, include administrator authentication information, and click OK.

To add a computer to the Server Monitor list:

1. Open the Server Monitor tool by choosing /Applications/Server/Server Monitor (**Figure 2.93**).

2. Click the Add Server button (**Figure 2.94**).

3. Enter the IP address or name of the server, and include the administrator authentication information (**Figure 2.95**).

   Remember, saving a password to the keychain will automatically log you in to that server from this point forward.

4. Click the OK button to add the server to your server list.

   Server Monitor will maintain a persistent connection to your server as long as it's in the list. You can repeat the process to add as many servers as you wish to monitor.

Xserve RAID

The Xserve RAID is a configurable double array of disks with one controller for each array. Each array can hold up to 7 disks, with a total of 14 disks and a possible total capacity of 3.5 Terabytes. You can configure these disks in a variety of RAID formats depending on your needs. An Xserve RAID also has dual power supplies and dual fans, and it can have dual Ethernet or fibre cards and dual backup batteries. You configure the Xserve RAID using the RAID Admin configuration tool.

USING SERVER MONITOR

To monitor a server:

1. If you haven't already done so, add your server to the Server Monitor list (see the previous task).

2. Select a server from the Server Monitor list, and then select the "Show detailed status" check box (**Figure 2.96**).

   Selecting this option shows you a more detailed monitoring view in the Status Summary column.

3. Click each tab in the middle of the window (Info, Memory, and so on) to monitor a specific category.

   Each tab shows a variety of information and statistics about your Xserve. For example, clicking Network monitors the network interface port (**Figure 2.97**).

4. From Server Monitor, you can remotely run a System Profiler report. Click the Info tab, and then click the Get Apple System Profiler Report button (**Figure 2.98**).

   Apple System Profiler, or System Profiler, lets you query a Mac OS X Client or Server for a variety of hardware and software information.

5. The Server Monitor log window appears, and the System Profiler Report is displayed (**Figure 2.99**).

   In this window, you can click the Save As button to save the log as a text file for future inspection.

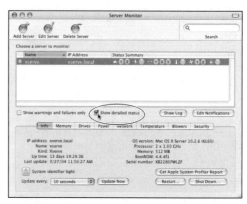

Figure 2.96 In the main Server Monitor window, select a server from the Server Monitor list, and then select "Show detailed status."

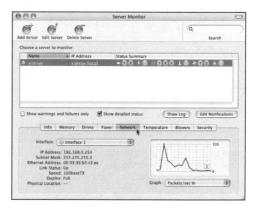

Figure 2.97 Clicking the Network icon shows the network status in the bottom half of the window.

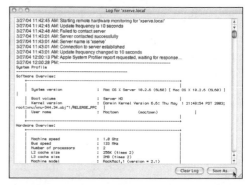

Figure 2.99 The Server Monitor log window shows the System Profiler report.

Figure 2.98 Click the Info tab, and then click the Get Apple System Profiler Report button.

Figure 2.100 Select a server from the Server Monitor list, and then click the Edit Notifications button.

Figure 2.101 Select the monitoring devices you want to be automatically notified about.

Figure 2.102 Configure an email account from which the Server Monitor should send its messages, and email accounts you want to receive the messages.

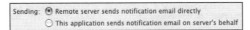

Figure 2.103 Choose an option to specify whether you want the current tool or the server itself to send the message.

Using Server Monitor without an Xserve

Server Monitor can connect to any type of hardware running Mac OS X Server. However, none of the hardware-monitoring features will work. But you can still perform some basic functions available from the Info pane, such as restarting, shutting down, and getting System Profiler reports.

To enable Server Monitor notifications:

1. If you haven't already added done so, add your server to the Server Monitor list.

2. Select a server from the Server Monitor list, and then click the Edit Notifications button (**Figure 2.100**).

   The Notifications dialog sheet drops down.

3. Select the monitoring devices you want to be automatically notified about (**Figure 2.101**).

   These buttons work as toggle switches: Clicking a button switches it between disabled and enabled.

4. In the Email Settings dialog, configure an email account from which the Server Monitor should send its messages (**Figure 2.102**).

5. Configure as many email accounts as you want to receive the messages. Also set the message priority, subject, and beginning message text.

6. *Choose one of the following options* to specify whether you want the current tool or the server itself to send the message (**Figure 2.103**):

   ▲ Remote server sends notification email directly

   ▲ This application sends notification email on server's behalf

   Remember, if this tool is to send the notification, then you must keep the tool running at all times.

7. Click the OK button to save the settings.

✔ Tip

■ If you're setting up Server Monitor notifications, it's a good idea to set up this feature on a client as opposed to the server. That way, if for some reason the server comes to a halt or has a network issue, the message will still be sent from the client.

Additional Server Tools

Mac OS X Server has other server tools that let you set up and configure optional hardware and software, such as RAID, NetBoot, and QuickTime Streaming. These tools are used to manage those hardware configurations and services.

RAID Admin tool setup

The RAID Admin tool is used to configure and manage an Xserve RAID array. It lets you view the current settings and configure the Xserve RAID in a variety of ways (**Figure 2.104**).

When you first launch the RAID Admin tool, you're presented with a window that shows all connected Xserve RAIDs. Clicking a RAID array shows information about the array in the tabs within the window. These tabs are as follows:

Info—Provides information about the RAID such as the name, location, contact email address, and controller status (**Figure 2.105**).

Arrays & Drives—Gives the status of your arrays and drives, such as how the drives are configured and their respective capacity (**Figure 2.106**).

Components—Tells you the status of the installed components, such as the left and right power supplies, blowers, RAID controllers, and network cards (**Figure 2.107**).

Figure 2.104 The RAID Admin tool lets you view the current settings and configure the Xserve RAID in a variety of ways.

Figure 2.105 The RAID Admin Info tab provides information about the RAID such as the name, location, contact email address, and controller status.

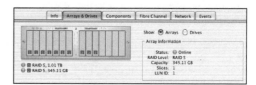

Figure 2.106 The RAID Admin Arrays & Drives tab gives the status of your arrays and drives.

Figure 2.107 The RAID Admin Components tab tells you the status of the installed components.

Figure 2.108 The RAID Admin Fibre Channel tab provides information for each fibre channel interface.

Figure 2.109 The RAID Admin Network tab provides information about each Ethernet interface.

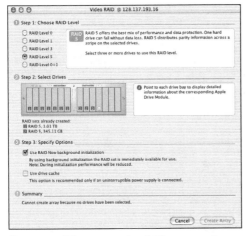

Figure 2.110 When you create a RAID array, you have several options about how that array is created.

Figure 2.111 In the RAID Settings System tab, set up the system configuration.

Fibre Channel—Provides information for each fibre channel interface (**Figure 2.108**).

Network—Provides information about each Ethernet interface (**Figure 2.109**).

Events—Describes monitored events, if any.

When you create an array, you have several options about how that array is created (**Figure 2.110**). Refer to Chapter 1 for references on the various levels of RAID.

To create a RAID Array:

1. Click the Create Array button ![Create Array] in the Toolbar (authentication is required).

2. Click the Settings button on the Toolbar. The RAID Settings window opens.

3. In the System tab, set up the system configuration (**Figure 2.111**).

   This includes the name of the array, the location and email address of the contact, the method of synchronizing the time (none, local time, or a Network Time Protocol server), a password, and system alert options.

4. In the Network tab, choose whether to use DHCP or manual addresses for each controller (**Figure 2.112**).

continues on next page

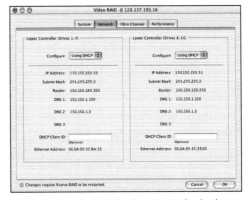

Figure 2.112 In the RAID Settings Network tab, choose whether to use DHCP or manual addresses for each controller.

ADDITIONAL SERVER TOOLS

5. In the Fibre Channel tab, set options such as the speed of the connections and the topology (**Figure 2.113**).

6. In the Performance tab, set your specifications (the cache setup for each controller) (**Figure 2.114**).

Once the configuration is finished, the RAID array is available for use by the Xserve.

Fibre Channel Utility options

The Fibre Channel Utility lets you change both the speed and topology of the Fibre card on the Power Mac or Xserve that's connected to the Xserve RAID (**Figure 2.115**).

You can select each port and change the options. Click the Apply button to commit the changes to the card.

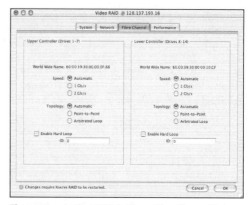

Figure 2.113 In the RAID Settings Fibre Channel tab, set options such as the speed of the connections and the topology.

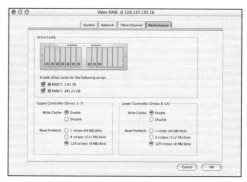

Figure 2.114 In the RAID Settings Performance tab, set your specifications (the cache setup for each controller).

Figure 2.115 The Fibre Channel Utility lets you change both the speed and topology of the Fibre card on the Power Mac or Xserve that's connected to the Xserve RAID.

Figure 2.116 Choose /Applications/Server/Network Image Utility...

Figure 2.117 ...to open the Network Image Utility and create NetBoot images.

Figure 2.118 Choose /Applications/Server/QTSS Publisher to open the QTSS Publisher tool.

Network Image Utility overview

The NetBoot service is unique in that it shares entire bootable volumes that Macintosh clients can start up over a network connection. You can use the Network Image Utility to create and manage a special type of disk image known as a *NetBoot disk image*. The NetBoot service uses these disk images to provide the remote startup services for your Macintosh clients (**Figures 2.116** and **2.117**).

Like most server administration tools, you can run the Network Image Utility on any Mac OS X Client or Server. Likewise, you can use the Server Admin tool to remotely manage the NetBoot service settings. For more information about the Network Image Utility and the NetBoot service, refer to Chapter 11, "Running a NetBoot Server."

QTSS Publisher overview

The Quick Time Streaming Server (QTSS) is used to deliver streamed audio and video content over your network or the Internet. Apple's QTSS stands out when compared to other streaming solutions due to its open standards compatibly, unlimited streaming capabilities, lack of licensing fees, and unparalleled ease of use. You are literally limited only by disk performance, CPU speed, and network bandwidth. This ease of use is made possible through a variety of comprehensive management tools. One such tool is the QTSS Publisher, which you can use to manage all of your previously recorded streaming audio and video content (**Figure 2.118**).

continues on next page

ADDITIONAL SERVER TOOLS

The primary objective for the QTSS Publisher is to provide content creators with an easy method of adding and managing QTSS media without having to use the more complicated administration tools (**Figure 2.119**). However, in order to properly set up a QTSS, you must also enable and configure the server settings via the System Admin tool. Thus, the server administrator can initially configure the QTSS and then delegate the task of populating the server with media to a less experienced user.

This chapter is designed to introduce you to the Mac OS X Server administration tools, so configuration of the QTSS goes beyond its scope. However, this topic discussed at length in Chapter 12, "QuickTime Streaming Server."

✔ Tip

■ QTSS Publisher is used to manage the streaming of previously recorded audio and video content. Use QuickTime Broadcaster to manage the streaming of live audio and video content.

QuickTime Streaming from Mac OS X Client

You can install the QuickTime Streaming Server on any Mac OS X Client. To do this, either select the QuickTime Streaming Server package in your Mac OS X Server CDs or download and install the Darwin Streaming Server from Apple's Open Source project. Although it's interesting and fun to experiment with the QuickTime Streaming Server/Darwin Streaming Server on Mac OS X Client, it isn't officially supported by Apple, and you won't receive phone support should you have questions or problems streaming from a Mac OS X Client.

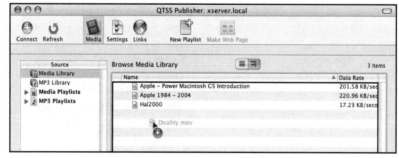

Figure 2.119 You can drag media files directly onto the QTSS Publisher window.

QuickTime Broadcaster overview

The QuickTime Broadcaster tool is used to compress audio and video in real time to facilitate live streaming over a network or the Internet. Typically, QuickTime Broadcaster is used in conjunction with one or more QuickTime Streaming Servers (QTSS) to share this live content with a large number of clients. The number of QTSSs and the amount of network bandwidth through which your broadcast relays directly affect the number of clients that can view your live stream. As expected, the more QTSSs and network bandwidth you have, the more clients you can stream to. Configuration of the QTSS goes beyond the scope of this chapter, but it's discussed at length in Chapter 12.

You need only one Macintosh running QuickTime Broadcaster to create the initial live stream. In fact, you can use QuickTime Broadcaster without being connected to a QTSS to stream content to a few clients.

✔ Tip

- You can install QuickTime Broadcaster on Mac OS X Client.

To set up a simple live broadcast:

1. Connect your audio and/or video source.
   QuickTime Broadcaster is compatible with most audio input devices and digital video devices. This includes Apple iSight cameras, digital video cameras, and analog-to-digital video converters.

2. Open the QuickTime Broadcaster tool by choosing /Applications/QuickTime Broadcaster (**Figure 2.120**).

3. When the tool first opens, it shows a compact window with only a few basic settings (**Figure 2.121**).
   Click the Show Details button to view all the options.

continues on next page

Figure 2.120 Open the QuickTime Broadcaster tool by choosing /Applications/QuickTime Broadcaster.

Figure 2.121 The Show Details button expands the QuickTime Broadcaster window.

ADDITIONAL SERVER TOOLS

71

4. Click the Audio tab, and then select the Enable Audio Stream check box (**Figure 2.122**).

You must select the compression preset and the audio source from the pop-up menus. Several built-in compression presets are good starting points; you can tweak them further with the settings that follow.

5. Click the Video tab, and then select the Enable Video Stream check box (**Figure 2.123**).

You must select the compression preset and the video source from the pop-up menus. Again, several built-in compression presets are good starting points; you can tweak them further with the settings that follow.

6. Click the Network tab (**Figure 2.124**).

Select Manual Unicast from the Transmission pop-up menu, and enter the IP address of the client you're sending the broadcast to.

7. Select Compress from the Preview pop-up menu in the main QuickTime Broadcaster window to preview the video feed with your current settings (**Figure 2.125**).

Verify the settings below the Preview window before you start streaming.

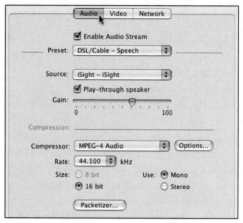

Figure 2.122 In the Audio settings dialog, select the Enable Audio Stream check box.

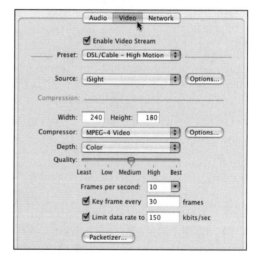

Figure 2.123 In the Video settings dialog, select the Enable Video Stream check box.

ADDITIONAL SERVER TOOLS

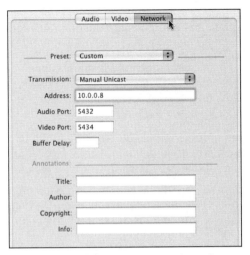

Figure 2.124 In the Network settings dialog, select Manual Unicast from the Transmission pop-up menu and enter the client's IP address.

8. Select File > Export > SDP to save the session description file (**Figure 2.126**).

A Save dialog appears, in which you can choose the destination and name for the session description file. The client uses this file as instructions for connecting to your broadcast.

9. In the QuickTime Broadcaster window, click the Broadcast button to begin the live media stream (**Figure 2.127**).

Selecting the "Record to disk" check box saves the streamed file to the local hard disk for future streaming.

continues on next page

Figure 2.125
Select Compress from the Preview pop-up menu to preview the video feed with your current settings.

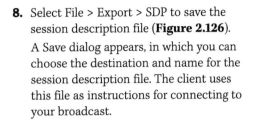

Figure 2.126 Select File > Export > SDP.

Figure 2.127 Click the Broadcast button to begin the live media stream.

10. Transfer the session description file to the client computer.

Open the file by double-clicking it (**Figure 2.128**).

11. QuickTime Player automatically opens, and the broadcast appears (**Figure 2.129**).

There will be a slight delay in the broadcast due to compression time and network overhead.

✔ Tips

■ As your stream is being broadcast, you can also monitor the video feed and connection settings from QuickTime Broadcaster.

■ Click the Stop button to stop the live media stream (**Figure 2.130**).

■ Each of the tools in this chapter is used to administer, manage, and edit parts and pieces of Mac OS X Server. It's good practice not to authenticate as root when running any of these tools (most tools won't let you, but some will, using both the short name *root* and the long name *System Administrator*). Doing so could have unexpected results such as failure to authenticate later as your administrator account, effectively locking you out of working with your server tools.

Broadcast Management Options

◆ QuickTime Broadcaster is used to manage the streaming of live audio and video content. Use QTSS Publisher to manage the streaming of previously recorded audio and video content.

◆ Real-time compression and streaming of audio and video are processor intensive. For this reason, QuickTime Broadcaster requires at least a G4-based Macintosh, if not a dual-processor G4 or G5 computer, for best results.

Figure 2.128 Double-click the SDP (Session Description Protocol) file to open it.

Figure 2.129 The QuickTime Player window opens, and you can view the live broadcast.

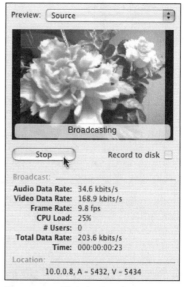

Figure 2.130 Click the Stop button below the broadcast Preview window to stop the stream.

OPEN DIRECTORY

Open Directory is Apple's way of implementing directory services. In order to understand Open Directory, you must first understand how directory services are set up and managed.

Think of a database, such as FileMaker Pro or Microsoft Excel. When you set up Microsoft Excel, you may have headers for each column, and the first column may contain a unique number for each entry in the table. FileMaker Pro can be set up to have data entered into fields, and the fields can be used to create forms, perhaps containing all information about a user or a product. A database is a container of information. A directory is really nothing more than a database that contains information—in this case, usually data about a user and/or group and other related facts.

The formation of directories structured in a certain fashion is called *directory services*. Some of the more popular directory services are Lightweight Directory Access Protocol (LDAP), NetInfo, eDirectory, and Active Directory. Both Active Directory and eDirectory are derivatives of LDAP, and Mac OS X Server uses LDAP as the basis of its Open Directory architecture. When you create a secondary directory for users (the initial directory service on both Mac OS X Client and Server is NetInfo), that directory is an Open Directory LDAP directory.

You can implement Open Directory a variety of ways, as you'll see in this chapter. Some of these techniques work with both Mac OS X and Mac OS X Server. One of the main differences between Mac OS X and Mac OS X Server with respect to Open Directory is the ability of Mac OS X Server to create the secondary directory for user information; this secondary directory is the focus of attention later, but for now this chapter will explore some basic functions of Open Directory.

Keep in mind that there are many potential types of configuration, and you should read this entire chapter before you attempt any tasks.

LDAP Overview

LDAP stands for Lightweight Directory Access Protocol, which indicates that LDAP is a *protocol*: a way to connect devices and share information. It is that, and more. LDAP is also a way to store information.

LDAP data is arranged in a fashion that may be foreign to some users. LDAP *schema* describe the overall structure of a directory. The schema contains entries, and the entries contain attributes. For example, attributes dictate such things as your short name, long name, password, user ID, and group ID. All of these things, when grouped together, form an *entry*. The items associated with the attribute (User ID, Group ID, and so on) can be defined as the data associated with that particular attribute. These terms may make you feel overwhelmed, but the basic setup of Mac OS X Server doesn't require you to know them. You need to understand the basics of LDAP because Mac OS X Server is extremely flexible. Attributes that don't exist by default in Mac OS X Server can be added, such as Address, City, State, Zip, and Phone Number.

The other reason to understand the basic terminology of LDAP is that you may need to map attributes from another LDAP server, such as a server running eDirectory, to your Mac OS X Server's Open Directory architecture. Although at first this seems overly complicated, essentially all you're doing is connecting the dots. For example, suppose you wish to connect to an eDirectory server. You know the Open Directory attribute for Group ID is called PrimaryGroupID. Now all you need to do is find out what eDirectory calls it, and match the names using the Search & Mappings tab of the Directory Access application (as you'll see later). If the attribute doesn't exist on the other directory service, you must either create that attribute or use an empty attribute and match the new name (**Figure 3.1**).

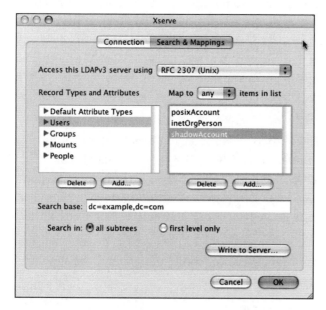

Figure 3.1 Directory Access's LDAP plug-in maps the attributes from one directory service to Mac OS X or Mac OS X Server.

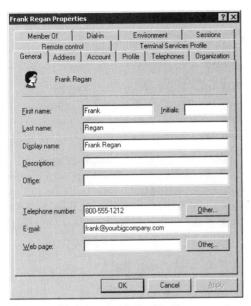

Figure 3.2 This is a typical Active Directory account, showing the various attributes of that account.

It's important to remember that most Mac OS X Server setups (especially the first Mac OS X Servers in an organization) will be Open Directory masters and will *not* connect to other directory services. As such, most of the plug-ins discussed in this chapter are unlikely to be configured on the initial Mac OS X Server by the administrator; however, they're configurable on any Mac OS X client. This doesn't diminish the importance of understanding the functionality and concepts behind these plug-ins.

Active Directory overview

Microsoft's Active Directory (AD) is another way of storing user data. Like Apple's Open Directory, it's based on the LDAP architecture. AD uses attributes, and these attributes store data. This book is only interested in the user data stored in AD.

Mac OS X Server administrators need to understand how AD works because in some cases, businesses that are running AD are reluctant to relinquish control of their user attribute data to Mac OS X Server. If this is the case, then Mac OS X Server can be configured to manage the AD users in a variety of ways without changing their actual data. In other words, Mac OS X Server is used to manage groups of users that exist on the AD server by creating the group on Mac OS X Server and managing the users in that group even though they exist on the AD computer.

Mac OS X Server administrators normally don't deal with AD servers, but it's worth seeing what a typical AD account looks like (**Figure 3.2**).

Directory Access overview

The Directory Access application is found on both Mac OS X Client and Server inside /Applications/Utilities/. It's used primarily to connect a Mac OS X computer to another directory service or system.

Directory Access has three tabs: one that lists all the services, one that shows the list of additional directory services from which a Mac OS X computer can obtain information, and a Contacts tab that lets applications read information from other directory services (**Figure 3.3**).

To understand how the Directory Access application works, you must be familiar with the concept behind what it does. Since Directory Access is based on a modular plug-in architecture, the application works differently depending on the plug-in used. Let's say you have another Mac OS X Server already in your organization, and you want this Mac OS X Server to see all the users and groups you've created on your first server. Or, you have a Microsoft AD server, and you wish to see all the users in that directory service (provided you have the proper access). You can choose from four different methods of connecting your Mac OS X computer (client or server) to another directory service. You'll see these options when you click the Services tab of Directory Access:

Active Directory—Use this plug-in to bind your Mac OS X computer to an AD machine (as you'll see later in this chapter).

BSD Flat Files and NIS—Use this plug-in to allow your Mac OS X computer to search locally for flat files containing user and group information and/or allow it to search the directory of an NIS computer, such as Linux or Solaris.

LDAPv3—Use this option when you're connecting to another Mac OS X Server or an OpenLDAP server running on another operating system.

NetInfo—You can use this plug-in when you're connecting a Mac OS X computer to an older parent NetInfo directory, such as Mac OS X Server 10.2 (Jaguar Server).

In short, when you're using the Directory Access application, understand that it's used to connect your Mac (client or server) to another directory service to obtain user name and password authentication, authorization information, and contact information.

Authentication paths

You can choose to get directory information from any of these methods, although with AD and NetInfo you're limited to binding to one server per plug-in. Once you've chosen a method and the information is retrieved correctly, you can then have your Mac OS X computer authenticate against that additional directory service.

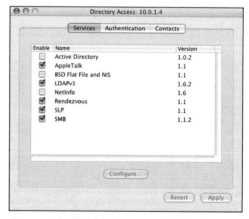

Figure 3.3 The Directory Access application allows you to connect or *bind* to another directory service.

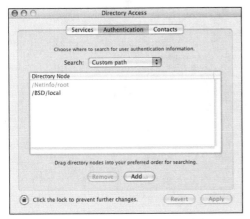

Figure 3.4 The Authentication tab allows various other locations to be searched for authentication information.

Figure 3.5 Choose Server > Connect in the Directory Access application.

Figure 3.6 Type in the address or name of the server and the administrator's name and password, and click Connect to connect to a remote Mac OS X Server's Directory Access application.

Whenever a user logs in, Mac OS X checks the local NetInfo directory first (Mac OS X and Mac OS X Server *always* check the local NetInfo directory first). If a user record isn't found in the local NetInfo directory, Mac OS X checks the authentication path for the username and password information, allowing the authenticated user to log in. That search list is handled by the Authentication tab of the Directory Access application (**Figure 3.4**).

For example, suppose you want your Mac OS X Client computer users to log in to their machines, and their user names and passwords are stored on another directory server. You don't have to create any entries in your local NetInfo directory—simply have your Mac OS X Server piggyback on another server for user names and passwords, and then add computer management using your Mac OS X Server.

Once you've chosen a plug-in, it's time to configure it. Let's start with the NetInfo plug-in.

✔ Tip

- If you're working on an Xserve or managing your server remotely, you can connect to your server's Directory Access application through yours. To do so, launch your Directory Access application located in /Application/Utilities/, and choose Server > Connect (**Figure 3.5**). Type in the address or name of the server and the administrator's name and password, and click the Connect button (**Figure 3.6**). You'll have to reauthenticate every five minutes while this application is open, so it's a good idea to get in, make your changes, save them, and get out.

NetInfo plug-in

The NetInfo plug-in is very basic. To configure your server to bind to a parent NetInfo directory, open the Directory Access application, click the Services tab, and select the NetInfo check box. Then click the Configure button (Configure…) to properly configure that plug-in (**Figures 3.7** and **3.8**).

You can find a parent NetInfo server three ways:

By IP address—Using this method ensures that you know exactly where the NetInfo parent is located. Typical NetInfo parents have the Server Tag name *network*.

By getting its parent information from a DHCP server—This entails having your Mac OS X Server get an address from a DHCP server that can also forward NetInfo information as part of its packet delivery.

By attempting to connect using the broadcast protocol—Using this approach, your Mac OS X Server sends out requests asking if any servers on the local network are parent NetInfo servers. Parents must know about the child NetInfo servers binding to them. If they don't, then your Mac OS X Server won't receive the proper information.

NetInfo is now legacy technology, and this is an unlikely scenario. However, if you aren't doing any NetInfo binding, it's important to unselect the NetInfo check box in Directory Access.

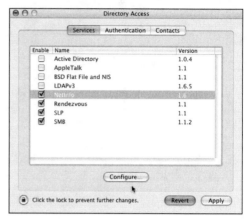

Figure 3.7 The Services tab of Directory Access includes the NetInfo plug-in.

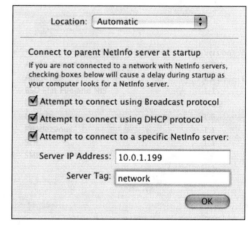

Figure 3.8 These options appear in the NetInfo plug-in after you click Configure in Directory Access.

LDAP OVERVIEW

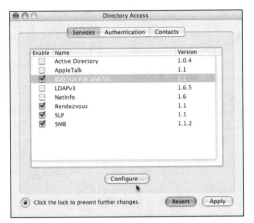

Figure 3.9 Select the BSD Flat File and NIS plug-in on the Services tab of Directory Access.

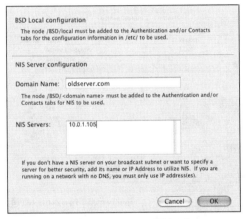

Figure 3.10 These options are available when you connect to an NIS system.

Flat Files

Before there were directories to store user information, it was stored (on various operating systems) in plain-text files on the computer. Mac OS X Client and Server still contain these plain-text files and permit an administrator to add these files in the authentication search path via the Directory Access application. See "To add flat-file searching to the authentication path," later in this chapter, for more information.

BSD Flat File and NIS plug-in

The second directory service technology this section will look at is Network Information Services (NIS). This technology is still used in certain places, and Mac OS X computers can authenticate against it using the BSD Flat File and NIS plug-in. It can also be used to authenticate against flat files that exist on the local disk, which can allow for the creation of a hidden account not found in the local directory.

To configure the NIS portion of the BSD Flat File and NIS plug-in:

1. Open the Directory Access application, located in /Applications/Utilities/, authenticate by clicking the lock in the lower-left corner of the dialog, click the Services tab, and select the BSD Flat File and NIS plug-in check box if it isn't already checked (**Figure 3.9**).

2. Click the Configure button [Configure...], and *do one of the following* (**Figure 3.10**):

   ▲ Add the domain name to the configuration to make the location of the NIS computer easier to find.

   ▲ Add the NIS server address(es).

3. Click OK to close the dialog, and click Apply [Apply] to confirm the changes.

continues on next page

LDAP OVERVIEW

4. Click the Authentication tab, and choose "Custom path" from the pop-up menu (**Figure 3.11**).

5. Click Add [Add...], and select /BSD/Local from the list.

Click Add again to add /BSD/Local to the Search path (**Figures 3.12** and **3.13**).

6. Click Apply [Apply] to commit the changes to your Open Directory architecture.

Your Mac OS X Server is now ready to have users authenticate from the NIS directory server.

✔ Tip

■ Again, this is legacy technology in most cases. It's unlikely that you'll use this technique in a newer Mac OS X Server system, unless compatibility with an NIS system is a must.

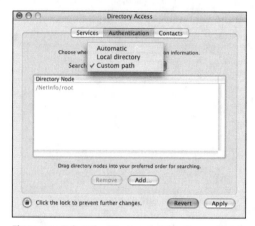

Figure 3.11 Select the "Custom path" option on the Authentication tab of Directory Access.

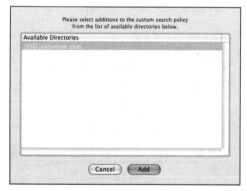

Figure 3.12 Select the BSD Flat File and NIS plug-in from the list of optional authentication methods.

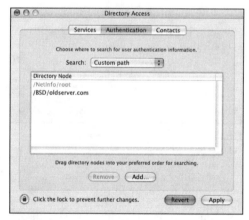

Figure 3.13 The final authentication path includes the BSD Flat File and NIS option.

LDAP OVERVIEW

Figure 3.14 Add a user in the Accounts Preference pane of System Preferences.

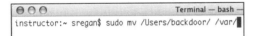

Figure 3.15 Use the mv command to move the home folder to another folder.

Figure 3.16 Delete the user account using the Accounts Preference pane of System Preferences.

To create a local user outside the NetInfo directory:

1. Use the System Preferences > Accounts Preference pane to create a user with the long name *Back Door* and the short name *backdoor* (**Figure 3.14**).

   This creates the home folder directory for the user backdoor (you can use any name that suits you).

2. Open the Terminal application, and type sudo mv /Users/backdoor/ /var/ (**Figure 3.15**).

   Press Return, and enter your administrator password when asked.

   This moves the home folder of the user backdoor away from the normal location in the /Users folder and places it in the hidden /var folder.

3. Open System Preferences, and delete the user backdoor by clicking on the Delete button below the list of users (**Figure 3.16**).

4. Confirm your deletion by clicking OK in the confirmation dialog (**Figure 3.17**).

continues on next page

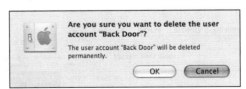

Figure 3.17 Click OK in the confirmation dialog to delete the user.

LDAP OVERVIEW

5. Open a new Finder window, choose Go > Go To Folder, and type /etc in the resulting dialog (**Figure 3.18**).

If you know Unix well, at this point you can change the contents of the file any way you see fit.

6. Drag the master.passwd file that resides in /etc to the Desktop.

Because you aren't the owner of the file, you may have to authenticate to copy it (**Figure 3.19**).

7. Open the file in a text editor, such as TextEdit.

You can't save this file with an extension, so be careful what application you use to open it.

8. Highlight the last line in the file, and copy it to a new line at the bottom of the file (**Figure 3.20**).

9. Change the short name, user ID, group ID, long name, home folder, and shell. Leave the colons and other zeros intact.

For example, in the line backdoor: *:501:501::0:0:Back Door:/var/backdoor:/bin/bash, from left to right:

▲ backdoor is the user's short name.

▲ The asterisk is a placeholder for the password that will be changed later.

▲ 501:501 is the user ID followed by the primary group ID.

▲ Back Door is the user's long name.

▲ /var/backdoor is the path to the home folder, which was moved into /var earlier.

▲ /bin/bash is the user shell type.

Figure 3.19 An Authenticate dialog appears when you attempt to copy a file from a location where the user doesn't have write access.

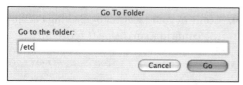

Figure 3.18 Use the Go To Folder option to connect to the /etc directory.

Figure 3.20 This master.passwd file shows the last line of the file being copied and pasted to a new line below.

Figure 3.21 Change the user's password in the master.passwd file using the passwd command.

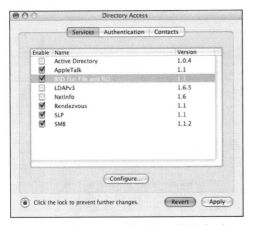

Figure 3.22 Select the BSD Flat File and NIS plug-in.

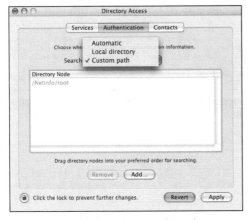

Figure 3.23 Choose the "Custom path" option.

10. Save the file.

Make sure the file is saved as plain text with *no* file extension.

11. Drag the file back into /etc/, and authenticate when necessary.

12. Open the Terminal, and change the password for your new user by typing sudo passwd −i file backdoor and pressing Return (**Figure 3.21**).

Enter *your* password first, because you started the command with sudo. Then enter and reenter the new backdoor user's password to change it.

13. While you're in the Terminal, type sudo chown −R backdoor:backdoor /var/ backdoor, and press Return.

This command reassociates the backdoor user with the backdoor home folder.

You've created a hidden user inside the local flat file. You must now add the local flat files to the authentication search path.

To add flat-file searching to the authentication path:

1. Open the Directory Access application located in /Applications/Utilities/, authenticate by clicking the lock in the lower-left corner of the dialog, click the Services tab, and select the BSD Flat File and NIS plug-in check box if it isn't already checked (**Figure 3.22**).

2. Click the Authentication tab, and choose "Custom path" from the pop-up menu (**Figure 3.23**).

continues on next page

LDAP OVERVIEW

3. Click the Add button <kbd>Add...</kbd>, and select /BSD/local from the list.

Click Add to add it to the Search path (**Figures 3.24** and **3.25**).

4. Click the Apply button <kbd>Apply</kbd> to commit the changes to your Open Directory architecture.

Your Mac OS X Server is now ready to have users authenticate from flat-file users.

5. Log out, and then log in with your new hidden account.

✔ Tip

- By making the user ID the same as your initial user, you guarantee that the backdoor user will see user 501's files.

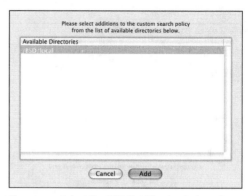

Figure 3.24 Select the BSD Flat File plug-in from the list of optional authentication methods.

Figure 3.25 The final authentication path includes the BSD Flat File option.

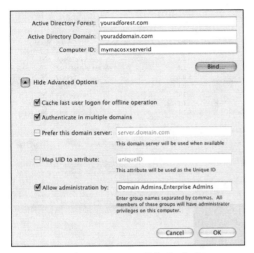

Figure 3.26 Select a computer ID in the Active Directory plug-in dialog of Directory Access.

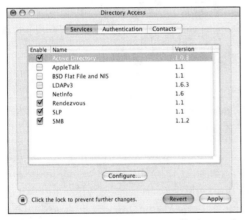

Figure 3.27 Select the Active Directory plug-in.

Figure 3.28 Enter the Active Directory forest, Active Directory domain, and computer ID.

Active Directory plug-in

When you're attempting to bind your Mac OS X computer to an Active Directory server, you must first know a few things about your AD setup. You need to know whether your AD server is in a forest and, if so, which forest. You must know the fully qualified name of the server, and you should pick a computer ID for your Mac OS X computer (**Figure 3.26**).

You'll choose from several options prior to binding.

✔ Tip

- *Never* use spaces in the name of your Computer ID when binding to an AD server. If you do, the binding process won't complete properly.

To bind Mac OS X to an Active Directory server:

1. Open the Directory Access application located in /Applications/Utilities/, authenticate by clicking the lock in the lower-left corner of the dialog, click the Services tab, and select the Active Directory plug-in check box if it isn't already checked (**Figure 3.27**).

2. Click the Configure button `Configure...`. The Active Directory configuration dialog opens.

3. Enter the Active Directory forest and domain, and add a computer ID (**Figure 3.28**).

continues on next page

4. Click the disclosure triangle next to Show Advanced Options, and add any criteria that suit your needs (**Figure 3.29**):

"Cache last user login for offline operation" allows a computer to be disconnected from the network but retain the authentication from the AD server.

"Authenticate in multiple domains" lets users be authenticated by several domains.

"Prefer this domain server" means that with several servers present, authentication is attempted with this server first, regardless of whether other servers are closer.

"Map UID to attribute" forces AD to use the entered attribute to hold the User ID.

"Allow administration by" allows groups entered here to have administrative rights when logging into a Mac OS X computer using their AD user name and password.

5. Click the Bind button [Bind...].

In the dialog that opens, enter the authorized AD name and password, and click OK (**Figure 3.30**).

The Computer OU or correct LDAP mappings should be automatically filled in.

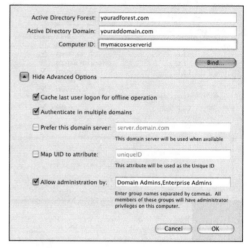

Figure 3.29 Clicking the disclosure triangle displays the Active Directory plug-in's additional options.

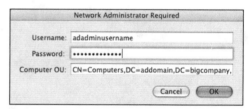

Figure 3.30 After you click the Bind button, the Active Directory authentication dialog appears.

AD Forests

An Active Directory *forest* is a collection of AD servers that are bound together, usually serving a single organization.

Active Directory and Mac OS X Server

Although you can do the previous task with Mac OS X Server, it's most commonly associated with Mac OS X Client. You would do this with Mac OS X Server to enable the management of local groups on Mac OS X Servers that contain aliases of users within the AD domain.

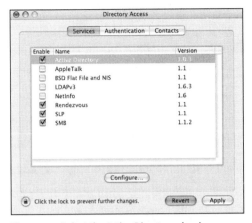

Figure 3.31 Select the Active Directory plug-in.

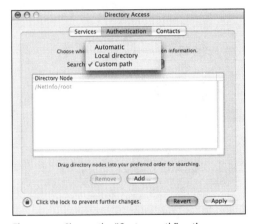

Figure 3.32 Choose the "Custom path" option.

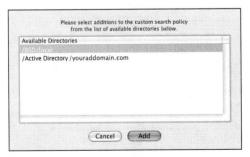

Figure 3.33 Select the Active Directory plug-in from the list of optional authentication methods.

To add Active Directory plug-in architecture searching to the authentication path:

1. Open the Directory Access application located in /Applications/Utilities/, authenticate by clicking the lock in the lower-left corner of the dialog, click the Services tab, and select the Active Directory plug-in check box if it isn't already checked. (**Figure 3.31**).

2. Click the Authentication tab, and choose "Custom path" from the pop-up menu (**Figure 3.32**).

3. Click the Add button ⟨Add...⟩, and select /Active Directory/ from the list.
   Click Add to add it to the Search path (**Figures 3.33** and **3.34**).

4. Click the Apply button ⟨Apply⟩ to commit the changes to your Open Directory architecture.

5. Log out, and then log in with your Active Directory account.

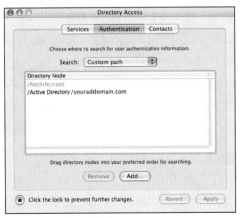

Figure 3.34 The final authentication path includes the Active Directory option.

LDAP OVERVIEW

LDAPv3 plug-in

The LDAPv3 plug-in lets Mac OS X Client and Server bind to another LDAP server and obtain authentication and authorization information from that server. This plug-in is different than the others in that it can contain many references to even *more* servers. Your Mac OS X Server can choose to authenticate against any number of servers, so the number of permutations is very high (**Figure 3.35**).

A look at the LDAPv3 plug-in reveals that you can also obtain LDAP information from a DHCP server on your network by opening the Directory Access application, selecting the LDAP plug-in, and clicking the Configure button (**Figure 3.36**). This subject is covered in more depth in Chapter 6, "Network Configuration Options."

Clicking the disclosure triangle from within the LDAP plug-in displays another area full of buttons, menus, and options.

To understand how to add an LDAP entry in this dialog, you must be familiar with the basics of LDAP; see the section "LDAP Overview," earlier in this chapter.

To set up a manual LDAP connection:

1. Open the Directory Access application located in /Applications/Utilities/, authenticate by clicking the lock in the lower-left corner of the dialog, click the Services tab, and select the LDAP plug-in check box if it isn't already checked. (**Figure 3.37**).

2. Click the Configure button ⬚Configure... .

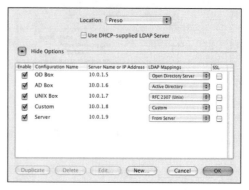

Figure 3.35 The LDAP plug-in of Directory Access has many different connections to other LDAP directory servers.

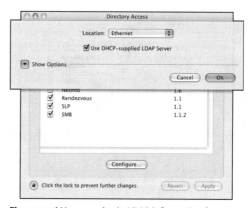

Figure 3.36 You can obtain LDAP information from a DHCP server on your network.

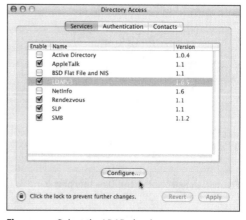

Figure 3.37 Select the LDAP plug-in.

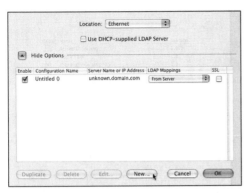

Figure 3.38 Click Show Options, and then click the New button.

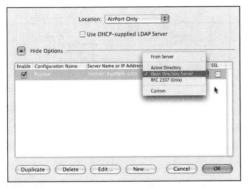

Figure 3.39 Select the initial LDAP mappings from the pop-up menu...

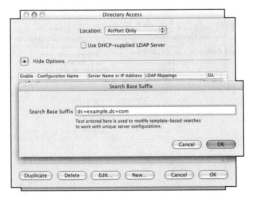

Figure 3.40 ...to open the Search Base Suffix dialog where you can enter the appropriate information.

3. Deselect the "Use DHCP-supplied LDAP Server" check box if it's selected.

Click the disclosure triangle next to Show Options (if it says Hide Options next to the triangle, then you're where you need to be) (**Figure 3.38**).

4. Click the New button, and *enter the following information*:

Configuration Name—The name you wish to give the server you're adding to the LDAP list. This name can be any combination of characters; you'll use it to identify the computer.

Server Name or IP Address—The Fully Qualified Domain Name (FQDN) or IP address of the server you're adding to the LDAP list.

LDAP Mappings—You can choose one of the following four popular server setups: From Server, Active Directory, Open Directory Server, or RFC 2307 (Unix). Or, you can make your own by choosing Custom (**Figure 3.39**).

SSL—Choose whether to encrypt traffic over secure sockets layer. This must be supported on the server you're binding to, as well.

5. Once you choose an LDAP mapping method (from the pop-up menu discussed earlier), a dialog pops up, asking for a search base suffix (**Figure 3.40**).

Without knowing much about LDAP, you can ask the administrator of the LDAP server you're connecting with to provide you with the search base. It typically looks something like dc=example,dc=com. You can also click OK without entering anything at this point and enter the suffix later.

continues on next page

LDAP OVERVIEW

6. Click the Edit button to edit the server connection and mappings (**Figure 3.41**).

7. Change the Configuration Name, Server Name or IP Address, and timeouts under the Connection tab, and click OK (**Figure 3.42**).

You have now set up a basic LDAP binding. It's likely that unless you're binding to another Mac OS X Server, you'll also need to manipulate the Search & Mappings tab, which is adjacent to the Connection tab (**Figure 3.43**).

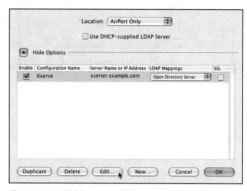

Figure 3.41 Clicking the Edit button in the LDAP plug-in dialog allows for further editing of that LDAP data.

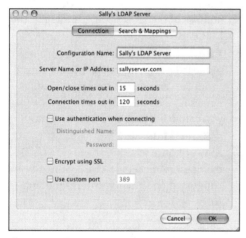

Figure 3.42 The Connection tab shows the fields associated with the current LDAP configuration.

Figure 3.43 The Search & Mappings tab lets you customize fields to permit the association of LDAP data between directory services.

✔ Tip

- All of these methods produce a result: You're binding to another directory to obtain user and group information that doesn't reside on your machine. Since you've spent all this time in Directory Access, you again must understand that this can be done on Mac OS X Client or Server. If you do this on Mac OS X Client, then users logging in to that client machine can authenticate against a directory that isn't on their local computer. If you do this on Mac OS X Server, users created in a third-party directory can be managed by Mac OS X Server management tools. Much thought went into Directory Access and the plug-ins that reside there.

LDAP Mappings

Each of the LDAP server mappings contains the attributes that are commonly found within the setups. For example, choosing Open Directory Server results in Open Directory mappings being shown. Choosing Custom lets you create your own mappings.

There is an Active Directory mapping set, but you should use the AD plug-in instead of the LDAP plug-in since the AD plug-in does a better job of addressing the issues surrounding AD. One exception to using the LDAP plug-in when binding to an AD server occurs when many additional attributes need to be mapped. In this case, the LDAP plug-in is a better choice.

LDAP OVERVIEW

NetInfo Overview

Whether it's Mac OS X or Mac OS X Server, the local directory is a NetInfo directory. NetInfo is a holdover from the days when Steve Jobs was CEO of a computer company called NeXT (after he left Apple). Some of Mac OS X is based on NeXT, so you need to be familiar with NetInfo to better your understanding of directory services.

When you create your initial user account on Mac OS X and Mac OS X Server, the user information is contained in the NetInfo directory. You can access this directory by using the NetInfo Manager application or by using command-line utilities such as `nicl` and `dscl`. Normally, most user changes are made using the Accounts Preference pane or Workgroup Manager; but under certain circumstances, you may wish to use these two command-line utilities. Although the NetInfo Manager application is located on both Mac OS X Client and Server, its usage when managing the NetInfo directory has been usurped by Workgroup Manager.

It's important to understand that when you install Mac OS X Client and Mac OS X Server (as a stand-alone server), you're working with the local directory. This has some restrictions. Although the NetInfo directory stores the user information, it doesn't store the password; the password is stored in a shadow hash file located in /private/var/db/shadow for Mac OS X Client. Also, global user authentication policies (covered later in this chapter) can't be implemented on an account with a shadow password.

To understand how NetInfo stores information, think about a database. A database uses fields to hold the data. NetInfo calls fields *properties* and the data in those fields *values*. So, for example, a NetInfo directory may have a user with the short name *sally*. A long name, user ID, and other information are tied to the user sally. Some properties are required (such as a short name), and others are optional for user data (such as a user picture).

What's in a Name?

NetInfo Manager uses the terms *properties* and *values* to describe what LDAP and Workgroup Manager call *attributes* and *values*. Understanding how NetInfo Manager lays out the directory is important, but ultimately you should use Workgroup Manager. Details about Workgroup Manager with users can be found in Chapters 2 ("Server Tools") and 4 ("User and Group Management").

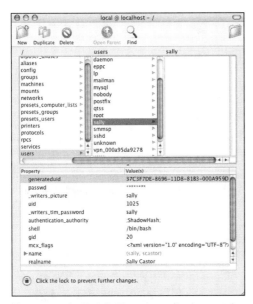

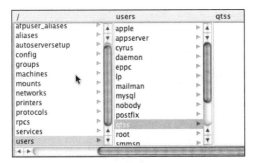

Figure 3.44 The NetInfo Manager application contains user records.

Figure 3.45 The upper-left corner of NetInfo Manager indicates the default directory.

Figure 3.46 Choose the users directory.

Think of the user with the short name sally listed with all other users. You now have a collection of users. Collections of items like this are called *records*; NetInfo divides data into records. You can see the local NetInfo directory with the records listed by opening NetInfo Manager in /Applications/Utilities/. The actual directory is located in /private/var/db/netinfo/local.nidb; it can't (and shouldn't) be accessed by anyone but root (**Figure 3.44**).

To use NetInfo Manager to show user records:

1. Launch NetInfo Manager, located in /Applications/Utilities/.

2. Locate the base of the directory above the left frame, as indicated by a forward slash (/) (**Figure 3.45**).

3. Click the forward slash to display collections of data that have been categorized in the middle column.

4. In the left column, scroll down if necessary, and choose the users directory (**Figure 3.46**).

    Doing this displays a list of users. You'll see your local administrator and any other users you've created in the local directory, as well as many users you didn't create. These are users that Mac OS X uses to manage specific services.

continues on next page

NETINFO OVERVIEW

5. Choose a user by clicking the short name.

That user's short name is displayed at the top of the next column (**Figure 3.47**).

6. Browse the Properties and associated values in the frame below the columns (**Figure 3.48**).

When you're finished with the user data, you can browse other categories. As long as you don't authenticate by clicking the lock at lower-left in NetInfo Manager, you'll be unable to effect any changes.

✔ Tips

- Prior to Mac OS X Server 10.3, you could create a NetInfo parent directory. This was a secondary directory that housed information in the same fashion as the local NetInfo directory. Users placed in the parent NetInfo directory could log in from another computer and access the services Mac OS X Server had to offer.

- Changes made directly to the NetInfo directory may render your computer unusable. If you aren't sure what you're doing, it's best to use NetInfo Manager to browse properties and values and use Workgroup Manager to change them.

- If you're installing Mac OS X Server 10.3 and don't need to upgrade from an older version of Mac OS X Server, you can skip the next section—it doesn't apply to you.

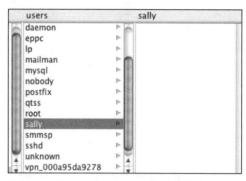

Figure 3.47 Choosing a user record in NetInfo Manager...

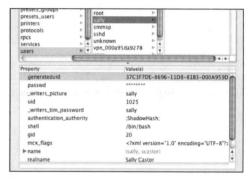

Figure 3.48 ...shows the attributes for that user.

Shadow Passwords

Shadow passwords keep passwords safer, compared to the way local passwords were stored prior to Mac OS X 10.3 (they were stored as a property in the local NetInfo directory). If you upgrade from Mac OS X 10.2 to Mac OS X 10.3, you have older, crypt passwords. Once passwords are changed, they are removed from the local NetInfo directory and stored in the shadow directory. This is mostly important to Mac OS X Client, because Mac OS X Server uses Password Server to store passwords.

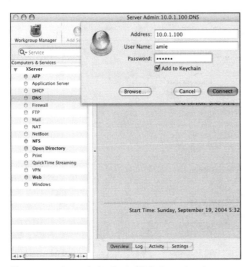

Figure 3.49 Launch the Server Admin tool and authenticate as an administrator.

Command-Line Directory Editors

Using the Terminal application lets you run both nicl (pronounced "nickel") and dscl (pronounced anyway you want), which stand for NetInfo Command Line editor and Directory Services Command Line editor, respectively. nicl isn't used much anymore because almost everything that nicl can do, dscl can do, and then some.

To run dscl, open the Terminal application, type dscl localhost, and press Return. Since dscl is an interactive tool, you're presented with a > symbol. Enter ls, and press Return to see a list of the Directory Service options. You can search your local directory from here. Type a question mark (?) and press Return to get information about the proper usage of dscl. When you're finished using dscl, type quit and press Return to get back to the command prompt.

Migrating older Mac OS X Server user records

Knowing how NetInfo stores information will help you understand how other directory services store their information. When you're using NetInfo, you have the option to migrate users' records. Before moving on to other directory services, let's examine what you need to do if you're upgrading a Mac OS X Server 10.2 to Mac OS X Server 10.3. You'll need to migrate your parent NetInfo directory to the newer LDAP directory in 10.3.

If you're upgrading from Mac OS X Server 10.2 to Mac OS X Server 10.3, you can migrate your parent NetInfo directory to an Open Directory directory by using the Server Admin tool. Ideally, you should back up your user data and install a fresh copy of Mac OS X Server 10.3, but sometimes this may not be possible. Before upgrading, *always* make a backup of the user data if possible.

To migrate user records to Mac OS X Server:

1. Install Mac OS X Server 10.3 as an upgrade on your Mac OS X Server 10.2 machine.

2. Open the Server Admin tool, located in /Applications/Server/, and authenticate as an administrative user (**Figure 3.49**). You can add the server to your Favorites menu if you wish.

continues on next page

NETINFO OVERVIEW

3. Click the disclosure triangle next to your server, and choose Open Directory from the Computers & Services list.

Click the Settings tab [Settings] and then the Protocols tab [Protocols] (**Figure 3.50**).

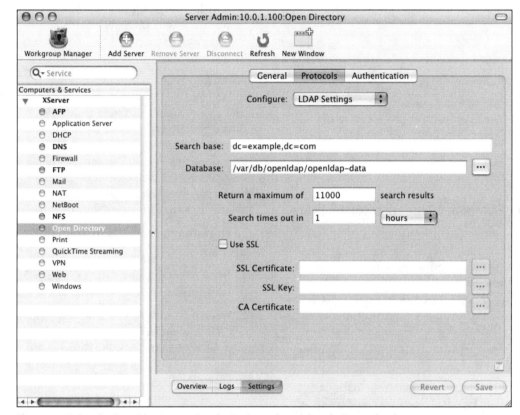

Figure 3.50 Select the Open Directory service, the Settings tab, and then the Protocols tab.

4. Select NetInfo Migration from the Configure drop-down menu (**Figure 3.51**).

You'll see that NetInfo is already running. Click the Migrate button; a dialog opens.

continues on next page

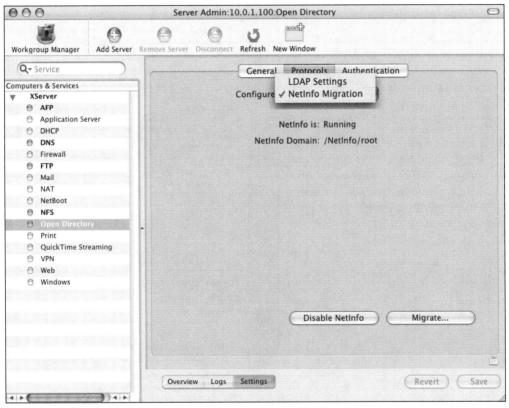

Figure 3.51 Choose NetInfo Migration from the Configure drop-down menu.

5. Enter the administrator's short name and password, the Kerberos realm (if known), and the search base (again, if known, which allows the Kerberos KDC to start up successfully) (**Figure 3.52**).

You also have the option to switch all existing NetInfo clients to LDAP. Click OK.

6. Observe the NetInfo migration and transition (**Figures 3.53** and **3.54**).

7. Your Mac OS X Server is still technically a NetInfo master, so older Mac OS X clients can bind to it. Change it to an LDAP master if you wish to continue to modernize your Mac OS X Server and take advantage of all the options Mac OS X Server 10.3 has to offer (**Figure 3.55**).

8. If necessary, you can choose to disable NetInfo if you're planning to move everything to LDAP. To do so, click the Disable NetInfo button in the Open Directory > Settings > Protocols path.

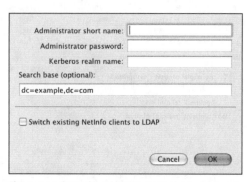

Figure 3.52 Enter the administrator's short name and password, the Kerberos realm (if known), and the search base (if known).

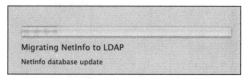

Figure 3.53 Observe the NetInfo migration and transition in the NetInfo migration progress bar...

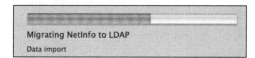

Figure 3.54 and the NetInfo conversion to LDAP progress bar.

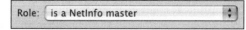

Figure 3.55 The Role pop-up menu shows the current role of the migrated server.

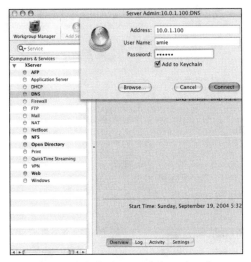

Figure 3.56 Launch the Server Admin tool, and authenticate as an administrator.

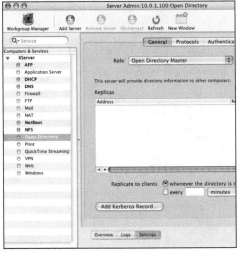

Figure 3.57 Select the General tab of the Open Directory service.

Connecting your server to another directory system

Mac OS X Server can also connect to another directory service, such as Microsoft's Active Directory or an OpenLDAP server running on a Unix computer. You use the Directory Access application located in /Applications/ Utilities/ to accomplish this task. As you've seen, the way you implement the connection of Mac OS X Server to another directory service is identical on both Mac OS X Client and Server. Once the connection has been established, you can proceed to change the behavior of your Mac OS X Server to allow it to become bound to another directory system.

This topic may not seem oriented toward Mac OS X Server, but it imparts the importance of understanding the Directory Access application.

To connect Mac OS X Server to another directory service:

1. Open the Server Admin application, located in /Applications/Server/, and authenticate as the administrator of the server (**Figure 3.56**).

2. Choose the Open Directory service from the Computers & Services frame.

   Select the Settings tab and then the General tab (**Figure 3.57**).

continues on next page

NETINFO OVERVIEW

3. Choose "Connected to a Directory System" from the Role pop-up menu, and make changes if necessary (**Figure 3.58**).

This option allows you to open the Directory Access application from here by clicking the Open Directory Access button.

4. Once you've opened Directory Access, you can choose one of the methods discussed earlier in this chapter as your binding method (NetInfo, LDAP, BSD/Local).

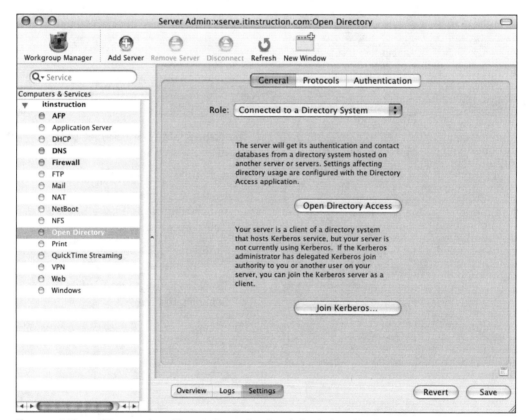

Figure 3.58 Choose "Connected to a Directory System" as the role for the Mac OS X Server.

Open Directory and the master directory

What if you don't want or need to connect to another directory system? What if you just bought an Xserve and want to start a new user directory? What if you've followed this book and already have a local, stand-alone server with 14 users in the local NetInfo directory? What if you want a robust, secure, extensible, directory service that allows users, groups, and computers to be managed?

You need to create a secondary directory on your Mac OS X Server. It will be an LDAP directory, not a NetInfo directory like the local one. This directory will be populated with the administrator who creates it; and you'll add users and groups to it. The extensibility, management, security, and power of Mac OS X Server are about to be unleashed.

A *master directory* is a secondary directory within your Mac OS X Server. You create the master directory using the Server Admin tool. Prior to creating a master, you need to ask yourself a few questions:

- ◆ Will this directory be used within a larger environment of servers?

- ◆ Will there be another Domain Name Server (DNS Server) in this environment?

- ◆ Will you be using a security method called Kerberos to handle authentication?

- ◆ Will *this* server be the Domain Name Server of your network?

The answers to these questions determine how you set up your master directory. This section assumes that your server is also the Domain Name Server and, therefore, must be running DNS. (Chapter 6, "Network Configuration Options," covers the setup and management of DNS.) Prior to creating a master, it's *highly* recommended that your Mac OS X Server either be running DNS itself or have a valid DNS entry in the Network Preference pane of your server. Failure to do this will result in unexpected behavior of your server down the road.

✔ Tip

- ■ Although you can create a master during the initial setup, doing so isn't recommended. DNS should be working properly and double-checked prior to the server's promotion to a master.

Getting It Right the First Time

Making sure your networking house is in proper order is the biggest challenge prior to promoting a stand-alone Mac OS X Server with a local NetInfo directory to a directory master that houses the local NetInfo directory and the master LDAP directory. You should ensure that your IP address is the one you want to stick with and that your subnet mask, router, DNS, and domain entries are correct and working properly prior to promoting the Mac OS X Server to a master.

To create a master directory:

1. Open the Server Admin application, located in /Applications/Server/, and authenticate as the administrator of the server (**Figure 6.59**).

2. Choose the Open Directory service from the Computers & Services frame, select the Settings tab, and then select the General tab (**Figure 3.60**).

3. Choose Open Directory Master from the Role pop-up menu (**Figure 3.61**).

   A dialog pops up, asking for information.

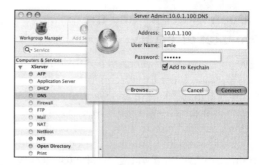

Figure 3.59 Launch the Server Admin tool, and authenticate as an administrator.

Figure 3.60 Select the Open Directory service, the Settings tab, and then the General tab.

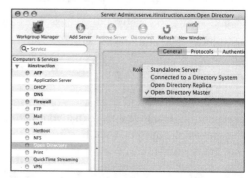

Figure 3.61 The various possible roles for a Mac OS X Server appear on the General tab of the Open Directory service.

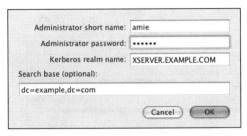

Figure 3.62 After you choose to create an Open Directory master, this dialog asks for pertinent information.

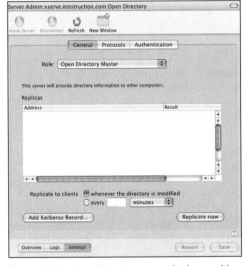

Figure 3.63 An Open Directory master is shown with no current replicas.

4. Enter the server administrator's short name and password (**Figure 3.62**).

   Click OK. If DNS is functioning properly on your network, you should see your Kerberos realm name and search base automatically populated.

5. Click the Save button [Save].

   An Open Directory Master screen with no replicas opens (**Figure 3.63**).

6. Click the Protocols tab to confirm your status as an Open Directory master.

   You can limit the number of searched records here and limit the timeout to a reasonable length (**Figure 3.64**).

   You can also move the LDAP Master directory, but doing so requires booting from another disk or partition so as not to corrupt the directory.

continues on next page

What Else Happens When You Create an Open Directory Master?

After you create an Open Directory master, you can open your Directory Access application, select the LDAP configuration, and click the Configure button. You'll see an entry for LDAPv3/127.0.0.1, which indicates that the Mac OS X Server is now bound to itself. That is, the process that creates the LDAP directory and the Kerberos Key Distribution Center (KDC; discussed later in this chapter) also creates the entry and places it in the Directory Services structure, which can be seen using the Directory Access application. In addition, the Authentication path now includes an entry for the new LDAP directory.

Figure 3.64 The Protocols tab shows the available options, such as limiting the number of records searched and encrypting transactions using SSL.

N**ET****I****NFO**** O****VERVIEW**

7. After allowing Mac OS X Server to write the necessary configuration files, click the Overview tab.

You should see all your services running (**Figure 3.65**).

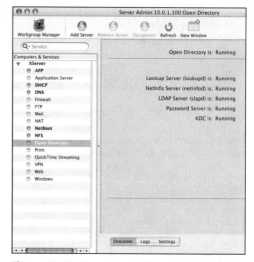

Figure 3.65 The Overview tab of the Open Directory service indicates that all pertinent services are running.

Replicas

Why buy one Xserve when you can buy two? One of the best uses of Mac OS X Server is its ability to function as a replica of another server. A *replica* is an exact duplicate of the LDAP and Password Server databases and the Key Distribution Center (KDC) on a master server. You can create replicas using the same method you used to create a master, but choose Open Directory Replica from the Role pop-up menu.

Once you choose that role, enter the following information (**Figure 3.66**):

◆ IP address of the LDAP master

◆ Root password on the LDAP master

◆ Domain administrator's short name on the master

◆ Domain administrator's password on the master

Click OK, and the replica server connects to the master; destroys its own directory, KDC, and Password Server; and replicates the master as its own.

From the master, you can see all your replicas and force them to update whenever the master is modified or at a given interval. You also have the choice to force a replication at any time.

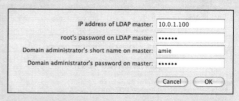

Figure 3.66 When you choose to make the Mac OS X Server a replica, this dialog appears.

NETINFO OVERVIEW

Applying Global User Authentication Policies

Now that you have an LDAP directory to store your users, you have a variety of options when choosing how those users authenticate to your server.

When you create users, you give them a long name, a short name, and a password. That's

Figure 3.67 The Authentication tab of the Open Directory service shows password server policies.

the minimum you need to create users on Mac OS X Server who can log in remotely and access folders and files needed for their work. Chapter 2, "Server Tools," examined how to quickly add users to a local directory. You probably haven't yet created a secondary directory, and it isn't necessary to do so if all you wish to do is let users log in remotely to access folders and files. You reduce the security and functionality by having the secondary directory, but it can be done.

When you create an Open Directory master, you then have the ability to set certain global authentication polices regarding user's password(s) (**Figure 3.67**). This is the case because user passwords are managed differently than those in the local directory. You've seen how to create that Open Directory master, but this chapter should help convince you that doing so is a wise decision. The global user authentication policies are listed in **Table 3.1**.

These policies help ensure security on your server by maintaining a better level of complexity when dealing with passwords.

Table 3.1

Global User Authentication Policies

DISABLE ACCOUNTS OPTION	USAGE
On *date*	Disables an account on a set date, such as when a contractor is set to leave a job site
After a set number of days	Disables an account after a set number of days, such as when a student has access for the number of days in a grading period
After a period of inactivity	Disables an account after the user doesn't log in for a set number of days, such as when a user stops using a particular file server
After a set number of failed login attempts	Disables an account after a user or hacker attempts to enter incorrect information a set number of times
PASSWORD POLICY OPTION	USAGE
Length policy	Dictates that a password must be at least a set number of characters long
Letter policy	Requires a password to contain at least one letter
Numeric character policy	Requires a password to contain at least one numeric character
Account name policy	Requires the password to be different from the account name
Reused passwords policy	Requires a password to be different from previous passwords
Password change policy	Requires a password to be changed after a set number of days, weeks, or months

To set the minimum length for passwords:

1. Open the Server Admin application, located in /Applications/Server/, and authenticate as the administrator of the server (**Figure 3.68**).

2. Choose the Open Directory service from the Computers & Services frame, select the Settings tab, and then select the Authentication tab (**Figure 3.69**).

3. Select the "Password must be at least ____ characters long" check box.

   You can also set other criteria, such as those specifying the use of letters and numeric characters.

4. Click the Save button to save the changes.

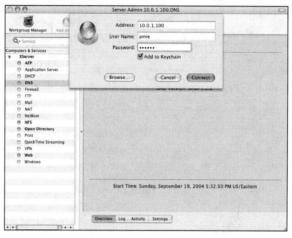

Figure 3.68 Launch the Server Admin tool, and authenticate as an administrator.

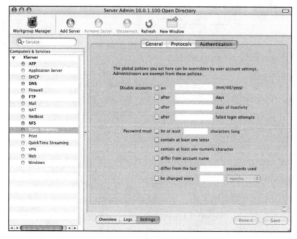

Figure 3.69 Set global password policies on the Authentication tab of the Open Directory service.

About authentication policies with Mac OS X Server

Mac OS X Server can authenticate users using several built-in methods. Depending on whether you upgraded your server or installed Mac OS X Server for the first time, you may need to change the type of password stored for each user.

Crypt passwords may have been used on a version of Mac OS X Server prior to 10.3. You can check this by opening Workgroup Manager, selecting a user, clicking the Advanced tab, and seeing whether the User Password Type pop-up window shows Crypt Password. Crypt passwords aren't as secure as other passwords and should generally be changed to a more secure method—in this case, Open Directory passwords. One reason to keep a user's password as a crypt password is if that user is connecting to your Mac OS X Server from an older Macintosh operating system, such as Mac OS 8.6. Users of Mac OS X Server who aren't promoting the server to a master (keeping it a stand-alone server) may wish to keep the crypt passwords as well, although this is a terrible security risk.

Open Directory passwords are more complex and are stored securely in a separate database. One of the advantages of using an Open Directory password is that the password database can be stored on another Mac OS X Server, thus allowing one server to be the file server and Web server and another server to be used solely for user authentication.

When you're using Open Directory passwords, there are several editable methods of authentication (*editable* means you can turn off these authentication methods to restrict access to your server via the methods):

SMB-NT is used for Windows clients.

SMB-LAN-MANAGER is used for Windows clients.

MS-CHAPv2 is used for VPN connections to the server.

CRAM-MD5 is used primarily for IMAP mail.

WEBDAV-DIGEST is used for Web-DAV connections.

APOP is used by the POP protocol when retrieving mail.

There are additional methods of authentication, but they aren't editable. You can't turn them off in the GUI; you must do so via the command line using NeST (a command-line utility that's used to manage Password Server and therefore has several functions). Not only can you turn off various authentication methods, but you can also disable Password Server and create a Password Server administrator, in case the administrator you have doesn't work.

✔ Tip

■ You may wish to check Workgroup Manager for your LDAP administrator account after you promote your server to a master. If you fail to see an administrator, you may need to use NeST to create one.

NeST

NeST stands for NetInfo Setup Tool—and yes, it's loaded with plenty of options for managing NetInfo directory connections. Although it may seem to be out of date with Mac OS X Server 10.3, you can use it in emergency situations to create a Password Server administrator with the NeST *-hostpasswordserver* command.

Kerberos overview

Understanding that Password Server exists isn't the end of the authentication options when you're dealing with Mac OS X Server. Once a master has been created, a Kerberos Key Distribution Center (KDC) is also created.

Kerberos is an authentication method in which a ticket is granted to a user by a KDC for presentation to a service to utilize that service. The KDC knows the user's password, and both the user's computer and the KDC use a complex method to determine if the password entered by the user is correct. Once the password has been approved by the KDC, additional conversations take place between the user's computer and the KDC. Ultimately, the user receives a ticket for a service, such as Apple File Protocol (when done from a Mac OS X Server). The ticket is presented to the service, and the service then grants access to (in this case) the share points the user has permission to access.

Mac OS X Server has made Kerberos mostly invisible. You can ensure the KDC is running by clicking the Overview button in the Open Directory service and viewing the status.

Note that on both the Mac OS X Client and Server, an edu.mit.kerberos file must be present for Kerberos to function properly; it's located in /Library/Preferences. When a Mac OS X Client is properly bound to a Mac OS X Server, this file is sent down from the Server to the client automatically.

Literally all you need to do is choose the services on Mac OS X Server for which you wish to use Kerberos. The currently available services are Apple Filing Protocol, FTP, and the Mail server (there are others, but Kerberos is already built into them). Mac OS X clients (Mac OS X 10.2 and later) can obtain Kerberos tickets for these services automatically. Refer to Chapter 5, "File Sharing," for more information about setting up Apple File Service and FTP, and see Chapter 8 ("Mail Services") to learn about Mail server setup.

Administrators use Kerberos to help reduce problems associated with traditional authentication methods, such as lack of encryption for passwords, packet sniffing, and attacks against services to compromise the computer and harvest passwords. By keeping the KDC in a locked room with an excellent administrator password and no root user active, you reduce your risk.

Kerberos

Kerberos was developed at MIT as a way to secure passwords on a separate computer, locked in a room. The idea was that the user's computer could access a service on a third computer without the third computer knowing the password, thus keeping authentication centralized on one server.

Kerberos also uses single sign-on: When a user logs in to the computer, the user can automatically use any Kerberized services without further authentication. In Mac OS X, the Login Window is Kerberized, and if the user has a home folder, this window mounts using a ticket obtained automatically if the user's home directory is being mounted using the AFP protocol.

Kerberos has many configuration options. However, Mac OS X applies some preconfigured settings that are therefore somewhat easy to use.

Not everyone will use Kerberos, and not all services can be Kerberized. But it's important to understand that as more and more services utilize Kerberos, the cost of setting up and managing those services will drop, and the advantages of Kerberos will become greater. The bottom line for first-time Mac OS X Server users is that Kerberos is there, whether you use it or not. It may be a good idea to experiment with the service to see if it suits you.

✔ Tips

- Mac OS X Client and Server have a Kerberos tool located in /System/Library/ CoreServices that you can use to obtain, view, and destroy tickets.

- A Kerberos *realm* is a way of identifying the KDC's area of responsibility. For example, a realm name may be YOURXSERVER.YOURCOMPANY.COM.

- A Kerberos *principal* is contained inside its realm. It can be a user or a service, such as amie@XSERVER.EXAMPLE.COM or mailservice/xserver.example.com@ XSERVER.EXAMPLE.COM.

Kerberos on Mac OS X Client

In addition to using the Kerberos tool to obtain, view, and destroy tickets, you can do these things from the command line. Use the klist -e command to view all your tickets, kinit to obtain a ticket, and kdestroy to remove and destroy a ticket.

GLOBAL USER AUTHENTICATION POLICIES

To view the Kerberos tool:

1. On Mac OS X Server, open a Finder window.

2. Navigate to /System/Library/CoreServices.

3. Locate and double-click the Kerberos tool.

4. Click the Get Tickets button (**Figure 3.70**). Your realm name appears in the resulting dialog (**Figure 3.71**).

5. Enter your administrator username and password, and click OK.

   A Kerberos ticket appears in the window (**Figure 3.72**). This ticket is valid for a certain amount of time, after which it will be destroyed.

6. Double-click the ticket to display information about it, such as encryption type, time stamp, IP address information, and more (**Figure 3.73**).

Figure 3.70 The Kerberos utility shows the realm that it sees.

Figure 3.71 You can get a ticket using the Kerberos utility.

Figure 3.72 A Kerberos ticket appears in the window.

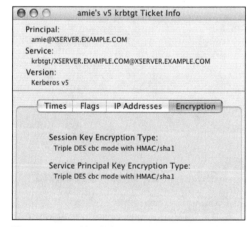

Figure 3.73 Double-clicking a ticket opens a dialog showing information associated with that ticket.

Understanding Directory Service Logs

It's important that your Mac OS X Server binding work properly. Most of the problems with binding arise from typos or mislabeled mappings. Knowing how to view and read the Directory Service log files is essential in discovering problems and fixing them.

To view the Directory Service logs:

1. Open the Server Admin application, located in /Applications/Server/, and authenticate as the administrator of the server (**Figure 6.74**).

continues on next page

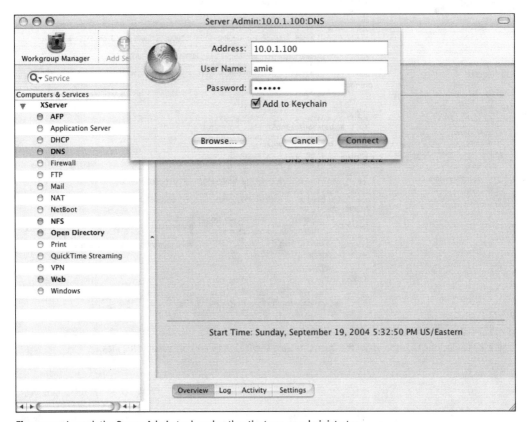

Figure 3.74 Launch the Server Admin tool, and authenticate as an administrator.

2. Choose the Open Directory service from the Computers & Services frame, and select the Logs tab.

From the Show pop-up menu, you can view many of the Open Directory log files (**Figure 3.75**).

✔ Tip

■ Prior to creating an Open Directory master, you should view the slapconfig.log in the /Library/Log directory.

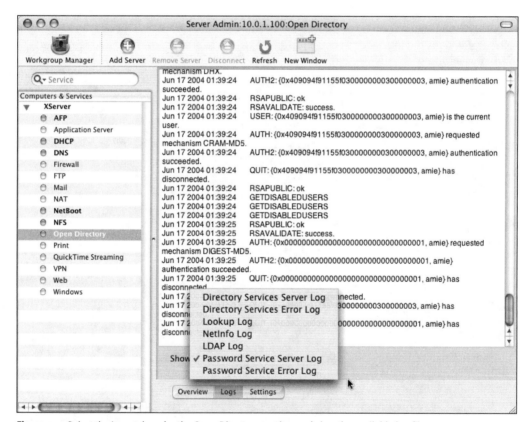

Figure 3.75 Select the Logs tab under the Open Directory service, and view the available log files.

User and Group Management

Populating a server with all your users and groups can be a potentially daunting task. Fortunately, the Workgroup Manager application, which is used to manage users, groups, computers, and sharing services, has a well-designed interface. Apple's renowned ease of use is apparent: Many of the advanced configuration options are easily accessible in this interface.

Workgroup Manager also includes numerous efficiency-enhancing features. For example, you can quickly make widespread changes by selecting and configuring multiple accounts simultaneously. A User Presets tool that can decrease the amount of time it takes to create similar user accounts is also available. Furthermore, Workgroup Manager has an Import option that lets you input new users from many types of external sources.

Before you begin setting up accounts, take time to consider how you're going to organize your users and groups. Keep in mind that on Mac OS X Server, groups are used for more than just individual file and folder permissions; they're also used to define access to share points, Web sites, email groups, and managed workgroup settings. Also, if you're configuring users and groups on an Open Directory (OD) master, it's important to consider how your groups will integrate with client computers. Remember, any groups in a shared directory are accessible to computers that authenticate against your OD master.

The reason for creating users here is if that you have anything but local users (you must have a shared directory), you can manage specific settings for each user when they log in from a Mac OS X Client that has been bound to the Mac OS X Server on which you're working. In other words, they have *no* account on the Mac OS X Client—only on the server—but they can authenticate and log in.

(You may find that an organizational tool such as a group outline or flowchart software (such as OmniGraffle from http://www.omnigroup.com) can help you plan the best implementation for your needs.)

Configuring Basic User Attributes

Workgroup Manager lets you reconfigure user attributes as many times as you want. Assuming you're a server administrator, you can configure any user account on any database hosted by that server. Otherwise, Workgroup Manager automatically prompts you for administrator authentication when attempting to make changes to a user directory you haven't already authenticated to.

This chapter assumes you've already created additional user accounts on your server. If you haven't, refer to the instructions for creating a basic user account in Chapter 2, "Server Tools."

To configure basic user attributes:

1. Launch the Workgroup Manager tool located in /Applications/Server, and authenticate as the administrator (**Figure 4.1**).

2. Click the Accounts icon ![icon] in the Toolbar and the User icon ![icon] in the account types tab (**Figure 4.2**).

   If you've added users previous to this task, they appear in the Name list.

3. Click the directory authentication icon ![Authenticated], and select the appropriate directory database from the pop-up menu (**Figure 4.3**):

   ▲ If you're working on the local directory, choose Local.

   ▲ If you're working on an Open Directory master, choose /LDAPv3/127.0.0.1.

   ▲ If you're connected to another database, choose Other, and select your database from there.

Figure 4.1 Open the Workgroup Manager tool, and authenticate as an administrator.

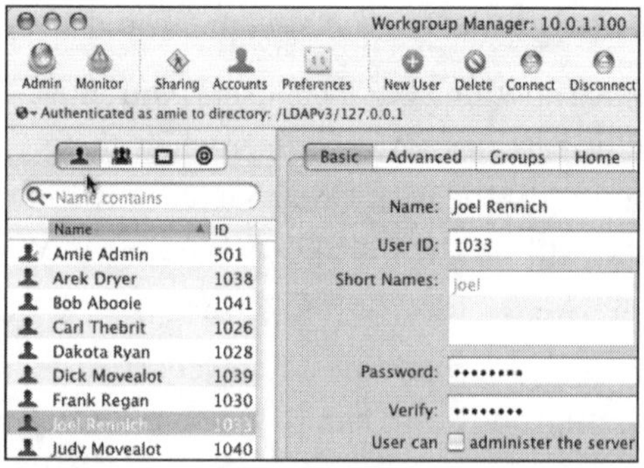

Figure 4.2 Click the Accounts button and the User tab in Workgroup Manager.

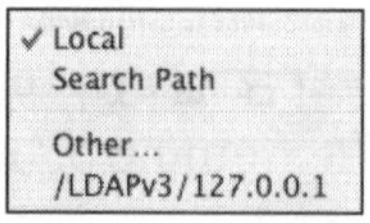

Figure 4.3 Select the appropriate directory database from the selection pop-up menu.

4. Select the user or users you wish to configure from the user list (**Figure 4.4**).

You can also create a new user by clicking the New User button  in the Toolbar.

5. In the user settings frame, click the Basic tab [**Basic**].

6. *Change any of the following* preexisting user account information (**Figure 4.5**):

- ▲ Name (long name)
- ▲ User ID
- ▲ Additional short names
- ▲ Password
- ▲ Administrator settings

Later, this chapter talks more about the administrator settings.

7. When you've finished making changes, click the Save button [**Save**].

Verify your changes by reviewing the account summary or by testing authentication from a client computer.

✔ Tip

- ■ Click the Revert button [**Revert**] if you made a mistake and don't want to apply the configuration changes.

Figure 4.4 Choose a user or users from the selected database.

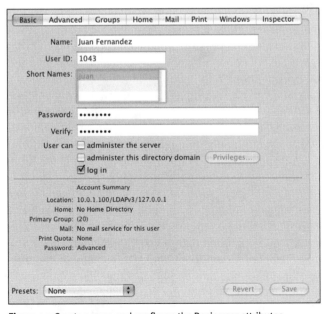

Figure 4.5 Create a user, and configure the Basic user attributes.

Configuring Multiple Users Simultaneously

There are two ways to select multiple accounts from the user list in Workgroup Manager:

◆ To choose a sequential list of accounts, select an account toward the top of the list and then, while holding down the Shift key on your keyboard, select an account further down the list. Workgroup Manager automatically selects all the accounts between your two selections.

◆ To select multiple accounts in a nonse-quential order, hold down the Command key on your keyboard and select multiple accounts. Workgroup Manager adds accounts to your total selection as you click each account individually.

After you've selected all the accounts you wish to change, continue by configuring settings as if you had selected only an individual user account. By clicking the Save button, you'll apply the configura-tion changes to all the user accounts you selected. The only settings you can't apply to multiple user accounts are Name, User ID, and Short Names.

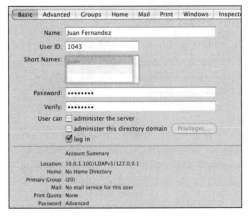

Figure 4.6 Navigate to the user account's Basic tab in Workgroup Manager.

Figure 4.7 Add an additional short name for a user.

Adding short names

The initial short name of a user in Mac OS X is the name of that user's home folder. Although you can add more short names, changing the original isn't a good idea unless you have a specific reason to do so. Apple recognizes this fact.

Toward that end, the only user attribute you can't change in the Basic tab of Workgroup Manager after you've created a user account is the user's short name. To remedy this situation, Mac OS X server lets you add several additional short names. Once they're configured, the user can use any short name they desire for authentication.

To add short names:

1. In Workgroup Manager, navigate to configure the user's Basic account attributes (**Figure 4.6**).

2. Double-click the area directly below the user's original short name.

   A text entry field appears, in which you can enter an additional short name (**Figure 4.7**).

3. Press the Enter key, and the Save button [Save] becomes available.
   Click Save.

✔ Tips

- You can add more short names by double-clicking the empty space below the last short name in the list.

- All short names, including additional short names that you add, must be unique within the entire system.

- Although the first short name is limited to 31 characters, additional short names may be longer.

"Changing" the Original Short Name

You really can't change the original short name. However, with some work, you can effectively do so by creating a new account with the desired short name and then moving the user's configuration and files to the new account. Follow these steps:

1. Create a preset using the user's old account (see "Using Presets for New Accounts," later in this chapter).

2. Create the new account using this preset.

3. Give the new account the same User ID value as the old account. The new account will have attributes and permissions similar to those of the old account.

Note that this solution does *not* move the user's email database or home folder files to the new account. You'll have to reconfigure those items manually.

Thoroughly test the new account before you delete the old one!

Figure 4.8 Open Workgroup Manager, and authenticate as an administrator.

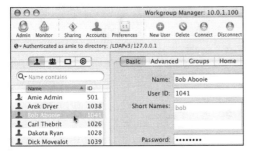

Figure 4.9 Click the Accounts button and the User tab in Workgroup Manager.

Figure 4.10 Select the appropriate directory database from the selection pop-up menu.

Administrative User Options

Administrative user accounts on Mac OS X Server are very similar to administrative user accounts on Mac OS X Client. Administrative users can configure any settings or file permissions on both Mac OS X Client and Server. Essentially, an administrative user account is any user who is also in the Admin group. Thus, it's important to restrict administrative user accounts to only those users who require such authority.

From an account management standpoint, administrators aren't that different from other user accounts. In fact, administrative users and regular users are only separated by one check box in the Workgroup Manager application.

This chapter assumes you've already created additional user accounts on your server. If you haven't, refer to the instructions for creating a basic user account in Chapter 2, "Server Tools."

To change administrative user options:

1. Launch the Workgroup Manager tool located in /Applications/Server, and authenticate as the administrator (**Figure 4.8**).

2. Click the Accounts icon ![icon] in the Toolbar and the User icon ![icon] in the account types tab.

   The user information is displayed (**Figure 4.9**).

3. Click the directory authentication icon ![Authenticated], and select the appropriate directory database from the pop-up menu (**Figure 4.10**).

continues on next page

4. Select the user or users you wish to configure from the user list (**Figure 4.11**).

5. In the user settings frame, click the Basic tab [Basic].

6. Depending on whether the user account is in a local or a shared directory, *do one of the following:*

- ▲ If the user account is in a local directory, select the "User can administer the server" check box (**Figure 4.12**).

- ▲ If the user account is in a shared directory, select the "User can administer the server" check box and the "User can administer this directory domain" check box (**Figure 4.13**). Clicking that check box invokes the administrator privileges dialog (**Figure 4.14**); click the OK button [OK] to accept the default settings.

7. When you've finished making changes, click the Save button [Save].

This user is now allowed to make changes to all server settings, file permissions, and user accounts.

✔ Tips

- ■ Administrative users can also become the root user by typing sudo –s in the Terminal and then pressing Return and entering their password.

- ■ To revert the administrative account back to a regular user account, deselect both administrator check boxes and save your changes.

- ■ An administrative user account in a shared directory can administer any computer that authenticates against that shared directory. In other words, if your client computers use the directory server, then server administrators also have administrative rights on client computers.

Figure 4.11 Choose a user from the selected database.

Figure 4.12 If the user account is in a local directory, select the "User can administer the server" check box.

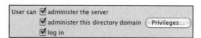

Figure 4.13 If the user account is in a shared directory, select the "User can administer the server" check box and the "User can administer this directory domain" check box. Doing so...

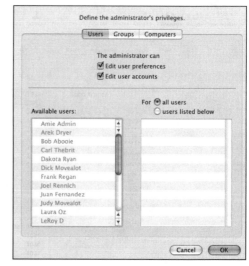

Figure 4.14 ...opens the administrator's privileges dialog.

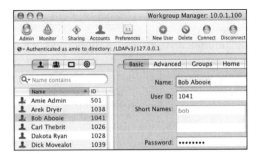

Figure 4.15 Click the Accounts button and the User tab in Workgroup Manager.

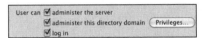

Figure 4.16 Verify that the "User can administer this directory domain" check box is selected.

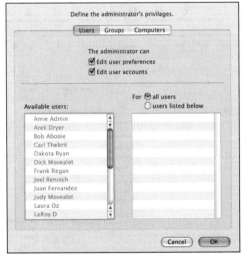

Figure 4.17 Click the Privileges button to display the administrator's editing privileges dialog.

Restricting administrator directory access

On Mac OS X Client, every administrative user is allowed to edit all settings, permissions, and user accounts. However, Mac OS X Server gives you more granularity when configuring administrative user permissions. Specifically, Mac OS X Server distinguishes administrators who can configure service settings from those who can configure account settings and share points. For example, server administrators can use the Server Admin tool, whereas directory administrators can use the Workgroup Manager tool.

In the task "To change administrative user options," you were instructed to enable unlimited server and directory administration rights for a user account, thus turning it into an administrative account. The following task explains how to restrict an administrator's directory permissions.

To restrict administrator directory access:

1. In Workgroup Manager, navigate to configure an administrative user's Basic account attributes (**Figure 4.15**).

2. Verify that the "User can administer this directory domain" check box is selected (**Figures 4.16**).

3. Click the Privileges button [Privileges...]. The administrator's privileges dialog drops down (**Figure 4.17**).

continues on next page

4. *Select one of the following* account types to edit:

▲ Users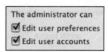

▲ Groups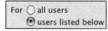

▲ Computers

At this point, the task assumes you've chosen the Users tab. The options are similar for each account type.

5. To configure the administrator's permissions, *select or deselect the following options* (**Figure 4.18**):

▲ "Edit user preferences" lets the administrator edit managed preferences for this account type.

▲ "Edit user accounts" lets the administrator edit account attributes for this account type.

6. Select the "For users listed below" radio button (**Figure 4.19**).

7. Drag and drop accounts from the "Available users" column to the right column (**Figure 4.20**).

8. Click the OK button to accept the changes.

The administrator's permissions dialog closes.

9. Click the Save button.

✔ Tips

■ When it's properly configured, you can safely delegate the task of managing accounts to other users with more time on their hands for such tasks. Keep in mind that every administrator can still become root in the terminal.

■ You can select more than one account at a time while in the administrator's privileges dialog by holding down the Shift or Command key on your keyboard while you make your selections.

Figure 4.18 Set the administrator permissions in the administrator privileges dialog.

Figure 4.19 Choose the option button that allows an administrator to administer certain users.

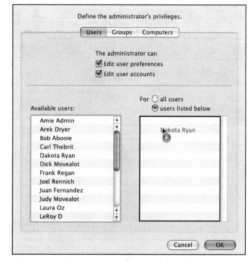

Figure 4.20 Drag users into the field to allow administration by a certain administrator.

Figure 4.21 Open Workgroup Manager, and authenticate as an administrator.

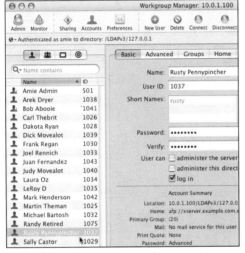

Figure 4.22 Click the Accounts button and the User tab in Workgroup Manager.

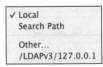

Figure 4.23 Select the appropriate directory database from the selection pop-up menu.

Figure 4.24 Choose a user from the selected database.

Advanced User Configuration

The Workgroup Manager tool affords a variety of advanced user configuration options that you may find useful. For example, you may not want a user to be able to log in remotely via the command line. Or, if they do have remote terminal access, you can dictate what type of shell they use.

This discussion assumes you've already created additional user accounts on your server. If you haven't, refer to the instructions for creating a basic user account in Chapter 2, "Server Tools."

To configure the shell type:

1. Launch the Workgroup Manager tool located in /Applications/Server, and authenticate as the administrator (**Figure 4.21**).

2. Click the Accounts icon in the Toolbar and the User icon in the account types tab.
   User information is displayed (**Figure 4.22**).

3. Click the directory authentication icon, and select the appropriate directory database from the pop-up menu (**Figure 4.23**).

4. Select the user or users you wish to configure from the user list (**Figure 4.24**).

5. In the user settings frame, click the Advanced tab.

continues on next page

ADVANCED USER CONFIGURATION

6. Click the Login Shell pop-up menu, and then choose a default shell (**Figure 4.25**).

The login shell permits users to use the Terminal to access the server remotely via the command line.

7. When you've finished making changes, click the Save button (Save).

Now, any time this user attempts to launch a command-line interface (generally, using the Terminal application), they will be presented with the shell type defined by this setting.

✔ Tip

■ You can define a custom shell type or script file by selecting Custom from the Login Shell pop-up menu.

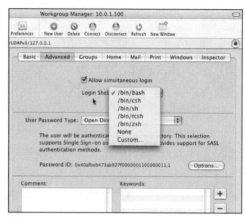

Figure 4.25 Choose an option from the Login Shell pop-up menu.

Does Susan Need to See a Shell?

A *shell* is Unix geek speak for a specific type of command-line environment. Believe it or not, there is more than one way to input cryptic strings of characters into the command line. Basically, the reason for all these different shell types boils down to user preference. For instance, the default shell for Mac OS X 10.3 is the bash shell, which is common among Linux systems. Prior to Mac OS X 10.3, the default shell was tsch, which is common among BSD Unix systems.

You can't really see a shell; you just know that when you type in commands, they belong to a particular shell type. Most users will be content with the bash shell, which is the default shell when you're creating users.

Configuring password types

Mac OS X Server 10.3 provides a variety of different password types for different services. The default password type for most users is Open Directory, because it provides the greatest security. (See Chapter 3, "Open Directory," for more information.) Occasionally, though, you may wish to change a user's password from one type to another. The most common reason for doing so is backward compatibility when you have older Mac OS clients (such as System 8.1) that need to connect to your Mac OS X Server.

The password types are as follows:

Open Directory passwords are the default type for Mac OS X Server 10.3. Open Directory provides single sign-on using Kerberos authentication. This service also provides authentication through a wide variety of other protocols including APOP, SMB-NT, DHX, CRAM-MD5, SMB-LAN Manager, and Web-DAV.

Shadow passwords are the default type for Mac OS X Client. If you as an administrator wish to use shadow passwords and not take advantage of the Open Directory password structure, you can do so.

Crypt passwords are the default type for Mac OS X version 10.1 and earlier. This type of password should only be used for backward compatibility.

To configure the password type:

1. In Workgroup Manager, navigate to configure the user's Advanced account attributes (**Figure 4.26**).

continues on next page

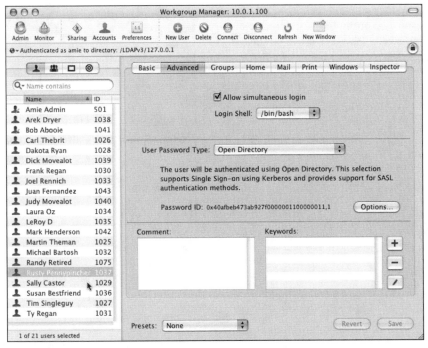

Figure 4.26 Navigate to the Advanced tab in Workgroup Manager.

ADVANCED USER CONFIGURATION

2. Depending on whether the user account is in a local or a shared directory, *select one of the following options* from the User Password Type pop-up menu:

▲ If the user account is in a local directory, your choices include Open Directory and Shadow Password (**Figure 4.27**).

▲ If the user account is in a shared directory, your choices include Open Directory and "Crypt password" (**Figure 4.28**).

3. Enter and verify a password, and click OK (OK) (**Figure 4.29**).

4. When you've finished making changes, click the Save button (Save).

Remember to test authentication from a client computer to verify the new password.

✔ Tip

■ When you're changing the password type, you'll be prompted to enter a new user password. However, it can be the same as the old password.

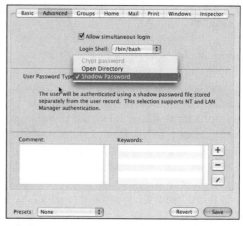

Figure 4.27 The User Password Type pop-up menu includes these options for a local user account...

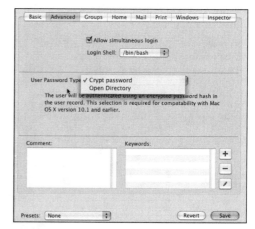

Figure 4.28 ...and these options for a network user account.

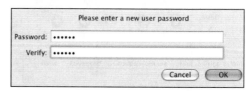

Figure 4.29 Enter a new password.

Adding comments to a user account

As an organizational aide, Mac OS X Server lets you add a comment to any user account. This comment is primarily used for administrators to add notes or information about a particular user. However, you can also use comments as part of your search criteria to find a specific account among a large list of users. (User searches are covered in the task "To search user accounts.")

To add a comment to a user account:

1. In Workgroup Manager, navigate to configure the user's Advanced account attributes (**Figure 4.30**).

2. Double-click in the Comment field, and enter your comment (**Figure 4.31**).

3. When you've finished making changes, click the Save button [Save].

✔ Tip

■ You can change a comment at any point by entering new text.

Adding keywords to a user account

As yet another organizational aide, Mac OS X Server lets you add keywords to any user account. A keyword provides an additional bit of information to quickly find specific accounts among a large list of users. Keywords help further define users through categories you create, such as *Temporary worker*, or your personal rating system for each user's computer experience and knowledge.

Say, for example, that you had 50 users. You could rate them with the following keywords: Novice, Intermediate, Expert, Certified, Mac OS X, Mac OS 9, Windows, and/or Unix. You could take that even further by entering application(s) they know well. You could also enter certifications they've received, such as Apple's ACHDS and ACTC. These keywords could be combined to allow you to search accounts for users who were trained or knowledgeable in a specific field. (User searches are covered in the task "To search user accounts.") Initially, no keywords are configured.

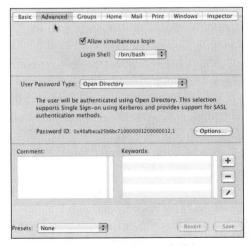

Figure 4.30 Navigate to the Advanced tab in Workgroup Manager.

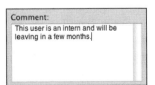

Figure 4.31 Double-click in the Comment field, and enter your comment.

To add a keyword to a user account:

1. In Workgroup Manager, navigate to configure the user's Advanced account attributes (**Figure 4.32**).

2. Click the Edit button ✎.

   The "Manage available keywords" dialog drops down (**Figure 4.33**).

3. Enter your keyword in the lower field, and click the Add button ⊕ to add that keyword to the list.

   To delete a keyword, select the word and then click the Delete button ⊖.

4. When you've finished managing the keyword list, click the OK button OK.

5. Click the Add button ⊕ next to the Keywords field.

   The Select dialog drops down (**Figure 4.34**).

6. Select the keywords you want to add to the user account, and then click the OK button OK.

7. When you've finished making changes, click the Save button Save.

✔ Tips

- You can always add more keywords at any time, or delete them by clicking the Delete button ⊖.

- Keywords are case sensitive. In other words, the keyword *Temporary* is different than the keyword *temporary*.

- You can select multiple items in the Select dialog by holding down the Command or Shift key on your keyboard while you make your selections.

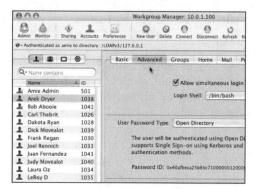

Figure 4.32 Navigate to the Advanced tab in Workgroup Manager.

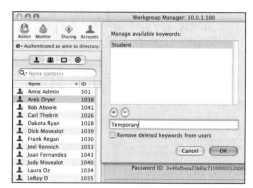

Figure 4.33 The "Manage available keywords" dialog drops down.

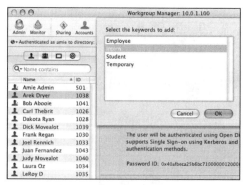

Figure 4.34 The Select dialog appears.

Figure 4.35 Open the Workgroup Manager tool, and authenticate as an administrator.

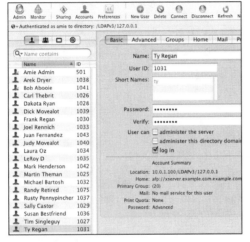

Figure 4.36 Click the Accounts button and the User tab in Workgroup Manager.

Figure 4.37 Select the appropriate directory database from the selection pop-up menu.

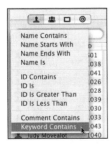

Figure 4.38 Select the search category you wish to use from the pop-up menu.

Figure 4.39 Entering a keyword search filters the user list.

Searching user accounts

Because Mac OS X Server has the potential to host thousands of user accounts, you may find it difficult to locate a specific account in the user list. Workgroup Manager lets you sort through the user list using a variety of search criteria, including Name, User ID, Comments, and Keywords. (For more about adding comments and keywords, see the previous tasks.)

To search user accounts:

1. Launch the Workgroup Manager tool located in /Applications/Server, and authenticate as the administrator (**Figure 4.35**).

2. Click the Accounts icon in the Toolbar and the User icon in the account types tab (**Figure 4.36**).

3. Click the directory authentication icon, and select the appropriate directory database from the pop-up menu (**Figure 4.37**).

4. Click the Spyglass icon above the user list, and select the search category you wish to use from the pop-up menu (**Figure 4.38**).

5. Enter your search criteria in the field above the user list.

   As you type, the list is automatically pared down to reveal the user accounts that fit your search criteria (**Figure 4.39**).

6. To bring your list back to its full length, delete the search criteria.

✔ Tip

■ Keyword searches are case-sensitive; name and comment searches aren't.

Creating Groups

Essentially, a group is nothing more than a list of users. Nevertheless, groups are used as a means to organize access to file and folder permissions, share points, Web sites, email groups, and managed workgroup settings.

This section discusses initial group configuration; the next section covers adding users to group lists. Implementation of groups in specific services is discussed in future chapters.

To create a group:

1. Launch the Workgroup Manager tool located in /Applications/Server, and authenticate as the administrator (**Figure 4.40**).

2. Click the Accounts icon ![icon] in the Toolbar and the Group icon ![icon] in the account types tab (**Figure 4.41**).

3. Click the directory authentication icon ![icon], and select the appropriate directory database from the pop-up menu (**Figure 4.42**).

Figure 4.40 Open the Workgroup Manager tool, and authenticate as an administrator.

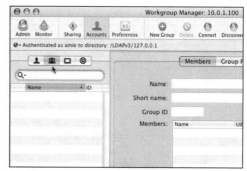

Figure 4.41 Click the Accounts button and the group tab in Workgroup Manager.

Figure 4.42 Select the appropriate directory database from the selection pop-up menu.

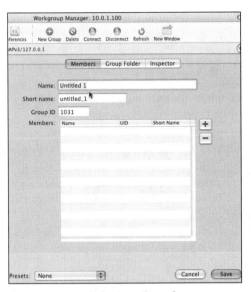

Figure 4.43 Enter the basic attributes for a group.

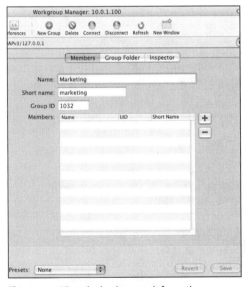

Figure 4.44 View the basic group information, including the group ID.

4. Click the New Group button ![New Group].

   The information in the Members frame is populated with a new untitled group (**Figure 4.43**).

5. Enter a new group name (long name), short name, and group ID.

   Using the automatically generated Group ID is usually acceptable (**Figure 4.44**). It's good practice to keep the long name and short name the same, although doing so isn't required.

6. When you've finished making changes, click the Save button ![Save].

   You can now begin populating this group with members; see the section "Adding Users to Groups."

✔ Tip

- As is the case for user accounts, no two group short names or group IDs should be the same.

Assigning group folders

Just as a user can have a home folder, a group can have a group folder. The group folder is used as a common access point for all members of that group. Group folders aren't required for remote login access or any other services; they're convenient locations for shared files. However, group folders must reside inside a share point that your client computers can access. Refer to Chapter 5, "File Sharing," for more information about configuring share points.

To assign a group folder:

1. In Workgroup Manager, navigate to the appropriate directory and group list that you wish to have a group folder (**Figure 4.45**).

   See steps 1–3 of the task "To create a group."

2. Select the group to which you wish to assign a group folder (**Figure 4.46**).

3. Click the Group Folder tab Group Folder (**Figure 4.47**).

4. Select the share point where the group folder will reside by *doing one of the following:*

   ▲ If this server has been configured with network mount share points such as sharing the Group folder, select one of those shares from the list (**Figure 4.48**). (See the task "To create additional network mounts" in Chapter 5.)

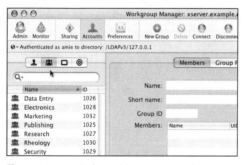

Figure 4.45 Use Workgroup Manager to navigate to the appropriate directory and group list.

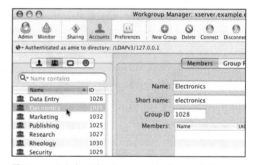

Figure 4.46 Select the group to which you wish to assign a group folder.

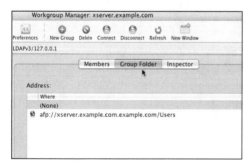

Figure 4.47 Click the Group Folder tab.

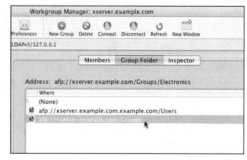

Figure 4.48 Select a group folder location from the network mount list.

CREATING GROUPS

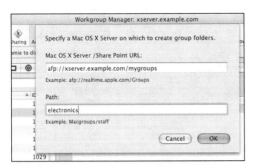

Figure 4.49 Specify the server's address, the share point, and the client's mount point.

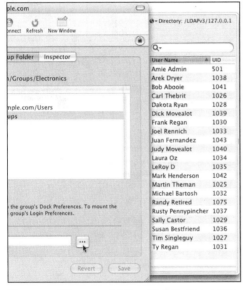

Figure 4.50 When you click the ellipsis button, a user drawer appears to one side of the main Workgroup Manager window.

▲ Click the Add button ⊕ , and specify a custom share point. You must specify the server's address, the share point, and the client's mount point (**Figure 4.49**).

5. To specify an owner for the group folder, click the ellipsis button ⋯ next to the Owner Name field.

A user drawer appears to one side of the main Workgroup Manager window (**Figure 4.50**).

6. Click and drag a user account from the user list to the Owner Name field (**Figure 4.51**).

7. When you've finished making changes, click the Save button Save .

The group folder will automatically be created overnight on the server, provided the server is left running.

✔ Tips

■ You can use command-line tools to enable disk usage quotas per group account. See "Setting disk quotas via the command line" for more information.

■ You can force the server to create the group folder immediately by entering the following command in the Terminal: `sudo creategroupfolder`.

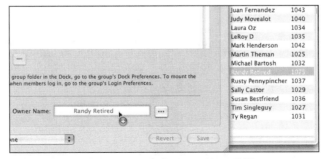

Figure 4.51 Drag a user account to the Owner Name field.

Adding users to groups

Groups are generally more useful when you add accounts to their member list. Fortunately, Workgroup Manager provides an easy-to-use interface for managing group members. The next task shows you how to add users to groups; conversely, the task after that shows how to add groups to users.

To add users to a group:

1. Launch the Workgroup Manager tool located in /Applications/Server, and authenticate as the administrator (**Figure 4.52**).

2. Click the Accounts icon ▲ in the Toolbar and the Group icon 👥 in the account types tab (**Figure 4.53**).

3. Click the directory authentication icon **⊘▾Authenticated**, and select the appropriate directory database from the pop-up menu (**Figure 4.54**).

4. Select the group to which you wish to assign users (**Figure 4.55**).

5. Click the Members tab **Members**, and then click the Add button **+** next to the Members list.

   A user drawer appears to one side of the main Workgroup Manager window (**Figure 4.56**).

Figure 4.52 Open the Workgroup Manager tool, and authenticate as an administrator.

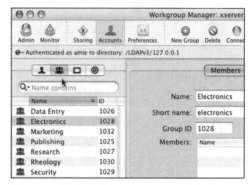

Figure 4.53 Click the Accounts button and the Group tab in Workgroup Manager.

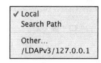

Figure 4.54 Select the appropriate directory database from the selection pop-up menu.

Figure 4.55 Select the group to which you want to add users.

6. Click and drag a user account or list of users from the user list to the Members field (**Figure 4.57**).

7. When you've finished making changes, click the Save button [Save].

✔ Tips

- To delete group members, click the account in the Members list, and then click the Delete button [−].

- On Mac OS X Server 10.3, you can't add a group to another group's user list.

- Administrative users are automatically placed in the Admin group user list.

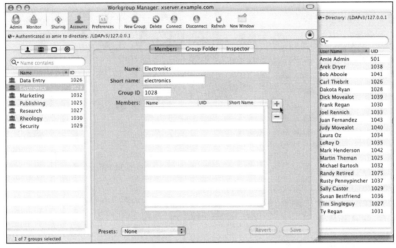

Figure 4.56 When you clicking the Add button, a user drawer appears to one side of the main Workgroup Manager window.

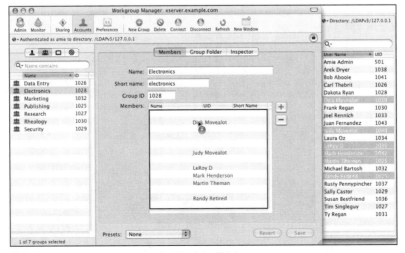

Figure 4.57 Drag user accounts to the Members field.

Adding groups to users

You may find it easier to manage groups by adding groups to users. However, it's important to understand that groups are only lists of user accounts. In Workgroup Manager, when you add a group to a user account, the system is actually adding the user account to that group's user list. This simulation of adding groups to users is another convenience provided by Mac OS X Server.

Figure 4.58 Open the Workgroup Manager tool, and authenticate as an administrator.

To add a group to a user:

1. Launch the Workgroup Manager tool located in /Applications/Server, and authenticate as the administrator (**Figure 4.58**).

2. Click the Accounts icon in the Toolbar and the User icon in the account types tab (**Figure 4.59**).

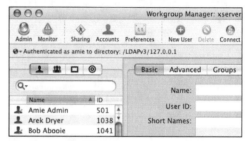

Figure 4.59 Click the Accounts button and the User tab in Workgroup Manager.

3. Click the directory authentication icon , and select the appropriate directory database from the pop-up menu (**Figure 4.60**).

4. In the user list, select the user or users you wish to add to a group (**Figure 4.61**).

Figure 4.60 Select the appropriate directory database from the selection pop-up menu.

Figure 4.61 Select the user or users you want to add to a group.

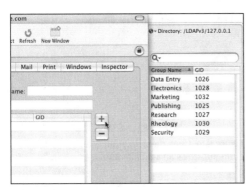

Figure 4.62 Clicking the Add button opens a group drawer to one side of the main Workgroup Manager window.

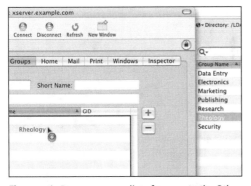

Figure 4.63 Drag a group or list of groups to the Other Groups field.

5. In the user settings frame, click the Groups tab Groups .

6. Click the Add button + next to the Other Groups list (**Figure 4.62**).

   A group drawer appears to one side of the main Workgroup Manager window.

7. Click and drag a group or list of groups from the group list to the Other Groups field (**Figure 4.63**).

8. When you've finished making changes, click the Save button Save .

✔ Tips

- To delete group memberships, click the group in the Other Groups list, and then click the Delete button − .

- Mac OS X Server recognize a maximum of 16 groups per user. In other words, you can have as many users as you want in a group list, but a user can belong to only 16 different groups.

- You can show the system groups by selecting Preferences > "Show system users & groups" in Workgroup Manager.

What Is a Primary Group?

Every user belongs to at least one group, their *primary group*. The default primary group for all users on Mac OS X Server is the Staff group (the Staff Group ID is 20). However, you can specify any group as a user's primary group in the user's Groups settings in Workgroup Manager.

You shouldn't remove the user from the primary group listing. You can, however, change the user's primary group, which removes them from the previous primary group.

The primary group is used by the system to determine the default permissions when a user creates a new file. Standard Unix behavior dictates that when a new file is created, the file's owner is the user who created it, and the file's group is the primary group of the user who created it. However, you can override this behavior in the AFP and SMB share point settings. (For more information on share points, see Chapter 5.)

CREATING GROUPS

Setting the Home Directory

User home directories are an integral part of any user account. Any user information stored outside of the directory database is stored in the user's home directory. For example, all of a user's personal documents and application preferences are stored in their home directory.

Local user home directories are usually stored on a local hard drive. For example, the primary server administrator's home directory is stored in the /Users directory. Most Mac OS X Clients keep local user directories in this location as well.

On the other hand, network user home directories must reside on a server configured with a network mount share point to which your clients have access. Network mount share points are like regular server share points, with one very important exception: Client computers automatically connect to network mount share points during startup. This is necessary because the Login window process on the client must have access to the home directories before any user can log in. (See Chapter 5, "File Sharing," for more information about configuring network mount share points.)

To create a user home directory:

1. Launch the Workgroup Manager tool located in /Applications/Server, and authenticate as the administrator (**Figure 4.64**).

2. Click the Accounts icon ![Accounts] in the Toolbar and the User icon ![User] in the account types tab (**Figure 4.65**).

3. Click the directory authentication icon ![Authenticated], and select the appropriate directory database from the pop-up menu (**Figure 4.66**).

Figure 4.64 Open the Workgroup Manager tool, and authenticate as an administrator.

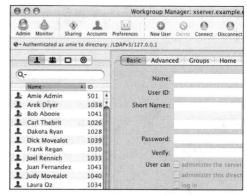

Figure 4.65 Click the Accounts button and the User tab in Workgroup Manager.

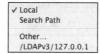

Figure 4.66 Select the appropriate directory database from the selection pop-up menu.

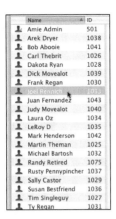

Figure 4.67 Choose a user or users from the selected database.

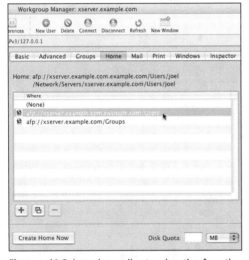

Figure 4.68 Select a home directory location from the network mount list.

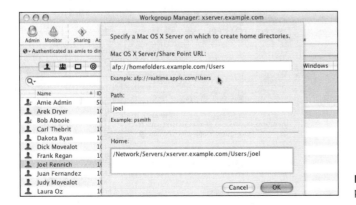

Figure 4.69 Specify a custom mount point for the user's home directory.

4. Select the user or users you wish to configure from the user list (**Figure 4.67**).

5. In the user settings frame, click the Home tab Home .

6. To select the share point where the home directory will reside, *do one of the following:*

   ▲ If this server has been configured with network mount share points, select one of those shares from the list (**Figure 4.68**).

   ▲ Click the Add button + , and specify a custom share point. You must specify the server's address, the share point, the name of the directory, and the client's mount point (**Figure 4.69**).

   It's easier to create the network mount share, but custom shares are more versatile. See the sidebar "Custom Mount Points" for more information.

7. When you've finished making changes, click the Save button Save .

8. Click the Create Home Now button Create Home Now to create the user's home directory immediately.

   Otherwise, the home directory will be automatically created the first time this user logs in.

   continues on next page

SETTING THE HOME DIRECTORY

✔ Tips

■ You can also create a home directory by typing `sudo createhomedir -a` from the Terminal.

■ If users are logging in from Windows computers that require a home directory, the home directory must be created prior to those users logging in.

■ Only local and AFP shared home directories are automatically created the first time a user logs in. For any other configuration, you must manually create the home directories.

■ It's strongly suggested that you thoroughly test a few network home directories before you implement this feature on a wide scale.

■ You can always change a user's home directory setting in the future. However, if you move a user's home directory location in the Workgroup Manager settings, the server won't move the user's data to the new location for you—you must manually move the user's data to the new location. Be sure to verify the ownership and permissions of the data after moving it to another location.

Custom Mount Points

When you choose custom mount points, you're allowing the mount point to go to another directory or possibly another server. This allows for a greater range of possible locations for the actual home folder. The three options for the custom mount point are as follows:

Share Point URL is the URL-style path to the user's home folder.

Path is the user's short name.

Home is the full path to the location of the home folder.

Figure 4.70 Open the Workgroup Manager tool, and authenticate as an administrator.

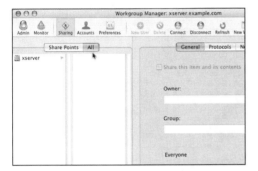

Figure 4.71 Click the Sharing button in Workgroup Manager, and click the All tab to see all mounted volumes.

Figure 4.72 From the server volume list, select a volume on which to enable disk quotas; then select the "Enable disk quotas on this volume" check box.

Setting User Disk Quotas

Mac OS X lets you set user disk quotas that limit the total amount of data a user is allowed to store on the server. These quotas work based on file ownership: Any file owned by a user applies to that user's disk quota.

Disk quotas are applied separately for each volume. In other words, a user with a 50 MB disk quota can store 50 MB of data on each volume to which they have write access.

To enforce disk quotas using Workgroup Manager, the user must have a home folder configured even if you never intend the home folder to be used. See the task "To create a user home directory."

To enable disk quotas:

1. Launch the Workgroup Manager tool located in /Applications/Server, and authenticate as the administrator (**Figure 4.70**).

2. Click the Sharing icon <img> in the Toolbar, and then click the All tab <img> (**Figure 4.71**).

3. From the server volume list, select a volume on which to enable disk quotas, and select the "Enable disk quotas on this volume" check box (**Figure 4.72**).

   Typically, you'll select the volume where the user's home folders will reside.

4. Click the Save button <img>, and then restart the server to enable quotas for the selected volume.

   Doing so creates the hidden quota configuration files and enables the quota service for the selected volume.

5. Repeat steps 3–5 for every volume on which you want to enforce disk quotas.

To set a user's disk quota:

1. In Workgroup Manager, navigate to configure the user's Home attributes **Home** (**Figure 4.73**).

2. In the user list, select the user or users you wish to configure (**Figure 4.74**).

3. Enter a number size in the Disk Quota field, and select MB (megabytes) or GB (gigabytes) from the pop-up menu (**Figure 4.75**).

4. When you've finished making changes, click the Save button **Save**.

   The next time this user logs in via AFP, the quota files will be configured for their account. You can always change the user's quota in the future.

✔ Tip

■ When you're using AFP, a malicious user can max out another user's disk quota by filling the other user's drop box with large files.

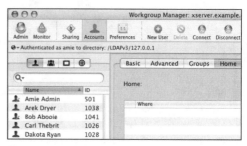

Figure 4.73 Click the Accounts button and the Home tab in Workgroup Manager.

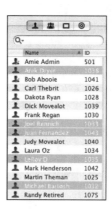

Figure 4.74 Select the user or users for whom you want to set quotas.

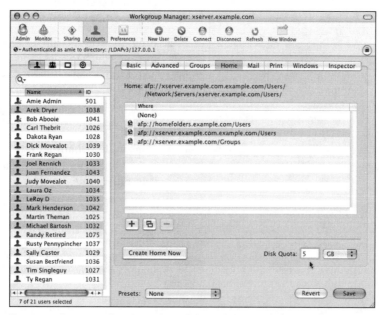

Figure 4.75 Enter a number size in the Disk Quota field, and select MB or GB.

Setting disk quotas via the command line

Enabling disk-usage quotas using the command-line tools gives you much greater control over quota settings than is available from Workgroup Manager. In fact, there are so many options that this section can cover only the basics.

The following task outlines the generally practiced method for setting quotas from the command line. Note that you must be the super user to configure disk usage quotas.

Quotas Expanded

You can use command-line tools to further edit user quotas—for example, by adding group quotas and/or specifying the quotas as *fixed* (hard quotas) or *malleable* (soft quotas). Hard quotas are implemented immediately, and soft quotas allow users to go over their quotas for seven days after the quota is in place, at which time the soft quota turns into a hard quota. The quota command-line tools are as follows:

◆ `quotaon` and `quotaoff`—Turn the quotas on and off

◆ `repquota`—Summarizes quotas

◆ `quota`—Displays disk quota use and limits

◆ `edquota`—Edits user and group quotas

◆ `quotacheck`—Ensures consistency

◆ `smbcquotas`—Used for NT File System (NTFS) quotas (NTFS is a Windows-based file system that isn't implemented on Mac OS X Server)

Refer to the section "Setting disk quotas via the command line" for more information about using these tools.

To set a disk quota from the command line:

1. *Do one of the following:*

   ▲ Log in to the command line as the root user.

   ▲ Log in with sudo -s.

   ▲ Preface every command with sudo.

2. *Do either of the following:*

   ▲ Use the quota files created by Workgroup Manager.

   ▲ Create the quota files .quota.user and .quota.ops.user at the root level of every volume on which you wish to enable quotas, by entering touch /.quota.user /.qouta.ops.user in the command line.

3. Configure the correct ownership and permissions for the quota files by entering chown :admin .quota* and then chmod 640 .quota* in the command line.

4. Update the quota files to reflect the current disk usage by entering quotacheck <volume name> in the command line.

5. Enable the quota system by entering quotaon <volume name> in the command line.

6. Configure the quota settings for your user accounts by using the edquota <user name> command.

   This utility uses vi, a command-line text editor, to configure the quota settings; Consult the man pages for proper use of vi.

7. Again, update the quota files to reflect the current disk usage by entering quotacheck <volume name> in the command line.

8. Use repquota <volume name> or quota <user name> to view the disk quota usage and settings.

✔ Tips

■ Although it isn't recommended, once you've configured quotas using the command-line tools, you can still use Workgroup Manager to configure quota settings.

■ Remember, it's always a good idea to experiment with quota settings on a test account before implementing quotas system wide.

■ It's a good idea to run quotacheck anytime a change is made to a user's quota settings.

■ You can also configure disk quotas based on group accounts by creating .quota.group and .quota.ops.group at the root level on any volume.

Figure 4.76 Open the Workgroup Manager tool, and authenticate as an administrator.

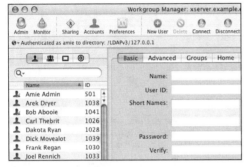

Figure 4.77 Click the Accounts button and the User tab in Workgroup Manager.

Figure 4.78 Select the appropriate directory database from the selection pop-up menu.

Figure 4.79 Select the user or users for whom you want to configure mail.

Adding Email to User Accounts

Mac OS X Server provides robust email services based on a Postfix/Cyrus open-source implementation. Primary configuration of the Mail service is available from the Server Admin application. Once the Mail service is configured, you use Workgroup Manager to enable and configure user-specific email settings.

There is much more to configuring an email server than is addressed in this topic. See Chapter 8, "Mail Services," for details regarding mail server configuration.

To add email to a user account:

1. Launch the Workgroup Manager tool located in /Applications/Server, and authenticate as the administrator (**Figure 4.76**).

2. Click the Accounts icon ![icon] in the Toolbar and the User icon ![icon] in the account types tab (**Figure 4.77**).

3. Click the directory authentication icon ![icon], and select the appropriate directory database from the pop-up menu (**Figure 4.78**).

4. In the user list, select the user or users you wish to configure (**Figure 4.79**).

continues on next page

5. In the user settings frame, click the Mail tab **Mail** (**Figure 4.80**).

The default setting for a user's mail is None (disabled).

6. Select the Enabled radio button (**Figure 4.81**).

7. If necessary, change the mail server address, set a mailbox quota (if the mail server is a Mac OS X Server 10.3 mail server), set the protocols by which the user(s) will receive their mail, or change where the mail box is stored (**Figure 4.82**).

8. When you've finished making changes, click the Save button **Save**.

✔ Tips

- If a user leaves your organization, you can forward their email to another email account automatically. Do this by selecting the Forward radio button and entering the new email address in the Forward To field (**Figure 4.83**).

- If you decide to change a user's mailbox location, you must first have moved the mailbox to that location. See Chapter 8 for more information.

- Setting the Mail Quota to 0 gives the user an unlimited mail quota, as if you hadn't set it at all.

Figure 4.80 Click the Mail tab.

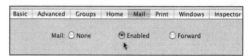

Figure 4.81 Enable mail for a user with Workgroup Manager.

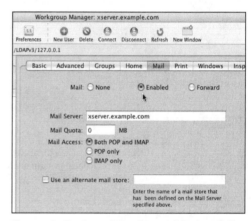

Figure 4.82 Configure the mail server location, mail quota, mail access protocols, and alternate mail store location.

Figure 4.83 You can forward email to another email account automatically.

Figure 4.84 Open the Workgroup Manager tool, and authenticate as an administrator.

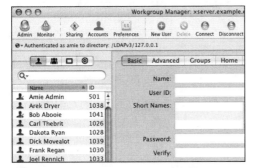

Figure 4.85 Click the Accounts button and the User tab in Workgroup Manager.

Figure 4.86 Select the appropriate directory database from the selection pop-up menu.

Figure 4.87 Select the user or users for whom printer quotas will be enforced.

Enabling Printer Quotas

Mac OS X Server lets you limit the number of pages a user can print to any queue hosted by your print server (as defined by the application from which the user is printing). Before you can enforce print quotas, you must first configure the print queues and enable the print server (see Chapter 7, "Printing Services").

To enable printer quotas:

1. Launch the Workgroup Manager tool located in /Applications/Server, and authenticate as the administrator (**Figure 4.84**).

2. Click the Accounts icon in the Toolbar and the User icon in the account types tab (**Figure 4.85**).

3. Click the directory authentication icon Authenticated, and select the appropriate directory database from the pop-up menu (**Figure 4.86**).

4. In the user list, select the user or users you wish to configure (**Figure 4.87**).

continues on next page

5. In the user settings frame, click the Print tab [Print] (**Figure 4.88**).

The default setting for a user's Print Quota is None.

6. Click the All Queues radio button (**Figure 4.89**).

The default, set at 0, allows this user unlimited printing on all queues.

7. Enter a number of pages per number of days quota limit in the associated fields (**Figure 4.90**).

8. When you've finished making changes, click the Save button [Save].

✔ Tips

■ If a user needs to print beyond their quota, you can reset the quota by clicking the Restart Print Quota button [Restart Print Quota].

■ The Print Service logs available from the Server Admin application show the number of pages and user for each individual print job.

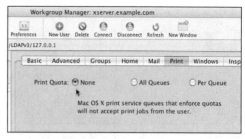

Figure 4.88 Click the Print tab.

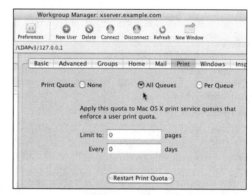

Figure 4.89 Clicking the All Queues radio button shows the default settings.

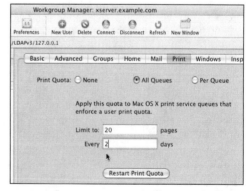

Figure 4.90 Enter a number of pages per number of days quota limit.

Figure 4.91 Click the Accounts button and the Print tab in Workgroup Manager.

Figure 4.92 Click the Per Queue radio button.

Figure 4.93 Enter a specific queue name and server, and either select Unlimited Printing or specify a pages and days printing limit.

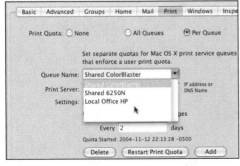

Figure 4.94 The Queue Name drop-down list shows all the quotas for this user.

Setting individual print quotas

Since printers range in capacity and capabilities, you may find it useful to set quotas for individual printers. You can do this in Workgroup Manager. Remember, you can only enforce quotas on printer queues set up in the Mac OS X Server print server service.

To set an individual printer's quota:

1. In Workgroup Manager, navigate to configure the user's Print attributes (**Figure 4.91**).

2. Select the Per Queue radio button and then click the Add button (Add) (**Figure 4.92**).

3. Enter the Queue Name and the Print Server address in the appropriate fields, and either select Unlimited Printing or specify a pages and days printing limit (**Figure 4.93**).

4. When you've finished making changes, click the Save button (Save).

5. Click the Add button (Add) to add additional queue quotas.

   Open the Queue Name drop-down list to view all the quotas for this user (**Figure 4.94**).

✔ Tip

■ If a user needs to print beyond their quota, you can reset it by clicking the Restart Print Quota button (Restart Print Quota).

ENABLING PRINTER QUOTAS

151

Understanding the Inspector Tab

The Inspector tab in Workgroup Manager provides unlimited access to the directory database information. It gives you the ability to edit account information outside the confines of the standard user interface. Using the Inspector gives you the power to add, delete, or edit any attribute for any item in the directory database as well as add many new attributes.

However, with great power comes great responsibility. Because you're allowed unfettered access to the directory database, you can very easily mess things up (as in, you can lock yourself out of your own server!). Also keep in mind that any changes you make using the Inspector are made while the directory is live. In other words, you can change an attribute that is currently in use by a user or system process. Needless to say, proceed with caution!

To change attribute values for users:

1. Launch the Workgroup Manager tool located in /Applications/Server, and authenticate as the administrator (**Figure 4.95**).

2. If you haven't already enabled the All Records tab and Inspector, do so now (see Chapter 2, "Server Tools").

3. Click the Accounts icon in the Toolbar and the User icon in the account types tab (**Figure 4.96**).

4. Click the directory authentication icon , and select the appropriate directory database from the pop-up menu (**Figure 4.97**).

   For this task, you should select the LDAP directory, listed as /LDAPv3/127.0.0.1.

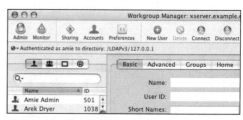

Figure 4.95 Open the Workgroup Manager tool, and authenticate as an administrator.

Figure 4.96 Click the Accounts button and the User tab in Workgroup Manager.

Figure 4.97 Select the appropriate directory database from the selection pop-up menu.

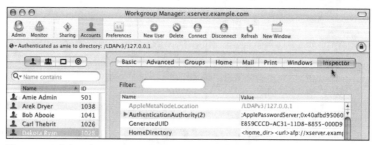

Figure 4.98 Select the user, and click the Inspector tab.

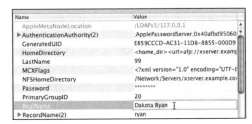

Figure 4.99 Double-click a value to make a change.

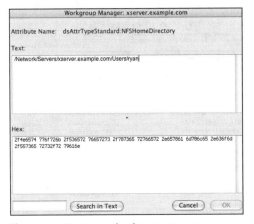

Figure 4.100 You can make changes to more complicated values in the attribute editing dialog.

Figure 4.101 Clicking the Options button lets you specify what is shown in the Inspector frame.

5. In the user list, select the user whose attributes you wish to edit, and then click the Inspector tab (**Figure 4.98**).

   The Inspector frame displays the user's account information as it appears in the directory database.

6. Find the value you wish to edit, and *do one of the following:*

   ▲ If the attribute's value is short, double-click it to make changes (**Figure 4.99**).

   ▲ If the attribute's value is long (typically any value that contains XML code), click the Edit button (Edit...) to make changes. The attribute editing dialog drops down, in which you can make changes to more complicated values (**Figure 4.100**). Click OK (OK) when you've finished editing the value.

7. When you've finished making changes, click the Save button (Save).

✔ Tips

■ Whenever you make account modifications with the Inspector, always thoroughly test your changes before you implement them on a wider scale. In fact, it's a good idea to create test user accounts so you can experiment with changes made using the Inspector.

■ Click the Options button to adjust how the Inspector list is presented. First-time users should deselect the two Prefix options under the Options tab (**Figure 4.101**).

UNDERSTANDING THE INSPECTOR TAB

Adding user attributes

Essentially, there is no limit to the number of attributes a record can have in either the local or the LDAP directory database provided by Mac OS X Server. You can configure as many attributes as you see fit. Keep in mind that attributes are nothing more than known storage locations for specific user account information.

Adding a custom user attribute to the directory is useful only if a specific system service or feature knows how to use that attribute. For example, you may need to add custom attributes in order for a Windows client to authenticate using your directory. (See Chapter 3, "Open Directory," for more information about directory services.)

To add user attributes:

1. In Workgroup Manager, navigate to the Inspector, and select the user account you wish to edit (**Figure 4.103**).

<aside>

Multiple-Value Attributes

Attributes can contain multiple separate values. To see a good example of this, use the Inspector to view the Authentication Authority attribute. Any attribute with more than one value shows the number of separate values in parentheses to the right of the attribute's name `▶ GroupMembership(2)`. There is also a small arrow to the left of the attribute's name; click it to reveal all the values for the attribute (**Figure 4.102**).

You can create multiple separate values for any attribute by selecting the attribute from the Inspector window and clicking the New Value button `New Value...`.

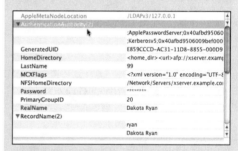

Figure 4.102 You can view all the values for an attribute.

</aside>

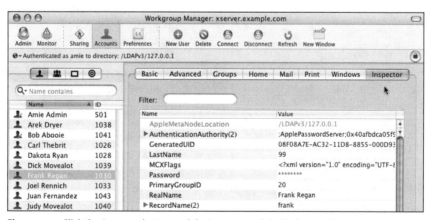

Figure 4.103 Click the Accounts button and the Inspector tab in Workgroup Manager.

2. Click the New Attribute button
New Attribute... .

An Attribute dialog drops down
(**Figure 4.104**).

3. From the Attribute Name menu,
select one of the preset attribute types
(**Figure 4.105**).

You can also enter a custom attribute
type to the right of the menu.

4. Enter the attribute's value in the Text field.
The system automatically populates the
Hex field (**Figure 4.106**).

continues on next page

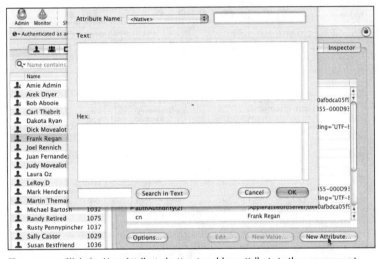

Figure 4.104 Click the New Attribute button to add an attribute to the user account.

Figure 4.105 Choose
an attribute type from
one of the many
preset attributes.

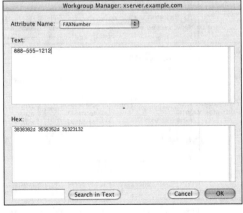

Figure 4.106 The system automatically populates the
Hex field.

5. When you've finished making changes, click the OK button (OK) to close the Attribute dialog, and then click the Save button (Save).

6. Locate your new attribute and associated value in the Inspector frame, and view the information (**Figure 4.107**).

The actual name of the attribute may vary from the name you chose in the list and the name that appears when it's saved.

Remember to always thoroughly test directory modifications before you implement them.

Figure 4.107 Locate the new attribute and its associated value.

Figure 4.108 Open the Workgroup Manager tool, and authenticate as an administrator.

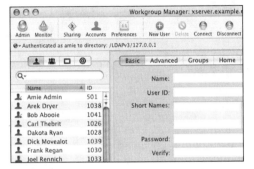

Figure 4.109 Click the Accounts button and the User tab in Workgroup Manager.

Figure 4.110 Select the appropriate directory database from the selection pop-up menu.

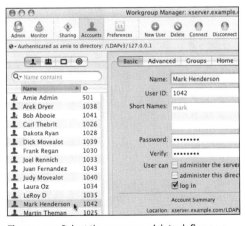

Figure 4.111 Select the user you wish to define as a preset.

Using Presets for New Accounts

If you've been reading this chapter sequentially, you've probably noticed that there are many settings to configure for a user account. Fortunately, you don't have to configure every single setting every time you create a new user. Workgroup Manager offers a time-saving feature that lets you save a preset for new user accounts. Once you define a preset, all new users you create will have the same configuration as the preset (the preset must be selected before you create the account). However, even when new users are created with the User Presets tool, you must still configure each user's name (long name), user ID, short names, and password.

To define a preset:

1. Launch the Workgroup Manager tool located in /Applications/Server, and authenticate as the administrator (**Figure 4.108**).

2. Click the Accounts icon in the Toolbar and the User icon in the account types tab (**Figure 4.109**).

3. Click the directory authentication icon , and select the appropriate directory database from the pop-up menu (**Figure 4.110**).

4. From the user list, select the account you wish to define as a preset (**Figure 4.111**).

continues on next page

5. From the Presets pop-up menu, select
Save Preset.

A dialog drops down from the title bar,
in which you can enter a name for your
preset (**Figure 4.112**).

6. Enter a name, and click the OK button
.

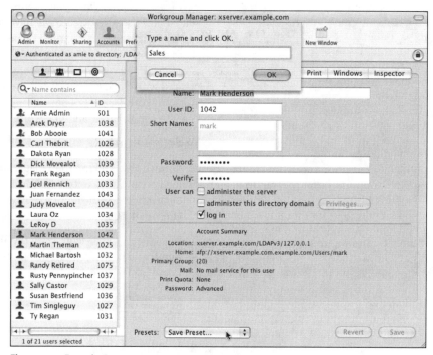

Figure 4.112 From the Presets pop-up menu, select Save Preset.

Figure 4.113 Open the Workgroup Manager tool, and authenticate as an administrator.

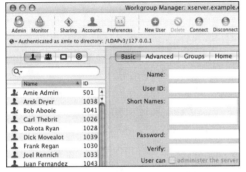

Figure 4.114 Click the Accounts button and the User tab in Workgroup Manager.

Figure 4.115 Select the appropriate directory database from the selection pop-up menu.

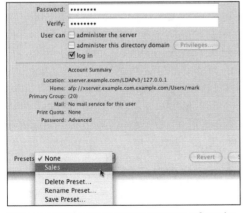

Figure 4.116 Select your custom user preset from the Presets pop-up menu.

Creating a user with a preset:

1. Launch the Workgroup Manager tool located in /Applications/Server, and authenticate as the administrator (**Figure 4.113**).

2. Click the Accounts icon in the Toolbar and the User icon in the account types tab (**Figure 4.114**).

3. Click the directory authentication icon , and select the appropriate directory database from the pop-up menu (**Figure 4.115**).

4. Select your custom user preset from the Presets pop-up menu (**Figure 4.116**).

5. Click the New User button to create a new account that will use this preset.

   Verify that your preset works by inspecting the attributes on the various account settings tabs: Advanced, Groups, and so on. Remember that you must still configure the Basic user attributes to complete this user account

6. When you've finished making changes, click the Save button .

✔ Tips

■ You can rename and delete presets from the Presets pop-up menu.

■ You can also create custom group presets. Repeat all the steps in the previous task; but, in step 2, click the Group icon instead of the User icon.

5

FILE SHARING

File sharing is by far the most common use for a server. For many organizations, file sharing is the only reason they have a server. Although Mac OS X Server is accomplished at tasks other than file sharing, it stands out as a robust and reliable multiplatform file server by providing file-sharing capabilities via the four most common sharing protocols: Apple File Protocol (AFP) for Mac OS clients, Server Message Block (SMB) for Windows-compatible clients, File Transfer Protocol (FTP) for almost any client, and Network File System (NFS) for Unix-based clients. Mac OS X Server is unique in its ability to share the contents of any directory via any of these protocols simultaneously.

For many administrators, the amount of time spent planning access to shared items outweighs the time spent configuring the server. Access to shared items is often a technical and political issue. As a server administrator, you're often charged with figuring out how to configure server resources so they fit with your organizational requirements. Therefore, it's a good idea to plan access to your shared items before you try to implement sharing services on your server. You should also set up users and groups before you enable your shared items, because Mac OS X Server uses Unix-style user and group permissions to control local and shared file access. (See Chapter 4, "User and Group Management," for detailed information on configuring users and groups.)

When you're ready to configure share points, you have two main areas of concern: setting up and configuring the protocols over which users connect, and the actual share point. This chapter examines both, moving back and forth between sharing protocol configuration and the share points.

Configuring Share Points

When a folder, disk, or volume and its contents are shared via Mac OS X Server, it's called a *share point*. You can also think of a share point as a mount point. In other words, when you make a folder a share point, you're defining a shared folder that the user can select and mount on their client computer. A user can access anything inside the share point, depending on file and folder permissions.

Mac OS X Server can host many share points simultaneously, including share points inside other share points. Using share points inside other share points is a great way to allow graduated access for complex file structures. Otherwise, you need to have a good understanding of file and folder permissions to facilitate proper access and security within your share points.

To configure new share points:

1. If the folder you wish to share doesn't yet exist on the server, create and properly name the folder using the Finder or the command-line tool `mkdir`.

   Putting your share points inside Shared Items is a good idea (**Figure 5.1**).

2. Launch the Workgroup Manager tool located in /Applications/Server, and authenticate as the administrator (**Figure 5.2**).

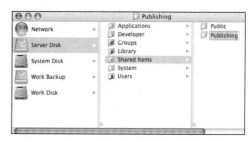

Figure 5.1 Create a new folder to be a share point in the Finder.

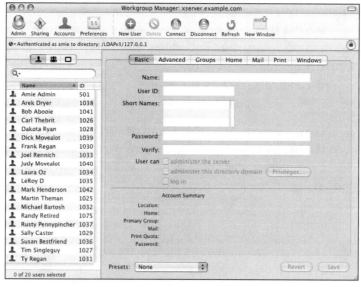

Figure 5.2 Open the Workgroup Manager tool.

CONFIGURING SHARE POINTS

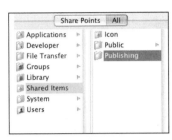

Figure 5.3 Select the folder in the share browser to be shared under the All tab.

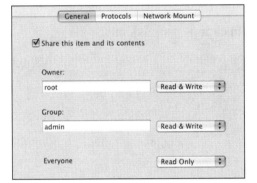

Figure 5.4 Checking the "Share this item and its contents" check box immediately creates the share point.

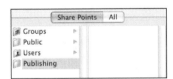

Figure 5.5 The Publishing folder share point is selected in the share browser.

3. Click the Sharing icon in the Toolbar and the All tab above the sharing browser.

Clicking the All tab shows all the server's local volumes and their contents.

4. The sharing browser works much like the Finder's column view. Select the folder, disk, or volume you wish to assign as a share point (**Figure 5.3**).

5. To the right of the sharing browser, click the General tab.

6. Select the "Share this item and its contents" check box (**Figure 5.4**).

7. When you've finished making changes, click the Save button.

8. Click the Share Points tab, and verify that your newly created share point is shown on the list with the other share points (**Figure 5.5**).

You may need to click the Refresh button in the Toolbar to update the shares shown.

Although the share point is now set, you'll probably need to configure permissions and file-sharing protocol options to fit your needs. Refer to the following tasks for more information about configuring permissions and file-sharing protocol options.

✔ Tips

■ When you select an entire disk or volume as a share point, authorized users will be able to see all items on the disk or volume.

■ You can expand the Workgroup Manager window and show more than just two columns when selecting share points.

CONFIGURING SHARE POINTS

Configuring File and Folder Permissions

Every file and folder on your Mac OS X Server is protected by Unix-style permissions, sometimes called *privileges*. An entire book could be dedicated to the technology behind file and folder permissions. However, they basically boil down to a few simple concepts:

◆ All items are associated with one owner and one group.

◆ Only the owner of the folder or file, or an administrative user, can change the permissions.

◆ All items have permissions defined at three levels: owner, group, and everybody else (called User, Group, and Other, in Unix-speak).

◆ At each level, you can have one of four basic access settings: none, read only, read and write, or (in the case of folders) write only.

◆ The permissions most specific to the user attempting to access the file are enforced.

◆ Permissions define access to an item's contents, not to the item itself.

If you're still confounded by the prospect of Unix-style permissions, you're not alone. Many experienced administrators learned permissions through trial and error. Experimenting with various permissions settings is often the best way to learn, and right now is a good time to start.

To change permissions:

1. Launch the Workgroup Manager tool located in /Applications/Server, and authenticate as the administrator (**Figure 5.6**).

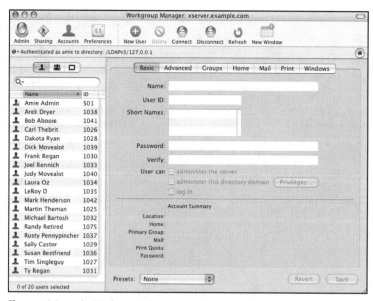

Figure 5.6 Open the Workgroup Manager tool.

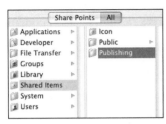

Figure 5.7 Select the item on which you wish to edit share permissions.

Figure 5.8 You can change ownership and permissions of a folder in the Users & Groups drawer.

Figure 5.9 Choose the appropriate database from which to select users.

Figure 5.10 Drag a new owner into the share point Owner box.

2. Click the Sharing icon, and then *do one of the following:*

▲ Click the Share Points tab to configure a share point or its contents.

▲ Click the All tab to configure any item on a local server volume.

3. From the sharing browser, select the item you wish to edit (**Figure 5.7**).

Click the General tab.

4. Click the Users & Groups button.

An account list drawer appears to one side of the main Workgroup Manager window (**Figures 5.8**).

5. At the top of the drawer, click the directory authentication icon.

From the pop-up menu, select the appropriate directory database (LDAPv3/127.0.0.1 indicates that you're looking at your LDAP [Master] database) (**Figure 5.9**).

6. To define a new owner, click the Users tab.

Click and drag an account from the user list to the Owner field, or type in the name of the user if you know it (**Figure 5.10**).

continues on next page

Command-Line Permissions

You can also configure file and folder permissions from the command line using the following utilities:

◆ `ls -l` lists the contents and permissions of a folder, disk, or volume.

◆ `chown` changes an item's ownership.

◆ `chgrp` changes an item's group.

◆ `chmod` changes an item's access rights.

7. To define a new group, click the Groups tab (**Figure 5.11**).

Click and drag an account from the group list to the Group field, or type in the name of the group if you know it (**Figure 5.12**).

8. To the right of the Owner, Group, and Everyone fields, select any one of the pop-up menus to define access rights (**Figure 5.13**).

9. When you've finished making changes, click the Save button 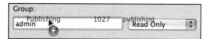.

10. If you're configuring the permissions for a folder and you want the permissions to permeate down the directory structure, click the Copy button 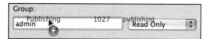 to copy the permissions of this folder to all items inside the folder.

✔ Tips

- Although doing so isn't recommended, you can also change file and folder permissions using the Get Info tool from the Finder. This approach may yield unexpected results, so it's always best to change file and folder permissions on Mac OS X Server using Workgroup Manager.

- Always test access to your shared items before allowing clients to use them.

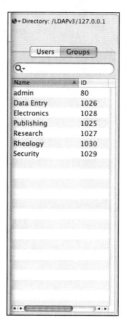

Figure 5.11 Select the appropriate group from the Groups drawer.

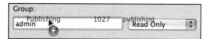

Figure 5.12 Drag a new group into the share point Group box.

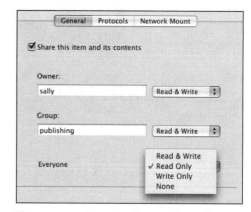

Figure 5.13 Set the appropriate permissions for everyone else (guests).

CONFIGURING FILE AND FOLDER PERMISSIONS

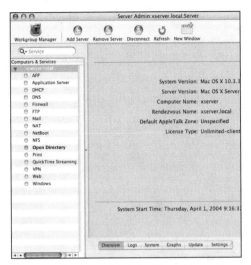

Figure 5.14 The Server Admin tool is used to configure sharing protocol options.

Figure 5.15 Select the AFP service from the Computers & Services list.

Figure 5.16 Click the AFP General tab under the Settings tab.

Configuring the Apple File-Sharing Service

The primary file-sharing protocol for Macintosh computers is the Apple File Protocol (AFP). The AFP service features full file-system compatibility for both Mac OS X and Mac OS 9 systems. In addition to providing robust sharing services, the AFP service offers secure authentication and encrypted data transport. AFP share points can also be used for home and group network mounts.

The following task shows you how to enable basic AFP file services. Refer to the remaining tasks in this section for more advanced AFP options.

To set AFP access options:

1. Launch the Server Admin tool located in /Applications/Server, and authenticate as the administrator (**Figure 5.14**).

2. Select the AFP service for your server in the Computers & Services list (**Figure 5.15**).

3. Click the Settings button [Settings] and then the General tab (**Figure 5.16**).

4. *Select the appropriate options:*

   "Enable Rendezvous registration" allows Mac OS X 10.2 or newer systems to browse to your server on the local network (sometimes defined as the local subnet).

   "Enable browsing with AppleTalk" allows pre-Mac OS X systems to browse to your server on the network using the older Chooser application.

continues on next page

CONFIGURING THE APPLE FILE-SHARING SERVICE

5. Click the Access tab (**Figure 5.17**).

6. *Select an authentication type* from the Authentication pop-up menu (**Figure 5.18**):

Standard uses the built-in AFP authentication.

Kerberos uses MIT's advanced key distribution system.

Any Method uses either of the two other methods of authentication.

See Chapter 3, "Open Directory," for more information about user authentication.

7. *Choose any of the following* AFP authentication options (**Figure 5.19**):

"Enable Guest access" enables access for users without accounts.

"Enable secure connections" enables secure data transport connections via SSH.

"Enable administrator to masquerade as any registered user" lets an administrator sign in to the server via AFP using a regular user's name but their own administrator's password.

8. Configure the maximum number of concurrent AFP client and guest connections (**Figure 5.20**).

You may have a limited number of AFP connections based on your server's software license type.

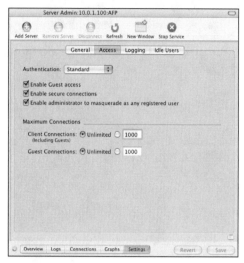

Figure 5.17 Click the Access tab under the Settings tab.

Figure 5.18 Choose an authentication method for others connecting to your server.

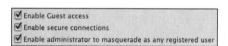

Figure 5.19 Select the appropriate options, such as guest access, number of users, and administration masquerading.

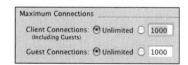

Figure 5.20 You can change the maximum number of user and guest connections.

Figure 5.21 You can see if the AFP service is running...

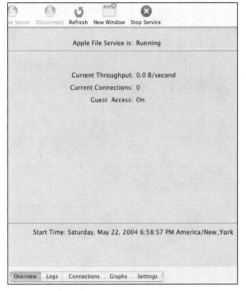

Figure 5.22 ...and start it using the Start Service button.

9. When you've finished making changes, click the Save button Save .

10. Click the Overview button Overview .

Verify that the AFP service is running (**Figure 5.21**). If it isn't, click the Start Service button Start Service to activate the AFP server (**Figure 5.22**).

Refer to the rest of the tasks in this chapter for more information about configuring the AFP service.

✔ Tips

- A small green dot ● to the left of the AFP service in the Computers & Services list indicates that the Apple File Service is running.

- In order to allow guest access, you must also enable guest access for each share point. See the task "To configure AFP share-point settings" for more information about enabling guest access for individual share points.

- The "Enable administrator to masquerade as any registered user" authentication option is very useful for testing share points and permissions.

CONFIGURING THE APPLE FILE-SHARING SERVICE

Connecting via AFP

Connecting to an AFP server from a Mac OS X client involves a few simple steps:

1. In the Finder, click the Network icon  Network to browse for your server. Mac OS X client can browse for AFP servers via the AppleTalk, SLP, or Rendezvous protocol.

   You can also connect directly in the Finder by selecting Go > Connect to Server from the menu bar and entering an AFP address or by pressing Command-K from the keyboard (**Figure 5.23**).

2. Authenticate to the server (**Figure 5.24**).

   You can also click the Options button Options... to configure client-side connection options (**Figure 5.25**).

3. Select the share point(s) you wish to connect to (**Figure 5.26**).

Default settings dictate that the share point's icon will mount on the Finder's desktop .

Figure 5.23 Use Go > Connect to Server to connect to servers.

Figure 5.24 Enter your username and password for authentication to access your server's share point.

Figure 5.25 You can change client-side options by clicking the Options button.

Figure 5.26 Select the shared item you wish to mount.

Figure 5.27 You can see the AFP settings by choosing the AFP service.

Logon Greeting:

The contents of this server belong exclusively to Example Co. Unauthorized use of this server will result in prosecution.

Figure 5.28 Enter the logon greeting you wish others to see.

☑ Do not send same greeting twice to the same user

Figure 5.29 You can choose not to send the same greeting twice to the same user.

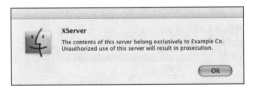

Figure 5.30 You can verify your logon greeting by logging in from a Mac OS X Client.

Login greetings

A *login greeting* is a string of text that appears as soon as a user attempts to log in from a client computer. Login greetings can be used for general service information or usage disclaimers for server access. More and more often, users must agree to the legal ramifications of using an employer's computer services. Using a login greeting is perfect for this task, because the user must click the OK button to dismiss the login greeting dialog and connect to your server. Such login greetings usually begin with, "By clicking the OK button you agree to...."

To add a login greeting:

1. Within Server Admin, navigate to your server's AFP service settings (**Figure 5.27**). Instructions for this step are detailed in steps 1–4 of the task "To set AFP access options."

2. On the General tab ⬜ General ⬜, enter your logon text in the Logon Greeting field (**Figure 5.28**).

3. To make the greeting appear only the first time a user logs in, select the appropriate check box below the Logon Greeting field (**Figure 5.29**).

   By default, the logon greeting appears every time a user logs in to your server via the AFP service.

4. When you've finished making changes, click the Save button ⬜ Save ⬜.

5. Verify the greeting by logging in to your server from the client (**Figure 5.30**).

✔ Tip

■ Deleting all the text in the Logon Greeting field disables the logon greeting dialog when a client connects.

Managing idle users

The AFP service requires a bit of overhead to maintain persistent server/client connections. The overhead per connection is quite low; however, when you have many connections simultaneously, this overhead can waste valuable server CPU and network resources. To remedy this situation, the server can automatically disconnect clients who are connected to your server but not actively using it. When this functionality is configured, idle disconnections on computers running software older than Mac OS X 10.3 should receive a message that that they have been disconnected.

To disconnect idle clients:

1. Within Server Admin, navigate to your server's AFP service settings (**Figure 5.31**).

   Instructions for this step are detailed in steps 1–4 of the task "To set AFP access options."

2. Click the Idle Users tab (**Figure 5.32**).

3. Select the "Disconnect idle users" check box, and enter a time in minutes (**Figure 5.33**).

4. Select any of the following idle-disconnect exceptions (**Figure 5.34**):

   Guests—Any users who didn't authenticate as users to your server.

   "Registered users"—Any users who have an authenticated connection.

Figure 5.31 You can access AFP settings by navigating to the AFP service from within Server Admin.

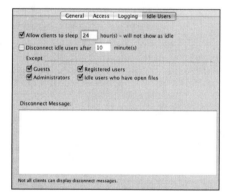

Figure 5.32 Use the Idle Users tab to manipulate options for users connected to your server via AFP.

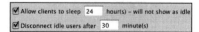

Figure 5.33 You can restrict the time allotted to disconnect client computers that are in sleep mode or idle.

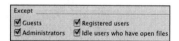

Figure 5.34 Choose which types of users are governed by the disconnect rules.

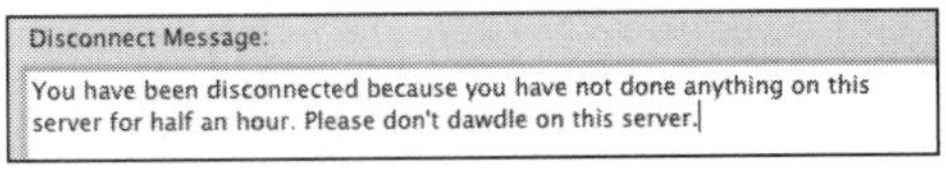

```
Disconnect Message:
You have been disconnected because you have not done anything on this
server for half an hour. Please don't dawdle on this server.
```

Figure 5.35 Set the disconnect message so users can be notified that they're no longer connected to the server via AFP.

Administrators—Any users who have an authenticated connection and are in the admin group.

"Idle users who have open files"—Any users who have a file that resides on the server but is open in an application running on their local computer. Severing the server connection while a file is open on the client is an excellent way to corrupt the file—in other words, it's a bad idea.

Selecting the check box next to an exception category allows that user type to remain connected regardless of the idle disconnect settings.

5. To configure a message to appear on the client computer when the server disconnects an idle user, enter a text string in the Disconnect Message field (**Figure 5.35**).

6. When you've finished making changes, click the Save button [Save].

✔ Tips

■ The "Allow clients to sleep" setting on the Idle Users tab lets the client computers sleep without counting as an idle connection. Computers sleeping and connected don't produce the extra overhead that running computers with idle connections do.

■ You should always select the idle disconnect exception for idle users who have open files.

■ Deleting all the text in the Disconnect Message field disables the message when an idle connection is disconnected.

Mac OS X 10.3 AFP Connections

Computers running Mac OS X 10.3 or later handle AFP idle disconnects in a very different manner. Your server still automatically disconnects, but the user shouldn't notice. The share point remains mounted to the client computer, yet the connection is idle. Essentially, the system hides the idle connection from the user. When the user tries to access the share again, the system automatically reconnects to your server. Furthermore, Mac OS X 10.3 or later attempts to reconnect to AFP connections that have been dropped due to network disconnects or sleep/wake cycles.

AFP share-point settings

When you create a share point on Mac OS X Server, it's automatically shared via AFP (as well as FTP and SMB), assuming the AFP service is running. Share points are also automatically configured for both registered user and guest access via AFP. Settings like these are individually configurable for each share point within the Workgroup Manager tool. See the "Configuring Share Points" section of this chapter for more information about creating share points.

To configure AFP share-point settings:

1. Launch the Workgroup Manager tool located in /Applications/Server, and authenticate as the administrator (**Figure 5.36**).

2. Click the Sharing icon [Sharing] in the Toolbar.

3. *Choose to do either of the following:*

   ▲ Configure an existing share point by clicking the Share Points tab [Share Points], and then select the share point you wish to edit from the sharing browser (**Figure 5.37**).

   ▲ Configure a new share point. See the "To configure new share points" task in this chapter for detailed instructions.

4. Once you've selected the share point you wish to configure, click the Protocols tab to the right of the sharing browser (**Figure 3.38**).

5. Directly below the Protocols tab is the Protocols pop-up menu. From this menu, select Apple File Settings (**Figure 5.39**). The Apple File Settings frame opens.

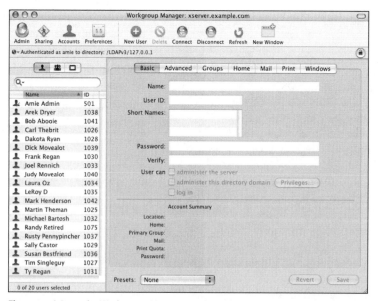

Figure 5.36 Open the Workgroup Manager tool.

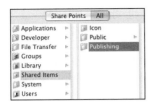

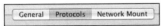

Figure 5.37 Use the Share Points tab in Workgroup Manager to see all the share points.

Figure 5.38 Once you've selected a share point, click the Protocols tab

Figure 5.39 You can see all the possible sharing protocols in the pop-up menu.

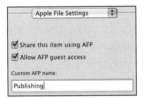

Figure 5.40 You can configure AFP share point protocol settings such as guest access and a custom name.

Figure 5.41 Decide which permissions model you wish to use for your AFP share point.

6. Configure AFP sharing and guest access for this particular share point (**Figure 5.40**).

   You can also configure a custom AFP share point name that differs from the original folder's name.

7. *Choose one of the following options* based on your permissions requirements (**Figure 5.41**):

   "Use standard Unix behavior"—The default behavior. New items created in this share point will be owned by the user who created the item, and the group will be set to that user's primary group. See Chapter 4, "User and Group Management," for more information about primary groups.

   "Inherit permissions from parent"— An optional behavior. New items created in this share point will have the same permissions as the share point itself. Refer to the section "Configuring File and Folder Permissions," earlier in this chapter.

8. When you've finished making changes, click the Save button (Save).

✔ Tips

- In order for guests to access a share point, its permissions must be set to give everyone read access.

- Disabling guest access to the AFP service in Server Admin disables AFP guest access for every share point regardless of individual share settings.

- Changing the name of a share point can help disguise a disk as a folder name but can also backfire if the user is looking for the folder's original share name. Sharing the same folder over several different protocols and using different share point names can quickly become difficult to manage.

Configuring the Windows File-Sharing Service

Mac OS X Server includes the open-source software Samba to provide Windows services. This means your Mac OS X Server can provide a variety of services to Windows clients, including the following:

◆ File sharing via the Server Message Block (SMB) protocol

◆ Print sharing, also via the SMB protocol

◆ Local network browsing via the Network Basic Input/Output System (NetBIOS) protocol

◆ Network browsing and name/address resolution via the Windows Internet Naming Service (WINS) protocol

◆ Network authentication and security services by acting as a Primary Domain Controller (PDC)

Initially, when you enable the Windows service, your Mac OS X Server acts as a standalone file server on the network. Windows and Mac OS X client computers can discover your server on the local network via the NetBIOS protocol, and connectivity is handled via the SMB protocol. The following task steps you through the process of enabling this basic configuration.

For more advanced Windows network configurations, see the remaining tasks in this section. For more information about Windows print sharing, refer to Chapter 7, "Printing Services."

✔ Tip

■ More information about Samba is available at http://www.samba.org/.

To set SMB access options:

1. Launch the Server Admin tool located in /Applications/Server, and authenticate as the administrator (**Figure 5.42**).

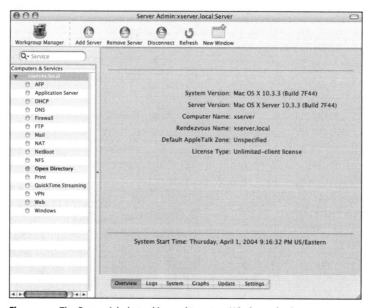

Figure 5.42 The Server Admin tool is used to set up Windows sharing.

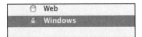

Figure 5.43 Select the Windows service to see all the sharing options.

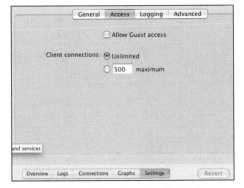

Figure 5.44 Choose the Access tab under Settings to...

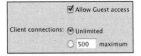

Figure 5.45 ...allow guest access and limit the number of connections for users over SMB.

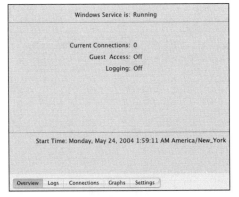

Figure 5.46 Use the Overview tab to confirm that the Windows (SMB) sharing service is running.

2. Select the Windows service for your server in the Computers & Services list (**Figure 5.43**).

3. Click the Settings button and then the Access tab (**Figure 5.44**).

4. Select the "Allow Guest access" check box to enable Windows guest connections (**Figure 5.45**).

You can also select the total number of simultaneous Windows connections. Mac OS X Server doesn't have any licensing restrictions on the number of simultaneous Windows connections.

5. When you've finished making changes, click the Save button [Save].

6. Click the Overview button [Overview].

Verify that the Windows service is running (**Figure 5.46**). If it isn't, click the Start Service button [Start Service] to activate the Windows server.

✔ Tips

- A small green dot [●] to the left of the Windows service in the Computers & Services list indicates that the Samba service is running.

- In order to allow guest access, you must also enable guest access for each share point. See the "To configure Windows share-point settings" task for more information about enabling guest access for individual share points.

- In Mac OS X Server 10.3, you don't have to configure any other settings for basic Windows authentication and sharing.

Connecting Mac OS X Clients via SMB

Connecting to an SMB server from a Mac OS X client involves a few simple steps:

1. In the Finder, click the Network icon 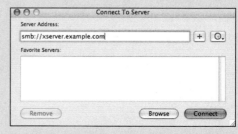 to browse for your server. Mac OS X client can browse for SMB servers via the NetBIOS protocol.

   You can connect directly in the Finder by selecting Go > Connect to Server from the menu bar and entering an SMB address or by pressing Command-K from the keyboard (**Figure 5.47**).

2. The SMB share point pop-up menu defaults to guest connection options at first (**Figure 5.48**). Select a share from the menu, and click OK; or, click the Authenticate button to gain availability to more share points. Either button will bring you to the SMB authentication dialog (**Figure 5.49**).

Default settings dictate that the share point's icon will mount on the Finder's desktop.

Figure 5.47 You can connect to a Windows (SMB) share point from Mac OS X by choosing Go > Connect to Server.

Figure 5.48 Pick which share point you wish to mount over SMB.

Figure 5.49 You must authenticate to have access to the SMB share point.

Connecting Windows Clients via SMB

Connecting to a Mac OS X SMB server from a Windows client involves the following steps (all the screenshots are from Windows XP):

1. In Windows Explorer, browse to your server as if it were another Windows computer (**Figure 5.50**).

   You can also manually add your server using the Add Network Place Wizard (**Figure 5.51**).

2. The authentication dialog is similar to that for any other Windows network connection (**Figure 5.52**).

Once you've authenticated, all the share points appear in the Windows Browser (**Figure 5.53**).

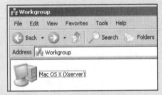

Figure 5.50 Use Windows Explorer to browse your network.

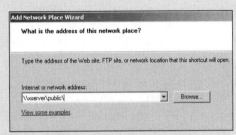

Figure 5.51 Add your Mac OS X share point in Windows with the Add Network Place Wizard.

Figure 5.52 Authenticate from Windows to your Mac OS X share point.

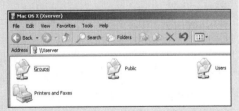

Figure 5.53 Mac OS X Server SMB share points show up just like other Windows share points, when viewed from Windows XP.

Advanced SMB roles

Large SMB networks use an organizational unit known as a *domain* to segregate computers and services. You can restrict access to items inside each domain by enabling domain authentication. Mac OS X Server can join a domain or even host a domain by becoming a Primary Domain Controller (PDC).

When you configure your server as a PDC, Windows clients can authenticate against your server for access to items inside the domain. Enabling your Mac OS X Server as a PDC also enables your Windows clients to change their passwords from their computers.

Because authentication is involved with hosting a PDC, your server must also be hosting an Open Directory (OD) database. Windows clients will use the same user accounts hosted in your OD database to log in to your domain. For more information about directory services and Open Directory, see Chapter 3, "Open Directory."

By default, your server will act as a Standalone Server (**Figure 5.54**). This means your server will create the workgroup you specify using the NetBIOS protocol. If this is all you need, enter server Description, Computer Name, and Workgroup values. When you've finished, click the Save button .

To enable Mac OS X Server as a domain member:

1. In Server Admin, navigate to your server's Windows service settings (**Figure 5.55**).

Instructions for this step are detailed in steps 1–3 of the task "To set SMB access options."

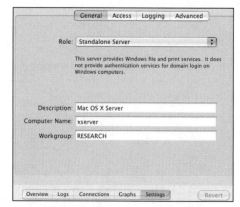

Figure 5.54 Mac OS X Server is a plain-Jane Windows server unless otherwise configured.

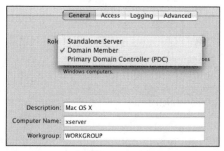

Figure 5.55 Navigating to the Windows service allows you to see the General and Settings tabs.

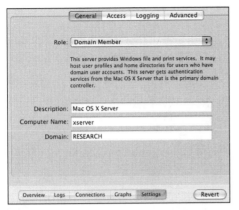

Figure 5.56 Begin making Mac OS X Server a domain member by choosing that option from the Role pop-up menu.

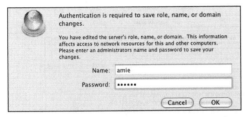

Figure 5.57 Authentication is necessary to change roles when you're dealing with the Windows share service.

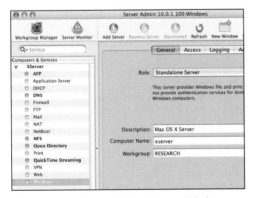

Figure 5.58 Use Server Admin to change Windows service options.

2. Click the General settings tab.

3. Select Domain Member from the Role pop-up menu (**Figure 5.56**).

4. Enter the following values:

   ▲ Description

   ▲ Computer Name

   ▲ Domain

5. Click the Save button [Save].

6. When you change SMB server roles, you must authenticate as an LDAP domain administrator for the PDC server (**Figure 5.57**).

To enable Mac OS X Server as a Primary Domain Controller:

1. Be sure you're an Open Directory master before proceeding.

   For more information about directory services and Open Directory, see Chapter 3, "Open Directory."

2. In Server Admin, navigate to your server's Windows service settings, and click the General settings tab (**Figure 5.58**).

continues on next page

3. Select Primary Domain Controller from the Role pop-up menu (**Figure 5.59**).

If your server isn't configured as an Open Directory master, then you'll receive an error dialog and you won't be able to continue.

4. Enter the following values:

▲ Description

▲ Computer Name

▲ Domain

5. Click the Save button [Save].

6. When you change SMB server roles, you must authenticate as an LDAP domain administrator for the PDC server (**Figure 5.60**).

✔ Tips

■ It's best if your server's computer name is the unqualified DNS host name (xserver, instead of xserver.example.com).

■ Windows workgroup and domain names are typically capitalized and can't exceed 15 characters.

■ On a Mac OS X Client, you can configure SMB network settings in the Directory Access application. This includes the ability to configure a specific workgroup or domain for the client.

■ Always verify client connectivity after you make SMB server role changes—especially from Windows clients, because domain authentication is vital to proper network functionality. See the sidebar "Connecting Windows Clients via SMB," earlier in this chapter.

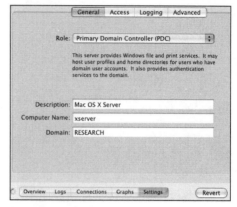

Figure 5.59 Choose Primary Domain Controller from the Role pop-up menu.

Figure 5.60 Authentication is necessary to change roles when you're dealing with the Windows share service.

Advanced SMB features

Mac OS X Server provides a variety of advanced SMB features that your Windows users may need. These features include support for alternate languages, improved network browsing, and hosting Windows home folders.

You can also participate in the election of workgroup master and domain master browsers and enable Windows Internet Naming Service (WINS). WINS allows Windows browsing across subnets and facilitates more efficient browsing.

The other option is to enable virtual share points, which provides easier configuration for Windows home directories. If your server is a PDC, a user's home folder automatically mounts when they log in to your domain from a Windows computer. In addition, users have the same home folder for both Windows and Mac OS X.

To enable advanced SMB features:

1. In Server Admin, navigate to your server's Windows service settings and click the Advanced tab (**Figure 5.61**).

2. The Code Page setting determines which language is used for Windows services. To change the Code Page, select the pop-up menu and choose from the list (**Figure 5.62**).

continues on next page

Figure 5.61 Server Admin is the tool you use to manage Windows service settings.

Figure 5.62 You can change the type of code the pages use.

Master Browsers

Master browsers are used to facilitate more efficient network browsing when using the NetBIOS protocol. This is the way Windows computers collect and display information when services are shared from Windows computers to Windows computers on a local subnet (local network).

A *domain master browser* is elected by choosing one of the master browsers on each local network. It collects and offers the list of services offered by Windows computers that resided on all the master browsers.

Selecting the Workgroup Master Browser and Domain Master Browser options doesn't guarantee that your server will become the master browser and/or the domain master browser if other computers are involved in the election.

CONFIGURING WINDOWS FILE-SHARING SERVICE

3. Select one or both of the Workgroup Master Browser and Domain Master Browser check boxes to have your server take part in the master browser elections (**Figure 5.63**).

4. *Choose one of the following* modes for WINS registration (**Figure 5.64**):

Off—Your server has nothing to do with WINS registration.

"Enable WINS server"—Your server is the WINS server that other machines register with.

"Register with WINS server"—Your server informs other WINS servers that you're providing Windows services. You must enter the IP address(es) of your WINS server(s). You can enter more than one server by separating the addresses with a comma and a single space.

5. Choose whether to enable virtual share points (**Figure 5.65**).

6. When you've finished making changes, click the Save button 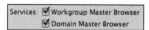.

✔ Tips

■ If your server is acting as a PDC, the Workgroup Master Browser and Domain Master Browser options aren't available. This is because a PDC *must* be the domain master browser for that particular domain.

■ On a Mac OS X Client, you can configure SMB network settings in the Directory Access application. This includes the ability for a client to register with WINS servers.

■ You should test these settings thoroughly from both Windows and Mac OS X client computers.

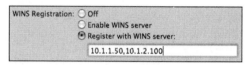

Figure 5.63 Checking these boxes allows your Mac OS X Server to become a workgroup master browser and/or domain master browser.

Figure 5.64 Set your WINS options.

Figure 5.65 You can also enable virtual share points for your Windows users.

Figure 5.66 Open the Workgroup Manager tool.

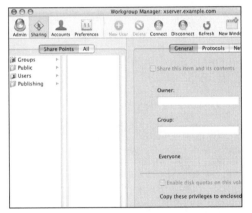

Figure 5.67 Use Workgroup Manager's Sharing icon to display and configure Windows share points.

Figure 5.68 You can select an existing share point or create a new one.

Windows share-point settings

When you create a share point on Mac OS X Server, it's automatically shared via SMB (as well as AFP and FTP), assuming the Windows service is running. Share points are also automatically configured for both registered user and guest access via SMB. You can configure such settings individually for each share point using the Workgroup Manager tool.

To configure Windows share-point settings:

1. Launch the Workgroup Manager tool located in /Applications/Server, and authenticate as the administrator (**Figure 5.66**).

2. Click the Sharing icon in the Toolbar (**Figure 5.67**).

3. Configure an existing share point by clicking the Share Points tab and then selecting the share point you wish to edit from the sharing browser (**Figure 5.68**).

4. Click the Protocols tab to the right of the sharing browser.

continues on next page

CONFIGURING WINDOWS FILE-SHARING SERVICE

5. Directly below the Protocols tab is the Protocols pop-up menu. From this menu, select Windows File Settings (**Figure 5.69**).

6. In this frame, you can configure SMB sharing and guest access for this particular share point.

You can also configure a custom SMB share point name that differs from the original folder's name (**Figure 5.70**).

7. *Choose one of the following options* based on your permissions requirements (**Figure 5.71**):

"Inherit permissions from parent"— New items created within this share point will have the same permissions as the share point itself. See "Configuring File and Folder Permissions," earlier in this chapter.

"Assign as follows"—This is the default behavior. It's similar to inherited permissions in that the owner and group assigned to each item are the same as those of the parent share point. The difference here is that you can configure specific access for the user, group, or everyone from the pop-up menus (**Figure 5.72**).

8. When you've finished making changes, click the Save button [Save].

✔ Tips

■ Changing the name of a share point can help disguise a disk as a folder name but can also backfire if the user is looking for the folder's original share name. Sharing the same folder over several different protocols and using different share point names can be difficult to manage.

■ In order for guests to access a share point, its permissions must be set to allow read access for everyone.

■ Keep in mind that the general Windows service settings may affect the settings you configure here. For instance, disabling guest access to the Windows service in Server Admin disables Windows guest access for every share point regardless of individual share settings. Remember to verify proper Windows service configuration in both Workgroup Manager and Server Admin.

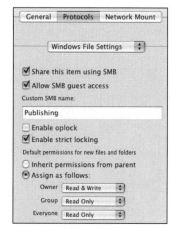

Figure 5.69 Choose Windows File Settings to manage share point options over SMB.

Figure 5.70 Decide if you want to share this item with guest access on or off and whether you wish to change the name of the share point.

Figure 5.72 Selecting "Assign as follows" lets you change permissions based on identity.

Figure 5.71 Choose a permissions model that best suits your needs.

File locking

The Windows file service offers a few unique features for managing files that reside on the server but are open on client computers. These file-locking options improve the performance and consistency of open files. You can configure these options individually for each share point.

Once configured, file locks are transparent to the users connected to the server. In addition, file-locking options don't conflict with any Windows service configuration in Server Admin.

To enable file locking:

1. In Workgroup Manager, navigate to a specific share point's Windows service settings.

   Instructions for this step are detailed in the first five steps of the task "To configure Windows share-point settings" (**Figure 5.73**).

2. *Choose one of the following* Windows file-locking options (**Figure 5.74**):

   "Enable oplock"—Opportunistic locking is disabled by default. Enabling this feature lets client computers cache changes to open files locally for improved performance.

   "Enable strict locking"—Enabled by default. Strict locking allows only one user at a time to open a particular file. This prevents the file corruption that occurs when applications attempt to edit files that are currently being edited by other users.

3. When you've finished making changes, click the Save button (Save).

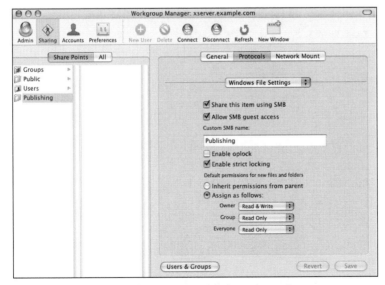

Figure 5.73 You use Server Admin to manage Windows share points.

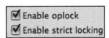

Figure 5.74 Decide on a file locking structure, if you want one.

Configuring the FTP File-Sharing Service

The File Transfer Protocol (FTP) service is by far the most ubiquitous file-sharing protocol available from Mac OS X Server. Almost anything with network access can connect to an FTP server, because FTP is a simple protocol to implement.

However, this simplicity is a double-edged sword from a technological standpoint. As a default, FTP is highly compatible and easy to implement because it uses clear-text passwords and unencrypted data transfers. This behavior is a potential security issue if any of your FTP traffic travels through insecure networks. A nefarious hacker can easily spot and intercept your FTP traffic. If security is an issue, then your alternative is to use the Secure FTP (SFTP) protocol. When you enable SSH on your Mac OS X Server, SFTP is automatically enabled. You don't need to enable FTP for SFTP to be enabled.

Other limitations of FTP include file-handling issues. Standard FTP can't handle folders because it only supports single file transfers. The FTP service also has problems with the forked files and Unicode filenames that are natively supported by Mac OS X.

You can easily overcome these limitations by using modern FTP client software that automatically archives and/or compresses requested files before they're transferred via FTP. The FTP service provided by Mac OS X Server includes support for automatic file archival and/or compression.

To set FTP access options:

1. Launch the Server Admin tool located in /Applications/Server, and authenticate as the administrator (**Figure 5.75**).

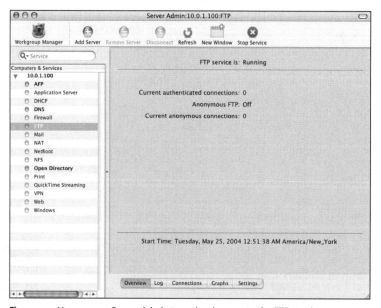

Figure 5.75 You can use Server Admin to make changes to the FTP service.

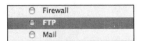

Figure 5.76 Select FTP from the services list to begin the process of setting up FTP service options.

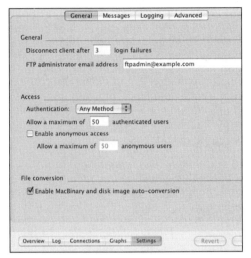

Figure 5.77 As with other services, click the Settings button and then the General tab to obtain access to the options.

Figure 5.78 The FTP service can be forced to use either standard authentication or Kerberos.

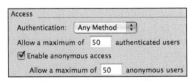

Figure 5.79 Enable anonymous access to your FTP site by checking "Enable anonymous access."

2. Select the FTP service for your server in the Computers & Services list (**Figure 5.76**).

3. Click the Settings button ⌈ Settings ⌉ and then the General tab ⌈ General ⌉ (**Figure 5.77**).

4. By default, FTP authentication via any method is allowed. Click the Authentication pop-up menu to configure a specific authentication method (**Figure 5.78**):

   Standard uses clear-text passwords.

   Kerberos uses MIT's advanced key distribution system.

   See Chapter 3 for more information about user authentication.

5. Select the "Enable anonymous access" check box to enable guest access via the FTP service (**Figure 5.79**).

   By default, anonymous FTP access is turned off.

6. When you've finished making changes, click the Save button ⌈ Save ⌉.

   If you make changes to the FTP service while it's running, you'll be prompted to restart the service (**Figure 5.80**).

   Be sure to check for connected users before restarting the service, so you don't kick them off.

continues on next page

Figure 5.80 Changes made to a running service, such as FTP, often require a restart of that service.

7. Click the Overview button [Overview].

Verify that the FTP service is running (**Figure 5.81**). If it isn't, click the Start Service button [Start Service] to activate the FTP server (**Figure 5.82**).

The rest of the tasks in this chapter provide more information about configuring the FTP service.

✔ Tips

- *Anonymous access* is another way of saying *guest access.*

- A small green dot [●] to the left of the FTP service in the Computers & Services list indicates that the File Transfer Protocol is running.

- In order to allow anonymous access, you must also enable guest access for each share point. Refer to the task "To configure FTP share-point settings" for more information about enabling guest access for individual share points.

- You can limit the number of simultaneous authenticated and anonymous users by entering values in the associated fields (**Figure 5.83**). The default of 50 users is a good starting point, because FTP servers are susceptible to performance issues if too many users connect.

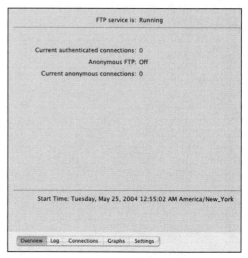

Figure 5.81 Verify that the FTP service is running.

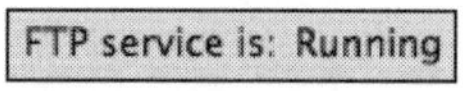

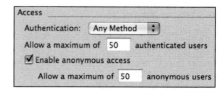

Figure 5.82 You can now see that the FTP service is running.

Figure 5.83 Limit the maximum number of users to keep from overloading the FTP service.

Connecting via FTP

Discussing the many third-party FTP clients for Mac OS X could easily fill a book. Try for yourself: Go to http://www.versiontracker.com/, and type `ftp client` in the search field. You'll probably find about two-dozen FTP clients for Mac OS X alone. As tempting as those options are, this book sticks to the FTP clients built into Mac OS X. For SFTP, search for and download Fugu, an SFTP application.

If you prefer the command line, you can use the `ftp` or `sftp` command to connect to your server. On the other hand, if you prefer the graphical user interface, do the following:

1. In the Finder, click the Network icon 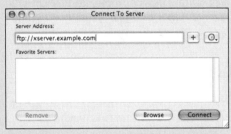 to browse for your server. Mac OS X Client can browse for FTP servers via the Rendezvous protocol.

   You can connect directly in the Finder by selecting Go > Connect to Server from the menu bar and entering an FTP address or by pressing Command-K from the keyboard (**Figure 5.84**).

2. Authenticate to the server (**Figure 5.85**). As an option, you can have the client computer remember your login.

3. With FTP, you don't select a share point; you're automatically sent to a default location set by the server's administrator. Default settings dictate that the FTP server icon mounts on the Finder's desktop .

You only have read access to an FTP share point when using the Connect to Server option. Use a third-party utility to enable read/write access to the FTP share point.

Figure 5.84 Choosing Go > Connect to Server lets you type in the name of the FTP server you wish to connect to.

Figure 5.85 FTP authentication takes place before you can mount the FTP share point.

FTP messages

When FTP was initially developed, all server connections were via the command-line environment. You didn't just connect to a shared folder, you actually connected to an FTP command-line environment. Upon initially connecting to the FTP server, you were greeted with a banner message. After authentication, you saw a welcome message. These messages usually contained information regarding server usage, availability, disclosure agreements, or anything else the administrator wished to communicate to connected users. Although FTP banner and welcome messages are rarely used by modern graphical FTP clients, Mac OS X Server still supports them.

To change FTP messages:

1. In Server Admin, navigate to your server's FTP service settings (**Figure 5.86**).

   Instructions for this step are detailed in steps 1–4 of the task "To set FTP access options."

2. Click the Messages tab.

3. Select the "Show welcome message" check box, and enter the desired text string in the field below the check box (**Figure 5.87**).

4. Select the "Show banner message" check box, and enter the desired text string into the field below the check box (**Figure 5.88**).

5. When you've finished making changes, click the Save button ![Save].

   If you make changes to the FTP service while it's running, you'll be prompted to restart the service.

   Be sure to check for connected users before restarting the service, so you don't kick them off.

6. Test these messages via the command line by entering ftp *serveraddress* and then authenticating to the server.

✔ Tips

■ You can disable either the welcome message or the banner message by deselecting the appropriate check box.

■ Connecting to an FTP server via the Finder in Mac OS X won't show you any FTP messages.

Figure 5.86 Server Admin is used to manage FTP service options.

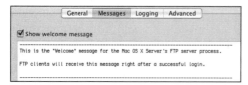

Figure 5.87 Enter your welcome message text.

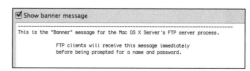

Figure 5.88 Enter your banner message text.

The FTP user environment

Typically, when an authenticated user connects to an FTP server, they don't get to choose a share point; they're dropped off in a predefined folder. Mac OS X Server lets you configure this aspect of the FTP user environment.

To configure the FTP user environment

1. In Server Admin, navigate to your server's FTP service settings (**Figure 5.89**).

   Instructions for this step are detailed in steps 1–4 of the task "To set FTP access options."

continues on next page

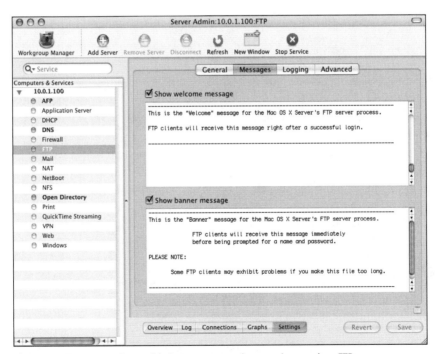

Figure 5.89 You can use Server Admin to manage various services, such as FTP.

CONFIGURING THE FTP FILE-SHARING SERVICE

2. Click the Advanced tab (**Figure 5.90**).

3. Click the "Authenticated users see" pop-up menu, and *select one of the following options* (**Figure 5.91**):

FTP Root and Share Points—Authenticated users connect to the FTP root folder (defined in step 4). In the FTP root folder, the system creates symbolic links to your other share points.

Home Directory with Share Points—Authenticated users connect to their home folder. They also have access to the other share points. If a user doesn't have a home folder, they're automatically connected to the FTP root folder.

Home Directory Only—Authenticated users are connected only to their home directory. If a user doesn't have a home folder, they're automatically connected to the FTP root folder.

4. The predefined FTP root folder is /Library/FTPServer/FTPRoot. To specify a custom FTP root folder, enter a new path to the appropriate field (**Figure 5.92**).

You can also click the ellipsis button to the right of the FTP root folder field to specify a new folder in a file browser dialog (**Figure 5.93**).

5. When you've finished making changes, click the Save button.

If you make changes to the FTP service while it's running, you'll be prompted to restart the service.

Be sure to check for connected users before restarting the service, so you don't kick them off.

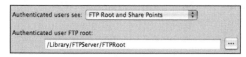

Figure 5.92 Modify the path to the FTP root folder by entering a path...

✔ Tips

■ See the sidebar "Connecting via FTP," earlier in this chapter, for more information about various FTP clients.

■ The initial administrative account always defaults to its home folder via FTP. However, folder permissions allow administrators to navigate outside their home folder.

■ Because FTP servers often fall victim to hackers, thoroughly test any access configurations you choose. You should also test access from various FTP clients so you know what to expect for your users.

Figure 5.90 Choose the Advanced tab in the FTP service.

Figure 5.91 You can choose what the user sees when they log in remotely.

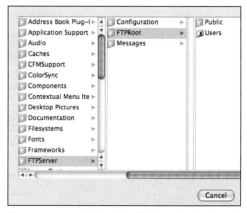

Figure 5.93 ....or clicking the ellipsis and selecting a new FTP root folder in the resulting window.

Figure 5.94 Open the Workgroup Manager tool.

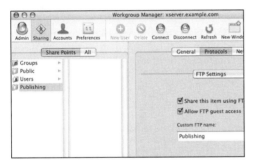

Figure 5.95 Click the Share Points tab, and click the Protocols tab to set the FTP share point options.

Figure 5.96 Choose FTP share-point setting options from the pop-up menu.

FTP share-point settings

When you create a share point on Mac OS X Server, it's automatically shared via FTP (as well as AFP and SMB), assuming the FTP service is running. Share points are also automatically configured for both registered user and anonymous access via FTP. You can configure such settings individually for each share point using Workgroup Manager. See the "Configuring Share Points" section of this chapter for more information about creating share points.

To configure FTP share-point settings:

1. Launch the Workgroup Manager tool located in /Applications/Server, and authenticate as the administrator (**Figure 5.94**).

2. Click the Sharing icon [Sharing] in the Toolbar.

3. *Choose to do one of the following:*

   ▲ Configure an existing share point by clicking the Share Points tab [Share Points] and then selecting the share point you wish to edit from the sharing browser (**Figure 5.95**).

   ▲ Configure a new share point. See the task "To configure new share points" for detailed instructions.

4. Once you've selected the share point you wish to configure, click the Protocols tab to the right of the sharing browser.

5. Directly below the Protocols tab is the Protocols pop-up menu. From this menu, select FTP Settings (**Figure 5.96**).

continues on next page

6. In this frame, configure FTP sharing and guest access (anonymous access) for this particular share point.

You can also configure a custom FTP share point name that differs from the original folder's name (**Figure 5.97**).

7. When you've finished making changes, click the Save button Save.

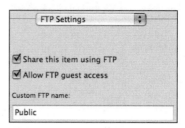

Figure 5.97 Edit the FTP share point name and guest access.

✔ Tips

■ In order for guests to access a share point, its permissions must be set to give everyone read access.

■ If you ever disable a share point, the symbolic link for FTP functionality may remain in the FTP root folder. You'll have to delete this symbolic link manually after you disable the share point. To do so, move the original item, delete the link, and move the original back.

■ Because FTP doesn't natively support multiple share points, the system creates symbolic links in the FTP root folder that point to your other share points.

■ Keep in mind that general FTP service settings may affect the settings you configure here. For instance, disabling anonymous access to the FTP service in Server Admin disables FTP guest access for every share point regardless of individual share settings. Remember to verify proper FTP service configuration in both Workgroup Manager and Server Admin.

■ Changing the name of a share point can help disguise a disk as a folder name but can also backfire if the user is looking for the folder's original share name. Sharing the same folder over several different protocols and using different share point names can quickly become difficult to manage.

Network File System Sharing

Although it's native to Mac OS X, the Network File System (NFS) service is very different than all the other file services available. The main difference is that the NFS service trusts the client's computer for authentication instead of the user. Specifically, rather than allowing the user to authenticate the connection, NFS requests the user identification number (UID). As long as the user's local UID matches a UID on the server, the NFS connection is authenticated. If the permissions allow everyone access, any UID that doesn't match a UID on the server is authenticated as a guest. For more information about UIDs, see Chapter 4, "User and Group Management."

To understand why NFS uses this type of authentication, you have to know where NFS comes from. The NFS service was first used by Unix terminals to access files on mainframe servers. Early Unix implementations relied on a unified directory service to authenticate users to any terminal computer. Because every user had to authenticate to the directory server before they had any computer access, it was safe to assume that once they were logged in to the terminal they were who they said they were. Thus, the NFS service requested the UID from the terminal computer.

In today's modern computing environment, which is rife with commodity personal computers, login authentication is often delegated to a local account. Even worse, on Mac OS X client computers, the local administrator accounts (UID 501) and root accounts (UID 0) have the same UIDs on your Mac OS X Server! However, this section discusses a variety of options that let you properly configure NFS share points, called *exports*, and protect them from such security risks.

To set up an NFS export:

1. Launch the Workgroup Manager tool located in /Applications/Server, and authenticate as the administrator (**Figure 5.98**).

continues on next page

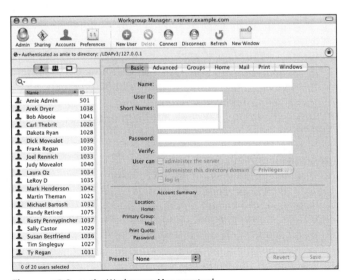

Figure 5.98 Open the Workgroup Manager tool.

2. Click the Sharing icon 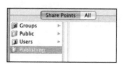 in the Toolbar.

3. To configure an existing share point, click the Share Points tab ![Share Points], and then select the share point you wish to edit from the sharing browser (**Figure 5.99**).

Figure 5.99 Select an existing share point from the Share Points list.

4. Click the Protocols tab to the right of the sharing browser (**Figure 5.100**).

Figure 5.100 After selecting the share point, click the Protocols tab to configure NFS share point options.

5. Directly below the Protocols tab is the Protocols pop-up menu. From this menu, select NFS Export Settings (**Figure 5.101**).

6. In the NFS frame, select the "Export this item and its contents to" check box to enable NFS for this share point (**Figure 5.102**).

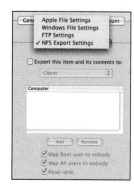

Figure 5.101 Select NFS Export Settings to see all the NFS share options.

7. To specify via IP address which clients can mount this export, *choose one of the following* from the Export pop-up menu (**Figure 5.103**):

Client limits this NFS export to a list of specific clients (**Figure 5.104**). Click Add or Remove to manage this list.

World allows any client to access this NFS export (**Figure 5.105**).

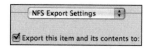

Figure 5.102 Select the "Export this item and its contents to" check box to begin NFS sharing.

Figure 5.103 You have three options when exporting via NFS.

Figure 5.104 This export list shows the 10.1.0 subnet. A single address could be added for one machine.

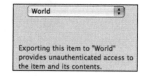

Figure 5.105 Exporting your share point to World allows everyone to access that share point.

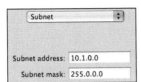

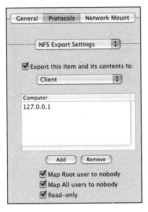

Figure 5.106 Subnets can be added to restrict access.

Figure 5.107 Remapping users is another way to restrict access.

Subnet limits this NFS export to a specific subnet of computers (**Figure 5.106**). Enter the subnet address and mask in the appropriate fields.

8. To further restrict access to this NFS export, *choose any of the following* (**Figure 5.107**):
   ▲ "Map Root user to nobody"
   ▲ "Map All users to nobody"
   ▲ "Read-only"
   Nobody in this case is an actual user with the name "nobody."

9. When you've finished making changes, click the Save button [Save].

10. Launch the Server Admin tool located in /Applications/Server, and authenticate as the administrator (**Figure 5.108**).

11. Select the NFS service for your server in the Computers & Services list (**Figure 5.109**).

continues on next page

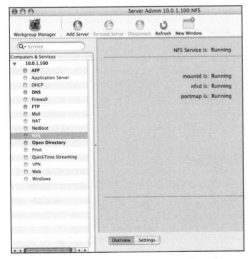

Figure 5.108 You use Server Admin to verify and edit services.

Figure 5.109 Select the NFS service for your server in the Computers & Services list.

NETWORK FILE SYSTEM SHARING

12. Click the Overview button Overview, and verify that the NFS service is running (**Figure 5.110**).

It should automatically start when you configure your first NFS export.

✔ Tips

- Aside from what you've configured here, all access to this share point is granted based on file-system permissions. See "Configuring File and Folder Permissions" for more information.

- In order for guests to access a share point, its permissions must be set to allow everyone read access.

- You can have only one World-viewable NFS export per server. Setting up your own World-viewable NFS export will interfere with the NetBoot service, because it uses a World-viewable NFS export to share boot images.

- To delete an NFS export, deselect the "Export this item and this contents to" check box, and then click the Save button.

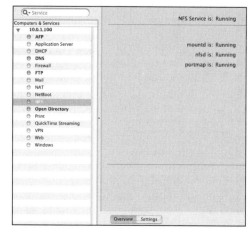

Figure 5.110 Like other services, you can see if the service is running.

NETWORK FILE SYSTEM SHARING

Connecting via NFS

You can connecting to an NFS export from a Mac OS X client as follows. In the Finder, click the Network icon Network to browse for your server. Mac OS X Client can browse for NFS exports via the Rendezvous protocol.

You can also connect directly in the Finder by selecting Go > Connect to Server from the menu bar and entering an NFS export server and path address or by pressing Command-K from the keyboard (**Figure 5.111**).

Default settings dictate that the share point's icon mounts on the Finder's desktop .

Figure 5.111 Choose Go > Connect to Server, and enter the address of the share point.

Resharing an NFS share point

The lack of secure NFS authentication prevents many people from implementing NFS services to desktop clients. Thus, authenticated protocols such as AFP and SMB are used instead. However, depending on the organization, large investments may have been made in NFS-based file servers that don't support AFP or SMB.

Mac OS X Server is unique in filling this gap by providing the NFS *reshare service*. Basically, your Mac OS X Server connects to another NFS export and then reshares that export via AFP or SMB. Clients connect securely via their native protocol to your Mac OS X Server, and it acts as a conduit to the other NFS server. This process lets you keep your current NFS-based server infrastructure and at the same time provide native and secure authentication to the desktop clients.

The system administrator for the originating NFS export must allow your Mac OS X Server root access to the export. This is required because the AFP service runs as root on your server. The security risk created

by allowing root access is overcome by configuring the NFS export to allow access only by your server. You can also set up a private network for this connection.

To reshare an NFS share point:

1. On your Mac OS X Server, use the Finder or the command `mkdir` to create a folder at the root of the system drive called nfs_reshares.

   This folder must be named exactly as shown, or the task will not work.

2. Although root doesn't have to own this folder, you must configure the permissions so root has access (see "Configuring File and Folder Permissions") (**Figure 5.112**).

   Use Workgroup Manager to configure the share point.

3. Inside the /nfs_reshares folder, create folders for each NFS export you plan to reshare.

   Give each folder the same name as the local mount name of the NFS export on your server. Once again, although root doesn't have to own these folders, you must configure the permissions so root has access. For example, if you have a Unix computer with a hard disk you want to share and the disk is called myhd, you'll create a folder in the nfs_reshares folder called myhd.

4. To make your server automatically mount the NFS exports at startup, you must configure network mount instructions in the server's local NetInfo database.

   Launch the NetInfo Manager tool, located in /Applications/Utilities on your server.

continues on next page

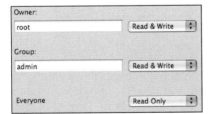

Figure 5.112 Root must have access to the reshared folder.

5. Click the lock icon , and authenticate as the server administrator (**Figure 5.113**).

6. In the NetInfo Manager directory browser, select the mounts directory (**Figure 5.114**). Click the New button to add a new directory item.

7. Double-click the name value in the NetInfo property browser to edit that item.

Change the value to match your original NFS export, using the following format: *<nfs server name>:/<nfs export path>* (**Figure 5.115**).

8. Choose Directory > New Property to add new properties (**Figure 5.116**).

Add two properties: vfstype and dir. The vfstype value is nfs. The dir value is the local mount point of the NFS export: /nfs_reshares/<share name> (**Figure 5.117**).

Don't worry if your properties are out of order; when you save the changes, they will reorder.

Figure 5.113 Authenticate within NetInfo Manager to set up the automounted share point.

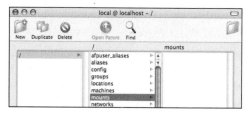

Figure 5.114 Select the mounts directory to create a new mount point.

Figure 5.115 Enter the appropriate value for the mount point.

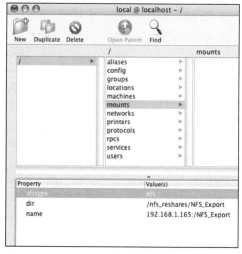

Figure 5.117 You must add properties to enable your mount point.

Figure 5.116 Add an additional property to your mount record.

Figure 5.118 Click Save to save your changes...

Figure 5.119 ...and click "Update this copy" to write it back to the database.

Figure 5.120 The NFS share appears inside the nfs_reshares folder.

9. When you've finished configuring the mount properties and values, click any other directory in the directory browser to initiate the save process.

   Continue through two verification dialogs to save your changes (**Figures 5.118** and **5.119**).

   You can add more NFS exports by repeating steps 6–9.

10. Quit NetInfo Manager, and restart your server.

    Verify that the NFS exports are auto-mounted. NFS reshares must always appear as mounted servers in the /nfs_reshares folder (**Figure 5.120**).

11. Launch the Workgroup Manager tool located in /Applications/Server, and authenticate as the administrator (**Figure 5.121**).

continues on next page

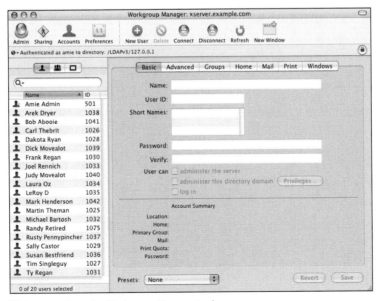

Figure 5.121 Open the Workgroup Manager tool.

NETWORK FILE SYSTEM SHARING

12. The NFS exports mounted in the /nfs_reshares folder automatically appear under the All tab 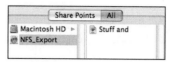 in the sharing browser (**Figure 5.122**).

13. Configure the NFS exports as you would any other share point on your server (see the task "To configure new share points," earlier in this chapter).

Figure 5.122 Once created, the share point appears under the All tab.

✔ Tips

■ Test the shares as you would any other secure share point. However, if the link between the original NFS server and your server is broken, the reshares will likewise be severed.

■ Be very careful when using NetInfo Manager, because changes are made live.

■ Workgroup Manager can also be used to create the NFS reshare.

NETWORK FILE SYSTEM SHARING

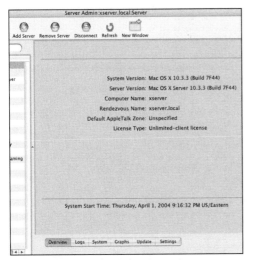

Figure 5.123 You can use the Server Admin tool to view certain log files.

Figure 5.124 Select a service from the Server Admin service list.

Name	Type	Address	Connected	Idle For
kevin	tcp	192.168.1.6	01:49	01:49
amie	tcp	192.168.1.19	01:43	01:42
leslie	tcp	12-202-23-226.client.	00:01	00:01

Figure 5.125 The connections frame shows currently connected users for the selected service.

Monitoring Sharing Services

Mac OS X Server provides a variety of statistics for monitoring sharing services. Using the Server Admin tool, you can monitor each file-sharing protocol in real time. The information provided by the monitoring tools is invaluable for troubleshooting connection problems and determining if resources are being properly used.

To view sharing service connections:

1. Launch the Server Admin tool located in /Applications/Server, and authenticate as the administrator (**Figure 5.123**).

2. Select the file-sharing service you wish to monitor in the Computers & Services list (**Figure 5.124**).

   You can choose to monitor service connections to AFP, FTP, and Windows services.

3. Click the Connections button [Connections].

   A connections frame appears, showing currently connected users for the selected service (**Figure 5.125**). AFP is the most extensive of all the file services. Note that idle connections appear grayed out compared to active connections.

   continues on next page

✔ Tips

- Click the Refresh button  to force Server Admin to refresh the connected user list immediately.

- You can select multiple users in the connected user list by holding down the Shift key or the Command key while you click the user names.

- In the AFP connections frame, you can send a message to a connected user. To do so, select a user from the connections list, and click the Send Message button `Send Message...`. A dialog appears, in which you can enter a message to the user (**Figure 5.126**). Click Send, and the user will be presented with a Message dialog (**Figure 5.127**).

- In both the AFP and SMB connections lists, you can disconnect a user. To do so, select a user from the connections list, and click the Disconnect button `Disconnect...`. A dialog appears, in which you can enter the amount of time before the user is disconnected along with a message to the user (**Figure 5.128**). After you click Send, the user will see the message, and the server will disconnect after the allotted time (**Figure 5.129**).

AFP share service throughput

The Server Admin tool provides a graphical interface for monitoring AFP service throughput. These graphs provide a visual reference that you can use to monitor your server's resource utilization.

Figure 5.126 Send a message to any user you wish.

Figure 5.127 This is the Message dialog box that the client sees.

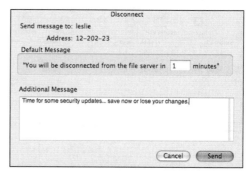

Figure 5.128 You can set the disconnect time and disconnect message.

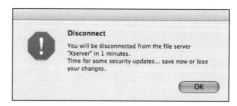

Figure 5.129 The client sees this Disconnect message.

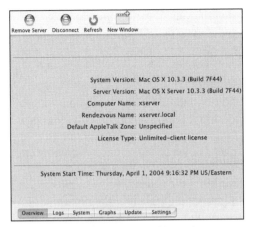

Figure 5.130 The Server Admin tool is used to measure service throughput.

Figure 5.131 Select the service you want to monitor, such as AFP.

To measure AFP share service throughput:

1. Launch the Server Admin tool located in /Applications/Server, and authenticate as the administrator (**Figure 5.130**).

2. Select the AFP service in the Computers & Services list (**Figure 5.131**).

   You can choose to monitor service connections to AFP, FTP, and Windows services.

3. Click the Graphs button `Graphs`.

   A graph frame appears.

4. The graph frame defaults to displaying Average Connected Users (**Figure 5.132**). Use the slider below the graph to manipulate the graph's sample timeframe.

5. Only in the AFP graph frame, you can click the pop-up menu and select Throughput.

   The resulting graph shows average AFP service network throughput (**Figure 5.133**).

✔ Tip

■ Click the Refresh button `Refresh` to force the Server Admin tool to refresh the connected user list immediately.

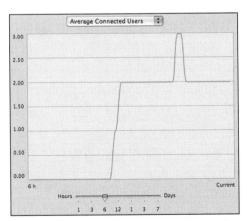

Figure 5.132 Use the graph to view your connected user totals.

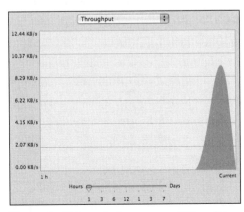

Figure 5.133 This graph shows average AFP service network throughput.

Creating a Home Directory Network Mount

Share points that are configured to automatically mount on your clients at startup are called *network mounts*. (In previous versions of Mac OS X Server, they were sometimes called *automounts*.) It's important to understand that network mounts are always available to any user on the client computer, whereas a share point located in the user's Startup Items is available only to that user and is mounted only when the user logs in.

Essentially, network mounts are instructions stored in a directory database that tell client computers to mount certain share points at startup. Thus, the Workgroup Manager tool can configure network mounts only for servers that are part of a directory service system. The server hosting the actual share points can be either an Open Directory master or connected to another directory server. In addition, your client computers must be configured as clients of the directory service system. (For more information about Directory Services and Open Directory, see Chapter 3.)

Network mounts are an important option because there are certain share points that client computers must have access to at all times. For instance, to provide network home directories for your users, the share point that hosts the home directories must be mounted on the client computer prior to user login.

To create a home directory network mount:

1. Launch the Workgroup Manager tool located in /Applications/Server, and authenticate to the server hosting the share points as the administrator (**Figure 5.134**).

2. Click the Sharing icon ![Sharing] in the Toolbar.

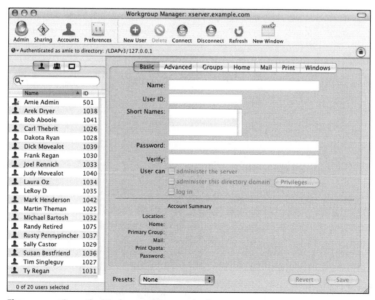

Figure 5.134 Open the Workgroup Manager tool.

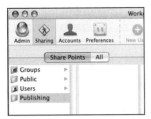

Figure 5.135 Select your share point from the list.

Figure 5.136 You get to the Network Mount tab by clicking any share point.

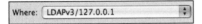

Figure 5.137 Choose the directory where the mount information will be located.

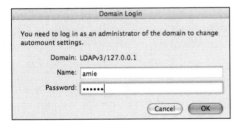

Figure 5.138 You must authenticate to add the mount point.

Figure 5.139 Select the "Create a mount record for this share point" to add the mount point.

3. *Do one of the following:*

▲ To configure the network mount option for an existing share point, click the Share Points tab [Share Points], and then select the share point you wish to edit from the sharing browser (**Figure 5.135**).

▲ To configure a new share point that also has the network mount option, see the task "To configure new share points" earlier in this chapter.

4. Once you've selected the share point on which you wish to enable the network mount option, click the Network Mount tab to the right of the sharing browser (**Figure 5.136**).

5. Select the directory server that will contain the network mount instructions from the Where pop-up menu (**Figure 5.137**). To the right of this pop-up menu, click the Lock icon [ ], and authenticate as an administrator of the selected directory server (**Figure 5.138**).

6. Select the "Create a mount record for this share point" check box (**Figure 5.139**).

continues on next page

CREATING A HOME DIRECTORY NETWORK MOUNT

7. From the Protocol pop-up menu, select either AFP or NFS as the share point's protocol (**Figure 5.140**).

AFP is the generally suggested way of handling network mounts.

8. Select the User Home Directories radio button (**Figure 5.141**).

9. When you've finished making changes, click the Save button (Save).

After restarting the client computers, verify the network mount. Home directory network mounts are found on the local clients at /Network/Servers/ *<servername>/<sharename>*.

✔ Tip

■ To configure individual network users' home directories, see the instructions in Chapter 4.

Figure 5.140 Choose AFP as your protocol of choice.

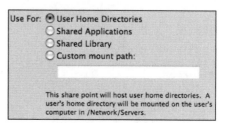

Figure 5.141 Select the User Home Directories option.

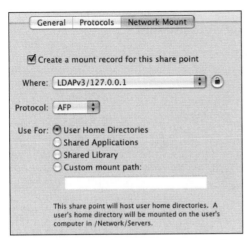

Figure 5.142 Choose another option for additional network mounts.

Creating additional network mounts

You may find it useful to add other types of share points as network mounts. Examples include a shared Applications folder, a shared Library folder, or any other share point you want to automatically mount to a specific point on the local client.

To create additional network mounts:

1. Use the Workgroup Manager tool to create a network mount share point.

   For detailed instructions, see steps 1–7 of the previous task, "To create a network home directory network mount."

2. *Select one of the following* radio buttons (**Figure 5.142**):

   Shared Applications—This network mount will automatically mount to the /Network/Applications directory. The client system will search this folder for available applications.

   Shared Library—This network mount will automatically mount to the /Network/ Library directory. The client system will search this folder for available resources, including fonts, frameworks, preference panes, or any other application or system support files.

   "Custom mount path"—This network mount will automatically mount to the path specified in the field below.

3. When you've finished making changes, click the Save button ⬚Save⬚.

   After restarting the client computers, verify the network mount. Additional directory network mounts are found on the local clients at the path you specified in the network mount configuration.

✔ Tip

■ You can view the network mount details using the Workgroup Manager Inspector.

Locally Configured Network Mounts

Instructions for automatic network mounts can be stored in any directory database, including the client's local NetInfo database. From the client in NetInfo Manager, you can add new mount directory entries. For an idea of how to do this, refer to steps 5–9 of the task "To reshare an NFS share point," earlier in this chapter. You need to add only a few properties and values for each mount entry:

◆ name = *<servername>*:/*<sharepoint>*

◆ dir = *<localmountpoint>*

◆ vfstype = url

◆ opts = net, url==*<serverurl>*

A typical network mount entry has the following properties (**Figure 5.143**):

◆ name = xserver:/Users

◆ dir = /Network/Servers/

◆ vfstype = url

◆ opts = net, url==afp://;AUTH=NO%20USER%20AUTHENT@10.1.1.5/Users

Figure 5.143 Add the mount information in NetInfo Manager.

NETWORK CONFIGURATION OPTIONS

What network-related services does Mac OS X Server offer, and how do you go about managing these services? Often, you'll want your Mac OS X Server to do double duty as a router, DHCP server, or DNS server, or do Network Address Translation (NAT). Perhaps you're replacing an older Windows NT server or upgrading an AppleShareIP server. Each of these services extends the functionality of your server. This chapter looks at setting up some of these services and discusses how they will benefit you.

DNS

Domain Name System. Domain Name Server. DNS is an acronym for both. DNS is both widely used and widely misunderstood.

The Domain Name System is used to make the Internet easy to navigate. Instead of typing numbers like `http://17.254.0.91`, you type `http://www.apple.com`; both addresses go to the same place, but the second is certainly much easier to remember. In order for DNS to work, Apple Computer must have a computer that has the name apple.com, which in turn knows about computers under its domain such as www.apple.com, training. apple.com, train.apple.com, and so forth. It's important to remember that it all starts with, in this case, apple.com.

Let's back up a bit. Suppose you wish to find an obscure Web site, such as http://www. thereisnothinghere.com. You'll probably start by searching the .com domain, which tells you where thereisnothinghere.com is, which, in turn, tells you where www.thereis-nothinghere.com is located. That computer is running a Web server and responds to your request by giving you back Web pages.

This concept works because almost all devices on the Internet that have an IP address associate that address with a name. This, in a nutshell, is how the Domain Name System works.

DNS and Mac OS X Server

Macintosh users never had to worry about maintaining a Domain Name Server before. Although Apple had software to do that (which ran under pre–Mac OS X operating systems), most users didn't need to use it.

Mac OS X Server, when running as an LDAP server and a Kerberos Key Distribution Center (KDC), relies heavily on DNS, so it's critical to discuss some key points about how to properly implement DNS on your system.

First, Mac OS X Server can be a Domain Name Server. That is, it can translate its IP address(es) into names and back. If your organization already has a Domain Name Server, it's *imperative* that you have the DNS administrator add zone records for your server. *Zone records* are text files kept on a DNS that convert names to IP addresses and IP addresses to names.

Many zone records can be used, but this chapter discusses forward and reverse records. If nothing else, you must have both forward and reverse records for your Mac OS X Server if you wish to use it as an LDAP server and a KDC (these particular records are known as *A records* and *PTR records*, and they will be shown later in this chapter).

Registering Your Server

If you don't have control of the Domain Name Server in your organization, ask the administrator to enter both forward and reverse records for your Mac OS X Server. You'll need to give the administrator the following information:

◆ The IP address of your server

◆ The name of your server

The *name* of your server means the *host name, as listed in the /etc/hostconfig file.* You gave your computer a host name when you initially set it up. Refer to Chapter 3, "Open Directory," for more information.

What if you have the ability to become your own Domain Name Server? How do you translate the IP address of your computer to its host name?

It starts with the initial setup. If your Mac OS X Server is going to host the example.com domain, then the host name of the server should be the name of the computer plus the domain. For instance, if the computer is named xserver, and it will be the computer that hosts the example.com domain, then the host name when setting up the computer is xserver.example.com. You enter this host name when the server is set up initially.

But just setting up the initial host name isn't enough. After the server has been through the initial setup, you must run a Domain Name Server on your Mac OS X Server before you promote your server to a master (see Chapter 3).

To set up simple forward and reverse zone records:

1. Open the Network Preference pane, and ensure you have the proper IP address, subnet mask, and router address (**Figure 6.1**).

2. Launch the Server Admin tool from /Applications/Server, and authenticate as the administrator (**Figure 6.2**).

3. Choose the DNS service from the Computers & Services list (**Figure 6.3**).

   Notice the four tabs at the bottom of the window:

   Overview shows whether the service is running and the current number of zones (**Figure 6.4**).

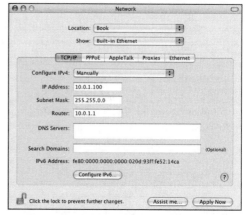

Figure 6.1 Check your network preferences before you proceed with setting up DNS.

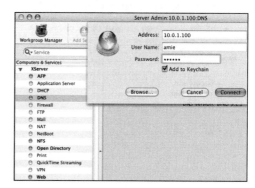

Figure 6.2 Launch the Server Admin tool, and authenticate.

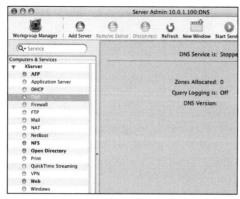

Figure 6.3 Choose the DNS service from the service list.

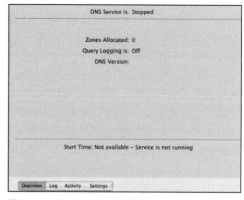

Figure 6.4 The Overview tab indicates service status.

DNS

Figure 6.5 The Log tab shows the DNS log files.

Log displays the DNS log (**Figure 6.5**).

Activity lists the number of requests and zone transfers, which allows other servers to see your zone files (**Figure 6.6**).

Settings displays three more tabs: General, Zones, and Logging. There are six types of logging. You can also restrict zone transfers and increase security with your DNS service (by turning off recursion) (**Figures 6.7**, **6.8**, and **6.9**).

continues on next page

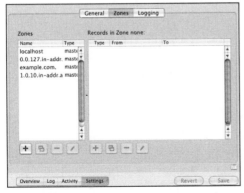

Figure 6.6 The Activity tab shows any requested zone transfers and current queries against the DNS service.

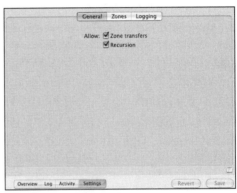

Figure 6.7 The Settings tab reveals three other tabs. The General tab lets you restrict zone transfers and recursion.

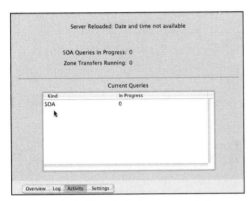

Figure 6.8 The Zones tab lets you enter zone and record data.

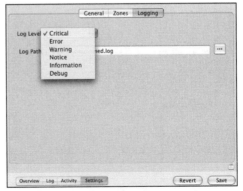

Figure 6.9 The Logging tab lets you change the location of the log file and logging details.

DNS

4. Select the Zones tab, and view the preset zones for loopback (127.0.0.1).

Click the Add button ➕ to add a new zone (**Figures 6.10** and **6.11**).

5. Enter the zone name (in this case, `example.com.`) and the Source of Authority (SOA—the name of the computer running the zone—in this case, `xserver.example.com.`) (**Figure 6.12**).

Enter an email address at the zone listed. Because Mac OS X Server uses BIND 9, you can use the @ symbol here, although a period will also suffice.

Click Save, and entries will appear in the Zone window and the Records window. This is the namespace record (**Figures 6.13** and **6.14**).

Figure 6.10 A preset zone is created automatically.

Figure 6.11 Add a new zone using the zone entry dialog entry fields.

Figure 6.12 When you enter initial zone data, don't forget the periods at the end of each line of text.

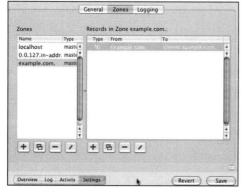

Figure 6.13 Saving the entries results in the zone file being created.

Figure 6.14 The newly created zone file has a namespace record.

Figure 6.15 Enter values for the critical address record, and be sure to select "Create reverse mapping record."

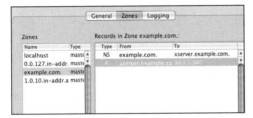

Figure 6.16 Both the forward and reverse zone records now appear in the Zones list.

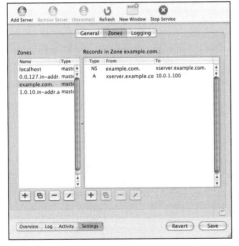

Figure 6.17 Clicking the Save button writes the changes to the zone files.

6. Click the Add button ⊞ under the Records window.

A drop-down dialog appears. Choose Address record (A) type from the menu.

7. *Do the following* (**Figure 6.15**):

▲ In the "Map from" box, enter the fully qualified domain name, such as xserver.example.com. (*with* the period at the end).

▲ In the "Map to" field, enter the IP address of the server (without a period).

▲ Select the "Create reverse mapping record" check box. This is *very* important: It creates the record that maps the IP address back to the name.

You now have two zone records: a forward zone record and a reverse zone record, as indicated by the Zones list (**Figure 6.16**).

8. Click the Save button and then the Start Service arrow button 🔘 to start the DNS service (**Figure 6.17**).

DNS

The Most Important Part, Period.

When you're entering data into zone files, it's important to remember to add a period to the end of any lines that have text in them. Failure to add a period at the end of each line will result in DNS not working properly, subsequent failure of the KDC to start, and potentially other problems as well.

Checking your work

It's important that you double-check your DNS settings before you move on. Problems with DNS records will cause problems elsewhere in the system. A good rule of thumb is to get your DNS house in order before turning on any other services or promoting your machine to a master.

To check your DNS handiwork:

1. After starting the DNS service, head back to your Network Preference pane, and enter the DNS IP address and the search domain (**Figure 6.18**).

2. Open the Terminal application on your server, located in /Applications/Utilities.

   Type hostname and press the Return key to return your fully qualified domain name, such as xserver.example.com (**Figure 6.19**).

3. Copy the returned text.

   On a new Terminal line, type host, press the spacebar, paste in your fully qualified domain name, and press Return (**Figure 6.20**). Your IP address is returned.

4. Copy your IP address.

   On a new line, type host, press the spacebar, paste in your IP address, and press Return to see your IP address resolve to your domain name (**Figure 6.21**).

   This confirms that your computer sees itself correctly; you are now assured that the basic DNS setup is working properly. Additional testing is needed if you have aliases, Mail Exchange (MX) records, or other types of zone records.

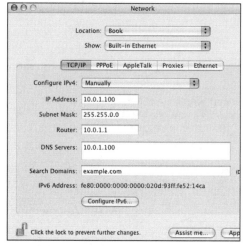

Figure 6.18 Enter the DNS server and search domain in the Network Preference pane.

Figure 6.19 Use the Terminal to retrieve your host name.

Figure 6.20 Use the host command to ensure that your fully qualified domain name maps correctly to your IP address.

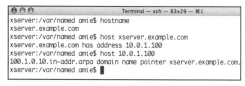

Figure 6.21 Use the host command to ensure that your IP address maps correctly to your fully qualified domain name.

DNS

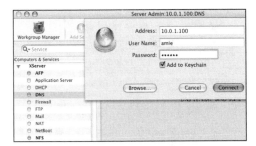

Figure 6.22 Launch the Server Admin tool, and authenticate.

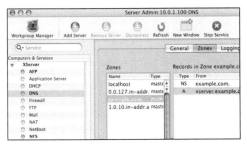

Figure 6.23 Choose the DNS service from the service list.

Figure 6.24 Add a new alias record for a Web server.

Adding other DNS record types

There are plenty of other record types that you may need to add to your DNS service:

◆ Address records

◆ Alias records

◆ Mail Exchange (MX) records

◆ Pointer records

◆ Namespace records

◆ Text records

◆ Other types of records

For example, you may want to add a Web server record or a mail server record. Maybe your server needs to have two names answer to the same IP address. These are all reasons to add records to your zone file.

To add other record types to your zone file:

1. Launch the Server Admin tool from /Applications/Server, and authenticate as the administrator (**Figure 6.22**).

2. Choose the DNS service from the Computers & Services list.

    Select the Settings tab and then the Zones tab (**Figure 6.23**).

3. In the Records in Zone window, click the Add button ➕ to add a new record.

    A drop-down dialog appears (**Figure 6.24**). In this case, you're adding an alias record for a Web server.

continues on next page

DNS

4. Save the changes, and stop and start the DNS service by clicking the Stop Service button ![Stop Service].

Click Start Service to restart the service ![Start Service] (**Figure 6.25**).

Depending on your DNS configuration, you may still need to add an address record for your Web server.

✔ Tip

■ Usually, the DNS service restarts itself and rereads the DNS zone files when you click Save. However, due to the critical nature of DNS, stopping and starting the DNS service ensures a proper rereading of the files.

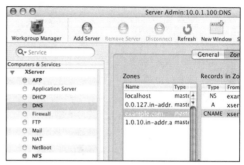

Figure 6.25 The new record shows up in the zone file.

Hit Records

The most popular types of zone records are address records, alias records, and mail exchange records:

◆ Mail Exchange records are used when you're setting up a mail server.

◆ Alias records are used for Web servers.

◆ Address records are used to define other machines.

An abundance of material is available on DNS and the process behind it, called Berkeley Internet Name Domain (BIND). Try the Glossary pages at http://www.menandmice.com/online_docs_and_faq/glossary/glossarytoc.htm.

DNS for Life

This isn't the last word on DNS. Setting up and running a Domain Name Server is one of the most critical pieces of a sound network infrastructure. If running a DNS service is one of your primary job responsibilities, take the time to learn more about other options that can affect the security and performance of your DNS server. Apple's interface for setting up and managing DNS (the Server Admin tool) provides a fraction of what can be added and manipulated via the text files that are created when configuring DNS. Those files are as follows:

◆ /private/etc/named.conf tells the DNS service where to find the zone files.

◆ /private/var/named/ (any files inside this folder) is the location of the actual zone files.

DNS

DHCP Services

Devices like computers, printers, routers, and servers all communicate via IP addresses. But where do these addresses come from? There are routable addresses and nonroutable addresses, or public and private addresses. Chapter 3, "Open Directory," discusses these address ranges.

You now need to decide how you can best manage computers connected to your network. Perhaps they will obtain an address from your server; if that's the case, then understanding how to setup DHCP services is an essential piece of Mac OS X Server. Prior to turning on your DHCP service, you need to ask anyone else on your network if their computer is acting as the DHCP server. Having two DHCP servers on the same network can wreak havoc on the network and should be avoided at all costs.

You can also quickly change the setting of any client computer to DHCP and see if it obtains anything but a 169.254.x.x address. Getting a 169.254.x.x address is called a *self-assigned address*, indicating that there is no DHCP server on the local network.

Passing out information via DHCP

Assuming you've done your homework and you wish your Mac OS X Server to be a DHCP server for your network, decide what addresses you want to pass out to the client computers. You should also decide whether passing out extra information with the address is necessary for your network. For example, Mac OS X DHCP server can pass out the following information to a client:

◆ IP address

◆ Subnet mask

◆ Router address

◆ DNS addresses

◆ Search domains

◆ LDAP information

◆ Windows WINS information

All this information is transferred from the server to the client when the client asks for an address.

DHCP basics

Before you begin to dole out addresses, let's examine what takes place when a DHCP server is on the network:

1. The client machine starts up and searches for a DHCP server.

2. The DHCP server responds to the client and offers the client an IP address and other information.

3. The client formally requests the information from the server, and the server sends it down to the client.

4. The client asks anything else (other computers, printers) on the network if the address offered is already taken.

5. If no one responds that they have the IP address in question, the client then proceeds to commit the information to memory. The client is *leasing* the address from the server.

This process takes place every so often during the day. If you tell your server to give out addresses for eight hours, then your client will ask the server if it can renew the address it has at four hours, or half the lease time.

Having leases that run for six months can be useful when you have only a handful of computers; but if you have laptops that come and go, and people hopping on and off their computers all day, a better idea for the lease time is to set it for 16 hours. This way, during a standard eight-hour day, you're assured the client computers will ask for a renewal, thus potentially freeing up addresses for others to use the following day. This feature is examined in the following task, "To change DHCP service settings."

Again, before you start the DHCP service on your Mac OS X Server, be *sure* no one else is providing DHCP services on your network.

To change DHCP service settings:

1. Launch the Server Admin tool from /Applications/Server, and authenticate as the administrator (**Figure 6.26**).

2. Choose the DHCP service from the Computers & Services list (**Figure 6.27**). Notice the four tabs at the bottom of the window:

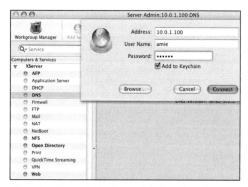

Figure 6.26 Launch the Server Admin tool, and authenticate.

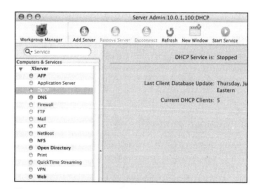

Figure 6.27 Choose the DHCP service from the Computers & Services list.

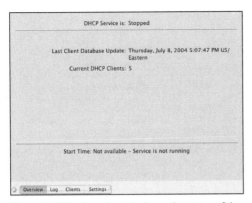

Figure 6.28 The Overview tab shows the status of the DHCP service.

Overview shows whether the service is running and the current number of leases (**Figure 6.28**).

Log displays the current log file for the DHCP service (**Figure 6.29**).

Clients shows all the client machines that are using an address given to them by the DHCP service (**Figure 6.30**).

Settings shows how many networks (called *subnets*) you're serving addresses to and what network interface you're using for each address range. This tab also lets you set the level of logging desired (**Figures 6.31** and **6.32**).

continues on next page

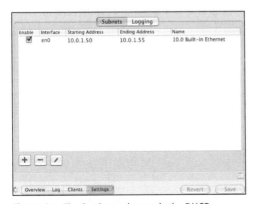

Figure 6.29 The Log tab shows the log information.

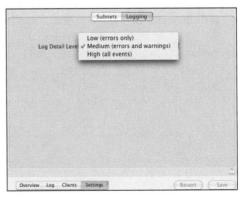

Figure 6.30 The Clients tab shows a list of clients who have received DHCP information from this server.

Figure 6.31 The Settings tab reveals the DHCP subnet(s) and Logging tabs.

Figure 6.32 The Logging tab lets you change the level of logging for the DHCP service.

DHCP SERVICES

3. Select the Settings tab, select the Subnets tab, double-click the General tab or select the subnet you wish to edit, and click the Edit icon 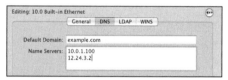.

The Editing Subnet window appears (**Figure 6.33**). Click the return arrow to return to the subnet window. For first-time setup, you can use the default subnet shown earlier in Figure 6.31.

To create a new subnet, click the Add button.

Clicking the Delete button with a subnet selected deletes that subnet.

4. Enter the information necessary in the General window (**Table 6.1**).

5. Click the DNS tab, and enter the appropriate DNS information you want the client computers to receive.

You may enter more than one DNS and search domain (**Figure 6.34**).

6. Save your changes by clicking the Save button.

7. Start the DHCP service by clicking the Start Service arrow button (**Figure 6.35**).

✔ Tip

■ You can set up two DHCP subnets on the same interface. You might do this if you already have a printer or a server within the range of addresses you wish to use. For example, if you have a server or a printer with an IP address of 192.168.1.50, you can have two DHCP ranges—the first going from 192.168.1.2 to 192.168.1.49 and the second range going from 192.168.1.51 to 192.168.1.200, thereby skipping the address users already know.

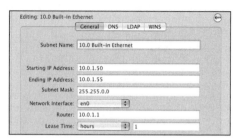

Figure 6.33 Double-clicking the DHCP subnet reveals the four settings tabs for that particular subnet. The General tab allows entry of standard DHCP data.

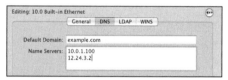

Figure 6.34 Data entered in the DNS tab is pushed down to the client with the IP information.

Figure 6.35 Clicking the Save button starts the DHCP service.

Table 6.1

General DHCP Service Parameters

Name	Function
Subnet Name	Name to identify the network
Starting IP Address	IP address to begin the range
Ending IP Address	IP address that ends the range
Subnet Mask	Mask that allows the network to be segmented
Network Interface	Built-in Ethernet 1 or 2, or any other interface card recognized by Mac OS X Server
Router	IP address of the router that clients will receive
Lease Time	Time in months, weeks, days, or hours until the lease for that address expires

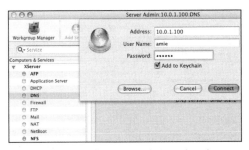

Figure 6.36 Launch the Server Admin tool, and authenticate.

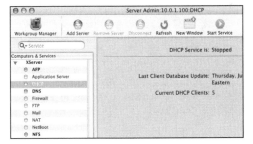

Figure 6.37 Choose the DHCP service from the service list.

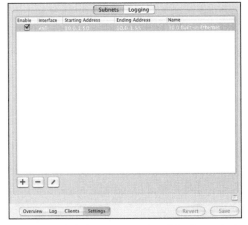

Figure 6.38 Click the Settings tab and the General tab to get to the subnet.

DHCP and LDAP

You've just learned how to push down IP address information that allows users to connect to your network. But what if your needs are bigger? What if you have home directories on your server, and you want the client machines to automatically find them? As discussed in Chapter 3, you can make a Mac OS X Server an LDAP server; one function of that is allowing home folders to exist on the server.

If you have more than 200 client machines, going to each machine to point it to the server is tedious and time consuming. A better way is to allow the DHCP server to push down the information to each client along with the IP address information.

To set up the DHCP service to propagate LDAP information:

1. Launch the Server Admin tool from /Applications/Server, and authenticate as the administrator (**Figure 6.36**).

2. Choose the DHCP service from the Computers & Services list (**Figure 6.37**).

3. Click the Settings tab, and double-click the subnet you want to edit (**Figure 6.38**). Click the LDAP tab.

continues on next page

DHCP SERVICES

4. *Enter the appropriate information* in the LDAP entries (**Figure 6.39**):

▲ Server Name is the fully qualified domain name of your server, such as xserver.example.com (this entry is different than those of DNS and should *not* have a trailing dot at the end of the name).

▲ Search Base is the LDAP search base of your server. In most cases, this looks something like dc=example,dc=com, which parses your domain name into standard LDAP structure. You can determine what information to enter here by reading the task "To create a master directory" in Chapter 3.

▲ Choose another port for the information to go over if you like.

▲ Choose to secure your connection over Secure Socket Layer (discussed in Chapter 10, "Security").

5. Save the changes by clicking the Save button ⎡ Save ⎤ .

If the DHCP service is already running, you'll be prompted to restart the service. Doing so implements your changes (**Figure 6.40**).

✔ Tip

■ Recall that the LDAP information is needed so the client machine can see the server. In this manner the client can authenticate against the server and obtain a home folder or other shared folders. If the client machines are already configured to accept a DHCP address all you have to do is ensure that the LDAP information is passed down along with the IP information.

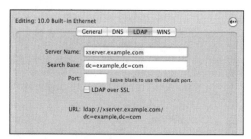

Figure 6.39 Double-click the subnet, and enter the LDAP data to be pushed down to the client.

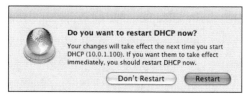

Figure 6.40 This dialog asks if you want to restart the DHCP service.

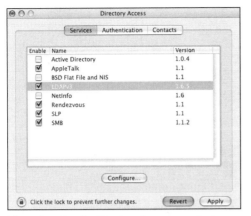

Figure 6.41 Opening Directory Access on a client machine to check the LDAP plug-in status.

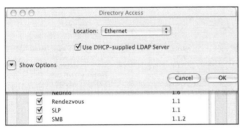

Figure 6.42 Be sure the LDAP plug-in is selected, allowing the client to obtain LDAP information from the DHCP server.

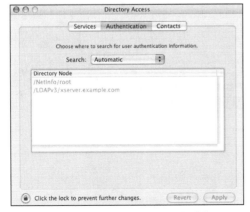

Figure 6.43 Check the Authentication tab of the Directory Access application. LDAP information is being pushed down from the DHCP server.

To set up the client to search for DHCP-supplied LDAP information:

1. On the client machine(s), open the Directory Access application in /Applications/ Utilities, authenticate by clicking the lock ![lock icon] at lower left, and click the Services tab (**Figure 6.41**).

2. Ensure that the LDAP plug-in is selected. Double-click the LDAP plug-in, and make sure the Use DHCP-supplied LDAP Server check box is selected (**Figure 6.42**). Click the OK button.

3. Click the Authentication tab, and ensure that the path which Open Directory searches for authentication information is set to Automatic (**Figure 6.43**).

   If your client machine is getting the DHCP LDAP information, you should see your server's information in the authentication list. If you don't, be sure your DHCP server is sending down the appropriate information.

   Your client machine is now ready to look for LDAP information.

✔ Tip

■ One other set of data can be pushed down to a client machine: WINS data. Windows Internet Naming Service (WINS) is used by Windows computers to locate one another on a network across subnets. If you have Windows clients obtaining an address from a Mac OS X Server, you configure the DHCP server to push down the WINS information.

DHCP SERVICES

To push WINS information via DCHP:

1. Launch the Server Admin tool from /Applications/Server, and authenticate as the administrator (**Figure 6.44**).

2. Choose the DHCP service from the Computers & Services list (**Figure 6.45**).

3. Click the Settings tab, double-click the subnet you want to edit, and then click the WINS tab (**Figure 6.46**).

4. Enter the appropriate information given to you by your Windows administrator.

   You have the options of adding both primary and secondary WINS server addresses as well as pushing down NetBIOS information.

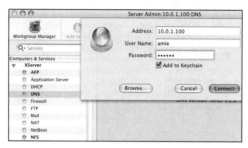

Figure 6.44 Launch the Server Admin tool, and authenticate.

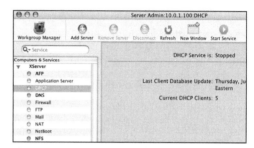

Figure 6.45 Choose the DHCP service from the service list.

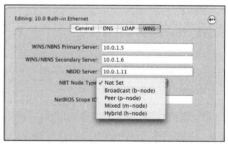

Figure 6.46 Enter WINS data in the current DHCP subnet's configuration window.

Figure 6.47 This dialog asks if you want to restart the DHCP service.

5. Save the changes by clicking the Save button (Save).

   If the DHCP service is already running, you're prompted to restart the service (**Figure 6.47**). Doing so implements your changes.

✔ Tip

- Using Mac OS X Server as a DHCP server is an excellent way to reduce dependency on an existing Windows server that can now be retired.

The ipconfig Tool

You can always check your server to ensure you're pushing down the appropriate information, but how do you tell from the client side if the information makes it down to the client? When you're utilizing any DHCP server, you can check what information is being handed down to the client by using a command-line tool called ipconfig (**Figure 6.48**).

You use the command ipconfig getpacket enx (where x is the number of your Ethernet connection—en0, en1, en2, and so on) to see what information your DHCP server is sending down to your client. To do so, open the Terminal, type the command, and press Return. You'll see all the information your DHCP server is sending you.

Using en0 tells the command to look at your built-in Ethernet connection. Use en1 if you want to look at the DHCP information that's gathered from a computer with an airport card.

```
Terminal — bash — 70x29 — ⌘1
instructor:~ sregan$ ipconfig getpacket en0
op = BOOTREPLY
htype = 1
dp_flags = 0
hlen = 6
hops = 0
xid = 1491112754
secs = 0
ciaddr = 0.0.0.0
yiaddr = 10.0.1.52
siaddr = 10.0.1.100
giaddr = 0.0.0.0
chaddr = 0:d:93:52:14:ca
sname = xserver.example.com
file =
options:
Options count is 9
dhcp_message_type (uint8): ACK 0x5
server_identifier (ip): 10.0.1.100
lease_time (uint32): 0xdec
subnet_mask (ip): 255.255.0.0
router (ip_mult): {10.0.1.100}
domain_name_server (ip_mult): {10.0.1.100}
domain_name (string): example.com
ldap_url (string): ldap://xserver.example.com/dc=example,dc=com
end (none):
instructor:~ sregan$
```

Figure 6.48 Use ipconfig getpacket en0 from a client machine to obtain information about the DHCP server and what it passed down to the client.

Restricting DHCP

There may be a time when you wish to specify which computers receive an IP address. For example, you may have two Mac OS X Servers serving up DHCP to many clients. Perhaps half of these Macs are supposed to obtain their IP address from one server, and the other half will obtain an IP address from the other server. You can restrict which computers receive an IP address from a Mac OS X Server DHCP service by using the NetBoot service interface.

To restrict IP addresses to specific computers:

1. Launch the Server Admin tool from /Applications/Server, and authenticate as the administrator (**Figure 6.49**).

2. Choose the NetBoot service from the Computers & Services list (**Figure 6.50**).

3. Choose the Settings tab and then the Filters tab to get to the NetBoot filter. Select the "Enable NetBoot filtering" check box (**Figure 6.51**).

4. Click the Add button ➕ , and add the hardware address of the built-in Ethernet interface of the machines you want to allow or deny an address from the DHCP service (**Figure 6.52**).

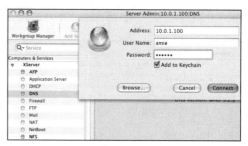

Figure 6.49 Launch the Server Admin tool, and authenticate.

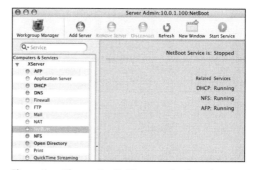

Figure 6.50 Choose the NetBoot service from the service list.

Figure 6.51 In the Filters pane under the Settings tab of the NetBoot service, select the "Enable NetBoot filtering" check box.

Figure 6.52 Add hardware addresses to be used in the DHCP/NetBoot filter.

Figure 6.53 Use NetInfo Manager to view the DHCP config record and see the Allow property with the Ethernet addresses placed in the list.

Figure 6.54 Use NetInfo Manager to show both Allow *and* Deny lists to further define DHCP clients.

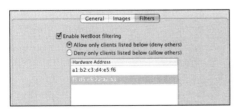

Figure 6.55 The NetBoot filter window has been enabled.

You can only allow *or* deny all addresses in the list here. It's possible to edit the NetInfo database config record directly to see a list of all Allows *and* a list of all Denys (**Figures 6.53** and **6.54**).

5. Click Save [Save] to save the changes (**Figure 6.55**).

It isn't necessary to enable the NetBoot service in order for the filter to function.

6. Choose the previously configured DHCP service from the Computers & Services list, and click the Start Service button to start the DHCP service (**Figure 6.56**). Your DHCP service will now only allow addresses (or deny addresses) to the computers in your filter list, although you can't implement this if the DHCP service is already running. You must restart the DHCP service and have the client machines all request a new address; this is easily done by restarting the client machines.

✔ Tips

- The NetBoot filter is really a DHCP filter. It shows up here instead of the DHCP service configuration because many users of NetBoot want to restrict who obtains an IP address from the server.

- This example uses NetInfo Manager to view and edit data. You can also use Workgroup Manager to do the same thing.

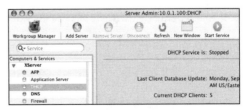

Figure 6.56 Start the DHCP service using the Start Service button when you select the DHCP service.

DHCP SERVICES

Network Address Translation

Mac OS X Server can perform Network Address Translation (NAT), which takes requests (for example, a request for a Web page) from machines connected to one network interface and submits them as if the server had made the request. Enabling NAT doesn't require two network interfaces, but it's suggested. Any Macintosh that supports Mac OS X Server can perform NAT. This function is also found in inexpensive wireless routers, such as Apple's AirPort Base Station.

There are a few reasons to use NAT:

◆ Shortage of IP addresses

◆ Security

◆ Control

Perhaps your organization doesn't need to have every computer use a public IP address. Using public IP addresses for each computer can, of course, lead to security issues, because every computer can be seen by the outside world. You still need all your computers to access the Internet and send and receive email, but you don't want to take the security risk of having those public IPs. NAT is for you.

Or, maybe you want to watch all requests to Web sites so you can monitor them for unauthorized use. NAT is for you.

Perhaps you purchased an Xserve and have no need to purchase many public IP addresses, which can be very expensive. NAT is for you.

Enabling NAT is simple.

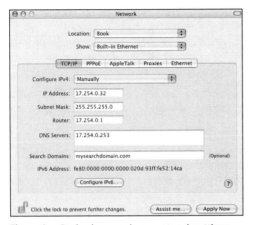

Figure 6.57 Recheck your primary network settings.

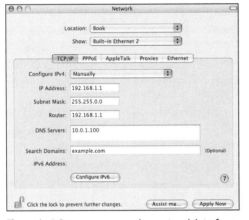

Figure 6.58 Set up your secondary network interface.

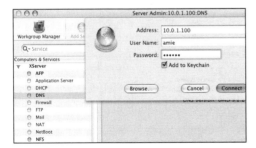

Figure 6.59 Launch the Server Admin tool, and authenticate.

To configure NAT:

1. Ensure that your primary network interface is set up properly and that you can connect to the network properly (**Figure 6.57**).

2. Set up your secondary network interface with the appropriate IP information for your internal network (**Figure 6.58**). You must have both network interfaces active to make NAT function.

3. Launch the Server Admin tool from /Applications/Server, and authenticate as the administrator (**Figure 6.59**).

4. Choose the NAT service from the Computers & Services list (**Figure 6.60**).

continues on next page

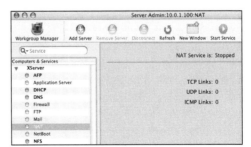

Figure 6.60 Choose the NAT service from the service list.

NETWORK ADDRESS TRANSLATION

5. Select the Settings tab, choose the primary interface to share, and click the Save button ▭ **Save** ▭ (**Figure 6.61**).

The interface you select is the interface that connects to the public network. In most cases, this is the network interface that connects to the Internet.

6. Start the NAT service by clicking the Start Service button 🔵 **Start Service**.

7. Choose the Firewall service from the Computers & Services list.

Start the Firewall service using the Start Service button 🔵 **Start Service** (**Figure 6.62**). The firewall must be running, but it doesn't need to be fully configured for NAT to function.

Client machines can now connect to the Internet, but no device on the Internet can contact your client machines, because they don't really exist on the Internet. As far as other devices on the Internet are concerned, all requests for information are coming from your Mac OS X Server.

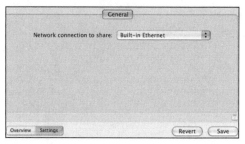

Figure 6.61 Choose the primary network interface before starting NAT.

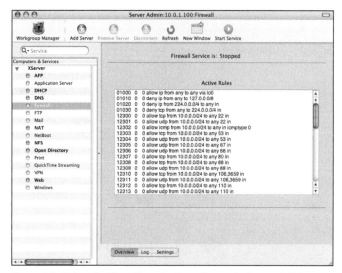

Figure 6.62 Select the Firewall service from the service list, and click Start Service.

NETWORK ADDRESS TRANSLATION

Acting as a Router

Another useful feature of Mac OS X Server is that it can do *IP forwarding*, which allows requests from one network to be sent to another network. This is necessary when you have a Mac OS X Server with two network interfaces and you wish to have information passed from one network to the other. IP forwarding differs slightly from NAT in that your internal network is likely to have public IP addresses, whereas NAT makes all requests as if those requests were coming from the server (the clients have private IP addresses).

When you're deciding how and where a Mac OS X Server should go, one consideration is whether the server will be a link between two different networks. For example, you could have your Mac OS X Server's built-in Ethernet interface go from the server to a switch, and then have the switch connect 40 or so computers that have public IP addresses (they exist on the Internet as separate devices). These computers would use the Mac OS X Server's Built-in Ethernet IP address as their router address. All information sent out of those 40 Macs would flow through the Mac OS X Server's built-in Ethernet interface.

Now, perhaps this is an Xserve with a second built-in Ethernet card, or maybe another Macintosh with a second Ethernet card added. Regardless, the second Ethernet interface is probably connected to another network; possibly this interface is connected to the Internet. It has different IP information than the first built-in Ethernet interface. If this scenario is something you want your Mac OS X Server to do, then you'll be enabling IP forwarding.

continues on next page

You've probably already set up your network information to connect you to the Internet. It's important to note that when you wish to enable IP forwarding, your secondary network should be below your primary network in the network interface list in your Network Preference pane (**Figure 6.63**). Once that's accomplished, open the Terminal, and change the system control parameters to allow this to occur by typing `sudo sysctl -w net.inet.ip.forwarding=1`.

✔ Tips

■ IP forwarding is only set for this instance. If you want it to be on in case of a server reboot, open the file hostconfig in the /etc directory, and change the word NO to YES next to IPFORWARDING. Recall that this file is only writable by root (**Figure 6.64**).

■ This chapter has looked at four services that are sometimes handled by routers or other servers. Mac OS X Server can handle and run these services; however, it's likely that not all the services Mac OS X Server can deploy will be handled by the same server.

■ If you can, it's a common best practice to have one Mac OS X Server do NAT, DHCP, NetBoot, and possibly DNS for the secondary network. Another Mac OS X Server may handle IP forwarding, or this function is handled by a router. Other Mac OS X Servers are then placed in the network to handle home directories, Web and mail, and file sharing.

Figure 6.63 Check the order of your network settings for IP forwarding.

```
IPFORWARDING=-NO-
```

Figure 6.64 Change the line IPFORWARDING=-NO- to IPFORWARDING=-YES- in the file hostconfig located in /etc.

ACTING AS A ROUTER

7

PRINTING SERVICES

Modern printers usually fall into two categories: inexpensive local printers that require a host computer, and more expensive stand-alone shared network printers. For many, sharing fewer high-end printers is a better solution than using individual inexpensive printers. Although they're more expensive, shared network printers are often economically more efficient from a cost-per-page standpoint and are usually technically superior as well, yielding faster and better prints. However, when shared-printer demand increases beyond capacity, resource contention among your users may cause problems. Thus, many administrators resort to print servers that monitor printer traffic and manage printer resources.

Mac OS X Server can be configured to provide such a printing service. Essentially, your server can act as an intermediary between your users and the printers. Print jobs are sent to your server, where they're placed in a queue; then, depending on their configuration, they're sent to the printer, put on hold, or denied. As the server administrator, you can configure how print jobs are handled. You can manually adjust print jobs, or you can define user print quotas that instruct the server to automatically disable a user's ability to print after their allowance is used up.

The print server also lets you share non-network printers and reshare network printers using different printing protocols. Specifically, you can create and share a print queue for any printer that Mac OS X can print to. This includes both raster and postscript printers available to your server via AppleTalk, Windows (SMB), LPR, IPP, HTTP, Rendezvous, Bluetooth, USB, and FireWire. Furthermore, Mac OS X Server can share any of its printer queues via AppleTalk, Windows (SMB), and LPR (with Rendezvous) network printing protocols.

Creating Printer Queues

On Mac OS X Client, when you add a printer to the printer list, you create a local print queue for the computer. Whenever you print from an application, the print job is temporarily stored in the print queue until the job is sent to the printer. The same is true for Mac OS X Server. When you create a print queue on a server, you can then enable print sharing, thus allowing other computers to use your server's print queues. In other words, every printer you have configured in the server's printer list is a queue that can be shared.

The default method for setting up printer queues on Mac OS X Server is to use the Server Admin tool. This tool lets you add printers to the server's printer list and then enable sharing for each printer queue. Similar to Mac OS X Client, you can use the Printer Setup Utility locally on the server to configure printers for the print server. (See the section "Configuring Printers on Clients," later in this chapter, for more information about using the Printer Setup Utility.) However, the Printer Setup Utility doesn't let you enable the shared queue settings; nor does it allow

for remote administration. Basically, you can add a printer with the Printer Setup Utility or the Server Admin tool, but in order to share the printer, you must use the Server Admin tool.

Before you create any printers, you must understand the different ways a printer can be connected (the accompanying figures are from the choices given when adding a print queue using the Server Admin tool):

AppleTalk creates a print server queue for an AppleTalk printer (**Figure 7.1**). If your network has AppleTalk zones, select the appropriate zone from the pop-up menu. In either case, AppleTalk printers automatically populate in the list. Select the printer from the list, and click OK.

LPR creates a print server queue for an LPR/IP printer (**Figure 7.2**). Enter the IP address or DNS name of the printer. For most printers, you'll leave the "Use default queue on server" check box enabled. However, if the destination printer has multiple queues, deselect the check box and enter the queue name in the appropriate field. When you're done, click OK.

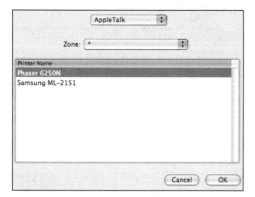

Figure 7.1 In the Printer Setup Utility, you can add an AppleTalk printer...

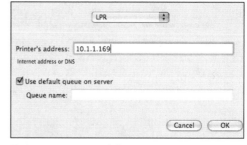

Figure 7.2 ...or an LPR (IP) printer...

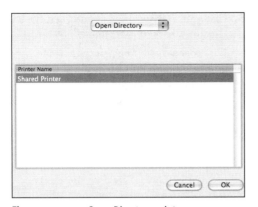

Figure 7.3 ...or an Open Directory printer.

Open Directory creates a print server queue for a printer listed in a directory system (**Figure 7.3**). For this option to work, your server must be configured to connect to a directory system. (See Chapter 3, "Open Directory," for more information.) If your server is properly configured, select the printer from the list and click OK.

To create a printer queue:

1. Launch the Server Admin tool located in /Applications/Server, and authenticate as the administrator (**Figure 7.4**).

continues on next page

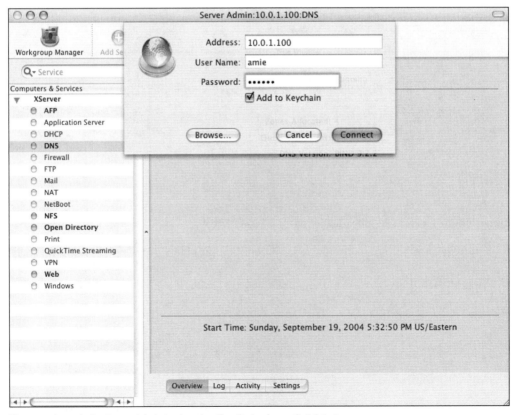

Figure 7.4 Launch the Server Admin tool, and authenticate as an administrator.

CREATING PRINTER QUEUES

2. Select the Print service for your server in the Computers & Services list (**Figure 7.5**).

3. Click the Settings button and then the Queues tab.

For most servers, the print queues list is empty (**Figure 7.6**). On the other hand, any printer connected to your server via USB automatically appears in this list.

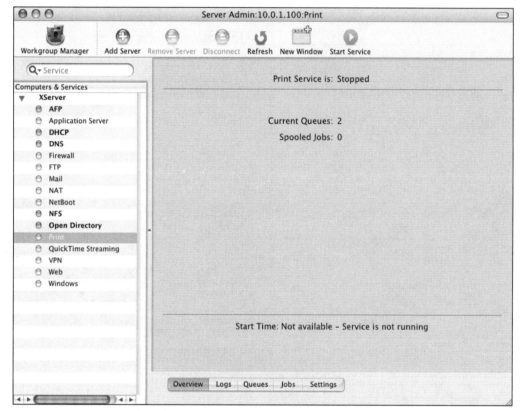

Figure 7.5 Select the Print service from the Computers & Services list.

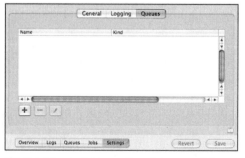

Figure 7.6 For most servers, the print queues list is empty.

CREATING PRINTER QUEUES

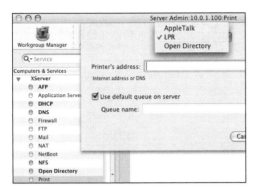

Figure 7.7 Choose one of the print protocol options for creating a print queue.

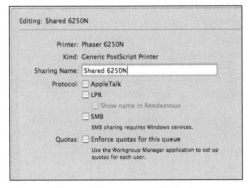

Figure 7.8 These options are available in the queue Editing frame.

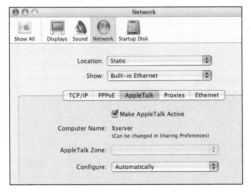

Figure 7.9 Be sure AppleTalk is selected in the Network Preference pane.

4. Click the Add button ⊕.

   The Create Print Queue dialog drops from the title bar.

5. Click the Print Protocol pop-up menu, and *select one of the following options* (**Figure 7.7**):

   ▲ AppleTalk

   ▲ LPR

   ▲ Open Directory

6. Once you've added the printer queue, the queue Editing frame opens (**Figure 7.8**). Feel free to change the sharing name of the print queue. (Note that in the figure, the printer's original name is different than the shared queue's name.)

7. To enable the shared queue, *select one or more of the following protocol check boxes*:

   AppleTalk shares this queue via the AppleTalk protocol. Make sure AppleTalk is enabled in the Network Preference pane on your server (**Figure 7.9**).

   LPR shares this queue via the LPR protocol. If LPR is selected, you can then click the "Show name in Rendezvous" check box and subsequently browse for this shared queue on Mac OS X 10.2 or newer computers via any Print window.

   SMB shares this queue via the SMB (Windows printing) protocol. Make sure the Windows service is also enabled on your server. (See the section "Configuring the Windows File Sharing Service" in Chapter 5 for more information.)

   continues on next page

CREATING PRINTER QUEUES

8. To enable quotas for this queue, select the "Enforce quotas for this queue" check box.

To configure user quota settings, you must use the Workgroup Manager tool; refer to the section "Enabling Printer Quotas" in Chapter 4.

9. When you're done making changes, click the Save button.

10. Click the Back button 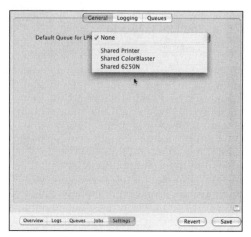 to return to the print queues list view in Server Admin.

11. Click the General tab (**Figure 7.10**).

From the Default Queue pop-up menu, select a queue to act as a catch-all for any print job not destined for a specific queue on your server.

Figure 7.10 Select the default queue under the General tab.

12. Click the Overview tab.

If the Print service isn't running, click the Start Service button on the Server Admin Toolbar to start the service (**Figure 7.11**).

✔ Tips

■ You can create more queues by clicking the Add button ⊕ . To edit a queue, select the queue from the print queues list and click the Edit button . Finally, you can delete a queue by selecting it and clicking the Delete button ⊟ .

■ Printer Sharing, available in the Sharing Preference pane on Mac OS X clients, is disabled on Mac OS X Server in favor of the Print service.

■ If you create a print queue for a network printer, Mac OS X Server can't prevent your users from bypassing this print queue and printing directly to a networked printer. One way to control printing to a given set of printers is to attach them to a switch or hub and connect that to a second Ethernet interface on your server.

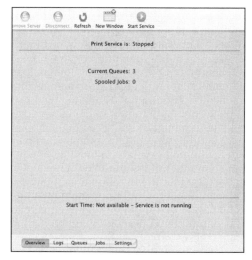

Figure 7.11 The Overview tab of the Print service indicates the Print service status.

CREATING PRINTER QUEUES

Common Unix Printing System (CUPS)

Mac OS X uses an open-source technology known as the Common Unix Printing System (CUPS) to handle printing. CUPS is a sort of magic black box that takes a print job, converts it to whatever format the printer needs, and communicates with the printing device to get the job done. Like most open-source technologies adopted by Apple, CUPS has many advantages:

◆ Web-based administration via http://127.0.0.1:631/ (you can also use the hostname of the server in the URL) **(Figure 7.12)**

◆ Command-line administration via the `lpadmin` utility

◆ A plethora of technical documentation and support, available at http://www.cups.org

◆ A legion of Unix geeks who create hundreds of third-party printer drivers, which are available at http://gimp-print.sourceforge.net

Although Mac OS X Server doesn't use CUPS to share the print queues, it does use CUPS as its printing back end. Thus, if you prefer, you can use the CUPS command-line or Web-based administration tools to create and edit your server's print queues. You must also use the Server Admin tool to configure sharing for each print queue.

Figure 7.12 You can manage printers using the CUPS Web interface.

Configuring Printers in Open Directory

Mac OS X supports discovery of LPR print services via directory services. Any Mac OS X Server that is acting as an Open Directory master can be configured to maintain a list of shared printers. You can configure any printer information you wish in Open Directory, regardless of print server settings. In other words, Open Directory doesn't care where the shared or network printers reside. You use Open Directory to maintain a list of printers that your client computers can easily discover through directory services. Obviously, in order for client computers to discover printers via directory services, they must be configured to access your directory server. See Chapter 3, "Open Directory," for more information about directory services.

To configure a printer in Open Directory:

1. Launch the Workgroup Manager tool located in /Applications/Server, and authenticate as the administrator (**Figures 7.13** and **7.14**).

   You can find detailed instructions for this step in Chapter 2, "Server Tools."

2. If you haven't already enabled the All Records and Inspector tabs, do so now.

   Detailed instructions for this step can also be found in Chapter 2.

3. Click the Accounts icon on the Toolbar and the All Records button  on the account types tab (**Figure 7.15**).

Figure 7.13 Authenticate as an administrator to use Workgroup Manager.

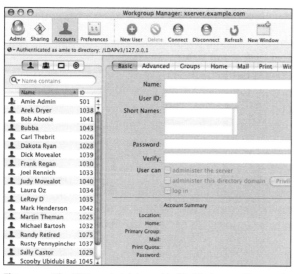

Figure 7.14 The All Records tab is enabled in Workgroup Manager's main view.

Figure 7.15 Click the Accounts icon and the All Records button in Workgroup Manager.

Figure 7.16 Choose the LDAPv3 directory if it isn't already selected.

Figure 7.17 Choose the Printers record from the All Records list in Workgroup Manager.

4. Click the Directory Authentication icon beneath the Toolbar ⊙▾Authenticated , and choose LDAPv3/127.0.0.1 if it isn't already selected (**Figure 7.16**).

5. Below the All Records icon is a record selector pop-up menu. Click this pop-up menu, and you'll be presented with a large list of record types to choose from (**Figure 7.17**).

   For the purposes of this task, choose Printers.

6. Click the New Record button ⊕ New Record to add a new printer record initially called untitled_1.

7. The Inspector frame displays the attributes and values for this new printer record (**Figure 7.18**).

   Double-click the first instance of the printer record's name in the Value column to edit the printer record's name (**Figure 7.19**).

continues on next page

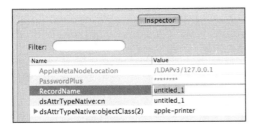

Figure 7.18 The Inspector frame shows the default attributes of a new printer record.

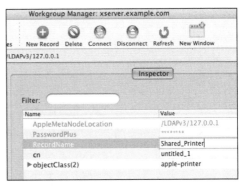

Figure 7.19 Change the RecordName value of the new printer record.

CONFIGURING PRINTERS IN OPEN DIRECTORY

8. Click the New Attribute button
[New Attribute...] , and the attribute-editing
dialog drops from the title bar
(**Figure 7.20**).

From the Attribute Name pop-up menu,
choose PrinterLPRHost, and then enter
the network address of the printer in the
Text field (**Figure 7.21**). Click OK to
close the dialog.

9. If the default queue for the printer is
acceptable, then you can skip this step.
However, if you need to define a specific
queue, click New Attribute [New Attribute...] .
Choose PrinterLPRQueue from the
Attribute Name pop-up menu, and then
enter the queue name in the Text field
(**Figure 7.22**). When you're done, click OK.

10. To specify the printer model driver to
use, add another attribute and choose
PrinterType from the Attribute Name
pop-up menu.

The text you enter here must exactly
match the model name used by the
PPD (**Figure 7.23**). When you're done,
click OK.

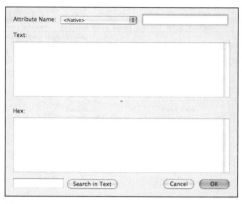

Figure 7.20 Open the attribute-editing window of the
newly created printer record.

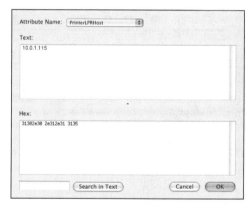

Figure 7.21 Add the PrinterLPRHost attribute IP
address for the new printer record.

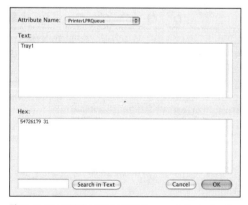

Figure 7.22 Add the PrinterLPRQueue attribute for the
new printer record.

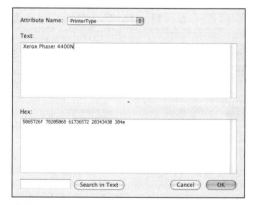

Figure 7.23 Add the PrinterType attribute for the new
printer record.

11. When you've finished making changes, click the Save button ⟨ Save ⟩.

Workgroup Manager will automatically duplicate your settings for directory service compatibility. Your printer record should match that shown in **Figure 7.24**.

✔ Tips

■ You can delete a printer record by selecting it and clicking the Delete button ⟨ Delete ⟩.

■ Click the Options button to adjust how the attribute list is presented.

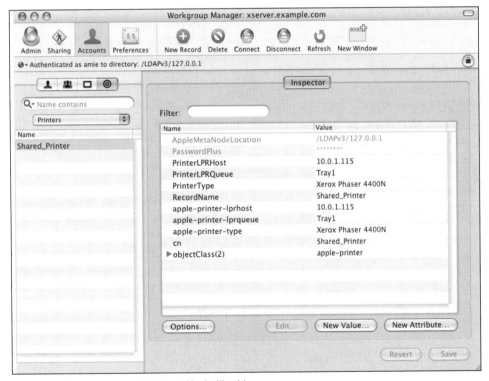

Figure 7.24 The completed printer record looks like this.

Configuring Printers on Clients

Mac OS X Client supports many types of printers, including network and directly connected printers. This section, however, focuses specifically on using the Printer Setup Utility to add printers shared from a Mac OS X Server. These printers are available to all users on the client.

To create a printer:

1. On a client, launch the Printer Setup Utility located in /Applications/Utilities.

   The Printer List window appears (**Figure 7.25**).

2. Click the Add Printer button  on the Toolbar.

   The Add Printer dialog drops from the title bar.

3. Click the Printer pop-up menu at the top of the dialog, and select one of the following options (**Figure 7.26**):

   AppleTalk—If your AppleTalk network is configured with multiple zones, select the appropriate zone from the pop-up menu. In either case, AppleTalk printers automatically populate in the list. Select the printer from the list, and click Add (**Figure 7.27**).

Figure 7.25 The Printer List window opens after you start the Printer Setup Utility.

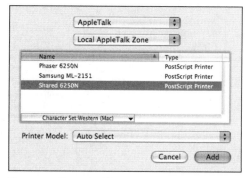

Figure 7.26 There are several default ways available to add a printer using the Printer Setup Utility.

Figure 7.27 You can add a printer using the AppleTalk protocol...

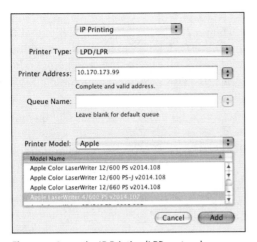

Figure 7.28 ...or the IP Printing/LPR protocol.

IP Printing/LPR—From the Printer Type pop-up menu, choose LPD/LPR. Enter the server's address and, optionally, the queue name. If you want to specify a printer driver other than the Generic driver, you may do so by selecting it from the Printer Model pop-up menu. When you're done making changes, click Add Add (**Figure 7.28**).

Open Directory—You can use this option if your client is configured for Open Directory and you've added printer records to your master Open Directory server. See the task "To configure a printer in Open Directory," earlier in this chapter, for more information. Otherwise, select the printer from the list, and click Add Add (**Figure 7.29**).

Rendezvous—If your server and client are on the same subnet, you can use Rendezvous to discover printers. Printers or shared queues configured with Rendezvous automatically populate in the list. Select the printer from the list, and click Add Add (**Figure 7.30**).

continues on next page

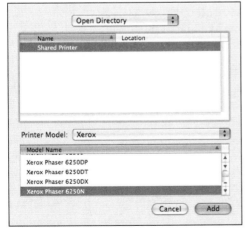

Figure 7.29 You can use Open Directory to add a printer that was set up with Workgroup Manager.

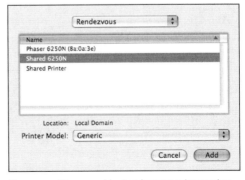

Figure 7.30 You can add a Rendezvous printer using the Printer Setup Utility.

CONFIGURING PRINTERS ON CLIENTS

Windows Printing—If your Windows network is configured with multiple workgroups, select the appropriate workgroup from the pop-up menu. Initially you'll be presented with computers running Windows (SMB) printer sharing. Select a computer from the list, and click the Choose [Choose] button (**Figure 7.31**). You'll have to authenticate with a user account (**Figure 7.32**). Then, select the printer from the list, and click Add [Add] (**Figure 7.33**).

USB—With USB printing, plugging in the USB printer is usually enough. You may need to install the printer drivers and printer description files if a CD is included with your printer. Consult the directions and CD that came with your USB printer in that case.

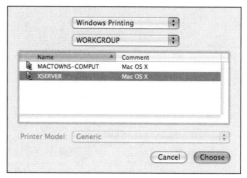

Figure 7.31 Windows workgroups may contain printers using the Windows Printers selection of the Printer Setup Utility.

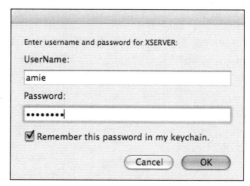

Figure 7.32 An authentication dialog appears before you choose a Windows printer.

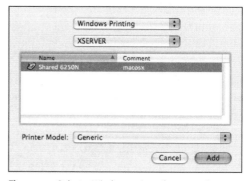

Figure 7.33 Select a Windows printer from a workgroup after authentication.

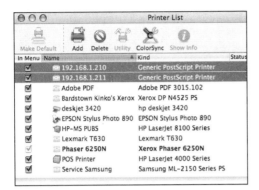

Figure 7.34 The Printer List window confirms all added printers.

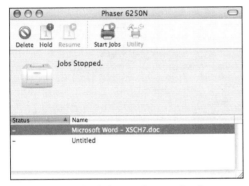

Figure 7.35 Double-click any printer to view its queue.

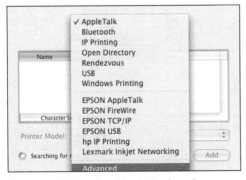

Figure 7.36 Holding down the Option key when you click the Add Printer button shows an additional Advanced option at the bottom of the list.

4. Verify that the printer you just selected has been added to your Printer List window (**Figure 7.34**).

Remember to quit the Printer Setup Utility when you're finished.

✔ Tips

- You can delete a queue by selecting it and clicking Delete 🔘 on the Printer List Toolbar.

- Double-click a printer in the list to view its local print job queue (**Figure 7.35**).

- You can also get to advanced options by holding down the Option key when you click the Add Printer button 🖥 (**Figure 7.36**).

- You can edit a printer's configuration by selecting it in the Printer List window and clicking the Show Info button ⓘ.

Creating Printer Pool Queues

Mac OS X supports a special type of printer queue called a *printer pool*, which can load-balance print jobs between multiple printers. Essentially, a printer pool is a queue that automatically sends a print job to the next available printer on a list you define. It takes only a few steps to enable a shared printer pool on Mac OS X Server.

To create a printer pool:

1. On the server, open the Printer Setup Utility, and add all the printers you wish to pool together.

2. Select all the printers you wish to pool by holding down the Command key while you make your selections (**Figure 7.37**).

3. Choose Printers > Pool Printers (**Figure 7.38**).

   The Printer Pool dialog drops down from the Printer List title bar.

4. Edit the pool's name, and click Create (**Figure 7.39**).

5. Return to the Server Admin tool's printer queue list to find your new printer pool queue.

   Enable print sharing for the printer pool queue as you would for any other printer.

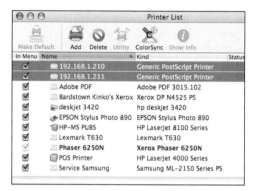

Figure 7.37 Select the printers you wish to add to the printer pool.

Figure 7.38 Choose Printers > Pool Printers.

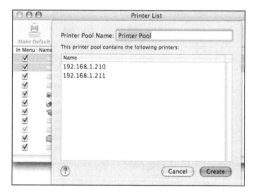

Figure 7.39 The Printer Pool dialog shows all printers in the pool.

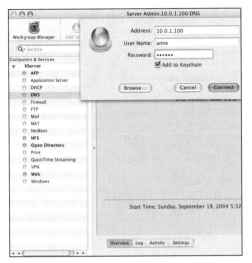

Figure 7.40 Launch the Server Admin tool, and authenticate as an administrator.

Figure 7.41 The Print service's Queues frame displays all current print queues and their status.

Figure 7.42 The Print service's Jobs frame displays all current jobs for a given print queue.

Managing Print Jobs

One of the primary reasons to configure a print server is that doing so gives administrators greater control over print jobs. The Server Admin tool in Mac OS X Server lets you monitor every print job that is sent through your print queues. Further, you can hold or delete print jobs waiting in the queue, thus allowing other jobs to print sooner.

To manage print jobs:

1. Launch the Server Admin tool from /Applications/Server, and authenticate as an administrator (**Figure 7.40**).

2. Select the Print service, and then click the Queues tab `Queues` at the bottom of the window.

   The Queues frame appears. It shows all your active print queues and the number of jobs in each queue (**Figure 7.41**). Notice in the figure that the selected queue is stopped.

3. *Do either of the following:*

   ▲ To stop all the jobs in a print queue, select the queue and click the Stop button `■`.

   ▲ Click the Start button `▶` to resume the print queue.

4. Click the Jobs tab `Jobs`.

   The Jobs frame appears. It shows all the active print jobs for a specific queue (**Figure 7.42**). Notice that the selected job is on hold.

continues on next page

MANAGING PRINT JOBS

5. Select the queue you want to view or manage from the Jobs on Queue pop-up menu (**Figure 7.43**).

6. *Do any of the following:*

▲ To hold a print job, thus letting other jobs in the queue print sooner, select the job and click the Pause button 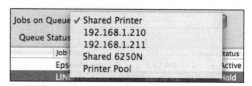.

▲ Select a job and click the Start button ▶ to put the print job back on normal print status.

▲ Select a job and click the Delete button − to delete the job from the print queue.

Figure 7.43 Select a queue in the Jobs frame to view the jobs in that queue.

✔ Tips

■ Although the Server Admin tool automatically refreshes, it may not refresh often enough for you to see all the jobs. This is the case because the print server is so fast that it may receive and send the print job in less time than it takes for the Server Admin tool to display the job in the list.

■ In the Queues list shown in Figure 7.41, you'll notice the acronym PAP in the Shared Via column. Printer Access Protocol (PAP) is the part of AppleTalk that is responsible for printing.

■ Click the Refresh button ⟳ to force the Server Admin tool to refresh the print queue or print job list immediately.

Figure 7.44 Launch the Server Admin tool, and authenticate as an administrator.

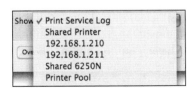

Figure 7.45 The Logs frame shows the Print Service log.

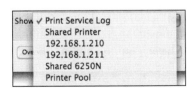

Figure 7.46 Choose which queue log to view.

Viewing Print Logs

If you're having printing problems on your Mac OS X Server, your main troubleshooting resource is the print logs. Every time a queue is modified or a print job is processed, the information is written to the print logs. The logs include print accounting information that isn't available in any other administration tool.

To view print logs:

1. Launch the Server Admin tool from /Applications/Server (**Figure 7.44**), and authenticate as the administrator.

2. Select the Print service, and then click the Logs tab $\boxed{\text{Logs}}$ at the bottom of the window.

   The Logs frame appears. By default, it shows you the Print Service log (**Figure 7.45**). This log includes general print service information, including adding/deleting print queues, starting/pausing print queues, starting/stopping the print server, and print service error messages.

3. Click the Jobs tab $\boxed{\text{Jobs}}$.

   The Jobs frame appears.

4. Click the Show pop-up menu, and choose a printer queue to view its log (**Figure 7.46**).

continues on next page

VIEWING PRINT LOGS

5. The Logs frame shows the log file for the selected print queue (**Figure 7.47**).

This log lists print-job details such as user name, print job, and number of pages. Held and deleted print jobs are also reported.

✔ Tips

■ The Server Admin tool is convenient in that you can view log files remotely; however, it lacks some of the log-reading tools available in the Console utility. If you have local access to your server, you can launch the Console utility located in /Applications/Utilities (**Figure 7.48**). Note that the location of the print service logs is /Library/Logs/PrintService.

■ Click the Refresh button 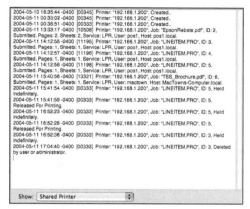 to force the Server Admin tool to refresh the log file immediately.

■ When you're viewing logs from the Console utility, use the Filter field to narrow the log file to the specific items you're looking for.

Figure 7.47 The Logs frame shows a printer queue.

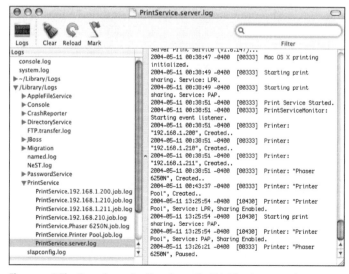

Figure 7.48 The Console application shows the PrintService server log.

MAIL SERVICES

The technologies within Mac OS X Panther Server that provide Mail services have been substantially upgraded from previous versions. In fact, once again Apple has leveraged solutions available from the open-source community to provide entirely different yet altogether more robust Mail services. Although the Server Admin tool provides a unified interface for configuring services, Panther Server uses a variety of interconnected but separate processes to provide a total mail solution. The segregated nature of the Mail service is a reflection of the separate protocols required to facilitate electronic mail transfers.

The Simple Mail Transfer Protocol (SMTP) is used to send outgoing mail from client to server and from one server to another server; Mac OS X Server uses the Postfix process to provide SMTP services. Clients receive incoming mail from their server via either the Post Office Protocol (POP) or the Internet Message Access Protocol (IMAP); Mac OS X Server uses the Cyrus process to provide POP and IMAP services. Other optional services provide ancillary mail features: Mac OS X Server includes the SquirrelMail process to provide Web site–based mail access and Mailman scripts to provide mailing list services.

These items are open-source solutions with many configuration options that go well beyond the scope of the Server Admin tool and this book. You can visit their Web sites for more information: http://www.postfix.org/, http://ags.web.cmu.edu/cyrus/, http://www.squirrelmail.org/, and http://www.list.org/.

Configuring Mail Services

SMTP is used to send mail, and IMAP or POP is used to receive mail, but one other service is absolutely necessary for your mail server to send and receive mail on the Internet. Obviously, you need static real-world IP addresses if your mail server is to send and receive mail from other servers on the Internet. Further, your mail server must have an Address (A) record and a Mailbox Exchange (MX) record on a Domain Name Server (DNS) if it's to be found by other mail servers on the Internet. Most mail clients are configured to find their mail server via DNS as well.

Even if your mail server will only be used internally on a closed network, you should have a DNS record for it, because the mail server won't allow SMTP services unless it can resolve its own IP address to a registered DNS name. If you don't have access to configure another DNS server on your network, it's simple to set up your mail server as a DNS server for itself. For more information about the DNS service, see Chapter 6, "Network Configuration Options."

To enable Mail services:

1. Test the MX record for your mail server by launching the Network Utility located in /Applications/Utilities (**Figure 8.1**).

   The Network Utility only tests the connection from the computer it's running on. So, if possible, you should run this utility on the server.

2. In the Network Utility, click the Lookup tab <kbd>Lookup</kbd>, and then select Mailbox Exchange from the lookup type pop-up menu (**Figure 8.2**).

3. Enter your mail domain address in the lookup field, and click the Lookup button <kbd>Lookup</kbd>.

   If DNS is appropriately configured, the lookup should return the name and IP address of your mail server (**Figure 8.3**).

Figure 8.1 Network Utility's default Info tab is shown when you open the Network Utility.

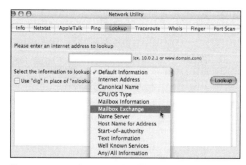

Figure 8.2 Use the Network Utility to check your MX record on your DNS server.

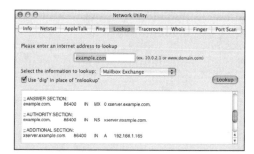

Figure 8.3 This is an example of a typical MX lookup return in the Network Utility.

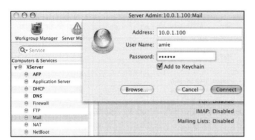

Figure 8.4 Launch the Server Admin tool, and authenticate.

Figure 8.5 Select the Mail service in the Computers & Services list.

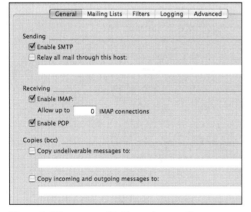

Figure 8.6 You can enable the various mail servers from within the General Mail service settings.

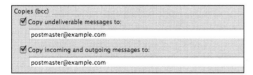

Figure 8.7 The Blind Carbon Copy options are enabled and configured for this mail server.

4. If the MX record is correct for the mail server, then you can proceed. Otherwise, the person in charge of DNS services needs to properly configure the MX record for your mail server.

5. Launch the Server Admin tool located in /Applications/Server, and authenticate as the administrator (**Figure 8.4**).

6. Select the Mail service for your server in the Computers & Services list (**Figure 8.5**).

7. Click the Settings button `Settings` and then the General tab `General`.

8. In the General mail settings frame, *select any of the following* (**Figure 8.6**):

Enable SMTP to enable the Postfix mail-sending service.

Enable IMAP to enable the Cyrus mail-delivery service. Enter a number in the "IMAP connections" field to limit the number of connections. Otherwise, leave the field at its default value of 0 for unlimited connections.

Enable POP to enable the Cyrus mail delivery service.

9. Optionally, you can configure Blind Carbon Copy (bcc) options by selecting the appropriate check boxes and entering a delivery address in the appropriate fields (**Figure 8.7**).

continues on next page

CONFIGURING MAIL SERVICES

...k the Advanced tab Advanced, and ...ify that your mail server's MX record ...ncluded among the Local host aliases (**Figure 8.8**).

If it isn't, double-click the first entry to make the appropriate changes.

11. Optionally, you can configure an alternate primary mail store location by redefining its default directory path (**Figure 8.9**).

You can manually enter a new path or click the ellipsis button ... to use the browse dialog (**Figure 8.10**).

12. When you've finished making changes, click the Save button Save.

13. Click the Overview button Overview, and verify that the Mail services are running (**Figure 8.11**).

If they aren't, click the Start Service button  to activate the Mail services. Although the Mail services are enabled, no mail accounts are enabled by default. The next task explains how to enable mail accounts.

✔ Tips

- It's good practice to stop the mail server, make your changes, then restart the Mail service each time you make a configuration change.

- You may have to shut down and restart the entire server to enable SMTP services for the first time to initially create the configuration files.

- To configure WebMail, refer to Chapter 9, "Web Services."

Figure 8.8 Verify that your server's host name appears in the Advanced Mail service settings.

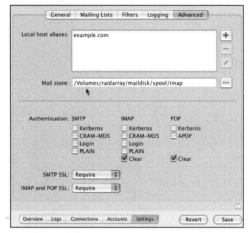

Figure 8.9 Configuring an alternate mail store is a common practice on busy mail servers.

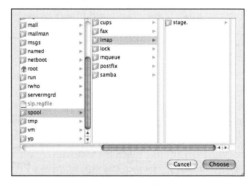

Figure 8.10 You can specify an alternate mail store location from this browse dialog.

Mail Service is:	Running
Outgoing SMTP:	Enabled
Incoming SMTP:	Enabled
POP:	Enabled
IMAP:	0 connected users
Mailing Lists:	Disabled

Figure 8.11 The various Mail services are enabled on this server.

Enabling mail accounts

Even though your server may be running Mail services, by default, no user account is configured to use them. If the user accounts have already been created, you must manually enable Mail service for the users. If you have yet to populate your server with user accounts, then you can save time by defining an account preset in which mail is enabled. This way, every new user you create will automatically be configured with their mail account enabled. For more information about creating user accounts, see Chapter 4.

Mail Configuration Files

Postfix and Cyrus have been around for quite some time, and many Unix administrators are familiar with their associated configuration files. Originally these services had no graphical interface, and all setup was done by editing plain-text configuration files. Although the Server Admin interface is nice, some options are still available only in the configuration files:

◆ The Postfix SMTP service configuration files are /etc/postfix/main.cf. and /etc/postfix/master.cf.

◆ The Cyrus IMAP/POP service configuration file is /etc/imapd.conf.

You need to remember a couple of rules when you're editing the Mail service configuration files. First and foremost, always back up any configuration file before you change it! Also, to activate any changes, you must restart the Mail service.

To enable mail accounts:

1. Launch the Workgroup Manager tool located in /Applications/Server, and authenticate as the administrator (**Figure 8.12**).

2. Click the Accounts icon in the Toolbar and the User icon in the account types tab (**Figure 8.13**).

3. Click the directory authentication icon , and select the appropriate directory database from the pop-up menu (**Figure 8.14**).

4. Select the user or users you wish to configure from the user list (**Figure 8.15**).

5. In the user settings frame, click the Mail tab Mail .

6. By default, Mail services for user accounts are set to None (**Figure 8.16**).

Figure 8.12 Launch the Workgroup Manager tool, and authenticate.

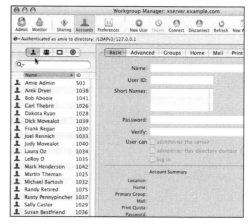

Figure 8.13 Select the User icon in the Workgroup Manager window.

Figure 8.15 Select an account from the user account list. Here, the Susan Bestfriend account is selected.

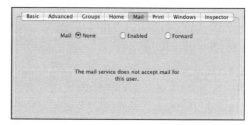

Figure 8.14 Select the appropriate directory database from this pop-up menu.

Figure 8.16 By default, no user has a mail account enabled.

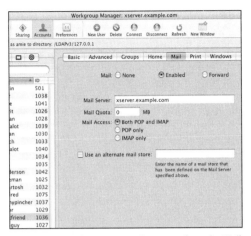

Figure 8.17 Enable a user's mail account from the Mail tab in Workgroup Manager.

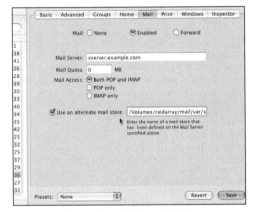

Figure 8.18 This user's mail is stored at in an alternate location.

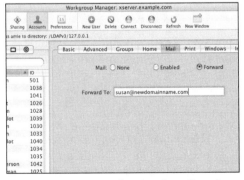

Figure 8.19 This user's mail account is configured to forward all mail to another server.

7. Click the Enabled radio button to activate and configure the selected user's mail settings (**Figure 8.17**):

   ▲ If it isn't already populated, enter the fully qualified domain name of your mail server in the Mail Server field.

   ▲ The Mail Quota is, by default, set for unlimited size with the 0 value. To restrict a user's mailbox quota, enter the desired number of megabytes.

   ▲ To restrict a user's access to either POP or IMAP, choose the appropriate radio button. Otherwise, this account may use either protocol.

   ▲ Optionally, you can configure an alternate mail store location for just this account by redefining its default directory path. To do so, select the "User an alternate mail store" check box, and manually enter a new directory path (**Figure 8.18**).

8. When you've finished making changes, click the Save button. Save.

   You have now enabled basic email service.

✔ Tips

■ If a mail user moves to another service provider, you can forward their mail by clicking the Forward radio button and specifying the user's forwarding address (**Figure 8.19**).

■ You can select multiple accounts from the user list by holding down the Shift or Command key while you make your selections.

■ It's common practice to configure a postmaster mail account on your server as a contact for other administrators to report mail delivery problems to you.

CONFIGURING MAIL SERVICES

Configuring SMTP relay usage

As with any new service, you should thoroughly test the configuration before going live. It's also a very good idea to consider enabling some of the advanced SMTP relay and security features to avoid mail spammers and hackers. Please refer to the other tasks in this chapter for instructions on how to secure your server from common mail server attacks.

Electronic mail servers were originally conceived with a more utopian world view in mind. If mail intended for another server was accidentally delivered to your mail server, the server would kindly relay that message to the correct server. This relay system also allowed administrators to distribute mail servers across their networks for better performance. Mac OS X Server lets you configure the mail server to send all outgoing messages through an SMTP relay server or to become a relay server for other mail servers.

Today, if your mail server acts as relay, then it's a prime target for spammers. They will use your mail server as a relay for delivering spam messages, making it more difficult to trace the spammer's origins. One way to combat this problem is to change the default SMTP relay settings for your server by using a relay filter.

Mail Storage, Backups, and Corruption—Oh My

The default location for temporarily storing outgoing messages is /var/spool/postfix/. This directory is usually small, because messages are only temporarily held there until they're sent. For this reason, Apple didn't include an easy-to-use interface for changing its location. If desired, you can change the outgoing mail store manually by editing the Postfix configuration file.

The default location for storing incoming mail and user mailboxes is /var/spool/imap/. This directory can become large, because it permanently stores all of your users' mail messages. As shown in the previous two tasks, it's easy to specify an alternate mail storage location using the administrative tools. It's common practice to place the mail store on a RAID for improved performance and reliability.

Before you back up either of these directories, you need to stop the mail server. Backing up the mail stores while the Mail service is active will probably result in a corrupted mailbox database backup. A backup solution that temporarily halts the mail server and performs a quick incremental backup is the best option. If you do corrupt the mailbox database, you can attempt to repair it using the `reconstruct -m` command from the Terminal.

Figure 8.20 Launch the Server Admin tool, and authenticate.

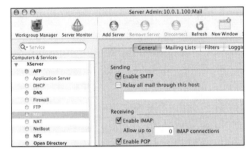

Figure 8.21 The Mail service is selected in the Computers & Services list.

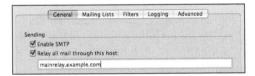

Figure 8.22 All outgoing mail can be relayed through another mail server.

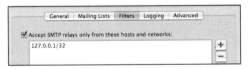

Figure 8.23 Initially, a mail server will only allow SMTP relaying to itself.

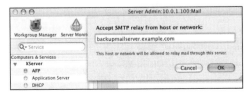

Figure 8.24 Enter additional allowed SMTP relay hosts or networks in this dialog.

To configure SMTP relay usage:

1. Launch the Server Admin tool located in /Applications/Server, and authenticate as the administrator (**Figure 8.20**).

2. Select the Mail service for your server in the Computers & Services list, and click the Settings button (**Figure 8.21**).

3. Configure *either of the following options:*

   ▲ To send all outgoing mail from your server through another relay, click the General tab ⬚General. Then, select the "Relay all mail through this host" check box, and enter the address of the destination relay server (**Figure 8.22**).

   ▲ To accept SMTP relay from other hosts through your mail server, click the Filters tab (**Figure 8.23**), and then click the Add button ⬚+. A drop-down dialog appears in which you can enter a host or network address (**Figure 8.24**). To modify an address, double-click its entry in the relays.

4. When you've finished making changes, click the Save button ⬚Save.

✔ Tips

■ You can test your mail server's relay configuration by attempting to Telnet into the server over port 25.

■ You should always stop and restart the Mail service whenever you make configuration changes.

■ Any mail account hosted on your server can relay through the server without authentication. For this reason, you should consider requiring SMTP authentication to prevent spammers from sending messages as one of your users. See the task "To configure advanced mail authentication" for more information.

CONFIGURING MAIL SERVICES

Handling junk mail

Junk mail, commonly known as *spam*, is unsolicited bulk electronic mail sent through your server or to your users. Unfortunately, junk mail is an unavoidable nuisance when you provide Mail services. One way Mac OS X Server can cut down on spam is by rejecting mail from known spam servers.

To reduce spam:

1. Launch the Server Admin tool located in /Applications/Server, and authenticate as the administrator (**Figure 8.25**).

2. Select the Mail service for your server in the Computers & Services list.

   Click the Settings button and then the Filters tab (**Figure 8.26**). Initially, Mac OS X Server doesn't reject mail destined for your users from any hosts or servers.

3. To refuse messages from known spammers, select the "Refuse all messages from these hosts and networks" check box (**Figure 8.27**).

   Click the Add button ; a drop-down dialog appears in which you can enter a host or network address (**Figure 8.28**). To modify an address, double-click its entry in the filters list.

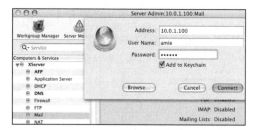

Figure 8.25 Launch the Server Admin tool, and authenticate.

Figure 8.26 The Mail service is selected in the Computers & Services list, and the Settings button and Filters tab are shown.

Figure 8.27 Initially, no incoming mail filters are enabled.

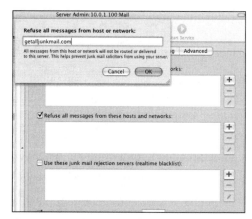

Figure 8.28 Enter blocked hosts or networks in this dialog.

Figure 8.29 Enter real-time black-list server addresses in this dialog.

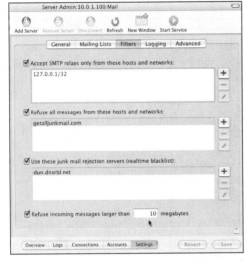

Figure 8.30 On the Filters tab, you can limit the size of all incoming messages.

SpamAssassin

Mac OS X Server doesn't include, but is compatible with, a highly effective spam filter known as SpamAssassin. This filter system uses a range of advanced rule-based filtration tests to identify spam. SpamAssassin is open source and freely available at http://spamassassin.apache.org/. For more information regarding the installation and setup of SpamAssassin on Mac OS X Server, the Apple Developer Connection offers an excellent tutorial at http://developer.apple.com/server/fighting_spam.html.

---

4. To refuse messages based on a continuously updated list of known spammers (maintained by blackhole servers on the Internet), select the "Use these junk mail rejection servers" check box.

Click the Add button [+]; a drop-down dialog appears in which you can enter a server address (**Figure 8.29**). A default link to the Domain Name Real-time Black List is provided for you. To modify an address, double-click its entry in the filters list.

5. When you've finished making changes, click the Save button [Save].

✔ Tips

- You should always stop and restart the Mail service whenever you make configuration changes.

- Any mail account hosted on your server is allowed to relay through the server without authentication. For this reason, you should consider requiring SMTP authentication to prevent spammers from sending messages as one of your users. See the task "To configure advanced mail authentication" for more information.

- You can also filter out unusually large messages to cut down on mail storage size (**Figure 8.30**).

CONFIGURING MAIL SERVICES

Using mail host aliases

Users have a penchant for mistyping electronic mail host names. For this reason, it's a good idea to set up local host aliases, also known as *virtual domains*. Doing so lets your mail server accept mail from more than one domain name. This is also useful if you wish to host mail for a variety of different domain names.

Before you add additional host names, make sure the names are configured with both a forward and reverse DNS record. For more information about the DNS service, see Chapter 6.

To set up mail host aliases:

1. Launch the Server Admin tool located in /Applications/Server, and authenticate as the administrator (**Figure 8.31**).

2. Select the Mail service for your server in the Computers & Services list.

   Click the Settings button and then the Advanced tab (**Figure 8.32**). Initially, Mac OS X Server uses the host name configured for its primary interface (**Figure 8.33**).

3. Click the Add button ⊞.

   A drop-down dialog appears in which you can enter another host name (**Figure 8.34**). To modify a host name, double-click its entry in the aliases list.

4. When you've finished making changes, click the Save button (Save) to save and view your changes (**Figure 8.35**).

   As with any name service change, you should thoroughly test the configuration before going live.

✔ Tip

■ You should always stop the Mail service prior to making changes and restart it only after saving your changes.

Figure 8.31 Launch the Server Admin tool, and authenticate.

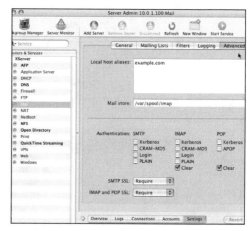

Figure 8.32 The Mail service is selected in the Computers & Services list, and the Settings button and Advanced tab are shown.

Figure 8.33 Initially, the main host name is the only host alias.

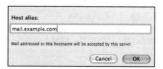

Figure 8.34 Enter additional host aliases in this dialog.

Figure 8.35 View the changes made to the mail alias list.

Mail Security

Amazingly, even though electronic mail has become one of the most valued and trusted communication methods, it's still one of the least secure transactions. Mail protocols were originally designed before security was an issue, to ensure maximum compatibility among disparate systems. Most servers' default settings are incredibly insecure: Sending mail via SMTP doesn't require any authentication, checking mail via either IMAP or POP uses clear-text passwords, and 100% of all mail messages are transferred in the clear. The lack of any real security on many mail servers has helped to fuel the proliferation of spam and mail viruses. In addition, as publicly available and highly insecure wireless networks become more popular, the need to ensure secure mail communication is paramount.

Because Mac OS X Server uses industry standard Mail service technologies, it's subject to the same insecure default mail settings. On the other hand, Mac OS X Server supports the latest secure mail authentication protocols and the Secure Socket Layer (SSL) protocol for message transfers. Configuring secure mail authentication is easy, as long as you have access to mail clients capable of supporting advanced authentication. Most contemporary mail clients, including Apple's free Mac OS X Mail application, support advanced authentication and SSL connections.

To configure advanced mail authentication:

1. Launch the Server Admin tool located in /Applications/Server, and authenticate as the administrator (**Figure 8.36**).

2. Select the Mail service for your server in the Computers & Services list.

   Click the Settings button and then the Advanced tab (**Figure 8.37**). Initially, Mac OS X Server uses no SMTP authentication and uses clear text for IMAP and POP authentication (**Figure 8.38**).

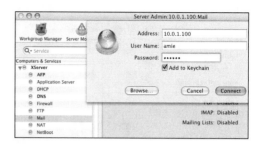

Figure 8.36 Launch the Server Admin tool, and authenticate.

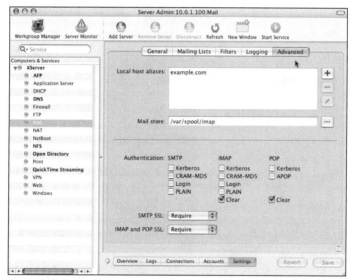

Figure 8.37 The Mail service is selected in the Computers & Services list, and the Settings button and Advanced tab are shown.

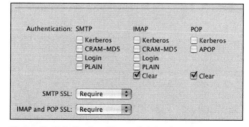

Figure 8.38 Default settings dictate clear-text authentication for IMAP/POP and no authentication for SMTP.

3. For each mail protocol, *choose an appropriate method of authentication* (**Figure 8.39**):

Clear—Only slightly better than nothing at all. All authentications are in clear text.

PLAIN—Similar to Clear; all authentications are in clear text.

Login—Passwords are encrypted and sent to be compared against the passwords on the server.

APOP (Authenticated POP)—All authentications are handled by a medium-strength encryption method.

CRAM-MD5 (Challenge-Response Authentication Mechanism—Method Digest v5)—All authentications are handled by a very strong encryption method. To take advantage of this protocol, user credentials must be saved in the Password Server. (For more information regarding the Password Server, see Chapter 3.)

Kerberos—All authentications are handled by a secret-key cryptography system. Kerberos is extremely secure and allows for single sign-on integration with the Login window. To take advantage of this protocol, user credentials must be saved in the Key Distribution Center (KDC).

4. When you've finished making changes, click the Save button (Save).

As with any service change, you should thoroughly test the configuration before going live.

✔ Tips

■ You may need to leave clear-text authentication temporarily enabled as you migrate your users to a more secure setting. Nonetheless, you should phase out and disable all insecure authentication protocols as soon as possible.

■ Securing mail authentication is a good first step, but your mail messages still remain in the clear. To ensure a completely secure message transfer, you should enable SSL support.

■ You should always stop the Mail service prior to making changes and restart it only after saving your changes.

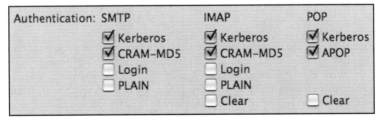

Figure 8.39 Select any authentication protocol you need. The higher it is on the list, the more secure the protocol.

MAIL SECURITY

Configuring Secure Sockets Layer

Once you've enabled a more secure mail authentication protocol, you should consider enabling Secure Sockets Layer (SSL) to encrypt the message data. This task covers how to enable SSL for the Mail service, but under the assumption that you've already obtained the proper SSL key and passphrase certificate files. Refer to Chapter 10, "Security," for detailed instructions on how to obtain SSL key and certificate files and where they are currently stored on Mac OS X Server.

To configure SSL:

1. Use your favorite plain-text editor to combine the contents of the SSL key and certificate files into one file.

   Specifically, copy the contents of the certificate file to the end of the key file, and save the resulting file with a .pem extension.

2. Make two copies of the .pem file.

3. From the server, open the Finder, select Go > Go to Folder, and navigate to the hidden /private directory (**Figures 8.40** and **8.41**).

4. Place one copy of the .pem file in the /etc/postfix/ directory and the other copy in the /var/imap/ directory (**Figure 8.42**).

Figure 8.40 The Go to Folder command in the Finder lets you navigate to hidden directories.

Figure 8.41 Most service configuration files are in the /private directory.

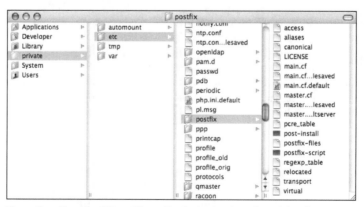

Figure 8.42 Place the SSL certificate files in the /var/postfix and /var/imap directories.

Figure 8.43 The Get Info command reveals the Get Info dialog in the Finder.

Figure 8.44 Use the Get Info dialog to change the ownership of the IMAP certificate file.

5. From the server, select the .pem file inside the /var/imap directory, and then select File > Get Info in the Finder (**Figure 8.43**).

   In the Get Info dialog, change the owner of the .pem file to the Cyrus user account (**Figure 8.44**). Close the Get Info dialog.

6. Launch the Server Admin tool located in /Applications/Server, and authenticate as the administrator (**Figure 8.45**).

7. Select the Mail service for your server in the Computers & Services list.

   Click the Settings button and then the Advanced tab (**Figure 8.46**). Initially, Mac OS X Server isn't configured to use SSL for SMTP, POP, or IMAP (**Figure 8.47**).

continues on next page

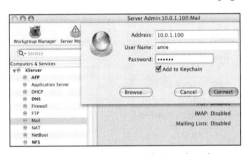

Figure 8.45 Launch the Server Admin tool, and authenticate.

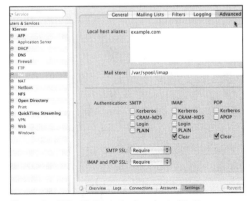

Figure 8.46 The Mail service is selected in the Computers & Services list, and the Settings button and Advanced tab are shown.

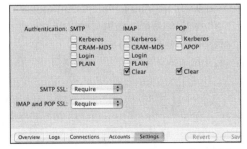

Figure 8.47 Initially, SSL connections are disabled for sending and receiving mail messages.

MAIL SECURITY

8. From the SMTP SSL pop-up menu, select either the Use or Require option (**Figure 8.48**).

Keep in mind that many other SMTP servers don't support SSL transactions. Thus, it's common practice to select the Use option here.

9. From the IMAP and POP SSL pop-up menu, select either the Use or Require option (**Figure 8.49**).

If you must support SSL clients that aren't SSL aware, then you should select the Use option here.

10. When you've finished making changes, click the Save button .

As with any service change, you should thoroughly test the configuration before going live.

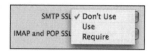

Figure 8.48 Enable IMAP/POP SSL mail data transfer with this pop-up menu.

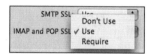

Figure 8.49 Enable SMTP SSL mail data transfer with this pop-up menu.

✔ Tips

■ You should always stop the Mail service prior to making changes and restart it only after saving your changes, including implementing SSL.

■ If you're familiar with the command line, feel free to perform steps 1–4 of the previous task using an SSH session to the server and the equivalent command-line utilities.

■ You may need to select the Use option from the SSL pop-up menus as you migrate all your users to a more secure setting. Nonetheless, you should phase out and disable as many insecure connections as possible.

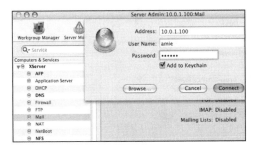

Figure 8.50 Launch the Server Admin tool, and authenticate.

Figure 8.51 The Mail service is selected in the Computers & Services list, and the Settings button and the Mailing Lists tab are shown.

Enabling Mail Lists

Mac OS X Server includes Mailman as its mailing list service. Mail lists are used to provide automated mail distribution to a group of electronic mail addresses. Subscribers to the list don't have to have mail accounts on your server; most mail lists allow users to subscribe or unsubscribe themselves via mail messages sent to your server. All an administrator has to do is create the mail lists and select list administrator accounts that are based on any email address.

You can use the Server Admin tool to enable the Mailman service initially. Once enabled, Mailman sports a variety of advanced mail-list organization and management features beyond those available in Server Admin. Typically, mail lists are managed via a Web browser interface or through an exchange of mail messages with the mail list server.

Because Mailman relies on Web and SMTP relay services, you must configure Apache and Postfix on your server before enabling mailing lists. See Chapter 9 for detailed instructions on how to enable a Web site. You can also refer to "Configuring Mail Services," earlier in this chapter, to learn how to enable the SMTP service.

To enable mail lists:

1. Launch the Server Admin tool located in /Applications/Server, and authenticate as the administrator (**Figure 8.50**).

2. Select the Mail service for your server in the Computers & Services list.

   Click the Settings button and then the Mailing Lists tab (**Figure 8.51**). You can see that initially, the Mailman service isn't configured or enabled.

continues on next page

ENABLING MAIL LISTS

3. Select the "Enable mailing lists" check box.

A dialog appears in which you can configure the first, and required, Mailman list (**Figure 8.52**). Enter an administrator password and as many administrator email accounts as you want, separated by carriage returns.

4. Click the OK button (OK), and verify that the mail list Mailman has been created (**Figure 8.53**).

You've now created the initial list. You can't delete this list, but you can remove all but one administrative account and ignore the list by not posting anything to it.

To create additional mailing lists:

1. Complete the previous task, "To enable Mail lists," and keep the Server Admin tool open to the Mail service, Settings tab, Mailing Lists tab (**Figure 8.54**).

Figure 8.52 In this dialog, configure the initial Mailman list.

Figure 8.53 The Mailman list is required, although you can unsubscribe all the accounts.

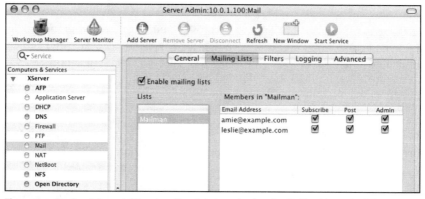

Figure 8.54 Begin adding additional mailing lists by selecting the Mailing Lists tab of the Settings button.

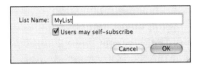

Figure 8.55 Enter additional mailing lists with this dialog.

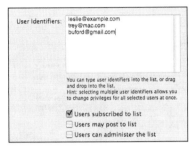

Figure 8.56 Enter mailing-list member accounts and options in this dialog.

Figure 8.57 From this drawer, you can select local user accounts.

2. Click the Add button ⊕ below the Lists list.

A dialog appears in which you can give the new list a name (**Figure 8.55**). Select the "Users may self-subscribe" check box if you want users to be able to subscribe or unsubscribe from this list without administrator intervention.

3. To add accounts to a list, select the list name, and *do one of the following*:

▲ To add any email account, click the Add button ⊕ below the Members list. A dialog appears in which you can enter as many email accounts as you want, separated by carriage returns (**Figure 8.56**). You can specify the accounts' mail list settings by selecting the appropriate check boxes (see step 4).

▲ To add a locally hosted email account, click the Users button (Users...) to reveal the Users & Groups drawer (**Figure 8.57**). Click and drag any user account from the drawer to the Members list (**Figure 8.58**).

continues on next page

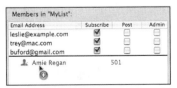

Figure 8.58 Drag and drop local user accounts into the Members list.

ENABLING MAIL LISTS

4. To modify an account's mail-list settings, select or deselect *any of the following options* next to the account name in the Members list (**Figure 8.59**):

Subscribe—Mail messages distributed by the list will be sent to this account.

Post—This account is allowed to send new messages to the list to be distributed to the other members.

Admin—This account can modify the advanced settings for the list.

5. To modify an account or list name, double-click its entry in the list (**Figure 8.60**).

You can also delete an account or list by selecting it in the list and clicking the Delete button $\boxed{-}$ at the bottom of the list.

6. When you've finished making changes, click the Save button $\boxed{\text{Save}}$.

7. Click the Overview button $\boxed{\text{Overview}}$, and verify that the mailing-list service is running (**Figure 8.61**).

As with any service change, you should thoroughly test the configuration before going live.

Figure 8.59 Select or deselect any member list options.

Figure 8.60 Double-click any member account or list name entry to edit it.

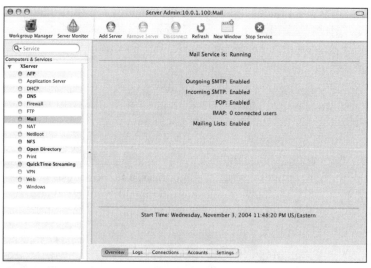

Figure 8.61 The mailing-list service is enabled on this server.

✔ Tips

- Considerably more detailed options for your mail lists are available at http://*serverhostname*/mailman/listinfo/ (**Figure 8.62**).

- You should always stop the Mail service prior to making changes and restart it only after saving your changes.

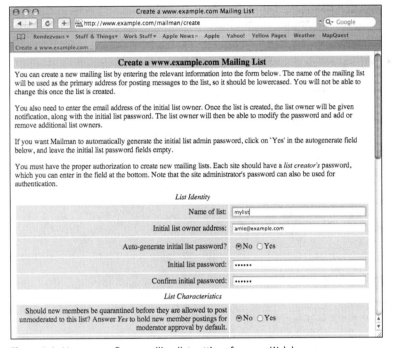

Figure 8.62 You can configure mailing-list settings from any Web browser.

Mailman Advanced Configuration and Files

Mailman has been around for a while, and many Unix administrators are familiar with its associated command-line utilities and configuration files. Although the Server Admin interface is fine, some options are still available only from the command line.

The /usr/share/mailman/bin/ directory holds all the advanced Mailman configuration utilities. Most of the utilities in this directory display their help pages when you enter the command's name with no options.

It may also help you to know that Mailman stores all of its configuration data in the /var/mailman/data/ directory.

Monitoring Mail Services

Mac OS X Server provides a variety of statistics for monitoring the Postfix and Cyrus mail services. Using the Server Admin tool, you can monitor individual mail connections, accounts, and Mail service log files. The information provided by the monitoring tools is invaluable for troubleshooting connection problems and determining if resources are being properly used.

To monitor Mail services:

1. Launch the Server Admin tool located in /Applications/Server, and authenticate as the administrator (**Figure 8.63**).

2. Select the Mail service for your server in the Computers & Services list.

   Click the Connections button Connections to view the current mail client connections (**Figure 8.64**). In this frame, you can monitor client host addresses, connection types, number of sessions, and connection length.

3. Click the Accounts button Accounts to view users' mail account status.

   In this frame, you can monitor user mailbox storage settings and quotas (**Figure 8.65**).

✔ Tips

■ If you've recently enabled your mail server, you'll have to wait until clients begin using the server before any data will appear.

■ Click the Refresh button Refresh to force the Server Admin tool to refresh the monitored data.

Figure 8.63 Launch the Server Admin tool, and authenticate.

Figure 8.64 You can monitor current Mail service connections in Server Admin.

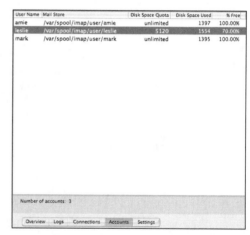

Figure 8.65 You can monitor mail account status in Server Admin.

MONITORING MAIL SERVICES

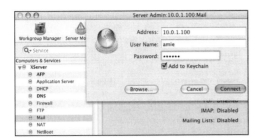

Figure 8.66 Launch the Server Admin tool, and authenticate.

Figure 8.67 The Mail service is selected in the Computers & Services list, and the Settings button and Logging tab are shown.

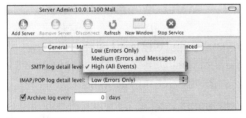

Figure 8.68 Configure log detail levels from the Logging Mail service settings.

Configuring mail logs

Although the Connections and Accounts charts in Server Admin are convenient, the real business of Mail service monitoring is in the log files. The Postfix and Cyrus mail servers can provide a great deal of information in their log files. You can even modify the log file level to meet your specific needs.

Each protocol has its own log, and the Mailman list service keeps several logs. The location of each log file varies based on the service: the SMTP log file is /var/log/mail.log, the POP and IMAP log file is /var/log/mailaccess. log, and mailing-list logs are located in the /var/mailman/logs/ directory. See the sidebar "Mail Log Analysis Tools" for more information about interpreting Postfix access logs.

To configure mail logs:

1. Launch the Server Admin tool located in /Applications/Server, and authenticate as the administrator (**Figure 8.66**).

2. Select the Mail service for your server in the Computers & Services list.

   Click the Settings button Settings and then the Logging tab Logging to view the current mail client connections (**Figure 8.67**). The Logging frame shows settings for both the SMTP and IMAP/POP service logs.

3. To adjust the log's level of detail, *select one of the following values* from either pop-up menu (**Figure 8.68**):

   Low—Logs only major service errors

   Medium—Logs all of the Low log's items plus mail messages

   High—Logs all of the Medium log's items plus any other message or service item

   continues on next page

MONITORING MAIL SERVICES

4. On extremely busy servers, the log files can become large; you may need to archive them to save space. To do so, select the Archive log check box, and enter the number of days between log rotations (**Figure 8.69**).

5. When you've finished making changes, click the Save button Save .

6. To view the logs, click the Logs button Logs .

7. Select the log file you wish to view from the pop-up menu at the bottom of the log window (**Figure 8.70**).

✔ Tips

■ You should always stop the Mail service prior to making changes and restart it only after saving your changes.

■ Click the Refresh button Refresh to force the Server Admin tool to refresh the logs immediately.

Figure 8.69 The Mail logs can be archived at set intervals.

Figure 8.70 A variety of mail logs can be viewed from Server Admin using the Logs button.

Mail Log Analysis Tools

Postfix access logs can be complicated and difficult to understand. You can try one of these Postfix log-analysis tools to help demystify the log files:

◆ Jimsun is a free, open-source tool that summarizes Postfix log entries: http://jimsun.linxnet.com/postfix_contrib.html.

◆ Sawmill is a commercial log-analysis tool that supports more than 500 different log types: http://www.sawmill.net/.

WEB SERVICES

No single shared service is more responsible for the explosive growth of the Internet than Web services. The World Wide Web is essentially the collective resource of all the computers on the Internet that share information via the common Hypertext Transfer Protocol (HTTP). Of these Web servers, no single implementation is more popular than the open-source Apache Web server.

For Apple, adopting Apache was a no-brainer. Apache is the most powerful, efficient, extensible, and secure HTTP Web server available. This is due to the open-source nature of the Apache server's development, which allows for constant refinement in an environment of shared programming knowledge. You can also appreciate the fact that Apache is completely free; in addition, legions of technically savvy folks constantly improve the product and can, in turn, help you with yours. For more information, visit http://httpd.apache.org/.

What can Apple do to improve on an already fabulous, not to mention free, product such as Apache? It should come as no surprise that Apple has done for Apache what Apple is most famous for: making complicated technologies easier to use. The developers at Apple have integrated Apache configuration into the excellent Mac OS X Server graphical administration tools. Further, Apple has integrated Apache with other Mac OS X technologies such as Open Directory, Quick Time Streaming Server, and the Mail Server, to name a few. On top of all these added features, Apple has further optimized the Apache service for improved performance.

Setting Up a Web Site

Configuring the Mac OS X Web server, although relatively simple, is only half of what you need to do in order to make your Web sites accessible to the Internet. Obviously, having static real-world IP addresses is necessary if your Web sites are to be accessed by anyone on the Internet. Further, because it's difficult for most people to remember IP addresses, Web sites usually have a DNS record name that makes them easier to find. You can certainly enable a Web site without a DNS record, but this isn't standard practice. As you may already know, Mac OS X Server can act as a DNS server (see Chapter 6, "Network Configuration Options"). Your Web server doesn't have to host these DNS records, because you may have a service provider already doing this for you.

Aside from making your Web sites easier to find, unique DNS names lets you host multiple Web sites on one Mac OS X Server using only one IP address. In order to have separate Web sites on one server, you must choose at least one of three unique host identifiers: Each Web site can be tied to a unique IP address, port number, or DNS name. Using multiple static IP addresses can be wasteful, because real-world addresses are limited and usually cost money. Using unique port numbers is free, but using any port number outside of the default for HTTP (port 80) requires a user to type in the custom port number after the address. Multiple DNS names are cost efficient—or free, if you host your own DNS server—and easiest for your users to access.

To set up a Web site:

1. Launch the Server Admin tool located in /Applications/Server, and authenticate as the administrator (**Figure 9.1**).

2. Select the Web service for your server in the Computers & Services list (**Figure 9.2**).

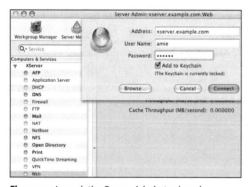

Figure 9.1 Launch the Server Admin tool, and authenticate.

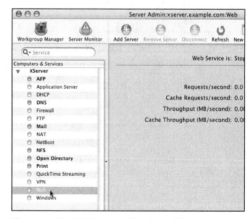

Figure 9.2 The Web service is selected in the Computers & Services list.

Figure 9.3 The Sites list contains one default Web site configuration.

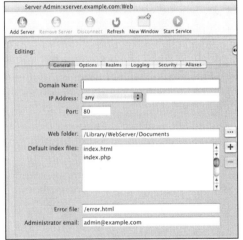

Figure 9.4 Each Web site has its own configuration frame within the Web server settings.

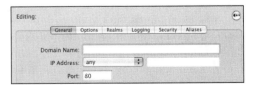

Figure 9.5 The three unique identifiers for a Web site are domain name, IP address, and port number.

3. Click the Settings button [Settings] and then the Sites tab [Sites].

Initially, the default Web site in the Sites list is configured with no Domain Name value and an asterisk for the Address (**Figure 9.3**).

4. To reconfigure the default Web site with your settings, double-click its entry in the Sites list to open an editing pane (**Figure 9.4**).

5. If it isn't already selected, click the General tab [General] to see this Web site's general settings.

6. Configure your Web site's unique host identifiers (**Figure 9.5**):

Domain Name—If you've registered a domain name for this Web site, enter it here. Otherwise, leave this field blank; the server will respond to requests based on the other two identifiers. This also may require editing your DNS entries. (See Chapter 6 for more information.)

IP Address—The default setting will respond to any request to any IP address the server may have (remember, a Mac OS X Server can be configured with multiple addresses). You can also select a specific address from the pop-up menu. Doing so directs all requests to the selected IP address. This also may require editing your DNS entries. (See Chapter 6 for more information.)

Port—The default setting is port 80, which is the default for all HTTP traffic. Enter a different port number if desired.

Remember, only one of these three settings must be unique from other Web sites.

continues on next page

SETTING UP A WEB SITE

7. *Choose to do one of the following:*

▲ Use the default location for your Web site's files: /Library/WebServer/Documents/ (**Figure 9.6**).

▲ Change the location of the files by typing a new path in the "Web folder" field or clicking the ellipsis button ⌐···⌐ to use the browse dialog (**Figure 9.7**). (To use the browse dialog, the folder must already exist on the server.)

8. *Choose to do one of the following:*

▲ Use the default filenames for your Web site's files: index.html and index.php.

▲ Replace the installed files with your Web site's files. To add new index filenames, click the Add button ⌐+⌐. To delete an index filename, click the Delete button ⌐–⌐.

9. In the "Error file" field, specify a custom HTML file that will appear when a user tries to access an invalid link on your Web site.

In the "Administrator email" field, specify the email address where users may contact you about Web site problems (**Figure 9.8**).

10. When you've finished making changes, click the Save button ⌐ Save ⌐.

11. Click the Back button ⌐⊙⌐ to return to the Sites list view (**Figure 9.9**).

Verify that your Web site's general settings have been updated in this list.

12. Click the Overview button ⌐ Overview ⌐, and verify that the Web service is running (**Figure 9.10**).

If it isn't, click the Start Service button ⌐ Start Service ⌐ to activate the Web server.

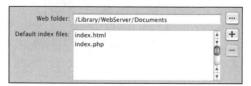

Figure 9.6 Configure the Web site's folder and index files using these fields.

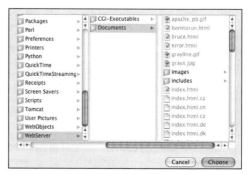

Figure 9.7 Select the appropriate file on your server using the browse dialog.

Figure 9.8 Configure the Web site's error file and administrator email.

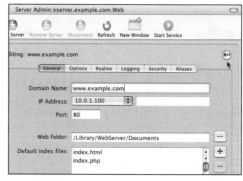

Figure 9.9 Selecting this Back button returns you to the Sites list view.

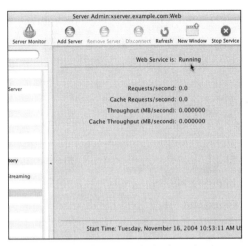

Figure 9.10 The Web service is indeed running.

Apache Configuration Files

Apache has been around for quite some time, and many Unix administrators are familiar with its configuration files. Originally, Apache had no graphical interface; all setup was done by editing the plain-text configuration files. Although the Server Admin interface is handy, some options are available only in the configuration files:

- The main Apache service configuration file is /etc/httpd/httpd.config.

- Each Web site has its own configuration file, saved in /etc/httpd/sites/.

You need to remember a couple of rules when you're editing the Apache configuration files. First, always back up any configuration file before you change it! Second, to activate any changes, you must restart the Apache Web service.

✔ Tips

- It's good practice to restart the Web service manually each time you make a configuration change. Also make sure to thoroughly test your Web site by opening any Web browser and entering the host name you configured.

- The Apache Web Server used by Mac OS X Server is very robust and can handle literally hundreds of requests every second, even on an older computer. To get the most out of your Web server, you can configure multiple Web sites by repeating steps 4–10 in the previous task.

- To duplicate an existing Web site to use as a template for a new Web site, select a site in the Sites list and then click the Duplicate button.

- To configure another new Web site, click the Add button +.

- To delete a Web site, select its entry in the Sites list and click the Delete button −.

- It's bad practice to leave the default placeholder Web site enabled. That Web page is a good indication to crackers that a server isn't fully configured and is possibly insecure.

- Configure multiple IP addresses using the Network Port Configurations view of the Network System Preference pane.

- The Server Admin tool should automatically restart the Web service when you click the Save button Save.

Configuring Web site options

In addition to the required settings for each of your Web sites found under the General tab, each Web site has a variety of options that let you customize its capabilities. As you turn on more options for your Web sites, you may need to enable new Apache modules. These modules, typically installed in /usr/libexec/httpd/, are coded extensions that add functionality to the Web server. Literally hundreds of freely downloadable Apache modules are available at http://modules.apache.org.

It's important to remember that the options settings are configured separately for each Web site. However, the module settings affect every Web site on your server. It's good practice to restart the Web service manually each time you make a configuration change. Also make sure you thoroughly test your Web site options by opening any Web browser and entering the host name you configured. Every option and module that you implement can potentially use more RAM, so you may want to keep an eye on RAM usage as you test the various options and modules.

To change Web site options:

1. Launch the Server Admin tool located in /Applications/Server, and authenticate as the administrator (**Figure 9.11**).

2. Select the Web service for your server in the Computers & Services list (**Figure 9.12**).

3. Click the Settings button `Settings` and then the Sites tab `Sites` (**Figure 9.13**).

4. In the Sites list, double-click the Web site you wish to configure.

   An Editing pane opens (**Figure 9.14**).

Figure 9.11 Launch the Server Admin tool, and authenticate.

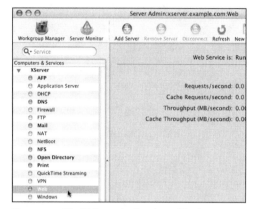

Figure 9.12 The Web service is selected in the Computers & Services list.

Figure 9.13 Select the Web site you wish to edit from the Sites list.

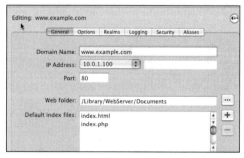

Figure 9.14 Each Web site has its own configuration frame within the Web server settings.

5. If it isn't already selected, click the Options tab to see this Web site's optional settings.

Enable any of the following optional settings (**Figure 9.15**):

Performance Cache—Enabled by default. Improves the server's response to static Web page requests by storing the Web site files in RAM. You may have to disable this option if your Web site uses dynamically generated Web pages.

Folder Listing—Lets you browse the contents of your Web folder with a standard Web browser (**Figure 9.16**). Typically, it's a good idea to leave this option off, because it may aid malicious users in trying to crack your Web site.

WebDAV—Enables WebDAV support for you Web site. See "Configuring WebDAV access," later in this chapter.

CGI Execution—Enables the Common Gateway Interface (CGI) system for your Web site. The CGI system is a common method used to facilitate dynamically generated Web pages based on user input. See the sidebar "Web Server Scripts" for more information about CGI scripts.

WebMail—Enables the SquirrelMail Web mail server for your Web site (**Figure 9.17**). Assuming this Web server is also running the Mail service (see Chapter 8, "Mail Services"), your users will be able to access their mail accounts at http://sitename/WebMail/. (For more information about SquirrelMail, visit http://www.squirrelmail.org/.)

continues on next page

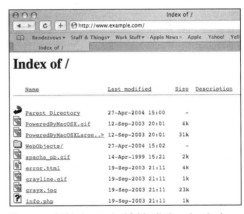

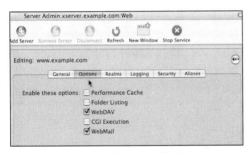

Figure 9.15 Enable any of the optional Web site features.

Figure 9.16 This is a typical folder listing view in the Safari Web browser.

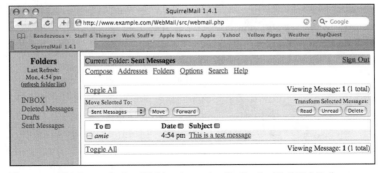

Figure 9.17 This is a typical mail folder view using the SquirrelMail WebMail server.

6. When you've finished making changes, click the Save button [Save].

7. Click the Back button [⟲] to return to the Sites list view (**Figure 9.18**).

8. To enable additional Web server modules, click the Modules tab [Modules].

In the Modules frame, you can enable additional Apache code modules for the entire Web server (**Figure 9.19**).

9. Select a check box to enable a specific Module from the list.

You can also click one of the editing buttons [+] [🖥] [−] [✎] below the Module list to do further configuration.

10. When you've finished making changes, click the Save button [Save].

If you aren't prompted by Server Admin, you may need to restart your server after making these changes.

Figure 9.18 Selecting this Back button returns you to the Sites list view.

Figure 9.19 The Modules frame lets you configure the Apache plug-in modules.

Web Server Scripts

Web scripts differ from regular Web site files in that they're coded instructions that let the server dynamically generate Web page information. Apache, through its extensive modules, supports common open-source scripting languages. The most commonly used scripts are CGI scripts written in Perl or Python and PHP scripts:

CGI option 1—The default location for CGI scripts available to all Web sites is /Library/WebServer/CGI-Executables/. In your Web browser, enter http://sitename/cgi-bin/script.cgi.

CGI option 2—If a script will be used by only one specific Web site, you can put it in that Web site's folder. In your Web browser, enter http://sitename/script.cgi.

PHP—Enable PHP script execution by selecting the php4_module in the Web server Modules list. PHP scripts can be located in any Web site's folder. In your Web browser, enter http://sitename/script.php.

Figure 9.20 Launch the Server Admin tool, and authenticate.

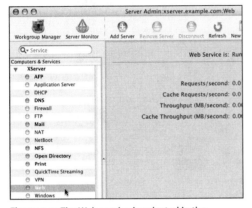

Figure 9.21 The Web service is selected in the Computers & Services list.

Configuring Secure Sockets Layer

Secure Sockets Layer (SSL) is a technology that facilitates a secure connection between your Web server and its users. Users trust your server based on its certificate of authenticity. Before you set up SSL for your Web site, you must first properly obtain and configure this certificate. (Refer to Chapter 10, "Security," for more about certificates.) Assuming you've already installed the certificate, the following task will guide you through the process of enabling SSL for a Web site.

To enable SSL:

1. Launch the Server Admin tool located in /Applications/Server, and authenticate as the administrator (**Figure 9.20**).

2. Select the Web service for your server in the Computers & Services list (**Figure 9.21**).

3. Click the Settings button ⬚ Settings ⬚ and then the Sites tab ⬚ Sites ⬚ (**Figure 9.22**).

4. In the Sites list, double-click the Web site you wish to configure.

   An editing window opens (**Figure 9.23**).

continues on next page

Figure 9.22 Select the Web site you wish to edit from the Sites list.

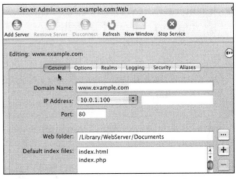

Figure 9.23 Each Web site has its own configuration frame within the Web server settings.

SETTING UP A WEB SITE

293

5. If it isn't already selected, click the Security tab Security to see this Web site's SSL settings (**Figure 9.24**).

6. Select the Enable Secure Sockets Layer check box (**Figure 9.25**).

7. Enter an appropriate password (read: long and complicated) in the Pass Phrase field (See Chapter 10, "Security," for more information about the passphrase).

8. Configure the Certificate File, Key File, and CA File *using one of the following methods:*

▲ Enter the absolute path on the server of each SSL file in its associated field.

▲ Click the ellipsis button ⋯ , and use the browse dialog to select the SSL files (**Figure 9.26**). To use the browse dialog, the files must already exist on the server.

▲ Click the Edit button ✎ , and use the edit dialog to paste a certificate into the SSL file directly (**Figure 9.27**). To use the edit dialog, the files must already exist on the server.

9. When you've finished making changes, click the Save button Save .

If you aren't prompted by Server Admin, you may need to restart your server after making these changes.

✔ Tips

■ It's important to remember that the SSL settings are configured separately for each Web site you have.

■ It's good practice to restart the Web service manually each time you make a configuration change.

■ Make sure you thoroughly test your secure Web site by accessing it from any Web browser.

■ To specify a secure connection to your Web server, append *s* after the *http* protocol specification in the host name: for example, `https://sitename/index.html`.

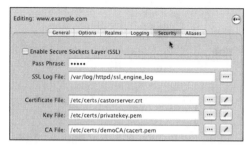

Figure 9.24 Enable and configure your Web site's Secure Socket Layer settings in the Security frame.

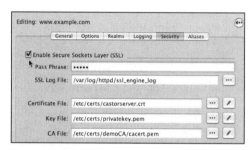

Figure 9.25 Select the Enable Secure Sockets Layer check box.

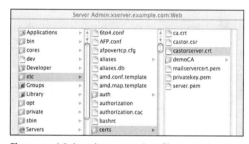

Figure 9.26 Select the appropriate file on your server using the browse dialog.

Figure 9.27 The SSL edit dialog lets you directly edit the security file.

Figure 9.28 Launch the Server Admin tool, and authenticate.

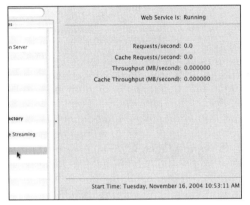

Figure 9.29 The Web service is selected in the Computers & Services list.

Adding Web site aliases

Web site aliases work very similarly to file aliases: They're items that act as pointers to another destination. Web site aliases are often used if you want a Web site to access documents that are on the local server but are outside of the Web site's folder. Another type of Web site alias, called a *redirect*, is used to let your Web site access documents on another Web server.

To configure a Web site alias:

1. Launch the Server Admin tool located in /Applications/Server, and authenticate as the administrator (**Figure 9.28**).

2. Select the Web service for your server in the Computers & Services list (**Figure 9.29**).

3. Click the Settings button Settings and then the Sites tab Sites (**Figure 9.30**).

4. In the Sites list, double-click the Web site you wish to configure.

   An editing window opens (**Figure 9.31**).

continues on next page

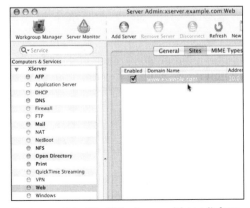

Figure 9.30 Select the Web site you wish to edit from the Sites list.

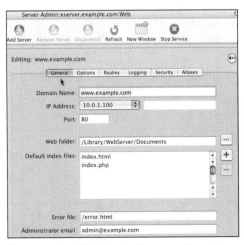

Figure 9.31 Each Web site has its own configuration frame in the Web server settings.

SETTING UP A WEB SITE

5. If it isn't already selected, click the Aliases tab ⟨ Aliases ⟩ to see this Web site's alias settings (**Figure 9.32**).

6. Click the Add button ⟨ + ⟩.

An editing dialog drops down from the title bar (**Figure 9.33**).

7. Click the Type pop-up menu, and *choose one of the following alias types* (**Figure 9.34**):

Alias—The Pattern field defines the name of the item to be accessed in the browser address. The Path field defines the location to which the alias is pointing (**Figure 9.35**). For example, when you enter `http://sitename/images/` in a Web browser, instead of accessing the folder called images in the Web site's folder, you access the /afpshare/images folder on the Web server's local volume.

Redirect—The Pattern field defines the name of the item to be accessed in the browser address. The Path field defines the Web server to which the redirect is pointing (**Figure 9.36**). For example, when you enter `http://sitename/calendar/` in a Web browser, instead of accessing the folder called calendar in your Web site's folder, you access http://calserver.example.com/.

AliasMatch/RedirectMatch—These types work similarly to standard aliases and redirects, but they allow the use of standard regular-expression matching.

Figure 9.32 The Alias frame lets you configure a list of Web site aliases and redirects.

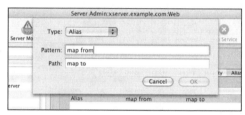

Figure 9.33 The alias edit dialog lets you add and manipulate Web site aliases and redirects.

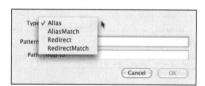

Figure 9.34 The Type menu in the alias edit dialog lets you select the alias type.

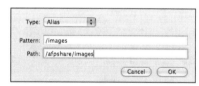

Figure 9.35 This edit dialog example shows a properly configured alias.

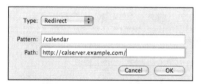

Figure 9.36 This edit dialog example shows a properly configured redirect.

SETTING UP A WEB SITE

8. Check your configuration by verifying the entries in the Aliases frame list (**Figure 9.37**).

9. When you've finished making changes, click the Save button Save .

   If you aren't prompted by Server Admin, you may need to restart your server after making these changes.

✔ Tips

- You can use the editing buttons ➕ 🗂 ➖ ✏ to further customize alias configurations.

- It's important to remember that alias and redirect settings are configured separately for each Web site you have.

- It's good practice to restart the Web service manually each time you make a configuration change.

- Be sure you thoroughly test your aliases and/or redirects by accessing them from any Web browser.

- Make sure you verify that the aliased folder has at least read privileges to the www user or group.

Figure 9.37 Verify your Web site's alias settings.

SETTING UP A WEB SITE

Setting Up Realms and WebDAV

The Apache Web server uses *realms* to control access to items in a Web site's folder. By default, everything in your Web site's folder can be read by everybody. However, once you specify a folder in your Web site's folder as a realm, you can enable restricted access to those Web site items based on user authentication. Configuring realms is also the first step required to enable secure Web Distributed Authoring and Versioning (WebDAV) support for your Web site.

To add a realm to a site:

1. Launch the Server Admin tool located in /Applications/Server, and authenticate as the administrator (**Figure 9.38**).

2. Select the Web service for your server in the Computers & Services list (**Figure 9.39**).

3. Click the Settings button Settings and then the Sites tab Sites (**Figure 9.40**).

4. In the Sites list, double-click the Web site you wish to configure.

   An editing window opens (**Figure 9.41**).

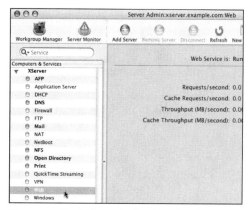

Figure 9.39 The Web service is selected in the Computers & Services list.

Figure 9.38 Launch the Server Admin tool, and authenticate.

Figure 9.40 Select the Web site you wish to edit from the Web Sites list.

Figure 9.41 Each Web site has its own configuration frame within the Web server settings.

5. If it isn't already selected, click the Realms tab [Realms] to see this Web site's realms settings (**Figure 9.42**).

6. Click the Add button [+].

An editing dialog drops down from the title bar.

7. Enter a name for the realm, and select an Authorization mode from the pop-up menu (**Figure 9.43**).

Digest authorization, although slightly more secure than Basic, requires that you

enable the digest Apache module. (See "Configuring Web site options," earlier in this chapter, for more information about Apache modules.)

8. *Do one of the following:*

▲ Specify a folder in your Web site's folder by entering the absolute path to the folder.

▲ Click the ellipsis button [...] to expand the dialog so you can choose the folder (**Figure 9.44**).

This is the folder for which access can be restricted in some fashion.

continues on next page

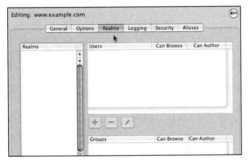

Figure 9.42 The Realms frame lets you configure Web site realms and access.

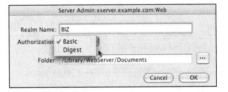

Figure 9.43 The edit dialog lets you configure a Web site realm.

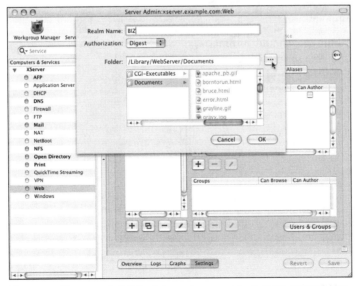

Figure 9.44 The expanded dialog lets you browse and select the realm's folder.

SETTING UP REALMS AND WEBDAV

9. When you've finished making changes, click the OK button (OK) and then the Save button (Save).

10. Verify that the realm was created, select it from the Realms list, and select the Can Browse check box for Everyone (**Figure 9.45**).

If you don't do this, then no one will be able to see the contents of the realm.

11. Click the Save button (Save).

If you aren't prompted by Server Admin, you may need to restart your server after making these changes.

✔ Tips

■ You can configure as many realms as you want for each Web site, including realms inside of other realms. However, you can only define a realm using the Web site's folder or anything in of that folder.

■ It's important to remember that realm settings are configured separately for each Web site you have.

■ You can always use the edit buttons (+ 🖺 − ✎) below the realms list for further configuration.

■ The Server Admin tool should automatically restart the Web service when you click the Save button (Save).

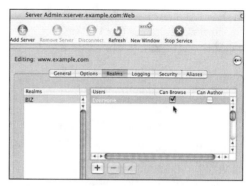

Figure 9.45 Select the Can Browse check box for Everyone.

Figure 9.46 Launch the Server Admin tool, and authenticate.

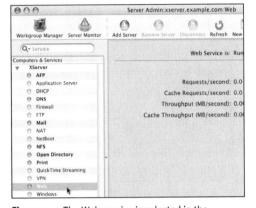

Figure 9.47 The Web service is selected in the Computers & Services list.

Adding users and groups to realms

One of the many enhancements Apple made to the Apache Web server includes directory services integration. This means the Apache Web server grants authenticated Web site access via any user and/or group accounts known to directory services. For this reason, you must properly configure Directory Access on the server hosting your Web sites. (See Chapter 3, "Open Directory," for more information about directory services.)

To add users and groups to a realm:

1. Launch the Server Admin tool located in /Applications/Server, and authenticate as the administrator (**Figure 9.46**).

2. Select the Web service for your server in the Computers & Services list (**Figure 9.47**).

3. Click the Settings button Settings and then the Sites tab Sites (**Figure 9.48**).

4. In the Sites list, double-click the Web site you wish to configure.

   An editing window opens (**Figure 9.49**).

continues on next page

Figure 9.48 Select the Web site you wish to edit from the Web Sites list.

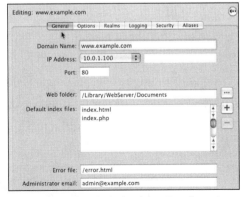

Figure 9.49 Each Web site has its own configuration frame within the Web server settings.

5. If it isn't already selected, click the Realms tab [Realms] to see this Web site's realms settings (**Figure 9.50**).

6. *Do one of the following:*

▲ If you haven't already configured the realms for your Web site, do so now by following the steps outlined in the task "To add a realm to a site."

▲ Select the realm you wish to configure from the Realms list (**Figure 9.51**).

7. Click the Users & Groups button [Users & Groups].

The Users & Groups drawer appears (**Figure 9.52**).

8. *Do one/or both of the following* to add a user and/or group account to the realm:

Users—Click the Users tab [Users], and then click and drag user accounts to the realm's Users list (**Figure 9.53**).

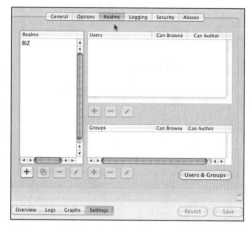

Figure 9.50 The Realms frame lets you configure Web site realms and access.

Figure 9.51 Select the realm you wish to configure from the Realms list.

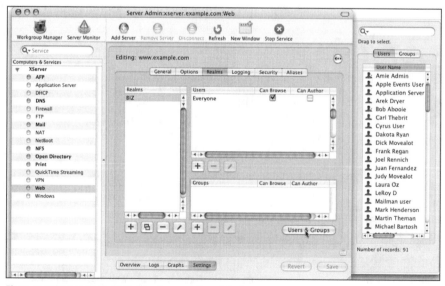

Figure 9.52 You can select users and groups from this drawer.

Figure 9.53 Drag a user into the realm's Users list.

Figure 9.54 Drag a group into the realm's Groups list.

Groups—Click the Groups tab **Groups**, and then click and drag group accounts to the realm's Groups list (**Figure 9.54**).

9. Deselect the Can Browse option for Everyone, and select the Can Browse option only for user and group accounts that need access to the realm.

10. When you've finished making changes, click the Save button **Save**.

If you aren't prompted by Server Admin, you may need to restart your server after making these changes.

✔ Tips

■ It's important to remember that realm settings are configured separately for each realm of each Web site you have.

■ Make sure you thoroughly test authenticated access to your realms by accessing them from any Web browser.

■ Mac OS X Server doesn't currently support very secure authentication for Web site access. If security is a concern, you should avoid using authenticated Web site access.

Connecting to an Authenticated Web Site

Once you've configured authenticated realm access, navigate to one of the files in the realm as you would any other file in your Web site. An authentication dialog appears, in which you can enter your user name and password (**Figure 9.55**). Notice that you can save your password to a keychain. Once authenticated, the Web site files should appear as normal.

Figure 9.55 Enter your user name and password in the Web site authentication dialog.

Configuring WebDAV access

Many people think of Web servers as only providing read access to shared items. However, Apache supports a technology known as Web Distributed Authoring and Versioning (WebDAV) that essentially allows users to write changes back to Web site items. The ability to read and write to a shared destination on a file server obviously makes WebDAV an alternative to standard file-sharing services such as AFP and SMB. Furthermore, WebDAV is an easy protocol to support, because free clients are available for every major operating system and all the network traffic runs across the standard port for HTTP (port 80, which is open on most firewalls).

WebDAV access is granted based on a Web site's realm configuration. In other words, you must already have realms configured for your Web site in order to use WebDAV. (See the previous two tasks for detailed instruction on configuring Web site realms.) In addition, when you're using WebDAV, you must set special file and folder permissions if you're going to allow users author, or write, access to Web site items. You must change the permissions so the group or user WWW has read and write access to the Web site items. This is necessary because, as a security measure, the Apache service only has access to items as the system user WWW and the system group WWW. (See Chapter 5, "File Sharing," for more information about permissions.)

To configure WebDAV access:

1. Launch the Server Admin tool located in /Applications/Server, and authenticate as the administrator (**Figure 9.56**).

2. Select the Web service for your server in the Computers & Services list (**Figure 9.57**).

Figure 9.56 Launch the Server Admin tool, and authenticate.

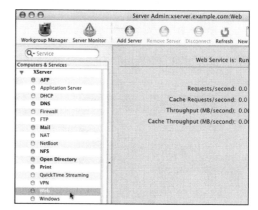

Figure 9.57 The Web service is selected in the Computers & Services list.

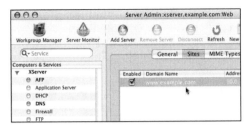

Figure 9.58 Select the Web site you wish to edit from the Web Sites list.

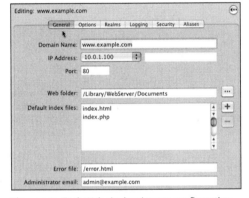

Figure 9.59 Each Web site has its own configuration frame within the Web server settings.

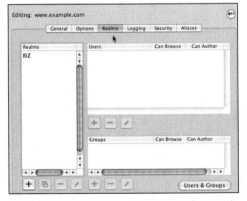

Figure 9.60 The Realms frame lets you configure Web site realms and access.

3. Click the Settings button Settings and then the Sites tab Sites (**Figure 9.58**).

4. In the Sites list, double-click the Web site you wish to configure.

An editing window opens (**Figure 9.59**).

5. If it isn't already selected, click the Realms tab Realms to see this Web site's realms settings (**Figure 9.60**).

6. *Do one of the following:*

- ▲ If you haven't already configured realm access for your Web site, do so now by following the steps outlined in the previous two tasks.

- ▲ Select the realm you wish to configure from the Realms list.

7. *Do one of the following:*

- ▲ If you want a user or group to have read access, select the Can Browse check box next to the desired account.

- ▲ If you want a user or group to have write access, select the Can Author check box next to the desired account (**Figure 9.61**).

continues on next page

Figure 9.61 Select the Can Author check box for the desired account.

SETTING UP REALMS AND WEBDAV

8. Click the Options tab [Options] to see this Web site's optional settings.

Select the WebDAV check box (**Figure 9.62**).

9. When you've finished making changes, click the Save button [Save].

If you aren't prompted by Server Admin, you may need to restart your server after making these changes.

✔ Tips

■ It's important to remember that realm settings are configured separately for each realm of each Web site you have.

■ Make sure you thoroughly test authenticated access to your realms by accessing them from any Web browser.

■ Mac OS X Server doesn't currently support very secure authentication for WebDAV access. If security is a concern, you should avoid using WebDAV access.

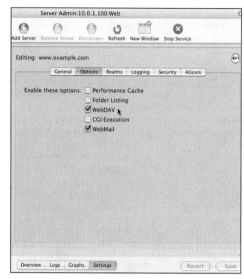

Figure 9.62 Select the WebDAV check box in the Web site's options frame.

Connecting via WebDAV

Connecting to a WebDAV server from a Mac OS X client involves the following steps:

1. In the Finder, select Go > Connect to Server, and enter a fully qualified HTTP address (**Figure 9.63**).

2. Authenticate to the server (**Figure 9.64**). Notice that you can also save your password to a keychain.

Default settings dictate that the share point's icon will mount on the Finder's desktop.

Figure 9.63 You can connect to WebDAV shares using the Connect To Server dialog in the Finder.

Figure 9.64 This is the WebDAV authentication dialog in the Finder.

Figure 9.65 Launch the Server Admin tool, and authenticate.

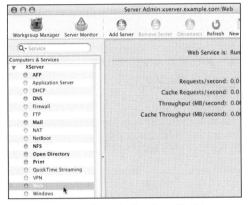

Figure 9.66 The Web service is selected in the Computers & Services list.

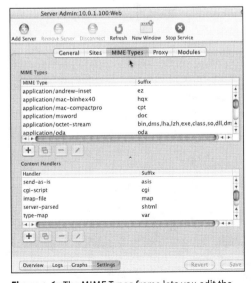

Figure 9.67 The MIME Types frame lets you edit the Web server's lists of MIME types and content handlers.

Editing MIME Types

Multipurpose Internet Mail Extension (MIME) is a standard protocol for defining how a user's Web browser handles files shared from a Web server. Typically, every file on your Web server has a file-type suffix appended to the end of the filename. MIME types define a specific action for a user's Web browser to take when it encounters a certain file-type suffix. Some examples of file-type suffixes configured with MIME types include .htm or .html for hypertext, .jpg or .jpeg for a picture file, and .qt or .mov for a QuickTime video file.

Mac OS X Server's Web server comes with a preconfigured list of standard MIME types. However, you may need to edit or add to your server's MIME types list.

To edit MIME types:

1. Launch the Server Admin tool located in /Applications/Server, and authenticate as the administrator (**Figure 9.65**).

2. Select the Web service for your server in the Computers & Services list (**Figure 9.66**).

3. Click the Settings button `Settings` and then the MIME Types tab `MIME Types`. The MIME Types pane displays your Web server's lists of MIME types and content handlers (**Figure 9.67**).

continues on next page

4. *Do one of the following:*

▲ Double-click the MIME type or suffix to edit it directly (**Figure 9.68**).

▲ Select a MIME type from the list, and then click the Edit button [✐]; an edit dialog drops from the title bar (**Figure 9.69**). To edit the Suffixes list in this dialog, click the Add or Delete icon [⬚]. When you've finished making changes, click the OK button [OK].

5. Verify your changes by checking the MIME Types list again.

6. When you've finished making changes, click the Save button [Save].

If you aren't prompted by Server Admin, you may need to restart your server after making these changes.

✔ Tips

■ It's important to remember that MIME type settings will affect every Web site on your server.

■ The Server Admin tool should automatically restart the Web service when you click the Save button [Save].

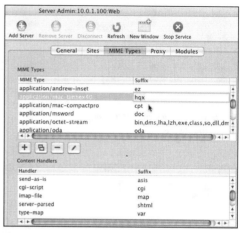

Figure 9.68 Double-click to edit a MIME type.

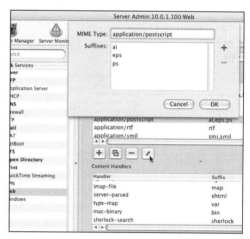

Figure 9.69 You can also edit a MIME type in this edit dialog.

Figure 9.70 Launch the Server Admin tool, and authenticate.

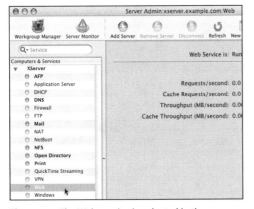

Figure 9.71 The Web service is selected in the Computers & Services list.

Figure 9.72 The MIME Types frame lets you edit the Web server's lists of MIME types and content handlers.

Editing content handlers

Content handlers are Java programs that define the Web server's response to file requests based on the file-type suffix. Typically, every file on your Web server has a file-type suffix appended to the end of the filename. Some examples of file-type suffixes configured with content handlers include as is, which sends the item as it's requested; bin, which transfers the file as a Mac Binary file; and cgi, which executes the file as a CGI script.

Mac OS X Server's Web server comes with a preconfigured list of standard content handlers. However, you may find it necessary to edit or add to your server's content handlers list.

To edit content handlers:

1. Launch the Server Admin tool located in /Applications/Server, and authenticate as the administrator (**Figure 9.70**).

2. Select the Web service for your server in the Computers & Services list (**Figure 9.71**).

3. Click the Settings button Settings and then the MIME Types tab MIME Types . The MIME Types pane displays your Web server's lists of MIME types and content handlers (**Figure 9.72**).

continues on next page

EDITING MIME TYPES

4. To edit a content handler, *do one of the following:*

- ▲ Double-click the content handler or suffix to edit it directly (**Figure 9.73**).

- ▲ Select a content handler from the list, and then click the Edit button ✎; an edit dialog drops from the title bar (**Figure 9.74**). To edit the Suffixes list in this dialog, click the Add or Delete icon ⊞. When you've finished making changes, click the OK button OK.

5. Verify your changes by checking the Content Handlers list again.

6. When you've finished making changes, click the Save button Save.

If you aren't prompted by Server Admin, you may need to restart your server after making these changes.

✔ Tips

- ■ It's important to remember that content handler settings will affect every Web site on your server.

- ■ The Server Admin tool should automatically restart the Web service when you click the Save button Save.

Figure 9.73 Double-click to edit a content handler.

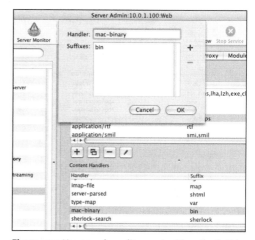

Figure 9.74 You can also edit a content handler in this edit dialog.

Figure 9.75 Launch the Server Admin tool, and authenticate.

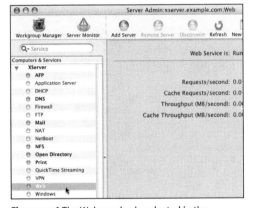

Figure 9.76 The Web service is selected in the Computers & Services list.

Enabling Web Proxies

Primarily, Web proxies are enabled to improve the performance of requests made to external Web sites by Web users on your local network. Many of your users visit the same Web sites throughout the day. A Web proxy caches this external Web site content; Web browsers on your local network then read the cached content rather than use your potentially slower Internet connection. Recently, though, Web proxies have fallen out of favor as high-speed Internet connections have become commonplace.

To enable a Web proxy:

1. Launch the Server Admin tool located in /Applications/Server, and authenticate as the administrator (**Figure 9.75**).

2. Select the Web service for your server in the Computers & Services list (**Figure 9.76**).

3. Click the Settings button [Settings] and then the Proxy tab [Proxy].
   The Proxy pane displays your Web server's proxy settings (**Figure 9.77**).

4. Click the Enable Proxy check box.

5. In the "Maximum cache size" field, set the maximum amount of space your Web server will use on the local hard drive for proxy cache files (**Figure 9.78**).

continues on next page

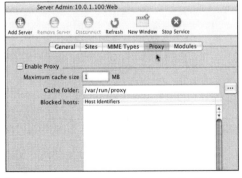

Figure 9.77 The Proxy pane lets you edit the Web server's proxy settings.

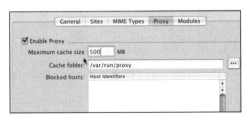

Figure 9.78 Edit the "Maximum cache size" field.

ENABLING WEB PROXIES

6. The default Web proxy cache folder is /var/run/proxy. To specify a different cache folder on the server's local drive, *do either of the following:*

▲ Enter the absolute path in the "Cache folder" field.

▲ Click the ellipsis button ••• to use the browse dialog (**Figure 9.79**).

7. When you've finished making changes, click the Save button Save.

✔ Tips

■ When the cache reaches the maximum size, the oldest files are deleted from the cache folder.

■ It's important to remember that proxy settings won't affect any of your Web site settings.

■ In order for your clients to use the Web proxy, you must configure them to use it. Client computers aren't configured to use a Web proxy by default.

■ If you have a slower Web server and a fast Internet connection, you may be better off without the Web proxy.

■ The Server Admin tool should automatically restart the Web service when you click the Save button Save.

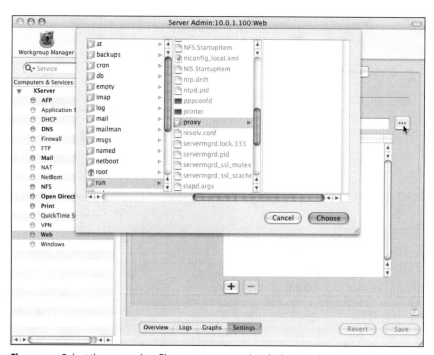

Figure 9.79 Select the appropriate file on your server using the browse dialog.

Configuring a Web Proxy on Clients

Configuring Web proxy usage on Mac OS X Client involves these steps:

1. Open the Network System Preferences pane by opening System Preferences under the Apple menu and selecting the appropriate network location and port configuration (**Figure 9.80**).

2. Click the Proxies tab Proxies (**Figure 9.81**).

3. Select the Web Proxy check box in the proxy list, and then enter the address to your proxy in the Web Proxy Server field (**Figure 9.82**).

4. When you've finished making changes, click the Apply Now button Apply Now, and close the System Preferences application.

Figure 9.80 Configure a computer's network settings using the Network Preferences pane.

Figure 9.81 Click the Proxies tab.

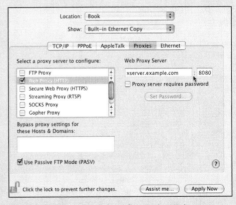

Figure 9.82 Enable and configure the Web proxy settings.

Configuring blocked Web sites

When you're using a Web proxy, all the Web traffic from your client computers must pass through the proxy server. You can take further advantage of this situation by creating a list of blocked Web site hosts. Doing so prevents your users from going to any Web site that you've defined in the list.

To block Web sites:

1. Launch the Server Admin tool located in /Applications/Server, and authenticate as the administrator (**Figure 9.83**).

2. Select the Web service for your server in the Computers & Services list (**Figure 9.84**).

3. Click the Settings button Settings and then the Proxy tab Proxy .

   The Proxy pane displays your Web server's proxy settings (**Figure 9.85**).

4. If it isn't already selected, select the Enable Proxy check box.

Figure 9.83 Launch the Server Admin tool, and authenticate.

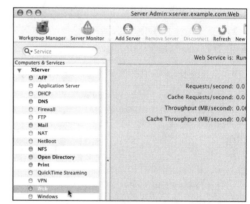

Figure 9.84 The Web service is selected in the Computers & Services list.

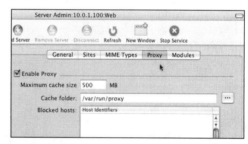

Figure 9.85 The Proxy pane lets you edit the Web server's proxy settings.

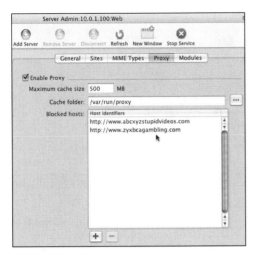

Figure 9.86 You can directly enter a fully qualified host name in the "Blocked hosts" list.

Figure 9.87 You can drag and drop a text file into the "Blocked hosts" list.

5. To add host names to the "Blocked hosts" list, *do either of the following:*

▲ Click the Add button ➕ , and enter the fully qualified host name (**Figure 9.86**). When you've finished entering the host name, press the Enter key.

▲ Drag and drop a plain-text file listing the fully qualified host names separated by tabs or commas (**Figure 9.87**).

6. When you've finished making changes, click the Save button ⬭ Save ⬭ .

✔ Tips

■ When you're dragging a text file to the "Blocked hosts" window, make sure there is a carriage return at the end of the last host name in the file. Otherwise, the last host-name entry will be ignored.

■ It's important to remember that proxy settings won't affect any of your Web site settings.

■ Client computers aren't, by default, configured to use a Web proxy. See the sidebar "Configuring a Web Proxy on Clients" for more information.

■ Once they're configured, you should verify that sites are indeed blocked to your users.

■ Any client that isn't configured to use your proxy server can bypass your list of blocked hosts. The best way to prevent this is to use a network firewall that only allows your proxy server to access external Web sites.

ENABLING WEB PROXIES

Monitoring Web Services

Mac OS X Server provides a variety of statistics for monitoring the Apache Web service. Using the Server Admin tool, you can monitor each Web site individually or the Web server as a whole. The information provided by the monitoring tools is invaluable for troubleshooting connection problems and determining if resources are being properly used.

To graph Web statistics:

1. Launch the Server Admin tool located in /Applications/Server, and authenticate as the administrator (**Figure 9.88**).

2. Select the Web service for your server in the Computers & Services list (**Figure 9.89**).

3. Click the Graphs tab Graphs .
   The Graphs frame defaults to requests per second (**Figure 9.90**).

4. Use the slider below the graph to manipulate the graph's sample timeframe.

5. Click the pop-up menu to *select any of the other graphs* (**Figure 9.91**):

   ▲ Throughput per second

   ▲ Requests per second using the performance cache

   ▲ Throughput per second using the performance cache

   The graphs that include the performance cache show two series; the lower series is the cache results (**Figure 9.92**).

Figure 9.88 Launch the Server Admin tool, and authenticate.

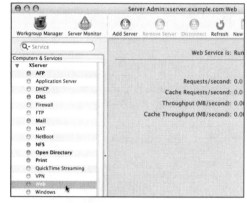

Figure 9.89 The Web service is selected in the Computers & Services list.

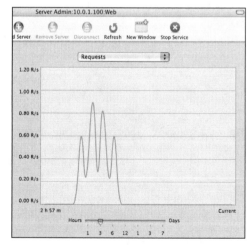

Figure 9.90 This is an example of a Web server throughput performance graph.

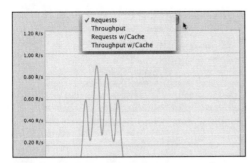

Figure 9.91 The pop-up menu lets you view different Web server performance graphs.

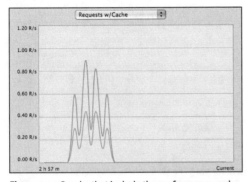

Figure 9.92 Graphs that include the performance cache show two series; the lower series is the cache results.

✔ Tips

- If you've recently enabled your Web server, you may have to wait some time for the graphs to react. You can always move things along by using a Web server benchmark utility. See the sidebar "Apache Benchmark Test" for more information.

- Click the Refresh button [Refresh] to force the Server Admin tool to refresh the performance graphs immediately.

- If you like to keep tabs on your Web server usage, you can leave the Server Admin tool running and on the graphs view. Server Admin will automatically update based on the refresh settings.

Apache Benchmark Test

You can always test your Web server by using a Web browser on another computer, or you can be a real geek and use the powerful ApacheBench command-line utility (**Figure 9.93**). It's always best to read the manual page of a command-line utility understand how it works; but to get you started, here are a few examples:

- ◆ To display ApacheBench usage information, enter the command *ab* –h.

- ◆ To send 1,000 sequential test requests to a server, enter *ab* –n 1000 http://*sitename*/.

- ◆ To send 1,000 concurrent test requests to a server, enter *ab* –n 1000 –c 1000 http://*sitename*/.

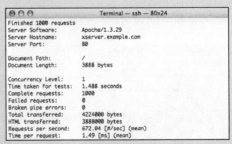

Figure 9.93 This is typical output from the ApacheBench command-line Web server benchmarking utility.

Using log files

Although performance graphs in the Server Admin tool are nice to look at, the real business of Web site monitoring is in the log files. The Apache Web server is renowned for the extensive detailed information available in its log files. You can even modify the log-file formatting to meet your specific needs.

To configure the Access and Error log files:

1. Launch the Server Admin tool located in /Applications/Server, and authenticate as the administrator (**Figure 9.94**).

2. Select the Web service for your server in the Computers & Services list (**Figure 9.95**).

3. Click the Settings button Settings and then the Sites tab Sites .

4. In the Sites list, double-click the Web site you wish to configure (**Figure 9.96**).

5. If it isn't already selected, click the Logging tab Logging to see this Web site's log settings.

   The Logging frame shows settings for both the Access and Error logs. For every site, there is an Error log that can't be disabled and an Access log that is enabled by default (**Figure 9.97**).

Figure 9.94 Launch the Server Admin tool, and authenticate.

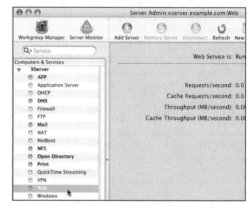

Figure 9.95 The Web service is selected in the Computers & Services list.

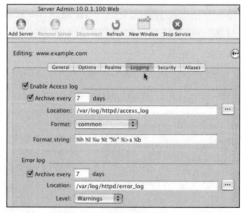

Figure 9.97 The Logging pane lets you configure the Access and Error log settings for each Web site.

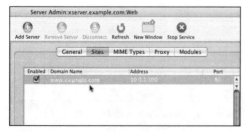

Figure 9.96 Select the Web site you wish to edit from the Web Sites list.

MONITORING WEB SERVICES

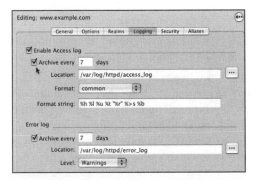

Figure 9.98 Archiving of the Access and Error logs has been enabled for this Web site.

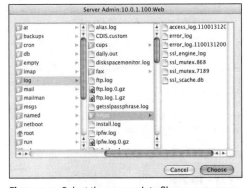

Figure 9.99 Select the appropriate file on your server using the browse dialog.

6. Select the Archive option, and enter the number of days between archives in the appropriate fields (**Figure 9.98**).

Neither the Access nor Error log is archived by default, and log files can become large on busy servers.

7. To specify a custom location for the log files, *do either of the following:*

▲ Type a new path in the Location field.

▲ Click the ellipsis button ••• to use the browse dialog (**Figure 9.99**).

8. To modify the Access log format string, *do either of the following:*

▲ Enter a custom string in the "Format string" field.

▲ Click the Format pop-up menu to specify a predefined format string (**Figure 9.100**).

9. To modify the Error log, click the Level pop-up menu and pick a log level (**Figure 9.101**).

Levels range from Emergency, which provides the least logging; to Debug, which provides the most logging.

continues on next page

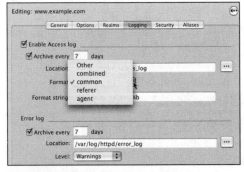

Figure 9.100 You can select a predefined Access log format string from this pop-up menu.

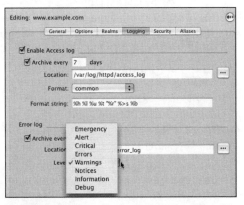

Figure 9.101 You can select an Error log level from this pop-up menu.

10. When you've finished making changes, click the Save button [Save].

11. To view the logs, click the Logs tab [Logs].

Notice that each Web site has its own Access and Error log. Select the log file you wish to view in the top list, and it appears in the pane below (**Figure 9.102**).

✔ Tips

■ The Server Admin tool should automatically restart the Web service when you click the Save button [Save].

■ It's important to remember that log settings are configured separately for each Web site you have.

■ See the sidebar "Apache Log Analysis Tools" for more information about interpreting Apache access logs.

■ Click the Refresh button [Refresh] to force the Server Admin tool to refresh the logs immediately.

■ If you like to keep tabs on your server usage, you can leave the Server Admin tool running and on the logs view. Server Admin will automatically update based on the refresh settings.

IP Address	Domain Name	Port	Type	Path
*	xserver.example.co	80	Access	/var/log/httpd/access_log
*	xserver.example.co	80	Error	/var/log/httpd/error_log
*	www.example.com	80	Access	/var/log/httpd/access_log
*	www.example.com	80	Error	/var/log/httpd/error_log

[Wed Jun 16 21:46:45 2004] [notice] Apache/1.3.29 (Darwin) DAV/1.0.3 PHP/4.3.2 configured -- resuming normal operations
[Wed Jun 16 21:46:46 2004] [notice] Accept mutex: flock (Default: flock)
[Wed Jun 16 21:46:46 2004] [warn] long lost child came home! (pid 20565)
[Wed Jun 16 21:46:55 2004] [notice] SIGUSR1 received. Doing graceful restart
Processing config directory: /etc/httpd/sites/*.conf
Processing config file: /etc/httpd/sites/0000_any_80_xserver.example.com.conf
Processing config file: /etc/httpd/sites/0001_any_80_www.example.com.conf
Processing config file: /etc/httpd/sites/virtual_host_global.conf
[Wed Jun 16 21:46:55 2004] [warn] module mod_WebObjects.c is already added, skipping
[Wed Jun 16 21:46:55 2004] [notice] Apache/1.3.29 (Darwin) DAV/1.0.3 PHP/4.3.2 configured -- resuming normal operations
[Wed Jun 16 21:46:55 2004] [notice] Accept mutex: flock (Default: flock)
[Wed Jun 16 21:46:55 2004] [warn] long lost child came home! (pid 20625)
[Wed Jun 16 21:49:05 2004] [notice] SIGUSR1 received. Doing graceful restart
Processing config directory: /etc/httpd/sites/*.conf

Figure 9.102 The Logs frame displays the Access and Error log for every Web site on your server.

Apache Log Analysis Tools

Apache access logs can be complicated to understand. You can read more about the log formats at http://httpd.apache.org/docs/logs.htm. Or, you can try one of the many Apache log analysis tools available:

AWStats—A free, Web-based, open-source log analysis tool: http://awstats.sourceforge.net/

Webalizer—Another free, Web-based log analysis tool: http://www.mrunix.net/Webalizer/

Urchin—A very popular commercial log analysis suite (**Figure 9.103**): http://www.urchin.com/

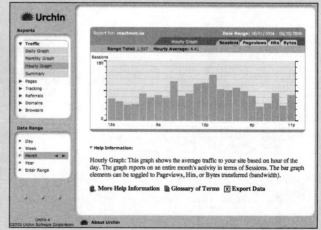

Figure 9.103 This is typical output of the Urchin Web log analysis tool.

SECURITY

Mac OS X was built to be secure. Ditto for Mac OS X Server. When you think about security, you may not consider what it entails. This chapter examines the ways to make your Mac OS X Server more secure: manipulating configuration files, starting certain processes, and providing physical security for the box itself.

First, ask yourself why you're reading this chapter. What do you wish to accomplish? Do you want to prevent people from seeing your data? to make it harder for people to guess your passwords? to reduce the entry points into your computer?

Mac OS X Server can help you accomplish these goals. Security on Mac OS X Server encompasses the following main areas:

◆ Physical security

◆ Open ports

◆ Passwords

◆ Encryption

This chapter focuses on these topics.

Physical Security

When you purchase Mac OS X Server, it's assumed you'll be using one of the several services on the server. This means data is being stored on the server—whether it's user information such as the LDAP directory or files stored by users—and that data must be protected.

If you set up your Mac OS X Server where anyone has access to the box, you're leaving it open to a physical attack. There are several ways in which someone can attack your server if they have physical access to the box:

◆ Opening the box and stealing the hard disk(s)

◆ Stealing the drive bays and disks out of an Xserve

◆ Shutting down the server by either holding down the power button or unplugging the power cable, and then booting into a less secure mode (**Table 10.1**).

Table 10.1

Keyboard Boot Methods		
BOOT DESCRIPTION	**STARTUP KEYBOARD SEQUENCE**	**RESULT**
FireWire Target Disk Mode	F	Computer boots into a mode where any FireWire connection to another running Mac shows the server disk(s) on the running Mac's Desktop.
Single User Mode	Command-S	Boots the computer into a mode where any person can, with a little Unix knowledge, wreak havoc.
Boot off CD/DVD	C	Boots the computer from a bootable Mac OS X or Mac OS X Server CD or DVD, which allows any person to change the password.
Bypass internal disks	Command-Option-Shift-Delete	Lets any person plug in a FireWire disk or other bootable media and force the server to boot off that disk, bypassing the internal boot disks.
NetBooting	N	Requires another Mac OS X Server running NetBoot on the same network. The user boots off the NetBoot image. (See Chapter 11, "Running a NetBoot Server.")
View all bootable media	Option	Permits any person to view (and boot from), as icons, any other bootable disks, partitions, and bootable media that contain a blessed and bootable system.

Figure 10.1 Install Open Firmware Password on your server.

Figure 10.2 Open Firmware Password's initial dialog informs you that you must be an administrator to change the password.

Preventing unauthorized logins

Using the methods listed in Table 10.1, any person can boot off another device and view, erase, change, or otherwise tamper with your server. To thwart these types of intrusion, download and install Open Firmware Password, which you can obtain from Apple's Web site (http://docs.info.apple.com/article.html?artnum=120095).

Once Open Firmware Password is installed, any person attempting any of the boot methods in Table 10.1 will be denied. The only variance is that Open Firmware Password allows any user to boot while holding down the Option key. However, when Open Firmware Password is implemented, the user sees only a padlock and an entry field rather than all possible bootable media. The user *must* know the Open Firmware Password application's password to view all the supported bootable media and subsequently temporarily change the boot disk to one of the available choices.

To use Open Firmware Password:

1. Download Open Firmware Password from Apple's Web site at http://docs.info.apple.com/article.html?artnum=120095, and install it on your server (**Figure 10.1**).

   The /Applications/Utilities folder is a common location for this application.

2. Double-click the Open Firmware Password icon to launch the program.

   You're presented with the program's initial dialog (**Figure 10.2**).

3. Click the Change button `Change`.

   A window opens in which you can enter a new password or phrase.

continues on next page

PHYSICAL SECURITY

4. Enter a password that you *will not forget* in both entry fields (**Figure 10.3**).

You can also require a password to change this setting in the future by checking the "Require password" check box.

5. Click the OK button (OK).

A window informs you of your success in setting or changing the password or phrase (**Figure 10.4**).

6. Restart your computer, and hold down the Option key to view the effects (**Figure 10.5**).

✔ Tip

■ Keyboard shortcuts aren't the only way data can be compromised. Xserves came with small keys that let you lock the drive bays so they can't be removed. Regardless of the version of Xserve you have, keeping the key in an extremely safe place is a good idea. Losing and reordering a key can cost you valuable time if you need to work on your Xserve.

Figure 10.3 Set the Open Firmware password using this dialog.

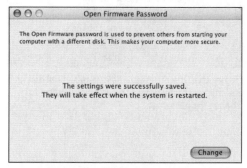

Figure 10.4 Open Firmware Password informs you of the success of setting/changing your password.

Figure 10.5 Hold down the Option key lets you view the effects once Open Firmware Password has been successfully enabled.

Securing the server room

The second piece of physical security is, of course, the room in which the server resides. This isn't just a Mac OS X Server issue, but it's worth mentioning that any good administrator limits access to the room where the servers are stored. Out of site, out of mind, as the old adage goes. If placing the server in a locked room isn't feasible, use the locking methods and remove the keyboard, mouse, and monitor unless they're absolutely necessary.

Remember, you can administer Mac OS X Server with a few main tools, all of which run remotely. Most of the tools can be found in the /Applications/Server directory. The Terminal application and Directory Access both reside in the /Applications/Utilities directory. Apple Remote Desktop, which you must purchase separately, lets you (from a remote computer) see and control the screen, keyboard, and mouse as if you were sitting in front of the server itself. These tools should be on your Mac OS X client computer.

Oops, I lost My Password!

If you lose or forget the Open Firmware Password application's password, you must shut down your server and make a physical change to the hardware of the server. This commonly involves taking out a RAM chip or two, rebooting the server (which erases the password), shutting the server back down, replacing the RAM, and booting the server once again.

Some people feel this makes Open Firmware Password insecure. On the contrary: If anyone can open the box on which

you're running Mac OS X Server, they have physical access to the disks, which means they can take them! Open Firmware Password doesn't protect or encrypt the disk(s); it places a password-protected lock on the firmware used to boot the computer.

If you're worried about someone gaining physical access to the innards of your server hardware, purchase a lock if the Macintosh model supports it; or, if it's an Xserve, use the key.

Open Ports

Your server has more than 65,000 ports, or doors. How many of them are used when you install Mac OS X Server? How do find out which ones are open and which ones may be relatively insecure? How do you close these doors?

Mac OS X Server comes with a powerful service called a *firewall*. Perhaps you're installing a server that's already behind your organization's firewall, and you don't see the need for another firewall inside your business. After all, you're protected from the outside world. But who is protecting you from others within your company? What about other people who wish to peruse this new Mac OS X Server without your permission? Instituting a firewall is an excellent idea, even if your users are all local.

Firewall basics

A firewall either permits or denies access to your Mac OS X Server from persons attempting to gain access to the server over the server's interfaces (usually, in the case of Mac OS X Server, your built-in Ethernet interfaces). If a person tries to access a service like FTP on your server, and the FTP service is running, then your server allows them in on port 21. If you have the Apple File Sharing service on, you're letting users connect over port 548.

Again, there are over 65,000 ports; so at first, managing a firewall may seem overwhelming. Keep in mind one simple rule: Close off *all* ports, and open ports only when people complain that they can't access certain services or when you have a given set of services open that most users will utilize. In this fashion, you open only what you know about, and you effectively shut out all other users by removing access to those ports.

The Old-Fashioned Way

There is another way to add rules to your firewall. The firewall (called ipfw) reads from two configuration files: ipfw.apple.conf and ipfw.conf, both located in /private/etc/ipfilter. When you make changes to the firewall using the Server Admin tool, it writes to the ipfw.apple.conf file. You can add your own rules to the ipfw.conf file using your favorite command-line editor.

When you start the firewall using Server Admin, ipfw reads from both of these files. This method introduces a potential conflict due to the fact you could accidentally create two rules that do exactly the opposite thing. Take care when you're editing files directly.

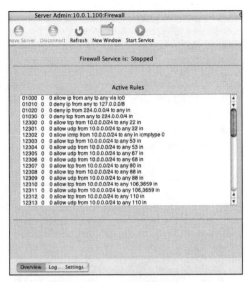

Figure 10.6 The Firewall service is selected, and the Overview tab indicates all current rules.

Figure 10.7 The Firewall service Log tab shows the Firewall log.

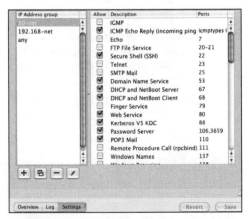

Figure 10.8 The Settings tab of the Firewall service shows both the IP Address group pane and the list of common ports.

The Firewall service

On Mac OS X Server, Apple has built in an interface for the firewall. Before you set a firewall in place, let's examine the Firewall window.

The Overview tab `Overview` shows the current firewall rules (**Figure 10.6**). They're listed in order of importance by the numeric value of the rule. For example, rule 65535 always allows all connections from any IP address to any IP address on your server. Rules that may restrict access are given a lower number and thus a higher priority.

The Log tab `Log` shows the Firewall log file (**Figure 10.7**). You can specify what gets logged in the settings window, as you'll see in a moment.

The Settings tab `Settings` displays three additional tabs (**Figure 10.8**):

◆ You'll do most of your firewall work in the General tab `General`. It displays two panes: "IP Address group" and a list of common ports. The "IP Address group" pane lets you create separate sets of rules, based on the IP address(es) of your server. The common ports window shows (what Apple considers) the ports most commonly associated with Mac OS X Server and its subsequent services. There are columns for activating the firewall on that port, the port number, and a description of the service that runs over that port(s).

continues on next page

OPEN PORTS

◆ The Logging tab Logging sets parameters for the logging that the firewall reports (**Figure 10.9**). It's important to remember that if you enable both allowed and denied packets, your log file will grow very quickly if your server does any sharing.

◆ The Advanced tab Advanced lets you add firewall rules that may need to be more specific or are missing from the General tab's common ports window (**Figure 10.10**).

IP address groups

Now that you're familiar with most of the pieces of the firewall, let's fit them together. The first thing you need to do is determine how your server is set up. This will determine how your firewall IP address groups will be oriented. For example, if you have just one interface connection, such as Built-in Ethernet, you may only wish to configure the IP address group associated with your server's IP address. If you have more than one network interface active, such as a server that's used as a router, you may want to enable different rules on different interfaces.

If you're new to the firewall and want to be sure you cover all your bases, you can choose the "any" group. Rules applied here apply to any network interface with any IP address (**Figure 10.11**). You can also use the editing buttons to add, delete, duplicate, or edit an IP address group (**Figure 10.12**).

Figure 10.9 You can set the type of logging for your firewall using the Logging tab of the Settings tab.

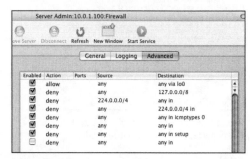

Figure 10.10 The Advanced tab of the Settings tab shows customized firewall rules.

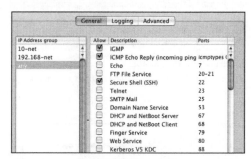

Figure 10.11 Select an IP address group to view the subsequent firewall rules for that group.

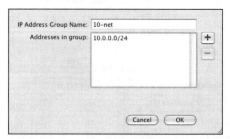

Figure 10.12 You can add IP address groups to the main list.

When you set up your server and turn on various services, the firewall IP address group associated with the topmost interface in your Network Preference pane automatically selects most of the services you currently have running. This is a safeguard against your accidentally turning on your firewall and being locked out of services you configured (**Figure 10.13**).

When you're ready to set up the firewall, take an inventory of the other services you're offering. You'll want to ensure you're providing proper access to those services. As soon

as you start your firewall, a "deny all" rule will take effect: This means that the only ports open to the outside will be those that are selected in the list of common ports.

✔ Tip

■ If you're using an Xserve and doing all remote administration, be very careful not to enable the firewall without ensuring that you have access using at least port 22 (ssh). If you deny access on all ports, how will you get in?

Figure 10.13 This expanded view of Server Admin shows several selected firewall rules that correspond with services that are running.

Turning on the basic firewall:

1. Launch the Server Admin tool located in /Applications/Server, and authenticate as the administrator (**Figure 10.14**).

2. Choose the Firewall service from the Computers & Services list (**Figure 10.15**).

3. Click the Settings tab [Settings], and select the appropriate group from the "IP Address group" list (**Figure 10.16**).

   Remember that you'll have a group for your IP address(es) and a group called "any".

4. Select any services you wish to be open for access from any network interfaces you've connected to any networks (**Figure 10.17**).

5. Click the Save button [Save] to write your changes to the ipfw.apple.conf file.

6. Start your firewall by clicking the Start Service button [ ] Start Service in the Server Admin Toolbar.

7. To test your firewall, go to any client computer on the same network as your server, open the Network Utility application in /Applications/Utilities, and click the Port Scan tab [Port Scan].

   Type in the IP address of your server, and click the Port Scan button. The list of open ports returned tells you whether your firewall is configured to your liking (**Figure 10.18**).

✔ Tip

■ Be careful not to enable or disable services on each IP address group unless you're sure that's what you want to do.

Figure 10.14 Launch the Server Admin tool, and authenticate.

Figure 10.15 Select the Firewall service from the Computers & Services list.

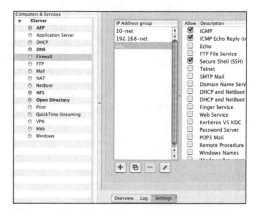

Figure 10.16 Click the Settings tab, and select the appropriate subnet from the "IP Address group" list.

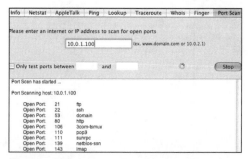

Figure 10.18 From a remote machine, use Network Utility to perform a port scan and confirm which services and ports are open and which are closed.

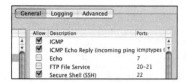

Figure 10.17 Select the services and associated ports that should be open; doing so opens the firewall to those services and ports.

Figure 10.19 Launch the Server Admin tool, and authenticate.

Figure 10.20 Select the Firewall service from the Computers & Services list.

Advanced FTP rules

A basic firewall is one order of protection. But what if you have ports you wish to open that aren't on the list of common ports? What if you always want your FTP service to respond to just one IP address only, and no other? Using the Advanced tab <kbd>Advanced</kbd> of the firewall settings, you can further define rules based on several other criteria.

To add an advanced FTP rule:

1. Launch the Server Admin tool located in /Applications/Server, and authenticate as the administrator (**Figure 10.19**).

2. Choose the Firewall service from the Computers & Services list (**Figure 10.20**).

3. Click the Settings tab <kbd>Settings</kbd>, and then click the Advanced tab <kbd>Advanced</kbd> (**Figure 10.21**).

4. Click the Add button <kbd>+</kbd>.

   The advanced setup dialog for a new rule opens (**Figure 10.22**).

continues on next page

Figure 10.21 Select the Advanced tab from the Settings tab in the Firewall service.

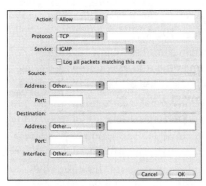

Figure 10.22 The advanced rule dialog shows all available fields.

OPEN PORTS

5. From the Action pop-up menu, *choose one of the following actions for the rule* (**Figure 10.23**):

▲ Allow

▲ Deny

▲ Other

In this case, choose to allow packets in.

6. From the Protocol pop-up menu, *choose one of the following protocols to allow* (**Figure 10.24**):

▲ UDP

▲ TCP

▲ Other

In this case, allow TCP. If you aren't sure which protocol to use, you can choose Other and enter the word all in the list (**Figure 10.25**).

7. Choose FTP File Service from the Service pop-up menu, and decide whether you want to log information related to this rule (**Figures 10.26** and **10.27**).

The corresponding port for this service appears under Port for the Destination.

8. In the Source section of the dialog, enter the IP address of the computer that is connecting to your server and the port from which the connection is coming (**Figure 10.28**).

You can choose from any IP address group in the Address pop-up menu, use a subnet, or use a range of IP addresses (**Figure 10.29**).

9. In the Destination section of the window, enter the IP address group or IP address of your server (**Figure 10.30**).

The port numbers (in this case, FTP) automatically fill in for you (from step 7).

10. In the Interface section, *choose which type of packets to allow* (**Figure 10.31**):

▲ In (incoming)

▲ Out (outgoing)

▲ Other

Figure 10.23 Choose an action for an advanced rule.

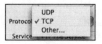

Figure 10.24 Choose a protocol for an advanced rule.

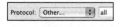

Figure 10.25 When you choose the Other option, you can enter the word all in the associated field to cover all potential protocols.

Figure 10.26 Choose from the list of possible preset services in the Service pop-up menu.

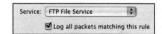

Figure 10.27 Select the FTP service, and choose to log all associated packets.

Figure 10.28 Configure the incoming (source) IP and port information.

OPEN PORTS

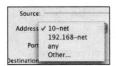

Figure 10.29 The Address pop-up menu shows the available options when you're choosing the source address.

Figure 10.30 Configure the destination IP address and port information for the server itself.

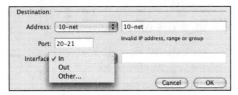

Figure 10.31 You can display interface-specific options via the pop-up menu.

Figure 10.32 Choose Other to refrain from limiting both incoming and outgoing access.

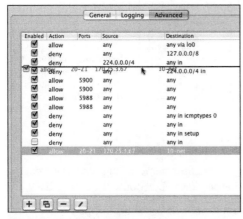

Figure 10.33 You can move rules up and down via drag and drop in the Advanced rule tab.

In this case, choose Other to refrain from limiting both incoming and outgoing access (**Figure 10.32**). Click the OK button ⬭OK⬮.

11. Click the Save button ⬭ Save ⬮ to save your settings.

You've added an advanced rule that allows connections to your server from a computer with the IP address 170.25.3.67. The next step would be to create a rule that denies all FTP packets. You can then move rules up or down for order of precedence in the Advanced tab ⬭Advanced⬮ (**Figure 10.33**).

✔ Tips

■ Obviously, there are thousands of rule combinations: rules that govern an interface entering your organization and an interface going out to the Internet, rules that are extremely restrictive or extremely lax, and the option of adding rules within Server Admin and within another file (/etc/ipfilter/ipfw.conf).

■ You can see all the firewall rules from the command line by typing sudo ipfw show.

■ You can erase any firewall rules by typing sudo ipfw flush from the command line. Of course, doing this leaves your server vulnerable to attack.

■ Once you use Server Admin to make changes to the firewall and save those changes, the rules are rewritten.

Password Security

It's unfortunate that this book must discuss this topic, but poor passwords or no passwords can lead to an insecure server. When you set up a server for the first time, you enter an initial administrator account. This account's password is also the password for the root account, which is enabled on Mac OS X Server by default. This situation presents several issues and several possible ways you can help reduce the risk of someone cracking or guessing your password.

For the user's short name, use a name that's difficult to guess. For example, you might make the administrator's short name q9tr73m1. It's a combination of both letters and numbers, which makes guessing the username even more difficult.

Set the password using the same complex method of combining letters and numbers—both uppercase and lowercase in this case.

You can even add an exclamation point in the mix to make the password harder to guess.

After the server is set up, you may wish to change the root password to something even *more* complex. Making the root password and the initial administrator account password different also increases security. In some circumstances, you might even disable root: for instance, if you have a server in your room, and you'd rather use sudo −s as an admin to become root rather than log in directly as root.

To change the root password:

1. Launch the Workgroup Manager tool located in /Applications/Server, and authenticate as the administrator (**Figures 10.34** and **10.35**).

Figure 10.34 Launch the Workgroup Manager tool located in /Applications/Server, and authenticate as the administrator.

Figure 10.35 The Workgroup Manager application shows the accounts in the LDAP database.

Be Careful!

◆ *Never* use capital letters in the initial administrator's short name. Doing so will prevent the server from properly setting itself up as a Kerberos Key Distribution Center (KDC).

◆ If you disable root, you may not be able to promote your server to be an Open Directory master.

◆ *Never* use a password that's easy to guess. You're asking for your server to be compromised.

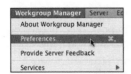

Figure 10.36 Choose Workgroup Manager > Preferences.

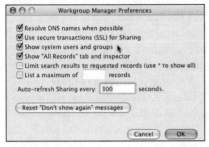

Figure 10.37 Select the "Show system users and groups" check box.

Figure 10.38 Select the LDAP directory from the directory authentication icon.

Figure 10.39 View the user database to show the System Administrator (root) account and change the password for that account.

Figure 10.40 Select the Local directory from the directory authentication icon.

2. Choose Workgroup Manager > Preferences (**Figure 10.36**).

A Workgroup Manager Preferences dialog opens.

3. Select the "Show system users and groups" check box (**Figure 10.37**).

Click the OK button (OK) to dismiss the dialog.

4. Click the directory authentication icon [🌐▾ Authenticated], and select the /LDAPv3/ 127.0.0.1 directory database from the pop-up menu (**Figure 10.38**).

5. Click the Accounts icon in the Toolbar, and click System Administrator in the Name list.

6. Enter and verify the new password in the Basic tab [Basic] (**Figure 10.39**).

7. Click the Save button (Save) to save the password change.

8. Go to step 4, and select the Local database from the directory authentication icon [🌐▾ Authenticated] (**Figure 10.40**).

Repeat steps 5–7 to change the password for the local root account.

You should change the root account for both databases at the same time, to avoid conflicts.

✔ Tip

- If you're upgrading from an older version of Mac OS X Server (like 10.2, aka Jaguar), you may wish to reset all passwords for all users. Doing so rewrites the passwords back into the upgraded Password Server database. It's possible that if you had users in a local database, they stored their passwords using the less secure crypt method, as opposed to the more secure Password Server methods.

PASSWORD SECURITY

Encryption

You can encrypt data sent between two devices so that no one can see, change, spoof, or subvert the packets. One of the devices is your Mac OS X Server. The other device can be any client computer that connects to your server. This section discusses how to enable encryption on your server so that various services can take advantage of better security.

The first type of encryption, Secure Sockets Layer (SSL), is the most common. Perhaps your Mac OS X Server is a Web server used to sell a product. Your Web site has pages that handle sensitive user data or credit card information. When users navigate to your Web site and enter a page that is secure, you should be ready. Or perhaps you wish to encrypt the transaction of sending and receiving mail, or the process of user authentication for home folders on your server.

The type of encryption this section discusses involves obtaining a certificate from a Certificate Authority (CA), creating your own certificate, or using one created for you by a non-CA. If you wish to obtain a certificate from a trusted source, you must be prepared to offer important business and personal information to Thawte, VeriSign, or another, smaller CA. To do so, navigate to the CA's Web site and ask for a certificate. Certificates come in various encryption levels and types, so you may want to choose one with a higher level if you have potential customers overseas. Chances are this certificate will cost you money, and you'll have to decide if the cost is worth the effort. Most CAs place great stock in making certain your business or organization is who it says it is. The cost of the certificate is profit for companies who have built their names on trust. Many Web sites today rely on these companies to verify them. However, some CAs don't charge as much as others. You must decide if your organization requires a name-brand certificate signed by a well-known CA, or if a lesser-known CA will do. There are no right answers here; it all depends on which CA you trust the most.

The reason for the cash transfer is that authentication has to start somewhere. If you're www.yourstore.com, how can people purchasing from your site know that you are who you say you are? You must prove to someone that you are indeed who you say you are and not a Web site that looks like you but is an imposter. By purchasing a certificate from a CA, you're telling people coming to your site that you underwent a thorough business check and that the CA says, "Yes, this site *is* the site they purport to be. I, Thawte, checked their background and had them issue me a certificate-signing request, which I signed. They now have a certificate registered with me so that when a customer's browser asks me to validate them, I can."

Private keys

Before you have a certificate to sign, you must create your own private key. Several parameters are involved when you create a key. In most cases, you'll want to create a 1024-bit private key, although you can create keys with a higher and lower encryption bit level and a different cipher, such as Blowfish, SHA-1, or MD5. Increasing the bit level for a key or changing the cipher may hinder others who try to connect to you; for as you know, people still use older, less secure operating systems to access the Internet.

To create a private key:

1. Open the Terminal application located in /Applications/Utilities.

   Become root by typing sudo -s, pressing Return, and entering the root password.

2. To create a private key, enter the command

   `openssl genrsa -des3 1024 > privatekey.pem`

   This tells the `openssl` command to generate an RSA-style key with a Triple-DES cipher at 1024 bits and to save the key as privatekey.pem (**Figure 10.41**).

3. Enter a passphrase that you will *not* forget!

✔ Tip

■ To expand on your understanding of the `openssl` command line tool, type `man openssl` in the Terminal.

```
xserver:~ root# openssl genrsa -des3 1024 > privatekey.pem
Generating RSA private key, 1024 bit long modulus
..++++++
...........++++++
e is 65537 (0x10001)
Enter pass phrase:
Verifying - Enter pass phrase:
xserver:~ root# █
```

Figure 10.41 Generate a Triple-DES, 1024-bit encrypted private key using openssl.

ENCRYPTION

Certificate Signing Requests

You've now created a private key, which only you have; do *not* give this key file to anyone! Now you must create a Certificate Signing Request (CSR) with that key.

CSRs are made on behalf of a server or service and presented to a CA. This process is done via the command-line interface on Mac OS X Server. Therefore, you must ensure that you make no typos, because the command-line interface (CLI) isn't forgiving.

To create a Certificate Signing Request:

1. In the Terminal, type the following command on one line (**Figure 10.42**):

   ```
   openssl req -new -key privatekey.pem
   -out mycsr.csr
   ```

   This command tells `openssl` to create a new key out of privatekey.pem and write it out as the file mycsr.csr.

2. Enter the passphrase that you used when you created your private key (**Figure 10.43**).

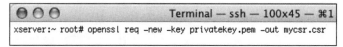

Figure 10.42 Create a CSR based on the private key using `openssl`.

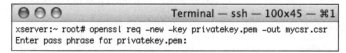

Figure 10.43 Enter the password associated with your private key to proceed.

ENCRYPTION

3. Enter the data required for the seven entries when creating the CSR (**Figure 10.44**):

- ▲ Country Name
- ▲ State Name
- ▲ Locality Name
- ▲ Organization Name
- ▲ Organizational Unit
- ▲ Common Name
- ▲ Email Address

Be sure the common name matches the Web address if you're using this certificate as a Web server certificate, as in Figure 10.42. You also have the option of adding two other entries before writing out the request.

They are:

- ▲ Challenge Password
- ▲ Optional Company Name

4. Send your CSR to Thawte, VeriSign, or one of the other CAs to start the process of obtaining your signed certificate.

Contact the appropriate Web site for instructions on how to submit the CSR.

✔ Tip

- ■ Apple has an in-depth document on **openssl** at http://developer.apple.com/internet/serverside/modssl.html.

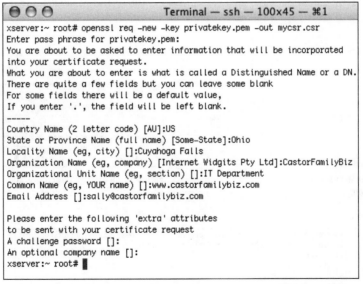

```
● ○ ○              Terminal — ssh — 100x45 — ⌘1
xserver:~ root# openssl req -new -key privatekey.pem -out mycsr.csr
Enter pass phrase for privatekey.pem:
You are about to be asked to enter information that will be incorporated
into your certificate request.
What you are about to enter is what is called a Distinguished Name or a DN.
There are quite a few fields but you can leave some blank
For some fields there will be a default value,
If you enter '.', the field will be left blank.
-----
Country Name (2 letter code) [AU]:US
State or Province Name (full name) [Some-State]:Ohio
Locality Name (eg, city) []:Cuyahoga Falls
Organization Name (eg, company) [Internet Widgits Pty Ltd]:CastorFamilyBiz
Organizational Unit Name (eg, section) []:IT Department
Common Name (eg, YOUR name) []:www.castorfamilybiz.com
Email Address []:sally@castorfamilybiz.com

Please enter the following 'extra' attributes
to be sent with your certificate request
A challenge password []:
An optional company name []:
xserver:~ root# █
```

Figure 10.44 Enter the appropriate information for the requested fields in the CSR using openssl.

ENCRYPTION

Acting as a Certificate Authority

Another possibility is that you don't need to pay for a CA to tell you that you're you. You know who you are, and you trust you. More important, your server may be inside a small school or organization where you don't need it for Web-page encryption but for encryption of another service (such as email) or to encrypt the transfer of data when requesting user data via the LDAP protocol. In these cases, you can sign your own certificate, thus avoiding the cost of having some else do it.

To act as your own CA:

1. Open the Terminal application located inside /Applications/Utilities.

   Become root by typing sudo –s, pressing Return, and entering the root password (**Figure 10.45**).

2. Create a folder called certs inside /private/ etc (any name will do, although the name cert or certs makes sense).

   Change directories so you're inside the certs folder (**Figure 10.46**).

3. *Do one of the following:*

   ▲ Move your private key into this folder.

   ▲ Create a new private key, as shown in step 2 of the task "To create a private key" (**Figure 10.47**).

4. Enter the following command in the Terminal (**Figure 10.48**):

   ```
   openssl req -new -x509 -days 365 -
   key privatekey.pem -out ca.crt
   ```

   The command creates a request for a new X509 certificate for 365 days based on the private key previously generated; the resulting file is named ca.crt.

Figure 10.45 Create a root shell on the server.

Figure 10.46 Change directories so you're inside the certs folder.

```
xserver:/private/etc/certs root# openssl genrsa -des3 1024 > privatekey.pem
Generating RSA private key, 1024 bit long modulus
......++++++
.....++++++
e is 65537 (0x10001)
Enter pass phrase:
Verifying - Enter pass phrase:
```

Figure 10.47 Create another private key to self-sign certificates.

Figure 10.48 Create an X509 certificate using openssl.

5. Enter the passphrase from your private certificate when asked (**Figure 10.49**).

6. Enter the required information when asked (**Figure 10.50**).

The common name should be the fully qualified domain name of your server.

7. Use the old CSR or create a new CSR, and enter all appropriate data (**Figure 10.51**).

continues on next page

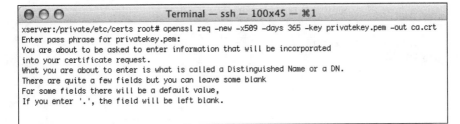

Figure 10.49 Enter your passphrase when requested.

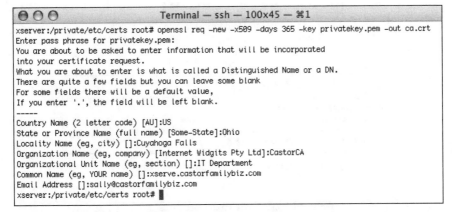

Figure 10.50 Enter the appropriate information when prompted.

```
⬤ ⬤ ⬤            Terminal — ssh — 100x45 — ⌘1
xserver:/private/etc/certs root# openssl req -new -key privatekey.pem -out castor.csr
Enter pass phrase for privatekey.pem:
You are about to be asked to enter information that will be incorporated
into your certificate request.
What you are about to enter is what is called a Distinguished Name or a DN.
There are quite a few fields but you can leave some blank
For some fields there will be a default value,
If you enter '.', the field will be left blank.
-----
Country Name (2 letter code) [AU]:US
State or Province Name (full name) [Some-State]:Ohio
Locality Name (eg, city) []:Cuyahoga Falls
Organization Name (eg, company) [Internet Widgits Pty Ltd]:CastorFamilyBiz
Organizational Unit Name (eg, section) []:Web Department
Common Name (eg, YOUR name) []:xserve.castorserver.com
```

Figure 10.51 Use the old CSR or create a new CSR, and enter all appropriate data.

8. Create a new folder called demoCA in the certs folder.

Create two folders in demoCA: private and newcerts (**Figure 10.52**).

9. Copy your ca.crt file from etc/certs to /etc/certs/demoCA, and rename it cacert.pem.

Move your privatekey.pem from the same original location to /etc/certs/demoCA/private, and rename it cakey.pem (**Figure 10.53**).

10. Create a file called index.txt in the demoCA folder.

Create another file called serial, containing the value "01" (**Figure 10.54**).

11. Navigate to the /etc/certs folder (**Figure 10.55**).

```
xserver:/private/etc/certs root# mkdir demoCA
xserver:/private/etc/certs root# cd demoCA/
xserver:/private/etc/certs/demoCA root# mkdir private
xserver:/etc/certs/demoCA root# mkdir newcerts
xserver:/private/etc/certs/demoCA root# █
```

Figure 10.52 Create two folders inside demoCA: private and newcerts.

```
Terminal — ssh — 100x45 — ⌘1
ate/etc/certs/demoCA/private root# cp /etc/certs/privatekey.pem cakey.pem
certs/demoCA/private root# cd ..
certs/demoCA root#
ate/etc/certs/demoCA/ root# cp /etc/certs/ca.crt cacert.pem
ate/etc/certs/demoCA/private root# █
```

Figure 10.53 Move and rename ca.crt and privatekey.pem.

```
xserver:/etc/certs root# touch demoCA/index.txt
xserver:/etc/certs root# echo "01" > demoCA/serial
```

Figure 10.54 Create two files, and enter data into one of them.

```
xserver:/etc/certs/demoCA root# cd /etc/certs
xserver:/etc/certs root# █
```

Figure 10.55 Navigate to the /etc/certs folder.

ENCRYPTION

12. Enter the following command in the Terminal to sign your own CSR (**Figure 10.56**):

```
openssl ca -policy policy_anything -in castor.csr -out castorserver.crt
```

13. Enter the letter y when asked about signing and again when asked about committing the certificate (**Figure 10.57**).

You now have, as far as your server is concerned, a signed certificate. You must copy the certificate to any client computers that you want to use the encryption.

✔ Tip

■ Some folders and files (like the demoCA folder) require certain names when dealing with self-signed certificates. Read the openssl.cnf file in /System/Library/OpenSSL/, which contains the default settings for using openssl with self-signed certificates.

```
xserver:/etc/certs root# openssl ca -policy policy_anything -in castor.csr -out castorserver.crt
Using configuration from /System/Library/OpenSSL/openssl.cnf
Enter pass phrase for ./demoCA/private/cakey.pem:
Check that the request matches the signature
Signature ok
Certificate Details:
        Serial Number: 1 (0x1)
        Validity
            Not Before: Sep 28 04:18:58 2004 GMT
            Not After : Sep 28 04:18:58 2005 GMT
        Subject:
            countryName               = US
            stateOrProvinceName       = Ohio
            localityName              = Cuyahoga Falls
            organizationName          = CastorFamilyBiz
            organizationalUnitName    = Web Department
            commonName                = xserve.castorserver.com
            emailAddress              = sally@castorfamilybiz.com
        X509v3 extensions:
            X509v3 Basic Constraints:
            CA:FALSE
            Netscape Comment:
            OpenSSL Generated Certificate
            X509v3 Subject Key Identifier:
            9B:25:F6:56:34:FD:90:70:B9:BD:22:72:44:85:4F:38:74:A8:CE:D9
            X509v3 Authority Key Identifier:
            keyid:9B:25:F6:56:34:FD:90:70:B9:BD:22:72:44:85:4F:38:74:A8:CE:D9
            DirName:/C=US/ST=Ohio/L=Cuyahoga Falls/O=CastorCA/OU=IT Department/CN=xserve.castorfamil
ybiz.com/emailAddress=sally@castorfamilybiz.com
            serial:00

Certificate is to be certified until Sep 28 04:18:58 2005 GMT (365 days)
Sign the certificate? [y/n]:█
```

Figure 10.56 Self-sign a certificate, and enter all the appropriate data.

```
Certificate is to be certified until Sep 28 04:18:58 2005 GMT (365 days)
Sign the certificate? [y/n]:y


1 out of 1 certificate requests certified, commit? [y/n]y
Write out database with 1 new entries
Data Base Updated
xserver:/etc/certs root# █
```

Figure 10.57 Confirm the signing and committing of the certificate.

To add the certificate to client computers:

1. Copy the file ca.crt from /etc/certs on your server to any client computers that need to know about the server.

   You should probably insure a secure copy from the server to the clients so no one can tamper with or see this file. Use a USB key drive, a FireWire drive, or secure connection to transfer the file from your server to client machines.

2. Once the certificate file is on the client computer, double-click it.

   The Keychain Access application opens and presents an Add Certificates dialog (**Figure 10.58**).

3. Click the View Certificates button  to be sure it's the correct certificate (**Figure 10.59**).

4. Click OK , and then click OK again to close the Add Certificate dialog.

   View the Keychain Access application, and locate your new certificate in the X509Anchors file (**Figure 10.60**).

   If this doesn't work, enter the following in the command line:

   ```
   sudo certtool i /etc/certs/ca.crt
   k=/System/Library/Keychains/
   X509Anchors
   ```

Figure 10.58 Double-click the certificate on the client to open an Add Certificates dialog.

Figure 10.59 Clicking the View Certificate button shows the contents of the certificate for visual verification.

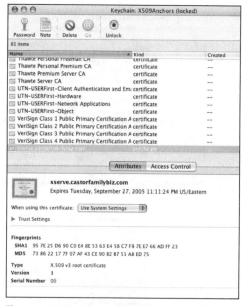

Figure 10.60 View the certificate in the keychain after you add the certificate to the X509Anchors file.

ENCRYPTION

Figure 10.61 Launch the Server Admin tool, and authenticate.

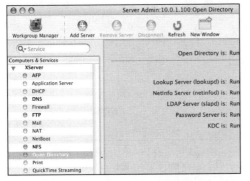

Figure 10.62 Select the Open Directory service from the Computers & Services list.

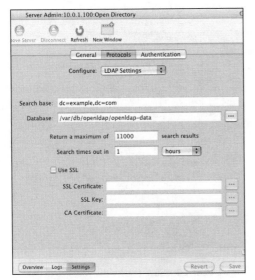

Figure 10.63 Select the Settings tab and then the Protocols tab, and select the Use SSL check box.

Implementing certificates

Whether you've created your own signed certificate or had a certificate signed by a CA, you can implement certificates in a variety of ways. Mac OS X Server can use certificates with the following services using the Server Admin tool:

◆ Open Directory

◆ Web sites

◆ Mail server

By default, if you're using a Mac OS X Server as an Open Directory master, all communications between your client computers and your server with regard to LDAP are passed as clear text. This is a potential security issue. You should set up the server to use Secure Sockets Layer (SSL) encryption and let the client computer know about this as well.

If you have a Web site, you should use the certificate to encrypt communications when customers come to your site.

If you're running a mail server, you should encrypt all email running through your server.

To encrypt Open Directory master communications:

1. Launch the Server Admin tool located in /Applications/Server, and authenticate as the administrator (**Figure 10.61**).

2. Choose the Open Directory service from the Computers & Services list (**Figure 10.62**).

3. Click the Settings tab Settings , and then click the Protocols tab Protocols (**Figure 10.63**).

continues on next page

ENCRYPTION

4. Select the Use SSL check box
(**Figure 10.64**).

Click the ellipsis buttons ⸱⸱⸱ , navigate to
the /etc/certs directory, and choose the
appropriate certificates and the private
key (**Figure 10.65**).

5. Click the Save button (Save) to save
the changes to the Open Directory settings (**Figure 10.66**).

Now, anyone connecting to your Mac OS X
Server via LDAP must have the required
certificate and have SSL active from the
client computer.

Figure 10.64 Select the check box to enable SSL.

Figure 10.65 Choose the appropriate certificates and
keys by using the ellipsis button to bring up a
navigation dialog.

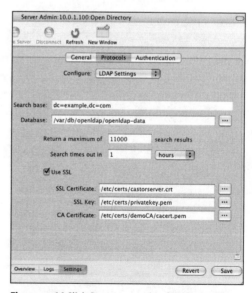

Figure 10.66 Click Save to save the changes to the
Open Directory settings.

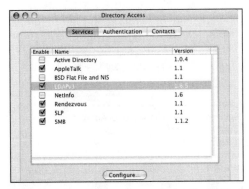

Figure 10.67 Use Directory Access to view the LDAP plug-in.

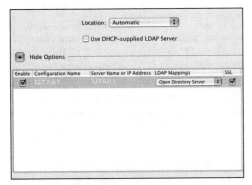

Figure 10.68 Check the SSL box to allow secure connections on the server.

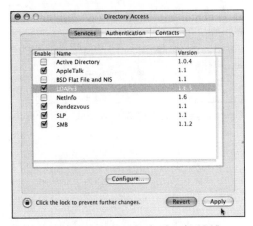

Figure 10.69 Deselecting and selecting the LDAP plug-in activates the Apply button.

Setting up Directory Access SSL LDAP

You must now tell your server to see itself over SSL. The same procedure outlined in the following task is done on the client machines when you bind to an LDAP server over SSL.

To set up Directory Access SSL LDAP:

1. On your server, open the Directory Access application located in /Applications/ Utilities, and authenticate as the administrator using the lock 🔒 (**Figure 10.67**).

2. Double-click the LDAP plug-in, click the disclosure arrow next to Show Options if necessary, and select the SSL check box (**Figure 10.68**).
   Click the OK button (OK).

3. Deselect the LDAP plug-in, and select it again.
   Doing so highlights the Apply button (Apply); click it (**Figure 10.69**).

4. Test thoroughly to ensure that your server certificates were created properly. If this doesn't work, it's possible that the certificate creation—especially the common name in the certificate setup—isn't correct.
   Once the server can see itself again (verified by a successful launching of Workgroup Manager and seeing the LDAP users), you can run through this list for clients that have the LDAP plug-in activated.

ENCRYPTION

DHCP LDAP SSL

If you set up your server as a DHCP server and you're pushing LDAP information down to your client, you should enable SSL there.

To enable SSL for the LDAP DHCP option:

1. Launch the Server Admin tool located in /Applications/Server, and authenticate as the administrator (**Figure 10.70**).

2. Choose the DHCP service from the Computers & Services list (**Figure 10.71**).

3. Click the Settings tab [Settings], double-click your subnet, and click the LDAP tab [LDAP].

4. Select the "LDAP over SSL" check box (**Figure 10.72**).

5. Click the Save button [Save].
   Your DHCP server will alert you that it needs to be restarted.

Figure 10.70 Launch the Server Admin tool, and authenticate.

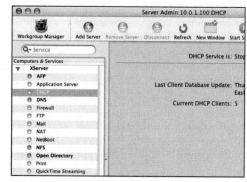

Figure 10.71 Select the DHCP service from the Computers & Services list.

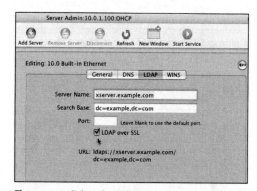

Figure 10.72 Select the "LDAP over SSL" check box.

Figure 10.73 Launch the Server Admin tool, and authenticate.

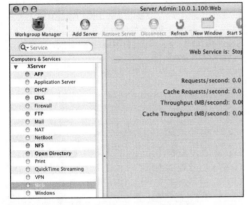

Figure 10.74 Select the Web service from the Computers & Services list.

Web SSL setup

When setting up your Web site for SSL, you must consider whether you wish to use the same certificate. This section assumes you're using the same certificate.

To enable SSL for the Web server:

1. Launch the Server Admin tool located in /Applications/Server, and authenticate as the administrator (**Figure 10.73**).

2. Choose the Web service from the Computers & Services list (**Figure 10.74**).

3. Click the Settings tab `Settings`, and then click the Modules tab `Modules`.
   Select the SSL module, and click the Save button `Save` (**Figure 10.75**).

4. Click the Sites tab, select your Web site, and click the edit button 🖊
   (**Figure 10.76**).
   An Editing dialog opens.

continues on next page

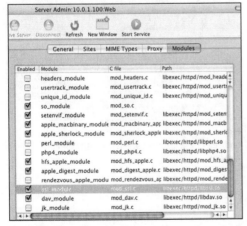

Figure 10.75 Select ssl_module on the Modules tab of the Settings tab.

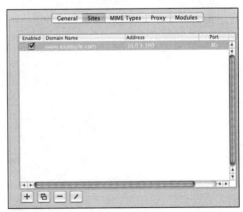

Figure 10.76 Choose the Sites tab, and select the Web site.

ENCRYPTION

5. Click the Security tab Security , and select the Enable Secure Sockets Layer check box (**Figure 10.77**.

Doing so enables SSL for this Web site.

6. Enter the passphrase from your Certificate Signing Request.

Click the ellipsis button ⋯ next to the SSL Log File field, and choose a file for the log (**Figure 10.78**).

7. Use the ellipses buttons ⋯ to open a navigation dialog and navigate to and select the following (**Figure 10.79**):

▲ Certificate file

▲ Private key file

▲ Certificate Authority file

8. Click the Save button Save .

Start the Web service using the Start Service button in the Server Admin Toolbar.

✔ Tip

■ To avoid having the Web server ask you repeatedly whether to restart, you can stop the Web service prior to this configuration and start it back up when you're finished.

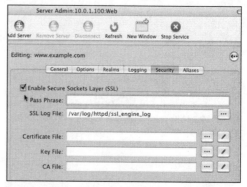

Figure 10.77 Click the Edit button and select the Security tab to reveal the Enable Secure Sockets Layer check box.

Figure 10.78 Enter your certificate passphrase, and choose a log file location.

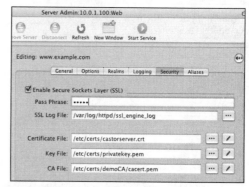

Figure 10.79 Use the ellipses buttons to navigate to and select the appropriate certificates and private key file.

Figure 10.80 Launch the Server Admin tool, and authenticate.

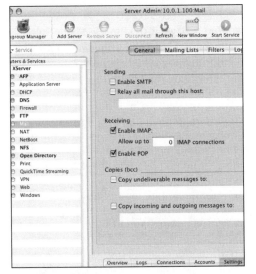

Figure 10.81 Select the Mail service from the Computers & Services list, and click the Settings tab.

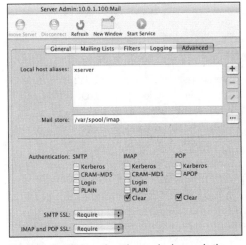

Figure 10.82 Clicking the Advanced tab reveals the SSL options for the Mail service.

Secure email

Another service that can take advantage of SSL is the Mail service in Mac OS X Server. There are many options for connecting to your mail server, but the mail itself is still transferred in clear text unless you enable SSL.

To enable SSL for mail:

1. Launch the Server Admin tool located in /Applications/Server, and authenticate as the administrator (**Figure 10.80**).

2. Choose the Mail service from the Computers & Services list, and click the Settings <kbd>Settings</kbd> tab (**Figure 10.81**).

3. Click the Advanced tab <kbd>Advanced</kbd> (**Figure 10.82**).

   To utilize SSL for both incoming (POP and IMAP) and outgoing (SMTP) mail from the pop-up menu next to the SMTP SSL and IMAP and POP SSL text, *choose one of the following methods* (**Figure 10.83**):

   Don't use doesn't use SSL at all.

   Use uses SSL if both the server and client mail application are configured properly.

   Require doesn't permit any unencrypted communications.

continues on next page

Figure 10.83 Choose a method to use SSL for incoming and outgoing mail.

ENCRYPTION

4. Click the Save button [Save] to save the changes.

Because of the way Cyrus and Postfix work with SSL, they have special requirements for enabling SSL.

5. Join the content of your server certificate and private key into one file, and move that file into both the /etc/postfix folder and the /var/imap folder (**Figure 10.84**).

Doing so allows Postfix and Cyrus to see the certificates. You could also make a symbolic link inside the postfix and cyrus directories pointing back to the /etc/certs directory.

Depending on how you copied the files, you may need to ensure that group mail has read access to the file server.pem inside the /var/imap directory.

6. Start the Mail service with the Start Service button [Start Service] in the Server Admin Toolbar.

✔ Tips

■ A symbolic link is like an alias. You create a symbolic link in the terminal with the command ln -s */path/to/ original/file /path/where/you/want/ the/link/to/go.*

■ You may want to stop the Mail service before you make any changes. Once all the changes are made and saved, you can restart the Mail service.

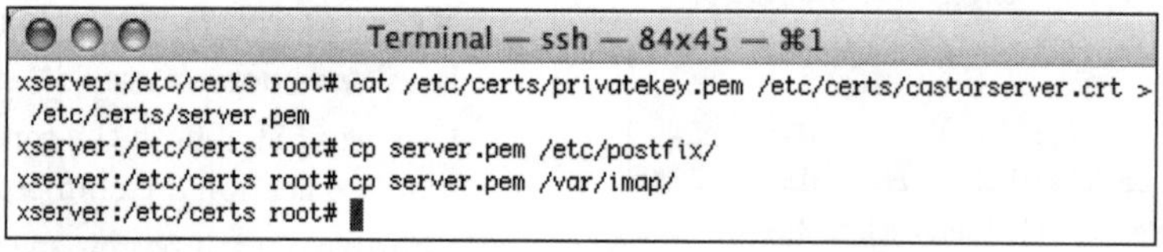

```
⬤ ⬤ ⬤          Terminal — ssh — 84x45 — ⌘1
xserver:/etc/certs root# cat /etc/certs/privatekey.pem /etc/certs/castorserver.crt >
 /etc/certs/server.pem
xserver:/etc/certs root# cp server.pem /etc/postfix/
xserver:/etc/certs root# cp server.pem /var/imap/
xserver:/etc/certs root# █
```

Figure 10.84 Create a new file with the combined contents of the private key and certificate.

Certificate Setup

If certificates don't work for one service, they're unlikely to work for another. Create your certificates, and test them with only one service before moving on.

The best service to test is the Web service, because failure won't cripple the server the way a failed test on Open Directory would. Because of the extra configuration steps involved in setting up SSL for mail, this also isn't a wise choice to test your first certificates.

If you're using self-signed certificates, and things aren't working, check DNS first and be sure your common name was correct in the certificate. If you feel there may have been errors, delete the certs folder inside /etc and start again. You can consult the /System/Library/OpenSSL/openssl.cnf file for more instructions.

ENCRYPTION

ssh keys

Another option when you're securing a server is to restrict who can access the server via ssh. Since ssh is turned on by default when you install and configure Mac OS X Server, a good password may not be enough to keep others out. You can use open-source software contained in Mac OS X Server to generate a key and then give the key to individuals who are permitted to log in via ssh.

To create an ssh key:

1. On a Mac OS X client computer, open the Terminal application located in /Applications/Utilities.

2. Enter the command ssh-keygen –t dsa, and press the Return key (**Figure 10.85**).

   This command generates the two files necessary for encryption using the type

dsa: id_dsa, which contains the private part of the key; and id_dsa.pub, which is the public part of the key.

3. You're asked to provide a filename, which you need not do.

   You're also asked for an optional passphrase, which you can add for even more security; it encrypts the private key with Triple-DES encryption.

4. Copy the id_dsa.pub file to your administrator's home folder on the server via any method you choose.

   If it doesn't already exist, create a folder called .ssh in the home folder on the server. Move the id_dsa.pub file into the .ssh/ folder, and rename it authorized_keys (**Figure 10.86**).

5. If you're remotely logged in to your server via ssh, log out.

continues on next page

```
● ● ●                 Terminal — bash — 100x45 — ⌘1
instructor:~ sregan$ ssh-keygen -t dsa
Generating public/private dsa key pair.
Enter file in which to save the key (/Users/sregan/.ssh/id_dsa):
Enter passphrase (empty for no passphrase):
Enter same passphrase again:
Your identification has been saved in /Users/sregan/.ssh/id_dsa.
Your public key has been saved in /Users/sregan/.ssh/id_dsa.pub.
The key fingerprint is:
b8:9a:ea:00:e4:c3:72:e0:52:b3:d1:12:a3:06:c8:00 sregan@instructor.local
instructor:~ sregan$ ▊
```

Figure 10.85 Create a public and private key using the ssh-keygen command.

```
● ● ●                  Terminal — ssh — 100
xserver:~ amie$ cd .ssh/
xserver:~/.ssh amie$ ls -la
total 8
drwxr-xr-x   3 amie  amie  102 29 Sep 01:19 .
drwxr-xr-x  18 amie  amie  612 29 Sep 00:54 ..
-rw-r--r--   1 amie  amie  613 29 Sep 01:17 id_dsa.pub
xserver:~/.ssh amie$ mv id_dsa.pub authorized_keys
xserver:~/.ssh amie$ ▊
```

Figure 10.86 Change to the .ssh directory on the server, and rename the id_dsa.pub file to authorized_keys.

ENCRYPTION

Attempt to log in again from the client computer that generated the keys, and enter the passphrase if you gave it one when requested (**Figure 10.87**).

If anyone else attempts to log in using your short name, they must also have the private key on their computer, which isn't likely.

✔ Tips

- Make a backup copy of the keys, and install them on all machines that may require other administrators to ssh into the server. You may also wish to copy the authorized_keys file from one administrator account to other accounts or to generate individual keys for each user.

- If you don't enter a passphrase when you generate a key, then when a user opens the Terminal and attempts to log in with the admin account, they won't be asked for a password or passphrase. This can be dangerous, because the client computer can access the server by opening the Terminal and typing in ssh admin_name@ ip_address.

- There are many other ways to make your server secure. These are just a few of the more popular ways, and most of them are also supported in the interface of Server Admin.

- Remember, security is never-ending. It all starts with a common-sense approach to guarding your passwords and data; then you work up from there.

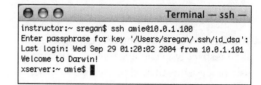

Figure 10.87 Attempt to log in from the client computer that generated the keys.

Running a
NetBoot Server

Setting the stage for Macworld Expo 1999, then-interim CEO Steve Jobs rolls out a huge rack of some 50 iMacs—all fully operational (one with a dead video card) and playing the same movie file without a single hard disk among them. However, Steve wasn't introducing the iMac, because it was old news by that time; he was introducing the first commercially available Mac OS X system. All the iMacs started up from a single copy of an operating system being hosted by a Mac OS X Server. That's right: One of the first public demonstrations of the future technology to drive all new Apple computers was a Mac OS X Server running the NetBoot service.

A server running the NetBoot service shares disk image files that contain the system software. Client computers, when instructed, automatically find and start up from any one of these disk images across the network. On a fast server with Gigabit Ethernet, more than 50 clients can start up from one disk image. Once booted, a client acts like any other computer that has been started from a local volume. Any changes made to the NetBoot client computer while running are lost upon restart, ensuring consistent system software across all your computers.

However, starting up over the network is only the tip of this iceberg. It's important to realize that an administrator can use the NetBoot service for a variety of time-saving administration techniques. For example, a special type of boot image, dubbed an *install image*, can be used to facilitate rapid mass deployment across your network. After you start up a computer, the install image can then automatically install onto the local volume all the software required for your system build. Another potential use for NetBoot is to create an image that contains all your favorite system mainte- nance and repair utilities. You can configure the ultimate administrator's toolkit, which is available to any computer on your network at any time—without having to carry a single CD or FireWire disk! The sky is the limit, because the NetBoot service is highly scalable. Each server can host 25 different images, and you can use as many

NetBoot servers as you need on your network. NetBoot servers will even automatically load-balance traffic for high-demand images if the same image is on multiple servers.

Upon further dissection, NetBoot is a combination of several different protocols, all working in concert to facilitate the remote booting of an operating system over the network. The services required to provide NetBoot include Dynamic Host Configuration Protocol (DHCP) to provide initial IP addressing information, Boot Service Discovery Protocol (BSDP) to advertise the location of the NetBoot server, Trivial File Transfer Protocol (TFTP) to deliver the initial boot files, and either Network File System (NFS) or Web services via HyperText Transfer Protocol (HTTP) to mount the system boot image. On the client side, the Open Firmware instructions built into the hardware of every modern Apple computer facilitate the NetBoot startup process.

Creating a Bootable Image

The Network Image Utility is one of the administrative tools included with Mac OS X Server. This application will serve as your main tool for creating boot and install images. Like all the other server administration tools, the Network Image Utility can run on your Mac OS X Server or any other computer running Mac OS X.

Before you start the Network Image Utility, you need to have access to a mountable volume that contains a copy of Mac OS X or Mac OS X Server. Your choices include the original installation CDs, disk image files created by Disk Utility, or any other available system volume besides the current startup disk.

The Network Image Utility essentially creates a copy of any system volume and then performs all the necessary modifications to make it a boot image. This gives you a great deal of freedom, because you can create boot images from any combination of system and application software you require.

To create a bootable image:

1. Choose /Applications/Server/Network Image Utility (**Figure 11.1**).

   The Network Image Utility opens.

2. Click the New Boot button in the Toolbar (**Figure 11.2**).

3. Under the General settings, fill out the Image Name, Image ID, and Description fields (**Figure 11.3**).

   Also choose the Default Language and sharing protocol.

   continues on next page

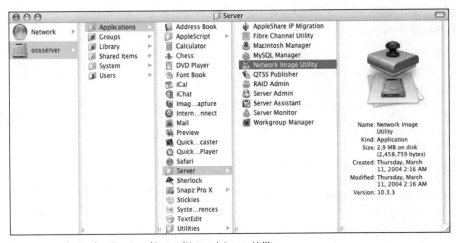

Figure 11.1 Choose /Applications/Server/Network Image Utility.

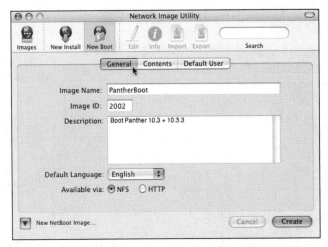

Figure 11.3 On the New Boot Image General tab, fill out the Image Name, Image ID, and Description fields.

Figure 11.2 Click the New Boot button.

CREATING A BOOTABLE IMAGE

4. Click the Contents tab (**Figure 11.4**).

From the Image Source pop-up menu, choose the volume, image file, or system CDs you wish to convert to a boot image.

5. If you're creating a boot image from Mac OS X install CDs, you need to define an administrator account. Click the Default User tab to specify the account settings (**Figure 11.5**).

Up to this point, you haven't created the image, so you can change almost anything before proceeding.

6. Click the Create button.

Continue through any other dialogs and license agreements that appear until the Save dialog box opens (**Figure 11.6**).

7. In the Save dialog box, choose the destination for the boot image.

If you're running the Network Image Utility on a server running the NetBoot service, it automatically chooses the NetBoot share point.

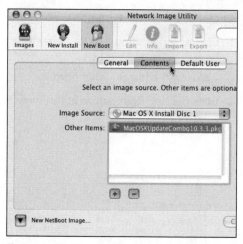

Figure 11.4 Click the New Boot Image Contents tab.

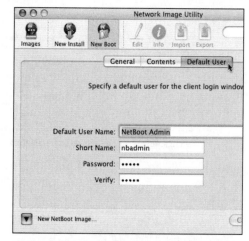

Figure 11.5 Click the New Boot Image Default User tab.

Figure 11.6 In the Save dialog, choose the destination for the boot image.

CREATING A BOOTABLE IMAGE

What's an Image ID?

The Image ID is a unique number of your choosing that client computers use to identify the boot image. If a boot image will be available from only one server, chose an ID number between 1 and 4095. However, if a boot image will be available from several servers, choose a number between 4096 and 65535.

If a client computer finds an image with the same ID on multiple servers, the client will assume they're identical image files and boot off the first image it receives from any of the servers containing that image. This has the effect of doing rudimentary load balancing between multiple NetBoot servers.

8. Click the Save button to initiate the creation process.

   Be patient; it may take a while to create the boot image. You can click the disclosure triangle in the bottom-left corner of the Network Image Utility to observe the creation process log (**Figure 11.7**).

✔ Tips

- Once boot images are created, they take up quite a bit of space. Be sure you have enough free space for your images prior to image creation.

- The freeware applications Carbon Copy Cloner and NetRestore Helper, created by Mike Bombich, can make boot images. Mike is an expert on disk imaging and system deployment, so a visit to his Web site is always a worthwhile trip: http://www.bombich.com/.

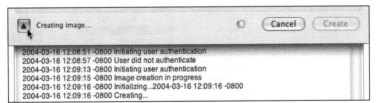

Figure 11.7 Click the disclosure triangle in the bottom-left corner of the Network Image Utility to see the New Boot Image process log.

Creating an Install Image

Install images are similar to boot images in that client computers can remotely boot from these image files if they're made available from a NetBoot server. However, when a client computer starts up from an install image, the user is presented with the Installer utility instead of the login window. At this point, the user experience is similar to booting up from the Mac OS X installer CDs: You step through a few simple windows in the Installer utility, and then the system from the install image is installed on the local computer's hard disk.

You can also create an automated install: In that case, having the client boot and choose an install image begins the process of installation. You never have to carry around an installation CD again.

To create an install image:

1. Choose /Applications/Server/Network Image Utility (**Figure 11.8**).
   The Network Image Utility opens.

2. Click the New Install button in the Toolbar (**Figure 11.9**).

3. Under the General settings, fill out the Image Name, Image ID, and Description fields, and choose the Default Language (**Figure 11.10**).

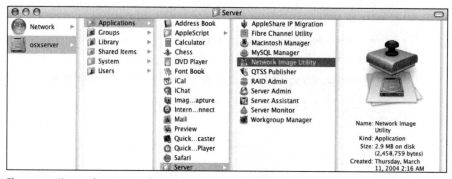

Figure 11.8 Choose /Applications/Server/Network Image Utility.

Figure 11.9 Click the New Install button.

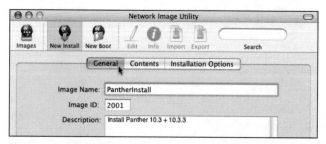

Figure 11.10 On the New Install Image General tab, fill out the Image Name, Image ID, and Description fields, and choose the Default Language.

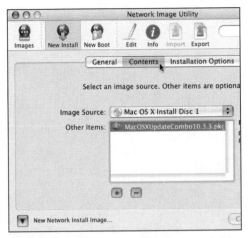

Figure 11.11 Click the New Install Image Contents tab.

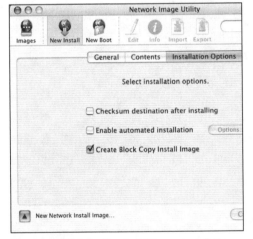

Figure 11.12 Click the New Install Image Installation Options tab.

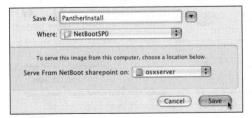

Figure 11.13 In the Save dialog, choose a destination for the install image.

4. Click the Contents tab (**Figure 11.11**).

From the Image Source pop-up menu, choose the volume, image file, or system CDs you wish to convert to an install image.

5. Click the Installation Options tab (**Figure 11.12**).

The options on this tab are discussed in the "Automating Installations" section later in this chapter.

Up to this point you haven't created the image, so you can change almost anything before proceeding.

6. Click the Create button.

Continue through any other dialogs and license agreements until the Save dialog box opens.

7. In the Save dialog box, choose the destination for the install image (**Figure 11.13**).

If you're running the Network Image Utility on a server running the NetBoot service, it will automatically choose the NetBoot share point.

continues on next page

CREATING AN INSTALL IMAGE

8. Click the Save button to initiate the creation process.

Be patient; it may take a while to create the install image. You can click the disclosure triangle in the bottom-left corner of the Network Image Utility to observe the creation process log (**Figure 11.14**).

✔ Tips

■ Once install images are created, they take up quite a bit of space. Be sure you have enough free space for your images prior to image creation.

■ If you select the "Checksum destination" option on the Installation Options tab, then after the install process completes, the computer will validate the installed files to ensure a complete copy. Checksum is a fancy way of ensuring that the image data maintains its integrity. That is, it makes sure all bits are exactly what they should be. This option increases the amount of time required to complete the installation.

■ A Block Copy Install Image uses asr (Apple Software Restore) to speed up the process of installation by doing a block-by-block copy.

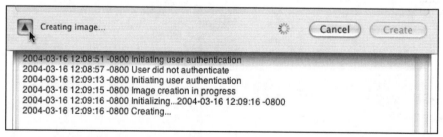

Figure 11.14 Click the disclosure triangle in the bottom-left corner of the Network Image Utility to see the New Install Image process log.

CREATING AN INSTALL IMAGE

Managing NetBoot Images

NetBoot images are really folders containing all the items necessary to facilitate booting over the network. These NetBoot image folders are easy to spot, because the name of the folder always ends with .nbi.

In order for a NetBoot server to use a NetBoot image, the image must reside in the NetBoot share points. The Server Admin utility automatically creates the NetBoot share points on every server volume in the Library/NetBoot/NetBootSP# folder. For each different server volume, the # is incremented by one, with the first column number being zero.

You can use the Network Image Utility as a centralized utility to manage your NetBoot images. The Network Image Utility maintains a list of all your NetBoot images for easy reference. If an image isn't in the Network Image Utility image list, you have to add it manually. More important, the Network Image Utility can be used to edit existing NetBoot images as your requirements change.

To add to the NetBoot image list:

1. Choose /Applications/Server/Network Image Utility (**Figure 11.15**).
   The Network Image Utility opens.

2. Click the Images button in the Toolbar (**Figure 11.16**).
   A list of images appears.

3. Select "Click here for image list options."
   A pop-up menu appears.

4. Select Add from the pop-up menu (**Figure 11.17**).
   Notice that you can also remove an image from the list.

continues on next page

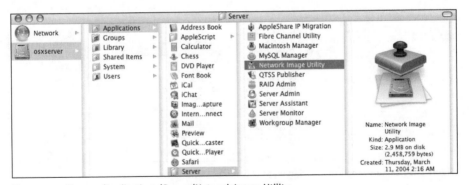

Figure 11.15 Choose /Applications/Server/Network Image Utility.

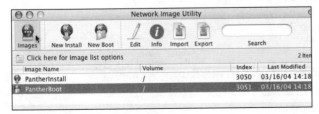

Figure 11.16 Click the Images button.

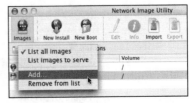

Figure 11.17 Select Add from the image options pop-up menu.

MANAGING NETBOOT IMAGES

5. A sheet drops down, allowing you to choose any .nbi folder on the local computer (**Figure 11.18**).

6. Click Select to add the NetBoot image to the image list.

✔ Tip

- Don't add .nbi folders from connected servers.

To modify a NetBoot image:

1. Choose /Applications/Server/Network Image Utility (**Figure 11.19**).
The Network Image Utility opens.

2. Click the Images button in the Toolbar. (**Figure 11.20**).
A list of images appears.

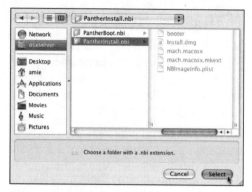

Figure 11.18 Choose any .nbi folder on the local computer.

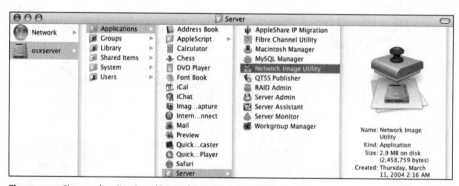

Figure 11.19 Choose /Applications/Server/Network Image Utility.

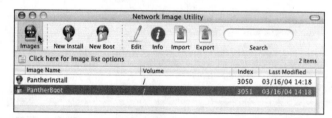

Figure 11.20 Click the Images button.

Figure 11.21 Authenticate as your server administrator.

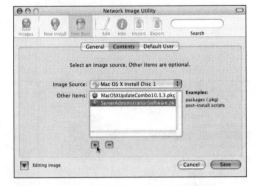

Figure 11.22 The Network Image Utility reverts to editing mode.

3. Select the image you want to modify from the images list.

Note that you can click the Info button to check the image settings before making any changes.

4. Click the Edit button in the Toolbar.

5. Authenticate as an administrative user (**Figure 11.21**).

6. The Network Image Utility reverts to editing mode (**Figure 11.22**).

You can make any changes to the image as if you were configuring a new image.

7. When you're done making changes, click the Save button.

Automating Installations

Setting up a NetBoot server with install images can be a huge time saver for administrators who need to install new software on many computers simultaneously. To save even more time, you can automate install images to facilitate a nearly hands-free approach.

To automate install images:

1. Choose /Applications/Server/Network Image Utility (**Figure 11.23**).

   The Network Image Utility opens.

2. *Do one of the following:*

   ▲ Click the New Install button in the Toolbar to configure a new install image (**Figure 11.24**).

   ▲ Click the Images button in the Toolbar, choose an existing install image from the list, and then click Edit (**Figure 11.25**).

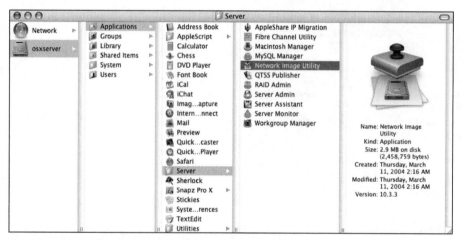

Figure 11.23 Choose /Applications/Server/Network Image Utility.

Figure 11.24 Click the New Install button.

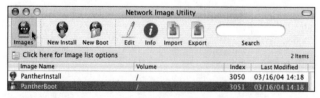

Figure 11.25 Select an existing image, and click Edit.

AUTOMATING INSTALLATIONS

3. Under the Installation Options tab of the Network Image Utility, select the "Enable automated installation" check box (**Figure 11.26**).

4. Click the Options button.

A drop-down sheet appears with a variety of Auto-Install Options to choose from (**Figure 11.27**).

5. Choose wisely, and then click the OK button.

6. *Do one of the following:*

▲ If this is a new install image, click the Create button to complete the image creation process.

▲ If you're editing an existing image, click the Save button to finalize your changes.

✔ Tip

■ For faster installation of Net Install images, select the Create Block Copy Install Image check box under the Installation Options tab (**Figure 11.28**).

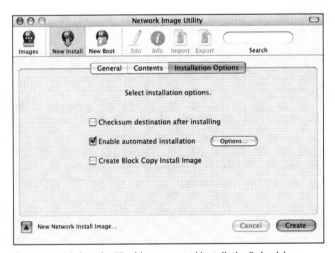

Figure 11.26 Select the "Enable automated installation" check box.

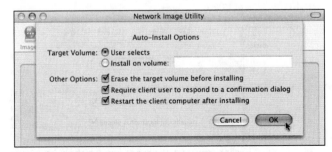

Figure 11.27 Select from the list of Auto-Install Options.

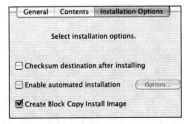

Figure 11.28 Choose the Block Copy check box.

Importing or Exporting Images

The Network Image Utility provides a unique function for moving images between Mac OS X Servers. The import and export functions can copy your NetBoot images among servers on the network. This copy service is facilitated through a Secure File Transfer Protocol (SFTP) connection.

To import a NetBoot image:

1. Choose /Applications/Server/Network Image Utility. (**Figure 11.29**).

   The Network Image Utility opens.

2. Click the Images button and then the Import button in the Toolbar (**Figure 11.30**).

   A dialog box drops down.

3. Enter the network address and the root user password of the server from which you're importing the image (**Figure 11.31**).

   Click the Connect button. A dialog sheet appears, listing .nbi files.

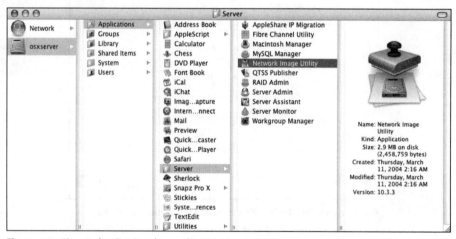

Figure 11.29 Choose /Applications/Server/Network Image Utility.

Figure 11.30 Click the Images button and then the Import button.

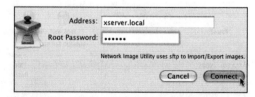

Figure 11.31 Enter the network address and the root user password of the server from which you're importing an image, and click Connect.

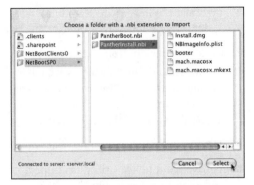

Figure 11.32 Select the .nbi files from the server.

Figure 11.33 In the Save dialog, choose the destination for the imported image.

4. Select the .nbi files from the server (**Figure 11.32**).

   Typically, the images are stored in /Library/NetBoot/NetBootSP#.

5. Click the Select button to continue.

   A Save dialog sheet appears.

6. In the Save dialog box, choose the destination for the imported image (**Figure 11.33**).

   If you're running the Network Image Utility on a server running the NetBoot service, it will automatically choose the NetBoot share point.

7. Click the Save button, and take a break.

   NetBoot images are typically over 1 GB in size and can take quite some time to transfer over a network connection, depending on the speed of that connection.

To export a NetBoot image:

1. Choose /Applications/Server/Network Image Utility (**Figure 11.34**).

   The Network Image Utility opens.

continues on next page

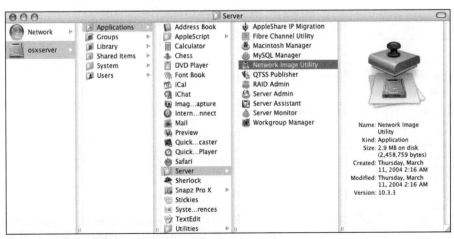

Figure 11.34 Choose /Applications/Server/Network Image Utility.

2. Click the Images button in the Toolbar.
A list of images appears.

3. From the image list, select the NetBoot image you wish to export (**Figure 11.35**).

4. Click the Export button in the Toolbar (**Figure 11.36**).
A dialog box drops down.

5. Enter the network address and the root user password of the server to which you're exporting the image.

Click the Connect button (**Figure 11.37**). A dialog sheet appears, showing volumes and folders.

6. Choose the destination location on the server to which you're exporting the image (**Figure 11.38**).

Typically, the images are stored in /Library/NetBoot/NetBootSP#.

7. Click the Select button, and take a break.
NetBoot images are typically over 1 GB in size and can take quite some time to transfer over a network connection, depending on the speed of that connection.

✔ Tip

- The Network Image Utility can import and export images to any Mac OS X computer, not just servers. All you have to do is turn on Remote Login in the Sharing System Preference pane and enable the root user in the NetInfo Manager utility.

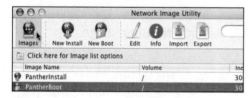

Figure 11.35 Select the image you want to export.

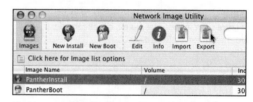

Figure 11.36 Click the Export button.

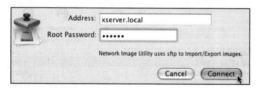

Figure 11.37 Enter the network address and root user password, and click Connect.

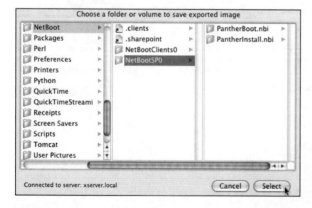

Figure 11.38 In the export location dialog, choose the destination location on the server to which you're exporting the image.

Enabling the NetBoot Service

Enabling the NetBoot server service requires a variety of server configuration changes. The Server Admin tool performs most of these changes for you, but you must enable a few related services in order for NetBoot to function properly. For example, the Apple Filing Protocol (AFP) and Network File System (NFS) services must be running in order for you to share your NetBoot images. The NFS service automatically starts when you configure NetBoot via the Server Admin utility, but you must enable the AFP service manually. (Refer to Chapter 5, "File Sharing," for instructions on how to enable the AFP service.)

A properly configured Dynamic Host Configuration Protocol (DHCP) server must also be available on your network in order for the NetBoot service to work. For many installations, the Mac OS X Server will act as the DHCP server. (Refer to Chapter 6, "Additional Network Configuration Options," for instructions on how to configure the DHCP service.)

What If I Already Have Another DHCP Server?

Many networks have another device that provides the DHCP service. You can still use the NetBoot service in these types of network environments. The DHCP service must be running on your NetBoot server because it's responsible for providing the Boot Service Discovery Protocol (BSDP), which allows client computers to automatically find it over the network. However, the DHCP service doesn't have to provide DHCP addresses. To prevent the DHCP service from providing configuration information to the network, unselect the Enable check box in the DHCP subnet settings (**Figure 11.39**).

Figure 11.39 Unselect the DHCP settings Enable check box.

To enable the NetBoot service:

1. Choose /Applications/Server/Server Admin (**Figure 11.40**).

   The Server Admin utility opens.

2. Connect and authenticate to the server you intend to configure (**Figure 11.41**).

3. Select NetBoot from the service list, click the Settings button, and then click the General tab (**Figure 11.42**).

4. From the network port list, select the check box(es) next to the network interface(s) on which you want to enable the NetBoot service (**Figure 11.43**).

5. From the volume list, select the check box(es) next to the volume(s) where you want to store the images and the client data (**Figure 11.44**).

   You must choose at least one volume for each column. The more volumes you enable, the more responsive your server will be.

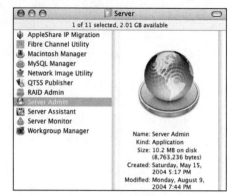

Figure 11.40 Choose /Applications/Server/Server Admin.

Figure 11.41 Authenticate as your server administrator.

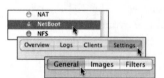

Figure 11.42 Select NetBoot from the service list, click the Settings tab, and then click the General tab.

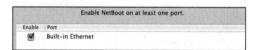

Figure 11.43 Make your network interface selection(s).

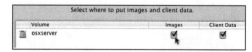

Figure 11.44 Select the volume storage options check box(es).

6. Click the Save button.

7. Click the Start Service button in the Server Admin Toolbar (**Figure 11.45**).

The Server Admin utility will configure the NetBoot server, share points, and user accounts.

8. Populate any NetBoot share points you have with .nbi image files.

Refer to the earlier tasks on image creation and image management for more details.

9. Click the Images button (**Figure 11.46**).

10. In the Enable column, select the check boxes next to the images you want to make available to NetBoot (**Figure 11.47**).

11. Click the Save button.

✔ Tips

■ You may have to restart the Mac OS X Server in order for NetBoot to function properly.

■ If you're experiencing problems with the NetBoot service, then check the log file for error messages. You can view the NetBoot log file in the Server Admin utility by selecting NetBoot from the service list and then clicking the Logs button (**Figure 11.48**).

■ To NetBoot across network subnets, check out the NetBoot Across Subnets utility created by Mike Bombich (http://www.bombich.com).

Figure 11.45 Click the Start Service button.

Figure 11.46 Click the Images button.

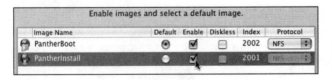

Figure 11.47 In the Enable column, select the check boxes next to the images you want to make available to NetBoot.

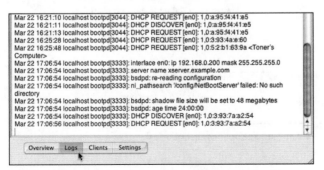

Figure 11.48 To view the NetBoot log file, select NetBoot from the service list and then click the Logs button.

ENABLING THE NETBOOT SERVICE

Storing Client Images

When any client computer boots from your NetBoot server, a client image is created on your server for temporary storage. This image is used to save any changes the user makes from the client computer while it's running. The client images are deleted as soon as the client computer shuts down or restarts. On a busy NetBoot server, a huge amount of data is written to and copied from these client images. In such cases, you can improve performance by moving the client image storage location to a different disk on your NetBoot server.

Figure 11.49 Choose /Applications/Server/ Server Admin.

To configure the client image location:

1. Choose /Applications/Server/Server Admin (**Figure 11.49**).

   The Server Admin utility opens.

2. Connect and authenticate to the server you intend to configure (**Figure 11.50**).

3. Select NetBoot from the service list, click the Settings button, and then click the General tab (**Figure 11.51**).

4. From the volume list, select the check box(es) in the Client Data column next to the volume(s) (**Figure 11.52**).

   The more volumes you enable, the more responsive your server will be.

5. Click the Save button.

Figure 11.50 Authenticate as your server administrator.

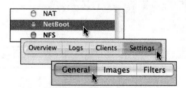

Figure 11.51 Select NetBoot from the service list, click the Settings button, and then click the General tab.

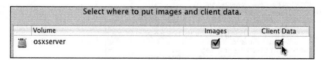

Figure 11.52 Select the volume storage options check box(es).

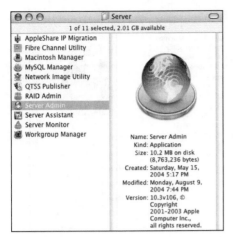

Figure 11.53 Choose /Applications/Server/
Server Admin.

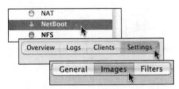

Figure 11.54 Authenticate as your server administrator.

Figure 11.55 Select NetBoot from the
service list, click the Settings button,
and then click the Images tab.

Choosing the Default Image

You can force a Macintosh computer to
search for a NetBoot server at startup by
holding the N key when you turn on the
computer. When you start a computer in
this manner, it always chooses the default
image on the NetBoot server. There can
be only one default image among all your
NetBoot servers, so choose wisely.

To choose the default image:

1. Choose /Applications/Server/Server
   Admin (**Figure 11.53**).
   The Server Admin utility opens.

2. Connect and authenticate to the server
   you intend to configure (**Figure 11.54**).

3. Select NetBoot from the service list, click
   the Settings button, and then click the
   Images tab (**Figure 11.55**).

4. In the Default column, select the radio
   button next to the image you want
   to make the default NetBoot image
   (**Figure 11.56**).

5. Click the Save button.

✔ Tip

■ It's a really, really bad idea to configure
  an automated install image as your default
  NetBoot image. An unsuspecting user
  could inadvertently NetBoot a client and
  end up accidentally erasing important
  data files on the computer's system disk.

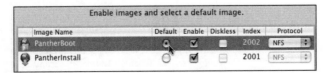

Figure 11.56 In the Default column, select the radio button next to the
image you want to make the default NetBoot image.

Enabling Diskless Mode

To increase NetBoot system performance, Mac OS X client computers store temporary cache and swap files, sometimes called *shadow files*, on their local hard disks. This performance-enhancing feature of NetBoot can be considered a limitation, because it doesn't allow for a truly diskless client computer. This feature also prevents you from using certain install and repair utilities on the local client's hard disk when you're using a NetBoot server. To remedy these situations, an optional diskless image mode disables shadow files.

To enable diskless mode:

1. Choose /Applications/Server/Server Admin (**Figure 11.57**).

   The Server Admin utility opens.

2. Connect and authenticate to the server you intend to configure (**Figure 11.58**).

3. Select NetBoot from the service list, click the Settings button, and then click the Images tab (**Figure 11.59**).

4. In the Diskless column, select the check box(es) next to the boot image(s) (**Figure 11.60**).

5. Click the Save button.

✔ Tip

- You can't enable diskless operation for install images because they're specifically designed to install data on the client's local hard disk.

Figure 11.57 Choose /Applications/Server/ Server Admin.

Figure 11.58 Authenticate as your server administrator.

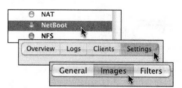

Figure 11.59 Select NetBoot from the service list, click the Settings button, and then click the Images tab.

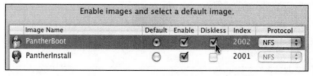

Figure 11.60 In the Diskless column, select the check box(es) next to the boot image(s).

Figure 11.61 Choose /Applications/Server/
Server Admin.

Figure 11.62 Authenticate as your server administrator.

Figure 11.63 Select NetBoot from the
service list, click the Settings button,
and then click the Filters tab.

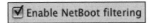

Figure 11.64 Select the "Enable
NetBoot filtering" check box.

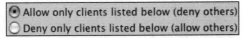

Figure 11.65 Select the appropriate NetBoot filtering
Allow or Deny radio button.

Enabling NetBoot Filtering

You can control client access to your NetBoot
server by enabling the NetBoot filter. The
NetBoot filter can be configured to allow or
deny specific client computers based on
their Ethernet address. This is useful when
you have computers that should *never* be
NetBooted, such as other servers; or computers that you *always* want NetBooted,
such as lab computers.

To enable NetBoot filtering:

1. Choose /Applications/Server/Server
   Admin (**Figure 11.61**).
   The Server Admin utility opens.

2. Connect and authenticate to the server
   you intend to configure (**Figure 11.62**).

3. Select NetBoot from the service list, click
   the Settings button, and then click the
   Filters tab (**Figure 11.63**).

4. Select the "Enable NetBoot filtering"
   check box (**Figure 11.64**).

5. Choose the appropriate radio button to
   create the allow or deny filter list
   (**Figure 11.65**).

continues on next page

6. *Do one of the following:*

▲ Click the Add button (**Figure 11.66**). A dialog sheet appears, allowing you to manually add a client's Ethernet address.

▲ Enter a client's host name, and then click the Spyglass button. The Server Admin utility queries the client for its Ethernet address. Click the Add button to add this address to your list (**Figure 11.67**).

7. Click the Save button.

✔ Tips

■ Click the Delete button to remove a client from the filter list (**Figure 11.68**).

■ You can view a list of all clients that have ever NetBooted for your server in the Server Admin utility by selecting NetBoot from the service list and then clicking the Clients button (**Figure 11.69**).

Figure 11.66 Click the Add button to manually add a client's Ethernet address.

Figure 11.67 Enter a client's host name and click the Spyglass button to have the Server Admin utility query the client for its Ethernet address. Then click the Add button to add the address to your list.

Figure 11.68 Click the Delete button to remove a client from the filter list.

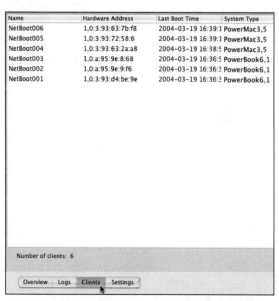

Name	Hardware Address	Last Boot Time	System Type
NetBoot006	1,0:3:93:63:7b:f8	2004-03-19 16:39:1	PowerMac3,5
NetBoot005	1,0:3:93:72:58:6	2004-03-19 16:39:1	PowerMac3,5
NetBoot004	1,0:3:93:63:2a:a8	2004-03-19 16:38:5	PowerMac3,5
NetBoot003	1,0:a:95:9e:8:68	2004-03-19 16:36:5	PowerBook6,1
NetBoot002	1,0:a:95:9e:9:f6	2004-03-19 16:36:3	PowerBook6,1
NetBoot001	1,0:3:93:d4:be:9e	2004-03-19 16:36:3	PowerBook6,1

Number of clients: 6

Overview   Logs   Clients   Settings

Figure 11.69 You can view a list of NetBoot clients in the Server Admin utility by selecting NetBoot from the service list and then clicking the Clients button.

Figure 11.70 Look for the NetBoot startup globe icon.

NetBooting the Client

After all the hard work involved in setting up your NetBoot server, it's time to test that sucker! There are two primary methods for configuring client computers to boot from your NetBoot server: You can select NetBoot at client startup or from the Startup Disk system preference pane. Selecting NetBoot at startup is only temporary, whereas setting the NetBoot option from Startup Disk is permanent. Also, selecting NetBoot on a lab full of computers allows that entire lab to boot off one image on your server.

To select NetBoot at startup:

1. *Do one of the following:*
   - ▲ Hold down the N key at startup.
   - ▲ Hold down the Option key at startup to invoke the Startup Manager. Select the NetBoot Globe icon, and click the Continue button.

2. Verify that you're booting from your NetBoot server by observing the Globe icon against the gray background (**Figure 11.70**).

NetBoot Client Compatibility

Mac OS X Server version 10.3 and higher only support NetBoot version 2. Apple computers with Firmware version 4.1.7 or newer are compatible with NetBoot version 2. Computers capable of using Firmware 4.1.7 or later include:

- ◆ G4 and G5 computers of any kind, except the very first G4 PowerMac
- ◆ All iBooks
- ◆ Slot-loading iMacs
- ◆ PowerBook G3s with FireWire

To select NetBoot from Startup Disk:

1. Open the System Preferences by choosing Apple Menu > System Preferences.

2. Click the Startup Disk icon (**Figure 11.71**).

   After a few moments, your individual NetBoot images appear in the Startup Disk window.

3. In the Startup Disk window, select the desired image (**Figure 11.72**).

4. Click the Restart button.

Figure 11.71 Click the Startup Disk icon.

✔ Tips

■ NetBoot clients require 128 MB of RAM and 100Base-T Ethernet connectivity. As always, configurations with more RAM or higher-speed network connectivity will have better performance.

■ You can't NetBoot over a wireless network or modem connection.

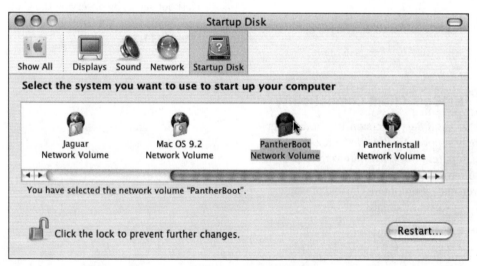

Figure 11.72 In the Startup Disk selection dialog, select the desired image.

QuickTime
Streaming Server

Apple has always been at the forefront when dealing with audio and video, so it should come as no surprise that the tool used to deploy audio and video in Mac OS X Server is capable of some neat tricks. Although it's part of Mac OS X Server, the QuickTime Streaming Server (QTSS) is a separate package that can be installed on Mac OS X Client. It comes with a different name—Darwin Streaming Server—but it's exactly the same underneath. It can also be installed on other operating systems.

QTSS is an audio and video deployment tool capable of streaming bits and bytes of your favorite home movie or child's recorded class recital over the Internet for all to hear. Some see QTSS as a distraction from the real business of Mac OS X Server, but others see it as an opportunity to provide training, information, and other verbal and visual assistance to thousands of users across the globe. Businesses utilize QTSS to stream safety videos to employee desktop computers, saving time and reducing the cost of employee training.

Couple QTSS with QuickTime Broadcaster (QTB), and you have a live streaming solution for your business. And whereas lesser streaming solutions from other companies make you pay licensing fees, Apple's Darwin Streaming Server is free to install on Mac OS X Client; whether you use that or QTSS on Mac OS X Server, you pay no licensing fees of any kind no matter how many users watch and/or listen to your content.

The last piece of this trio is the QTSS Publisher (Apple even shortened the name of this tool), which permits you to manage your playlists, MP3 files, and the like.

These are possibly the finest hidden gems in Mac OS X Server. They're relatively easy to configure, there are no license fees to worry about (always read the license agreement when you install, to make sure Apple hasn't changed its mind), and even when used for business meetings, they're fun! With these three tools properly configured, you can sit back and concentrate on creating the best content, as opposed to figuring out how to get streaming to work.

Understanding Bits and Bytes

Before you can begin streaming audio or video, you must do a little math.

Computer 101

In computer speak, files are measured in *bytes*. Generally, audio and video files tend to be large.

When you connect to the Internet with your computer, you do so at a given speed. The speed is measured in bits, *not* bytes. For example, a modem connection can try for 56 kilobits per second but usually falls short of that (near or less than 46 Kbps). A connection through your cable company can be as fast as 3.5 megabits per second (Mbps), although most such connections top out at 1 Mbps.

Video being streamed from your server must be properly prepared so users from all types of connections, from slow (modem) to fast (cable or better), can see it properly.

If you want to stream a 10 MB file to a user with a 1 Mbps connection, about how long will it take (**Table 12.1**)? It will take about 1.4 minutes for a 10 MB file to be downloaded from your server to a computer over the Internet using a 1 Mbps connection. Imagine how long it would take over a modem connection!

Next, you must ask how fast your connection to the network is. If you do some more math, you can figure that if 11 people, each with a 1 Mbps connection, all download the same file at the same time, the total bandwidth your server must contend with is near 923 Mbps (10 MB file x 11 users)! Most newer Macintosh computers contain Ethernet cards

that can transfer data at 1 gigabit per second (Gbps). You can see that 1000 megabits (1 gigabit) minus 923 Mb is 67 Mb. The 11 people have almost saturated a gigabit Ethernet connection, and it isn't likely that you have a gigabit connection from your server to the Internet.

This example illustrates the problem often faced by administrators using QTSS: quality versus quantity. You want a nice clear video that isn't the size of a postage stamp, and you want several people to view it at the same time. You should now realize that doing this has serious implications on your bandwidth.

✔ Tip

■ One note of caution: You should only stream content that you own. Streaming content that is copyrighted will probably violate copyright rules. Respect the rights of the owners of audio and video copyrighted material.

Table 12.1

Bits and Bytes

FILE TYPE	SIZE	MATH	RESULT
Megabytes	10	Multiply by 1024	10240
Kilobytes	10240	Multiply by 1024	10485760
Bytes	10485760	Multiply by 8	83886080
Bits	83886080	Divide by 1000	83886.08
Kilobits	83886.08	Divide by 1000	83.88608
Megabits	83.88608	Divide by 60	1.39

Hinting files for streaming

This section briefly discusses the process of *hinting*, which allows a video file to be prepared to be streamed over a network. For example, a video may be encoded at three different speeds: one for modem connections, one for cable and DSL, and one for local Ethernet (LAN) connections. When this is done, three separate files of the same video exist. QTSS can present a single file to the person connecting, and that person's

QuickTime Connection Speed settings determine which file they will receive (**Figure 12.1**). Hinting is basically the addition of an extra track that allows this to happen.

You can hint with a tool available from Apple called MakeRefMovie; you can also do it with iMovie. MakeRefMovie is a bit more involved.

To hint an iMovie file:

1. Open iMovie on any Mac OS X Client.

   It's generally located in the /Applications directory, but you as the administrator of your Mac OS X Client computer could have moved it anywhere on your system.

2. Open your last iMovie project, and choose File > Share (**Figure 12.2**).

   The Share dialog appears.

3. Click the QuickTime button, and choose Web Streaming from the Compress pop-up menu (**Figure 12.3**).

   Once you save the file, it's automatically hinted (that is, the hint track is added) for use with the QTSS. Chances are, however, that you'll be responsible for streaming the content, not creating it.

✔ Tip

- You can also use QuickTime Player Pro to export a movie as a hinted movie.

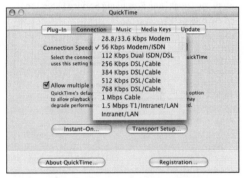

Figure 12.1 You set the QuickTime connection speed the same way on both Mac OS X Client and Mac OS X Server.

Figure 12.2 Choosing File > Share is the first step to hinting a movie.

Figure 12.3 Clicking the QuickTime button and selecting the compression for Web Streaming prepares the iMovie for streaming.

Setting Up the QuickTime Streaming Server

The first thing you'll need to do when setting up the QTSS is make a few key decisions. These decisions can always be changed later, but you should prepare for growth. A Mac OS X Server running other services like DHCP and file sharing and acting as an Open Directory master isn't the best possible solution for a full-blown QTSS setup. When you're seriously considering multiple connections and high-quality video, you must decide if a separate Xserve running Mac OS X Server with as much RAM as you can afford is within your budget.

Taking a tour of the QTSS setup is easy; you can do so using the Server Admin tool and a Web browser. After you've launched Server Admin and authenticated as an administrator, choose the QuickTime Streaming service from the Computers & Services list. From there, you have access to the following settings under the Settings tab:

◆ The General tab contains the settings for the directory containing the movies, the maximum number of connections, and the maximum throughput. When you're setting up a QTSS on the Internet, it's critical to limit the number of connections and the throughput during your testing phase to just two or three connections, because the default settings could bring your server to its knees (**Figure 12.4**).

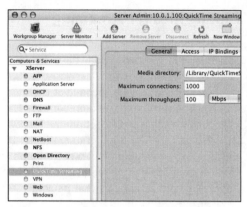

Figure 12.4 Click the General tab under the Settings tab of the QuickTime Streaming Service using the Server Admin tool.

Figure 12.5 The Access tab shows the password options.

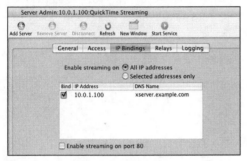

Figure 12.6 The IP Bindings tab permits the binding of the QTSS to more than one IP address.

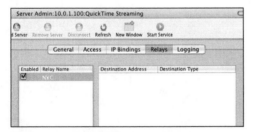

Figure 12.7 The Relays tab shows the addition of relays.

Figure 12.8 Error and access logging are enabled on the Logging tab.

◆ The Access tab lets you administer the QTSS via a Web page by allowing you to set a user name and password for that particular type of administration. The same is true for accepting incoming broadcasts to your server. You can also place streaming folders in every user's Sites folder and set an MP3 broadcast password, restricting access to your MP3 playlists (**Figure 12.5**).

◆ The IP Bindings tab allows streaming to take place over several IP addresses and Ethernet cards if you choose. You can also choose to stream over port 80, allowing users to access your QTSS over port 80, which is generally used for serving up Web sites (**Figure 12.6**).

◆ The Relays tab lets you enable relays. Relays allow the QTSS to pass its stream to others QTSS computers, thus reducing the overall load on the originating server. The relay servers must be configured to allow incoming broadcasts (**Figure 12.7**).

◆ The Logging tab lets you enable both the Access and Error logs (**Figure 12.8**).

Once you understand the settings, you can perform the proper configuration to enable the QTSS.

To enable a QTSS:

1. Launch the Server Admin tool from within /Applications/Server, and authenticate as the administrator (**Figure 12.9**).

2. Select the QuickTime Streaming service from the Computers & Services list. Notice the five tabs at the bottom of the screen (**Figure 12.10**):

   Overview shows whether the service is running, the current number of connections, and the current throughput.

   Log displays both the Error and Access logs, allowing you to monitor your QTSS (**Figure 12.11**).

   Connections shows the status of both active relays and connected users (**Figure 12.12**).

Figure 12.9 Launch the Server Admin tool, and authenticate.

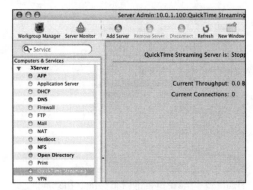

Figure 12.10 The QuickTime Streaming service Overview tab shows the status of the QTSS.

Figure 12.11 The QuickTime Streaming service Logs tab shows the Access and Error logs.

Figure 12.12 Choose the type of connections to be listed using the Connections tab.

Figure 12.13 Choose the type of graph to be viewed using the Graphs tab.

Figure 12.14 The General Settings tab shows the path to the movies and the settings for maximum number of connections and maximum throughput.

Figure 12.15 Check the path for the hinted movies to ensure it's correct.

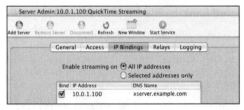

Figure 12.16 Check the IP Bindings to be sure the correct IP address is being used for streaming.

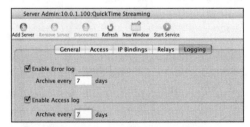

Figure 12.17 Enable logging to help troubleshoot and monitor your streaming.

Graphs indicates both the throughput and the number of active users (**Figure 12.13**).

Settings displays five more tabs, discussed earlier (**Figure 12.14**).

3. Select the Settings tab and then the General tab.

Be sure the movies to be streamed are in the correct directory listed in the Media Directory field (**Figure 12.15**).

4. Select the IP Bindings tab, and be sure streaming is permitted on the IP address you wish to use (**Figure 12.16**).

5. Select the Logging tab to enable both the Access and Error logs for later trouble-shooting and analysis (**Figure 12.17**).

6. Click the Start Service button ⬚ in the Toolbar to start the QuickTime Streaming Server service.

7. View your QTSS's status by clicking the Overview tab (**Figure 12.18**).

✔ Tips

- You can perform QTSS administration two ways: through Server Admin and via Web-based administration. You should learn both ways prior to implementing your QTSS.

- Before you can begin telling others about your QTSS, you must create at least one playlist.

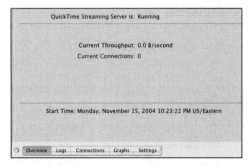

Figure 12.18 Click the Overview tab to view the QTSS's status.

Web-Based Administration

Another way to administer QTSS is through the use of a browser, such as Safari. Server Admin can be fine for the task of administration, but if you've installed the Darwin Streaming Server on another operating system or Mac OS X Client, you should be aware of Web-based administration.

When Web-based administration is enabled, you have access to the same settings found in Server Admin and QuickTime Streaming Server Publisher combined.

To enable Web-based administration:

1. Launch the Server Admin tool from within /Applications/Server, and authenticate as the administrator (**Figure 12.19**).

2. Click the QuickTime Streaming service, click the Settings tab, and then click the Access tab (**Figure 12.20**).

3. Select the "Enable web-based administration" check box.

    A dialog drops down in which you can set a user name and password for this task (**Figure 12.21**). You may need to click the Set Password button [Set Password...] if this has been done once before.

4. Click the Save button [Save] to save your changes.

5. For security reasons discussed later in this chapter, launch a Web browser of your choice on the server, type in the IP address of the server followed by a colon and the number 1220, and press the Return key (**Figure 12.22**).

    This represents the port number over which the QTSS Web-based administration tool runs.

Figure 12.19 Launch the Server Admin tool, and authenticate.

Figure 12.20 Select the Access tab to locate the Web administration options.

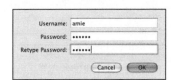

Figure 12.21 Selecting the "Enable web-based administration" check box brings up a user and password dialog.

Figure 12.22 Use a Web browser to type in the address and port number of a QTSS.

Figure 12.23 In the initial dialog box of the QTSS Web-based administration tool, enter the user name and password.

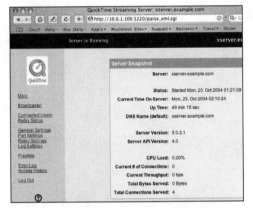

Figure 12.24 The QTSS Web-based administration tool displays options similar to those of Server Admin.

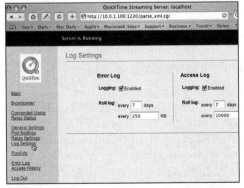

Figure 12.25 View the log files using the Web-based administration tool.

6. In the initial Web page that appears, enter the user name and password that you entered in step 3, and click the Log In button (**Figure 12.23**).

You can now manage the QTSS using the Web-based administration tool (**Figures 12.24**).

7. Click any link on the left to view various parameters of your QTSS (**Figure 12.25**).

Once you're finished changing settings, always log back out so you see the initial login screen (**Figure 12.26**).

✔ Tip

- It's not a good idea to use the same user name and password as your server administrator when you set up Web-based QTSS administration. The Web-based administration tool doesn't currently store the password in the same secure format as other Mac OS X and Mac OS X Server passwords.

Figure 12.26 Always log out of the Web-based administration tool when you're finished.

Secure Web-Based Administration

If you plan to use Web-based administration, you should consider implementing Secure Sockets Layer (SSL) using either your own self-signed certificate or one you've purchased. Doing so prevents others from gathering information about your QTSS when you use Web-based administration. You can learn more about SSL in Chapter 10, "Security" (**Figure 12.27**).

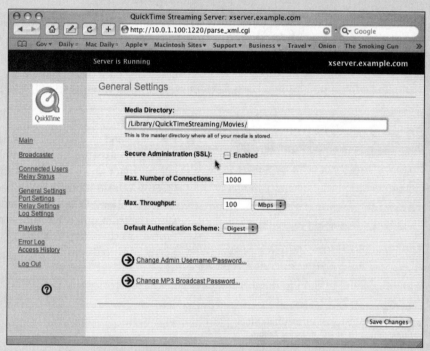

Figure 12.27 Enabling the SSL check box reduces the security risk associated with Web-based administration.

More User Names and Passwords

You must enter new user names and passwords with the QTSS Web-based administration tool and the Accept Incoming Broadcasts option because the QTSS isn't yet integrated with Apple's Open Directory structure. Since QTSS is built similar to the Open Source Apache Web server in the way it deals with users and groups, it has both users and groups files that contain the QTSS administrator entered in the previous task (for Web-based administration). These files can also be used to restrict access to your QTSS. The files are located in /Library/QuickTimeStreaming/Config and are called qtusers and qtgroups.

Figure 12.28 Launch the QTSS Publisher tool, and authenticate.

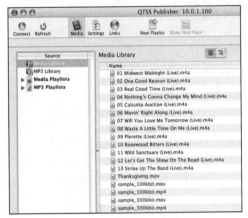

Figure 12.29 Drag your hinted video files into the Media Library window.

Creating Playlists

Playlists are collections of audio or video files that you wish to stream. Mac OS X Server includes a few sample files in the /Library/QuickTimeStreaming/Movies directory that you can work with prior to placing your own media files there.

There are two ways to add a playlist: one through the Web-based administration tool, and one using the QTSS Publisher tool. This section examines the QTSS Publisher tool.

You can create two types of playlists:

MP3 playlists are audio, based on MP3, and contain no video.

Media playlists contain video as well as different formats of audio files.

Before you can create playlists, video files must be hinted. Advanced Audio Coding files (AAC; used by iTunes) are considered video files and not MP3 files. MP3 files are also used by iTunes; you can encode your music as either AAC or MP3 with iTunes.

To create a video playlist:

1. Place your hinted video file(s) and MP3 file(s) in the /Library/QuickTimeStreaming/Movies directory on your server.

2. Launch the QTSS Publisher tool from /Applications/Server, and authenticate as the QTSS administrator (**Figure 12.28**).

3. Click the Media Library icon, and open the /Library/QuickTimeStreaming/Movies directory on your server.

   Drag your hinted video files into the Media Library window (**Figure 12.29**). This window shows all your media files and permits you to sort them based on the column criteria.

continues on next page

CREATING PLAYLISTS

4. Click the New Playlist button 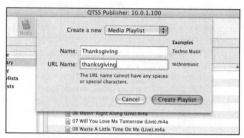 in the Toolbar.

In the resulting dialog, choose Media Playlist as the type of playlist you wish to create, enter the name of the playlist, and click the Create Playlist button (**Figure 12.30**).

5. Drag the media file(s) you want to add to the playlist from the media files pane to the Playlist Contents pane (**Figure 12.31**). Click the Apply button.

6. Choose to change the name and the Play Mode under the Playlist tab (**Figure 12.32**).

7. Click the Apply button to save any changes, and then click the Start button to start the broadcast (**Figure 12.33**).

Figure 12.30 Create a new media playlist by clicking the New Playlist button and entering the appropriate data.

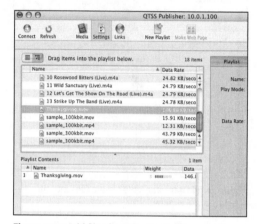

Figure 12.31 Add files from the Media Library to the new playlist.

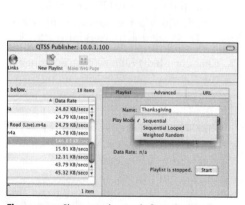

Figure 12.32 Choose a play mode from the list of options under the Playlist tab.

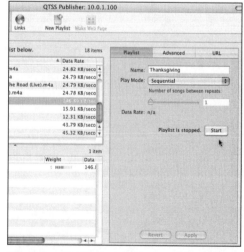

Figure 12.33 Click the Apply button to save the changes, and then click the Start button to start the stream.

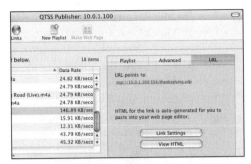

Figure 12.34 Viewing the URL link under the URL tab shows the exact path of the stream.

8. While you're still working on your server, click the URL tab (**Figure 12.34**).

   Click the link under "URL points to" to launch the QuickTime Player to test the media stream (**Figure 12.35**).

   After a successful test from your server to your server (to reduce troubleshooting to mostly non-networking issues, since the stream and the request are on the same computer), attempt to connect to the stream from another computer connected to the same network.

✔ Tip

■ It's possible to change the ending part of the URL when creating the playlist so others who have to access the playlist will reduce the chance they will make a typographical error when entering the playlist.

Figure 12.35 Test the video stream from a Mac OS X Client using QuickTime Player.

CREATING PLAYLISTS

Creating weighted random AAC playlists

Audio files come in various formats. One format used by iTunes is AAC. QTSS can't stream these files as audio files; instead, it streams them as video files that have no video!

When you're creating files for playlists, you can rate the media in the playlist from 1 to 10, with 10 being the highest rating a file can get. Rating media files in the Playlist Contents window lets media be streamed to the user in weighted random order (not in sequential order), based in part on the rating given each media file.

To create a weighted random AAC playlist:

1. Launch the QTSS Publisher tool from /Applications/Server, and authenticate as the QTSS administrator (**Figure 12.36**).

2. Click the Media Library icon, open the /Library/QuickTimeStreaming/Movies directory on your server, and drag your AAC audio files into the Media Library window (**Figure 12.37**).

   This window shows all your media files and permits you to sort them based on the column criteria.

3. Click the New Playlist button 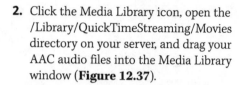 in the Toolbar.

   In the resulting dialog, choose Media Playlist as the type of playlist you wish to create, and click the Create Playlist button (**Figure 12.38**).

4. Drag the AAC file(s) (which appear as .m4a files) you want to be added to the playlist from the media files pane to the Playlist Contents pane (**Figure 12.39**). Click the Apply button.

Figure 12.36 Launch the QTSS Publisher tool, and authenticate.

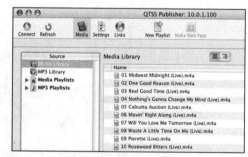

Figure 12.37 Clicking on the Media Library shows that all AAC files are now in the Library.

Figure 12.38 Add a new media playlist.

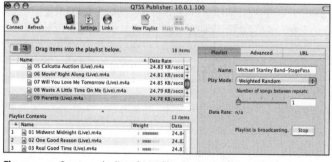

Figure 12.39 Create a playlist of AAC files, and set the name.

5. In the Playlist Contents pane, select each file and drag the Weight bars left or right to indicate a higher or lower preference for a file (**Figure 12.40**).

You're rating your AAC files as you would in iTunes.

6. Select Weighted Random from the Play Mode pop-up menu, click the Apply button, and click the Start button to start the broadcast (**Figure 12.41**).

7. While you're still working on your server, click the URL tab, and click the link under "URL points to" to launch the QuickTime Player to test the media stream (**Figure 12.42**).

The QTSS Publisher displays an overview of the Media Library and the playlist with the weighted media files (**Figure 12.43**).

After a successful test from your server to your server (to reduce troubleshooting to mostly non-networking issues, since the stream and the request are on the same computer), attempt to connect to the stream from another computer connected to the same network.

✔ Tips

■ It's possible to change the ending part of the URL when creating the playlist so others who have to access the playlist will reduce the chance they will make a typographical error when entering the playlist.

■ You create MP3 playlists just like you do an AAC playlist. However, when choosing the type of playlist to create, choose MP3 Playlist instead of Media Playlist.

Figure 12.40 Drag the Weight bars right or left to rate the media files.

Figure 12.41 Choose Weighted Random from the Play Mode pop-up menu for this playlist.

Figure 12.42 Locate the URL link under the URL tab to listen to this stream.

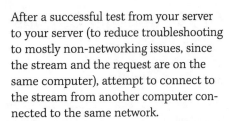

Figure 12.43 The QTSS Publisher displays an overview of the Media Library and the playlist with the weighted media files.

CREATING PLAYLISTS

QTSS Publisher Options

When you're using QTSS Publisher to create playlists, you have a few options as to how others receive the streams.

One option is to send the playlist to another broadcast server. To do this, open the QTSS Publisher application, select the playlist you want to stream, and click the Settings button [Settings] in the Toolbar. Click the Advanced tab, and fill in the IP address, user name, and password of the broadcasting server where you wish to send the playlist. Click the Apply button (**Figure 12.44**).

Another option is to use QTSS Publisher to create code that you can insert into Web pages you want others to visit. This code can be copied and pasted into the middle of other HTML (Web page) code. To obtain the code, open the QTSS Publisher application, click the Links button [Links] in the Toolbar, select the playlist you want, and click the HTML tab (**Figure 12.45**). Click inside the window containing the code, select it all, and copy it. Then, switch to your HTML application, and paste the code where you want it.

You can also vary the look of the link in both the QuickTime Player and any Web browser when users connect to your streaming server. If you wish to add an image, that image should be a JPEG or GIF image to be compatible with most Web browsers.

Figure 12.44 Send a playlist to another broadcast server using the Advanced tab.

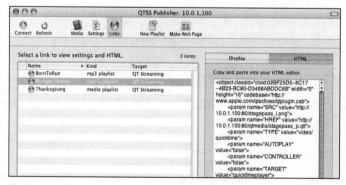

Figure 12.45 View the HTML code when selecting a playlist for Web-page streaming.

Figure 12.46 Launch the QTSS Publisher tool, and authenticate.

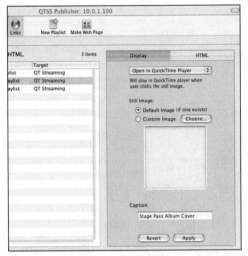

Figure 12.47 Clicking the Links button and then the selected playlist shows the default Display settings.

To add an image to your playlist:

1. Launch the QTSS Publisher tool from /Applications/Server, and authenticate as the QuickTime Streaming Server administrator (**Figure 12.46**).

2. Click the Links button [icon] in the Toolbar, select the media playlist you want, and click the Display tab (**Figure 12.47**).

3. Click the Custom Image option button, and navigate to where the image exists on your server.

   Select the image, and click the Open button to place it inside the window (**Figure 12.48**).

4. Optionally, you can add a caption in the Caption field (**Figure 12.49**).

5. Click the Apply button to save the changes.

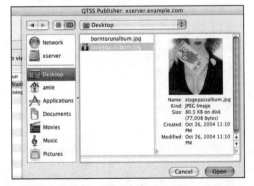

Figure 12.48 Select an image (in this case, an album cover) for the Web page to show while the stream is playing. (Image © Sony BMG Music Entertainment)

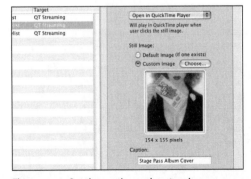

Figure 12.49 Set the caption and custom image.

How to use the image

Once an image is added, you need to choose how it will be used. You have three options in the Display pane, each of which generates different HTML code for use in a Web page:

Open in QuickTime Player allows the image to be embedded so that when you're viewing the stream from a QuickTime Player, the image will appear (**Figure 12.50**).

"Embed in Web page" places the image in a Web page and plays the stream when the user clicks the image (**Figure 12.51**).

"Auto-play in Web page" permits the stream to automatically begin playing when the user enters the Web page (**Figure 12.52**).

Remember, each option has different HTML code associated with it. If necessary, you need to copy that code and pasted it into the HTML code of your Web page(s).

✔ Tips

- Always click the Apply button after making changes.

- You may need to stop and restart the stream for the changes to take effect.

Figure 12.50 The Open in QuickTime Player option allows the image to be embedded.

Figure 12.51 "Embed in Web page" places the image in a Web page and plays the stream when the user clicks the image.

Figure 12.52 Applying the Auto-play function automatically starts the stream when a user enters the Web page with the link to the stream.

QTSS PUBLISHER OPTIONS

Figure 12.53 Launch the QTSS Publisher tool, and authenticate.

Figure 12.54 Select a playlist for the creation of a Web page.

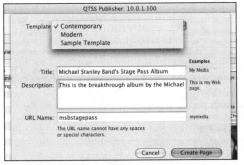

Figure 12.55 Click the Make Web Page button, select the type of Web page, and enter appropriate data.

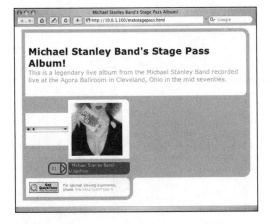

Figure 12.56 The Web page appears with the album art, text, and stream controls.

QTSS Publisher Web pages

QTSS Publisher also lets you create preformatted Web pages. These pages include all the code necessary for a Web page to be built so users can connect and view information about the playlist.

To create a preformatted Web page:

1. Enable your Web site, and start the Web service (see Chapter 9, "Web Services," for instruction on starting your Web service).

2. Launch the QTSS Publisher tool from /Applications/Server, and authenticate as the QuickTime Streaming Server administrator (**Figure 12.53**).

3. Be sure the playlist is broadcasting (see the earlier task "To create a video playlist").

4. Click the Links button in the Toolbar, and select the media playlist you want (**Figure 12.54**).

5. Click the Make Web Page button in the Toolbar.

6. In the resulting dialog, choose the type of Web page from the Template pop-up menu, enter the information you want on your Web page, and click the Create Page button (**Figure 12.55**). Your default Web browser opens and connects to the link you just created (**Figure 12.56**).

MP3 playlist links

MP3 playlists can also be embedded in Web pages and, more important, streamed to iTunes. The setup is similar to that for AAC (.m4a) files and video files; however, there are no options for images in QTSS Publisher. You must edit the Web pages directly to insert album art or other images.

To create an MP3 Web page:

1. Launch the QTSS Publisher tool from /Applications/Server, and authenticate as the QuickTime Streaming Server administrator (**Figure 12.57**).

2. Make sure the playlist is broadcasting (see the earlier task "To create a video playlist").

3. Click the Links button ![icon] in the Toolbar, select the MP3 playlist you want, and *do one of the following* (**Figure 12.58**):

   ▲ Click the Display tab, enter the text link that users will use to gain access to the stream as well as a caption to go with the stream (if you wish), and click the Apply button (**Figure 12.59**).

   ▲ Click the HTML tab, and view the HTML code, which you can copy and paste into your own Web pages (**Figure 12.60**).

Figure 12.57 Launch the QTSS Publisher tool, and authenticate.

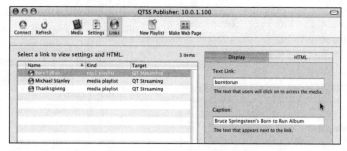

Figure 12.58 Select an MP3 playlist to prepare it for streaming.

Figure 12.59 Click the Display tab to set the text link and a caption.

Figure 12.60 View the HTML code, which you can copy and paste into an existing Web page.

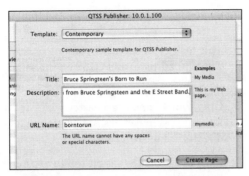

Figure 12.61 Create the Web page by clicking the Make Web Page button and entering all relevant information.

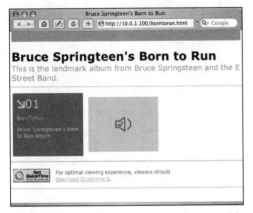

Figure 12.62 The Web page appears in a browser with all related text.

Figure 12.63 Click the link in the Web page to download the appropriate file.

Figure 12.64 Manually enter an MP3 link into the iTunes Enable Stream dialog.

4. Click the Make Web Page button in the Toolbar.

5. In the resulting dialog, choose the type of Web page from the Template pop-up menu, enter the information you want on your Web page, and click the Create Page button (**Figure 12.61**). Your default Web browser opens and connects to the link you just created (**Figure 12.62**).

6. Click the link in the Web page to download the appropriate file, which iTunes opens automatically (**Figure 12.63**).

You can also open iTunes directly, choose Advanced > Open Stream, type in the link to your stream, and click OK (**Figure 12.64**).

QuickTime Broadcaster

QuickTime Broadcaster is included with Mac OS X Server, but it isn't part of the server tools. It resides in the Applications directory. The primary job of QuickTime Broadcaster is to stream live audio and/or video content to others via the Real Time Streaming Protocol (RTSP). The Source options in both the Video and Audio tabs are the main considerations for this type of task.

QuickTime Broadcaster was covered briefly in Chapter 2, "Server Tools." To learn how to set up a basic live broadcast, refer to the task "To set up a simple live broadcast" in Chapter 2. This chapter discusses using QuickTime Broadcaster with QTSS.

To use QuickTime Broadcaster and QTSS to stream live content:

1. You should have a camera, a microphone, or some other supported AV input device connected.

If iChat launches when you plug in the device, quit iChat.

2. Complete the earlier task "To enable a QTSS."

This task assumes you're running Quick-Time Broadcaster and QTSS on the same Mac OS X Server.

3. Open QuickTime Broadcaster, which is located in your server's Applications directory (**Figure 12.65**).

4. Click the Show Details button to expand the window.

5. Click the Network tab, and *complete the following information* (**Figure 12.66**):

▲ Leave Transmission set at Automatic Unicast for the type of task being done here.

▲ Host Name is automatically filled in with either the fully qualified domain name or the IP address of your server.

▲ File is the name of the Session Description Protocol (SDP) file used to identify the stream. It's a good idea to use only lowercase letters and numbers— no spaces or other characters.

Figure 12.65 Launch QuickTime Broadcaster.

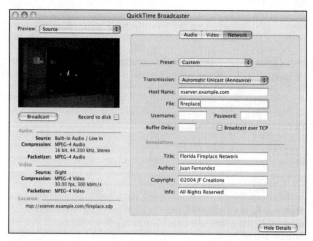

Figure 12.66 Set the Network settings in preparation for the broadcast.

▲ Username and Password can be used to restrict access to the stream.

▲ Buffer Delay allows for a build-up of data but causes a bigger delay in the delivery of live content.

▲ Broadcast over TCP permits the stream to travel over the TCP protocol, thus making the stream accessible behind certain networks.

▲ Annotations are used to further identify the broadcast stream.

6. Click the Video tab, and tweak the video input Source details to match the broadcast (**Figure 12.67**).

7. Click the Audio tab, and tweak the audio input Source details to match the broadcast (**Figure 12.68**).

continues on next page

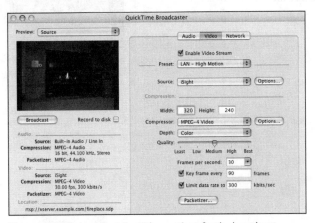

Figure 12.67 View and set the Video settings for the broadcast.

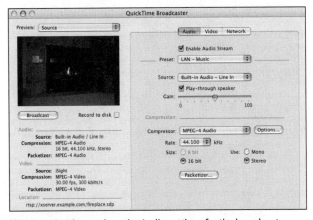

Figure 12.68 View and set the Audio settings for the broadcast.

QUICKTIME BROADCASTER

8. Choose File > Save Broadcast Settings in case you wish to use these settings for another broadcast session (**Figure 12.69**).

If you're finished tweaking the settings, click the Hide Details button [Hide Details] to reduce the size of the window.

9. Click the Broadcast button under the video feed to begin the Broadcast (**Figure 12.70**).

✔ Tip

■ Prior to beginning the broadcast, you can choose the "Record to disk" check box to save the broadcast directly to disk.

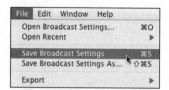

Figure 12.69 Save the broadcast settings for later use.

Figure 12.70 Click the Broadcast button to begin the broadcast.

Figure 12.71 Locate the link of a running broadcast.

Figure 12.72 Use QuickTime Player to view the broadcast.

Viewing your broadcast

When your broadcast is set up, you should view it on as many machines as possible over different connection speeds to check for variances in quality.

To prepare to view a live broadcast:

1. On your server, QuickTime Broadcaster should already be running. Be sure you can see it.

2. Locate the stream address in the QuickTime Broadcaster window under Location (**Figure 12.71**).

3. Open the QuickTime Player application in the Applications directory on another computer connected to the same network. Select File > Open URL in New Player (**Figure 12.72**). An Open URL dialog appears.

4. Type in the stream path from step 2, and click the OK button (**Figure 12.73**).

5. View your stream in the QuickTime Player window (**Figure 12.74**).

continues on next page

Figure 12.74 View your video stream using the QuickTime Player from Mac OS X Client.

Figure 12.73 Enter the information from the QuickTime Broadcaster Location into the QuickTime Player URL dialog.

QUICKTIME BROADCASTER

6. Choose Movie > Get Movie Properties (**Figure 12.75**).

The movie Properties window opens.

7. Choose Streaming Track from the pop-up menu on the left and Annotations from the pop-up menu on the right (**Figure 12.76**).

You can view all the annotations placed in the QuickTime Broadcaster window prior to beginning the broadcast.

Figure 12.75 Select Movie > Get Movie Properties.

✔ Tip

■ The Compression settings for both audio and video can be very complex and require background knowledge about color, video, compression, audio and video codecs, and more. When you're changing these settings, it's generally best to test thoroughly on several machines receiving the stream to ensure a quality broadcast.

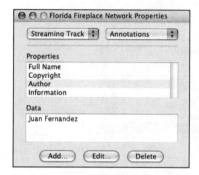

Figure 12.76 View the properties entered in the QuickTime Broadcaster Network tab as they appear in the final broadcast.

QUICKTIME BROADCASTER

Live Stream Precautions

Rebroadcasting copyrighted content is prohibited by law. Be sure to check with all parties involved prior to streaming any live audio or video.

CLIENT
MANAGEMENT

Many system administrators view a centrally controlled user environment as the ultimate management solution. The concept is simple: Instead of configuring user accounts individually at each computer, this management information is centralized on your servers. Thus an administrator can configure preferences for every account from one central location. For instance, you can prevent a specific user account from launching nonessential applications, or restrict printing on an expensive color printer to only a certain group of users, or set a preference that automatically shuts down every idle computer at the end of the workday. These are but a few examples of controlling Mac OS X clients by using the managed preference settings from your Mac OS X Server.

With such an extensive variety of managed preference options available, this simple concept can become complicated. Fortunately, the engineers at Apple have created a preference system that permits you to micromanage accounts while still working at the macro level. In other words, you can apply a specific setting to a broad range of accounts in a few steps. For starters, you can select multiple accounts and simultaneously apply managed preference settings for all of them in one step. Further, Mac OS X Server lets you define presets so newly created or imported accounts are automatically configured with your managed account settings. Most significantly, you can apply managed preference settings to workgroups or computer lists in addition to individual user accounts.

Prior to implementing managed preferences, you should consider all the options available and create a plan that will accomplish your administration requirements with the least amount of configuration.

(You may find that an organizational tool such as a group outline or flowchart software like OmniGraffle (http://www.omnigroup.com) can help you plan the best implementation for your needs.)

Managing Computer Lists

A *computer list*, as its name implies, is a list of computers. You can think of computer lists as groups for computers. If you want to manage preferences based on computers, you do so by using computer lists. In Workgroup Manager, you can add any Mac OS X computer to the computer list based on its hardware Ethernet address or Media Access Control (MAC) address.

You may have as many computer lists as you want, but a computer may be in only one list. Any computer outside of a list is automatically in the Guest Computers list. Windows computers have their own list (discussed in the task "To manage the Windows Computers list").

You can configure computer lists on any Mac OS X Server. However, computer lists are only functional on the server acting as an Open Directory master, because such servers are configured to share their directory information with other computers. Also, your client computers must be configured as clients of this directory service system. For more information about directory services and Open Directory, refer to Chapter 3, "Open Directory."

To create a computer list:

1. Launch the Workgroup Manager tool located in /Applications/Server, and authenticate as the administrator (**Figure 13.1**).

2. Click the Accounts icon in the Toolbar and the Computer Lists tab among the account types (**Figure 13.2**).

3. Click the directory authentication icon , and select the appropriate directory database from the pop-up menu. Computer lists are always hosted from a parent directory database (**Figure 13.3**).

Figure 13.1 Launch Workgroup Manager, and authenticate.

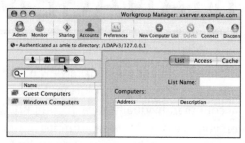

Figure 13.2 Select the Computer Lists tab to manage computer lists.

Figure 13.3 Select the appropriate directory database from this pop-up menu.

MANAGING COMPUTER LISTS

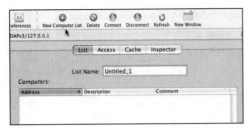

Figure 13.4 Add a new computer list.

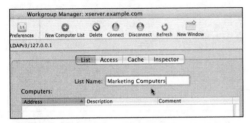

Figure 13.5 Enter your computer list's name.

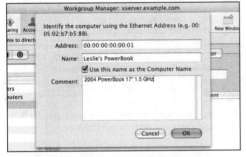

Figure 13.6 The computer list edit dialog lets you add or modify a computer in your computer list.

4. Click the New Computer List button.

The information in the List frame is populated with a new untitled computer list (**Figure 13.4**).

5. Enter an appropriate computer list name (**Figure 13.5**).

6. To add computers to this computer list, *do either of the following:*

▲ Click the Add button, and an edit dialog will drop from the title bar (**Figure 13.6**). Enter the computer's Ethernet address, name, and optional comment in the appropriate fields. When you've finished, click the Save button.

▲ Click the ellipsis button, and a browse dialog will open (**Figure 13.7**). Browse to and select the computer you wish to add to this list, and then click the Connect button.

7. Verify that the computers have been added to your computer list (**Figure 13.8**).

8. When you've finished making changes, click the Save button.

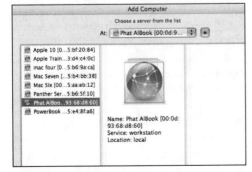

Figure 13.7 The browse dialog automatically discovers Mac OS X computers on your local network.

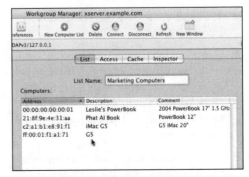

Figure 13.8 A few computers have been added to this computer list.

MANAGING COMPUTER LISTS

409

To modify a computer list:

1. Launch the Workgroup Manager tool located in /Applications/Server, and authenticate as the administrator (**Figure 13.9**).

2. Click the Accounts icon  in the Toolbar and the Computer Lists tab among the account types, and select the list you wish to edit (**Figure 13.10**).

3. If it isn't already selected, click the List tab **List**.

4. *Do either of the following:*

   ▲ Double-click the computer list item you wish to edit, and enter the new value (**Figure 13.11**). When you've finished, press Enter or click anywhere else.

   ▲ Select a computer from the Computers list, and then click the Edit button to open the computer list edit dialog.

5. To delete a computer from the list, select it from the Computers list, and then click the Delete button **—**.

To delete a computer list account:

1. Select the computer list account from the Accounts list.

2. Click the Delete button (**Figure 13.12**).

✔ Tips

■ You can have up to 2,000 computers in a computer list.

■ You may wish to explore the restricted workgroup access settings, the cache settings, and the managed preference settings for your computer list. Refer to the remaining tasks in this chapter for more information.

■ You can select more than one item in a list by holding down the Shift or Command key while making your selections.

Figure 13.9 Launch Workgroup Manager, and authenticate.

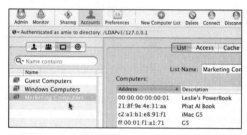

Figure 13.10 Select the Computer Lists tab to manage computer lists.

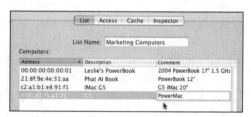

Figure 13.11 Modify any item in the computer list by double-clicking the appropriate field.

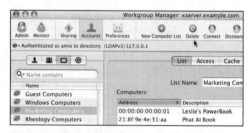

Figure 13.12 Select the computer list account, and then click the Delete button.

■ As is the case for user and group accounts, you can use account presets to automatically configure new computer lists. See Chapter 4, "User and Group Management," for more information.

Figure 13.13 Launch Workgroup Manager, and authenticate.

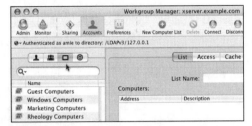

Figure 13.14 Select the Computer Lists tab to manage computer lists.

Figure 13.15 Select the appropriate directory database from this pop-up menu.

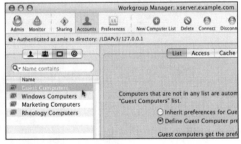

Figure 13.16 Select Guest Computers from the computer account list.

The Guest Computers list

Any Mac OS X computer that isn't defined in a custom computer list automatically uses the settings from the Guest Computers list. Generally, it's considered bad practice to allow any of your managed computers to fall into the Guest Computers list, because you should reserve this list for computers you don't want to manage. Take great care with your choices in the Guest Computers list, or you may inadvertently control computers you didn't intend to manage.

To manage the Guest Computers list:

1. Launch the Workgroup Manager tool located in /Applications/Server, and authenticate as the administrator (**Figure 13.13**).

2. Click the Accounts icon in the Toolbar and the Computer Lists tab among the account types (**Figure 13.14**).

3. Click the directory authentication icon , and select the appropriate directory database from the pop-up menu. Computer lists are always hosted from a parent directory database (**Figure 13.15**).

4. From the accounts list, select Guest Computers (**Figure 13.16**).

continues on next page

5. Click the Lists tab [List], and then *choose one of the following options:*

▲ "Inherit preferences for Guest Computers" is the default setting. Guest computers will inherit their managed preferences from your Open Directory server (**Figure 13.17**).

▲ "Define Guest Computer preferences here" means you wish to configure specific managed preferences for guest computers. This option lets you configure restricted workgroup access settings, cache settings, and managed preference settings for guest computers (**Figure 13.18**).

6. When you've finished making changes, click the Save button [Save].

✔ Tip

■ You may wish to explore the restricted workgroup access settings, the cache settings, and the managed preference settings for this computer list. Refer to the remaining tasks in this chapter for more information.

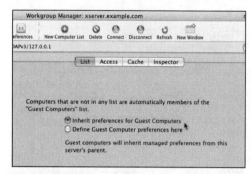

Figure 13.17 The Guest Computers List frame lets you set the Inherited preference option.

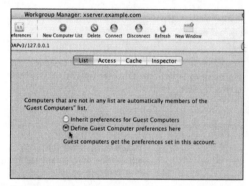

Figure 13.18 The Guest Computers List frame lets you set the Defined preference option.

Figure 13.19 Launch Workgroup Manager, and authenticate.

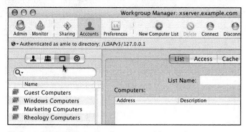

Figure 13.20 Select the Computer Lists tab to manage computer lists.

Figure 13.21 Select the appropriate directory database from this pop-up menu.

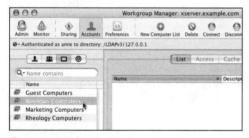

Figure 13.22 Select the Windows Computers account from the computer accounts list.

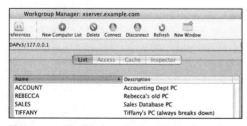

Figure 13.23 The Windows Computers List frame in Workgroup Manager lets you manage a list of Windows computers.

The Windows Computers list

One of the default computer lists automatically created by the server tools is the Windows Computers list. If your Mac OS X Server is configured as a Windows Primary Domain Controller (PDC), any Windows client supported by your server needs to be in this list. (See Chapter 5, "File Sharing," for more information about configuring your Mac OS X Server as a PDC.)

Windows computers can be in only one list, and there is only this one list for Windows, so they all appear here. The first time a Windows client joins your server's PDC, it's automatically added to this list. However, you can also manually configure Windows computers in this list using the instructions in the following task.

To manage the Windows Computers list:

1. Launch the Workgroup Manager tool located in /Applications/Server, and authenticate as the administrator (**Figure 13.19**).

2. Click the Accounts icon in the Toolbar and the Computer Lists tab among the account types (**Figure 13.20**).

3. Click the directory authentication icon , and select the appropriate directory database from the pop-up menu. Computer lists are always hosted from a parent directory database (**Figure 13.21**).

4. From the accounts list, select the Windows Computers account (**Figure 13.22**).

   You can only manage the computer list in the Windows Computers frame; all the other tab options are grayed out. Also, any Windows computer that has already joined your server's PDC is automatically added to this list (**Figure 13.23**).

continues on next page

MANAGING COMPUTER LISTS

5. To manually add a Windows computer, click the Add button ➕.

An edit dialog drops from the title bar (**Figure 13.24**).

6. Enter the Windows computer's NetBIOS name and an optional description in the appropriate fields.

Click the Save button ⬬ Save ⬬.

7. Verify that the Windows computer has been added to your computer list (**Figure 13.25**).

8. When you've finished making changes, click the Save button ⬬ Save ⬬.

Figure 13.24 The Windows Computers List edit dialog lets you add Windows computer.

✔ Tips

■ You can't modify the NetBIOS name of a Windows computer in the list. You can, however, modify the description by double-clicking the description you wish to edit and entering the new value (**Figure 13.26**). When you've finished, press Enter or click anywhere else.

■ To delete a computer from the list, select it from the Windows Computers list and then click the Delete button ➖. Don't delete the entire Windows Computers list!

■ Windows uses NetBIOS names to identify client computers. These names are typically in all uppercase letters and limited to 25 characters.

■ You can try to apply managed preference settings for these Windows computers, but they will ignore your settings. Windows is so different from Mac OS X that Workgroup Manager settings don't apply to Windows computers.

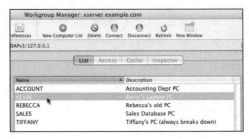

Figure 13.25 A few Windows computers have been added to this computer list.

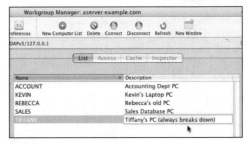

Figure 13.26 Modify the Windows computer description in the list by double-clicking the appropriate field.

Figure 13.27 Launch Workgroup Manager, and authenticate.

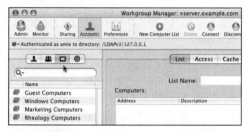

Figure 13.28 Select the Computer Lists tab to manage computer lists.

Figure 13.29 Select the appropriate directory database from this pop-up menu.

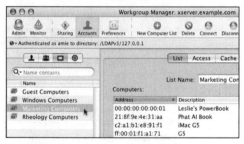

Figure 13.30 Select the computer list for which you wish to configure restricted workgroup access.

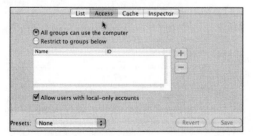

Figure 13.31 The computer account's Access frame lets you add workgroups to the computer account's access list.

Restricting login access

By default, any user in any group can log in to any client computer that is connected to your directory system. You can restrict user logins to your computers by combining computer lists with workgroups. In Workgroup Manager, you restrict user login to certain workgroups of users for a computer list. In other words, you assign users to workgroups, and then you assign workgroups to computer lists.

Obviously, in order for this approach to work, you must have already configured workgroups and computer lists. See Chapter 4, "User and Group Management," for more information. You can also find detailed information about managing computer lists earlier in this chapter.

To restrict login access:

1. Launch the Workgroup Manager tool located in /Applications/Server, and authenticate as the administrator (**Figure 13.27**).

2. Click the Accounts icon ![icon] in the Toolbar and the Computer Lists tab ![icon] among the account types (**Figure 13.28**).

3. Click the directory authentication icon ![Authenticated], and select the appropriate directory database from the pop-up menu. Computer lists are always hosted from a parent directory database (**Figure 13.29**).

4. From the accounts list, select the computer list for which you wish to configure restricted workgroup access (**Figure 13.30**).

5. Click the Access tab ![Access] to view this computer list's workgroup access settings.

   By default, any user belonging to any workgroup can log in to the computers in this list (**Figure 13.31**).

continues on next page

MANAGING COMPUTER LISTS

6. Select the "Restrict to groups below" radio button, and then click the Add button ![+].

A drawer appears in which you can select the workgroups you wish to assign to this computer list (**Figure 13.32**).

7. At the top of the drawer, click the directory authentication icon, and select the appropriate directory database from the pop-up menu.

The directory you are currently managing will be the default selection and, most likely, will be the one you want to use (**Figure 13.33**).

8. Click and drag workgroups from the drawer to the restricted groups list (**Figure 13.34**).

9. When you've finished making changes, click the Save button ![Save].

Now, when a user attempts to log in, their account will be compared to the workgroups assigned to the computer list this computer is in. If the user isn't part of a workgroup allowed to use this computer, then they won't be allowed to log in. If they belong to one of the allowed workgroups, they will continue to log in as normal. However, if a user belongs to more than one workgroup, they will be required to specify which workgroup they want to use for this session.

✔ Tips

- You can select more than one item in a list by holding down the Shift or Command key while making your selections

- You can further restrict login access to the computers in this list by disabling their access to local accounts. To enable this feature, deselect the "Allow users with local-only accounts" check box (**Figure 13.35**).

Figure 13.32 In this drawer, you can select workgroup accounts.

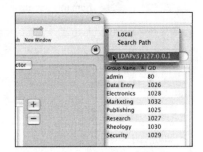

Figure 13.33 Select the appropriate directory database from this pop-up menu.

Figure 13.34 Drag and drop workgroups into the computer account's access list.

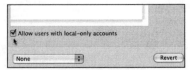

Figure 13.35 Disable local computer accounts by deselecting the "Allow users with local-only accounts" check box.

Figure 13.36 Launch Workgroup Manager, and authenticate.

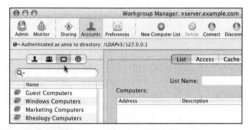

Figure 13.37 Select the Computer Lists tab to manage computer lists.

Figure 13.38 Select the appropriate directory database from this pop-up menu.

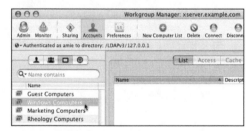

Figure 13.39 Select the computer list for which you wish to configure cache settings.

Configuring computer caches

To facilitate computers that may occasionally disconnect from your directory server, like laptops, and to improve directory service performance, managed preference settings are cached locally on client computers. In Workgroup Manager, you can configure how often this cache is automatically updated to the client if any changes are made on the parent directory server. Otherwise, the next time a user logs in to an account, the new account settings will be read, and the local cache file will be updated.

To configure computer cache settings:

1. Launch the Workgroup Manager tool located in /Applications/Server, and authenticate as the administrator (**Figure 13.36**).

2. Click the Accounts icon in the Toolbar and the Computer Lists tab among the account types (**Figure 13.37**).

3. Click the directory authentication icon, and select the appropriate directory database from the pop-up menu. Computer lists are always hosted from a parent directory database (**Figure 13.38**).

4. From the accounts list, select the computer list for which you wish to configure cache settings (**Figure 13.39**).

continues on next page

MANAGING COMPUTER LISTS

5. Click the Cache tab [Cache] to view this computer list's cache settings.

By default, the cache is set to reset every two days (**Figure 13.40**).

6. To change the cache intervals, enter a different value in the appropriate field, and then select a unit of time from the pop-up menu (**Figure 13.41**).

7. To immediately update the cache files on the computers in this list, click the Update Cache button [Update Cache].

8. When you've finished making changes, click the Save button [Save].

The cache files will be automatically updated based on the schedule you set or whenever a user logs in.

✔ Tips

■ To update the cached preferences on a client computer, hold down the Shift key when you log in. When a dialog appears, click the Refresh Preferences button to update the cached preference information.

■ You can select more than one item in a list by holding down the Shift or Command key while making your selections.

Figure 13.40 The computer account's Cache frame lets you configure a computer account's cached preference settings.

Figure 13.41 Select an appropriate time frame from this pop-up menu.

Managing Preferences

By default, Mac OS X Server doesn't have any managed preference settings enabled. Before you begin configuring these settings, you should consider all of your management options. For starters, Mac OS X Server lets you configure unique managed preferences separately for user, workgroup, and computer list accounts. In other words, you can configure some or all of the available managed preference settings for any account type independently of another account type's settings. To compound this already complicated situation, each user account can belong to multiple workgroups, and each workgroup account can belong to multiple computer lists.

With all these configuration options available, situations often arise in which a user account may have conflicting managed preference settings. Mac OS X resolves these conflicts by first narrowing the login to only one of each account type. Obviously, a user account is unique among other user accounts, but computers are also individually unique

because they can belong to only one computer list account. The only variable that can occur is when a user is part of multiple workgroups. However, during login, this situation is resolved, because users must choose one workgroup to belong to during their session.

Once the login is narrowed to a single user, workgroup, and computer list account, conflicting managed preferences pan out into one of the following three situations:

◆ A managed setting is configured for only one account type. In this case, there are no conflicts among settings, so the resulting preference is inherited based on the one managed account type.

◆ A managed setting is configured for multiple account types, and the result is overridden based on the most specific managed account type. User account options are the most specific, followed by computer list account options, followed by workgroup account options. Most managed preferences follow this override rule.

◆ A managed setting is configured for multiple account types, and the setting uses list-type options. In this case, the conflicting results are combined based on all the managed account types. The Application Items, Dock Items, Printer List, and Login Items managed preferences follow this combined rule.

✔ Tip

■ You may find that an organizational tool such as a group outline or flowchart software like OmniGraffle (http://www.omnigroup.com) can help you plan the best implementation for your needs.

Best Practices for Managed Preferences

A few best practices will help you avoid managed-preference conflict and, as a result, save time:

◆ Always start with a plan.

◆ Manage each preference only once at specific account types. For example, manage the Printer List settings only in the computer list accounts.

◆ Make exceptions only at the user account level. This approach keeps workgroups and your potential confusion to a minimum.

To configure managed preferences:

1. Launch the Workgroup Manager tool located in /Applications/Server, and authenticate as the administrator (**Figure 13.42**).

2. Click the Accounts icon ![Accounts] in the Toolbar and the Computer Lists tab ![tab] among the account types (**Figure 13.43**).

3. Click the directory authentication icon ![Authenticated], and select the appropriate directory database from the pop-up menu.

   Computer lists are always hosted from a parent directory database (**Figure 13.44**).

4. From the accounts list, select the user, workgroup, or computer list for which you wish to configure the managed preference settings (**Figure 13.45**):

Figure 13.42 Launch Workgroup Manager, and authenticate.

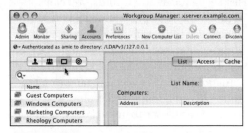

Figure 13.43 Select the Computer Lists tab to manage computer lists.

Figure 13.44 Select the appropriate directory database from this pop-up menu.

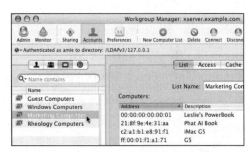

Figure 13.45 Select an account from the list. In this case, a computer list is selected.

▲ If you select a user or workgroup account, the Preferences frame appears, in which you can select 1 of 11 managed preference icons (**Figure 13.46**).

▲ If you select a computer list account, you have one additional managed preference icon (Energy Saver) (**Figure 13.47**).

continues on next page

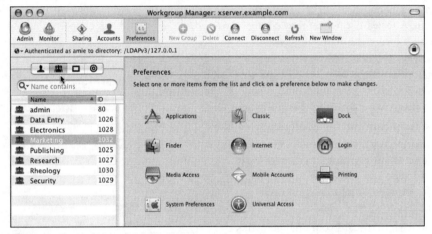

Figure 13.46 The Preferences frame shows 11 options when you're configuring a user or workgroup account...

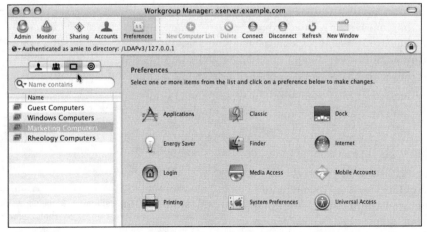

Figure 13.47 ...or 12 options when you're configuring a computer list account.

MANAGING PREFERENCES

5. Click the preference you wish to manage, to reveal the available options (**Figure 13.48**).

6. *Select one of these three options,* which appear at the top of every managed preference frame (**Figure 13.49**):

Not Managed—The default setting for every managed preference. For the selected account, this preference isn't managed.

Once—Available for all managed preferences. For the selected account, this preference is managed the first time a user logs in. Afterward, the user may configure their own custom preferences.

Always—Available for every managed preference. For the selected account, this preference is always managed; the user can't make any changes to this setting.

7. Make your configuration choices.

The options available for each managed preference are too varied to discuss here. Refer to specific tasks later in this chapter for more information about each managed preference.

8. If you wish to discard your changes, click the Revert button (Revert).

Otherwise, when you've finished making changes, click the Apply Now button (Apply Now).

9. Click the Done button (Done) to return to the managed preferences icon view (**Figure 13.50**).

The arrow icon next to a preference icon indicates that managed preferences are configured for this item.

The changes you've made will automatically be updated to the client computers based on the cache schedule set in the computer lists or whenever the user logs in next. (See the task "To configure computer cache settings," earlier in this chapter, for more information regarding cache settings.)

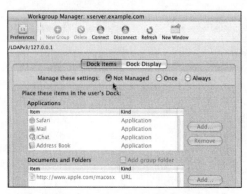

Figure 13.48 Click the preference you wish to manage, to reveal the available options. In this case, the Dock item was selected.

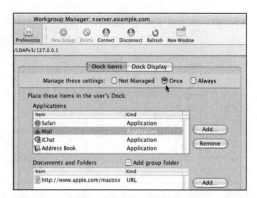

Figure 13.49 Each managed preference requires that you select one of these three options.

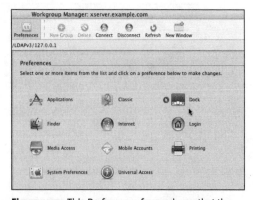

Figure 13.50 This Preferences frame shows that the Dock managed preferences are enabled for the selected account.

✔ Tips

- Refer to specific tasks later in this chapter for more specific information on each managed preference.

- To configure managed preferences for Mac OS 9 client computers, you must use the Macintosh Manager service and configuration tools.

- You can select more than one item in a list by holding down the Shift or Command key while making your selections.

- As is the case for group and user accounts, you can use account presets to automatically configure new computer lists. See Chapter 4, "User and Group Management," for more information.

MCX Is Behind the Scenes

Managed preference settings, like all other account settings, are stored in your Mac OS X Server's Open Directory database. However, due to the complexity of these settings, they go beyond the standard attribute/value data specification.

Managed preference settings use a format known as Machine Control XML (MCX). (More fun with acronyms—XML is short for Extensible Markup Language.) These MCX files consist of text formatted in a certain manner that is understood by the preference system on the client computers. In fact, the MCX text file format is similar to the format used for other Mac OS X preference files called *property lists*.

You can directly view and edit the MCX settings by using the Inspector view in Workgroup Manager (**Figures 13.51** and **13.52**). Take great care when editing this information directly, because human errors can cause some serious problems. See Chapter 4 for more information about using the Inspector.

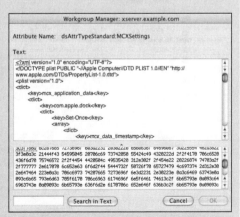

Figure 13.51 The Inspector frame in Workgroup Manager lets you view the MCX account settings.

Figure 13.52 The Inspector edit dialog in Workgroup Manager lets you view and edit MCX account settings.

The Applications managed preference

Before you read this section, be sure you're familiar with the concepts discussed in the task "To configure managed preferences," earlier in this chapter. The figures in this section show a variety of managed preference configurations. These are only examples, and they should not be interpreted as the most appropriate configuration for your needs.

The Applications managed preference ![Applications] lets you restrict the launching of applications on Mac OS X computers. More specifically, you can do the following (**Figure 13.53**):

◆ Specify a list of approved or unapproved applications

◆ Restrict the launching of local applications

◆ Restrict approved applications from launching other applications

◆ Restrict the use of Unix tools

The Applications managed preference is available to user, workgroup, and computer list account types. You can't manage this preference just once, because it's either unmanaged or always managed. If there are conflicting account settings, the resulting applications list is a combination of all the settings. Otherwise, all conflicting account settings for the Applications managed preference follow the override rule.

✔ Tips

■ Workgroup Manager automatically finds applications on the computer it's running on.

■ When you're creating the applications list, it's best to use Workgroup Manager from one of the clients you'll be managing.

Figure 13.53 The Applications managed preference lets you restrict the launching of applications on Mac OS X computers.

The Classic managed preference

Before you read this section, be sure you're familiar with the concepts discussed in the task "To configure managed preferences," earlier in this chapter. The figures in this section show a variety of managed preference configurations. These are only examples, and they should not be interpreted as the most appropriate configuration for your needs.

The Classic managed preference 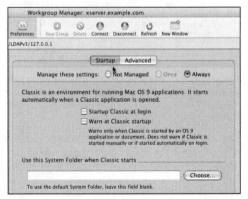 lets you configure the Classic environment and restrict access to Classic-related items on Mac OS X computers. More specifically, in the Startup tab you can do the following (**Figure 13.54**):

◆ Require that Classic launch after user login

◆ Warn the user before Classic attempts to launch

◆ Specify a custom location for the Classic system items

In the Advanced tab of the Classic managed preference, you can do the following (**Figure 13.55**):

◆ Allow special Classic startup modes

◆ Restrict access to Classic Apple menu items

◆ Specify the amount of time before Classic can go to sleep when idle, thereby saving both memory and CPU usage

The Classic managed preference is available to user, workgroup, and computer list account types. You can't manage this preference just once, because it's either unmanaged or always managed. If there are conflicting account settings, all Classic managed preferences follow the override rule.

✔ Tips

■ Classic managed preferences work only if a copy of Mac OS 9 is installed or available as a disk image on the client computer.

■ If you restrict access to the Classic Startup application using the Applications managed preference, then users won't be able to launch Classic.

Figure 13.54 The Classic managed preference lets you configure the Classic environment and restrict access to Classic-related items on Mac OS X computers.

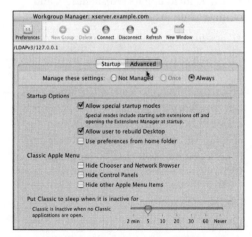

Figure 13.55 The Advanced tab of the Classic managed preference frame offers additional options.

The Dock managed preference

Before you read this section, be sure you're familiar with the concepts discussed in the task "To configure managed preferences," earlier in this chapter. The figures in this section show a variety of managed preference configurations. These are only examples, and they should not be interpreted as the most appropriate configuration for your needs.

The Dock managed preference 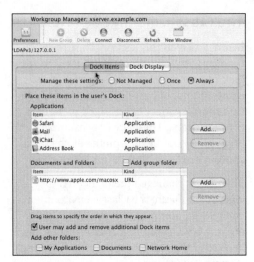 lets you define the contents of the Dock and define the Dock's visual settings on Mac OS X computers. More specifically, in the Dock Items tab you can do the following (**Figure 13.56**):

◆ Populate the Dock with applications or documents

◆ Restrict the user from modifying the contents of the Dock

In the Dock Display tab of the Dock managed preference, you can do the following (**Figure 13.57**):

◆ Specify all the visual aspects of the Dock, including its size, location, and magnification

◆ Specify the minimize window animation

The Dock managed preference is available to user, workgroup, and computer list account types. In addition to leaving this preference unmanaged, you can manage this preference once or always. If there are conflicting account settings, the resulting Dock Items list is a combination of all the settings. Otherwise, all conflicting account settings for the Dock managed preferences follow the override rule.

✔ Tip

■ Make sure any item you add to the Dock Items list is accessible to the client computers. Otherwise, those items will show up with a question mark icon in the Dock.

Figure 13.56 The Dock managed preference lets you define the contents of the Dock and define the Dock's visual settings on Mac OS X computers.

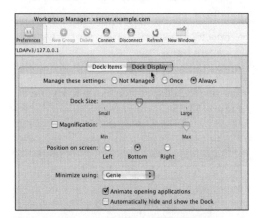

Figure 13.57 The Dock Display tab of the Dock managed preference frame offers additional options.

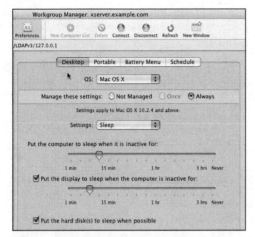

Figure 13.58 The Energy Saver managed preference lets you define the power-saving features for both desktop and probable Mac OS X computers.

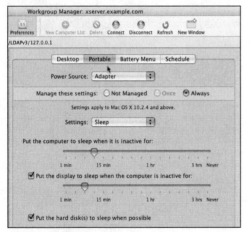

Figure 13.59 Additional options are available on the Portable tab...

The Energy Saver managed preference

Before you read this section, be sure you're familiar with the concepts discussed in the task "To configure managed preferences," earlier in this chapter. The figures in this section show a variety of managed preference configurations. These are only examples, and they should not be interpreted as the most appropriate configuration for your needs.

The Energy Saver managed preference lets you define the power-saving features for both desktop and probable Mac OS X computers. More specifically, in the Desktop tab you can do the following (**Figure 13.58**):

◆ Specify the amount of time the computer waits before it enters various sleep states

◆ Specify various wakeup options

◆ Specify unique sleep settings for either Mac OS X or Mac OS X Server

In the Portable tab of the Energy Saver managed preference, you can do the following (**Figure 13.59**):

◆ Specify the amount of time the computer waits before it enters various sleep states

◆ Specify various wakeup and processor usage options

◆ Specify unique Entergy Saver settings for either using the power adapter or battery power

continues on next page

MANAGING PREFERENCES

In the Battery Menu tab of the Energy Saver managed preference, you can do the following (**Figure 13.60**):

◆ Enable the battery status for portable computers

In the Schedule tab of the Energy Saver managed preference, you can do the following (**Figure 13.61**):

◆ Specify specific daily startup, sleep, or shutdown times

◆ Specify unique schedule settings for either Mac OS X or Mac OS X Server

The Energy Saver managed preference is only available to computer list accounts. You can't manage this preference just once, because it's either unmanaged or always managed. If there are conflicting account settings, all Energy Saver managed preferences follow the override rule.

✔ Tips

■ All of the Energy Saver managed preferences work only with Mac OS X 10.2.4 or above.

■ The Schedule settings work only with Mac OS X 10.3 or above.

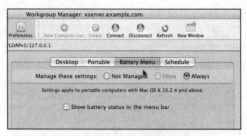

Figure 13.60 ...the Battery Menu tab...

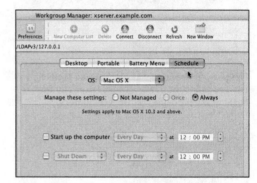

Figure 13.61 ...and the Schedule tab.

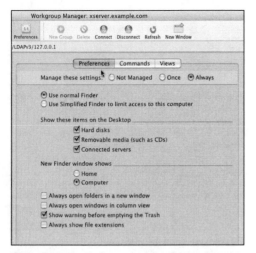

Figure 13.62 The Finder managed preference lets you define the Finder interface options for Mac OS X computers.

Figure 13.63 Additional options are available on the Commands tab...

The Finder managed preference

Before you read this section, be sure you're familiar with the concepts discussed in the task "To configure managed preferences," earlier in this chapter. The figures in this section show a variety of managed preference configurations. These are only examples, and they should not be interpreted as the most appropriate configuration for your needs.

The Finder managed preference Finder lets you define the Finder interface options for Mac OS X computers. More specifically, in the Preferences tab, you can do the following (**Figure 13.62**):

◆ Choose between normal or the more restrictive Simple Finder modes

◆ Specify the items that appear on the Desktop

◆ Specify various Finder view options

In the Commands tab of the Finder managed preference, you can do the following (**Figure 13.63**):

◆ Allow or restrict various Finder volume commands, such as ejecting disks or connecting to servers

◆ Allow or restrict the Go To Folder command

◆ Allow or restrict shutdown and restart commands

continues on next page

MANAGING PREFERENCES

In the Views tab of the Finder managed preference, you can do the following (**Figure 13.64**):

◆ Specify icon and list view settings separately for the Desktop, Default, and Computer views

The Finder managed preference is available to user, workgroup, and computer list account types. In addition to leaving settings in the Preferences tab and Views tab unmanaged, you can manage these settings once or always. Settings in the Commands tab can't be managed just once, because they're either unmanaged or always managed. If there are conflicting account settings, all Finder managed preferences follow the override rule.

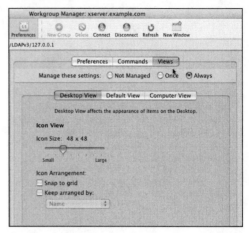

Figure 13.64 ...and the Views tab.

✔ Tip

■ The Simple Finder is a limited interface that is great for new computer users or kiosk computers that are open to the public.

The Internet managed preference

Before you read this section, be sure you're familiar with the concepts discussed in the task "To configure managed preferences," earlier in this chapter. The figures in this section show a variety of managed preference configurations. These are only examples, and they should not be interpreted as the most appropriate configuration for your needs.

The Internet managed preference lets you define the Internet settings on Mac OS X computers. More specifically, in the Email tab, you can do the following (**Figure 13.65**):

◆ Specify the default email application

◆ Specify the user's email account configuration

◆ Specify email server and protocol information

In the Web tab of the Internet managed preference, you can do the following (**Figure 13.66**):

◆ Specify the default Web browser application

◆ Specify Home and Search Web pages

◆ Specify the local location for downloaded files

The Internet managed preference is available to user, workgroup, and computer list account types. In addition to leaving this preference unmanaged, you can manage it once or always. If there are conflicting account settings, all Internet managed preferences follow the override rule.

✔ Tips

■ Be sure you allow access for the applications you define as the default email and Web browser if you're also using Applications managed preferences.

■ The Email Address field should be managed only at the user account level. You can, however, leave it blank if you wish to manage other email settings.

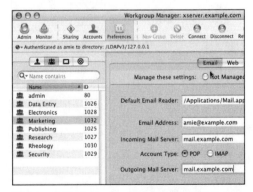

Figure 13.65 The Internet managed preference lets you define the Internet settings on Mac OS X computers.

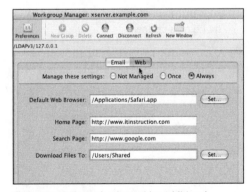

Figure 13.66 The Web tab provides additional options.

The Login managed preference

Before you read this section, be sure you're familiar with the concepts discussed in the task "To configure managed preferences," earlier in this chapter. The figures in this section show a variety of managed preference configurations. These are only examples, and they should not be interpreted as the most appropriate configuration for your needs.

The Login managed preference [icon] lets you define the Login window options for Mac OS X computers. More specifically, in the Login Items tab, you can do the following (**Figure 13.67**):

◆ Create a list of applications to launch and server volumes to connect after the user logs in

◆ Restrict users from adding their own login items and temporarily disabling login items by holding down the Shift key at login

In the Login Options tab of the Login managed preference, you can do the following (**Figure 13.68**):

◆ Choose between name and password fields or the user list to be displayed by the Login window

◆ Allow or restrict various Login window commands such as restart and shut down

◆ Enable fast user switching

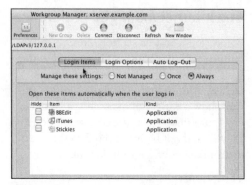

Figure 13.67 The Login managed preference lets you define the Login window options for Mac OS X computers.

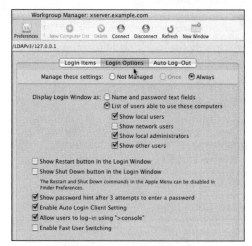

Figure 13.68 Additional options are available on the Login Options tab...

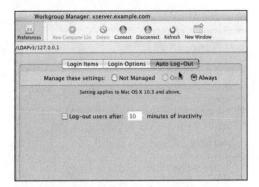

Figure 13.69 ...and the Auto Log-Out tab.

In the Auto Log-Out tab of the Login managed preference, you can do the following (**Figure 13.69**):

◆ Configure the amount of idle time that can pass before the system automatically logs out the user

Settings in the Login Items tab of the Login managed preference are available to user, workgroup, and computer list account types. However, settings in the Login Options tab and the Auto Log-Out tab are available only to computer list accounts.

In addition to leaving settings in the Login Items tab unmanaged, you can manage these settings once or always. Settings in the Login Options tab and the Auto Log-Out tab can't be managed just once, because they're either unmanaged or always managed.

If there are conflicting account settings, the resulting Login Items list is a combination of all the settings. Otherwise, all conflicting account settings for the Login managed preference follow the override rule.

✔ Tips

■ Be sure you allow access for the applications in the Login Items list if you're also using Applications managed preferences.

■ The Auto Log-Out settings work only with Mac OS X 10.3 or later.

The Media Access managed preference

Before you read this section, be sure you're familiar with the concepts discussed in the task "To configure managed preferences," earlier in this chapter. The figures in this section show a variety of managed preference configurations. These are only examples, and they should not be interpreted as the most appropriate configuration for your needs.

The Media Access managed preference ![Media Access] lets you define controlled access to removable media on Mac OS X computers. More specifically, in the Disk Media tab, you can do the following (**Figure 13.70**):

◆ Completely restrict access to optical disk media, or require administrator authentication

◆ Completely restrict access to recordable optical disk media, or require administrator authentication

In the Other Media tab of the Media Access managed preference, you can do the following (**Figure 13.71**):

◆ Completely restrict access to internal disks, or require administrator authentication

◆ Completely restrict access to external disks, or require administrator authentication

◆ Force removable media to be ejected when the user logs out

The Media Access managed preference is available to user, workgroup, and computer list account types. You can't manage this preference just once, because it's either unmanaged or always managed. If there are conflicting account settings, all Media Access managed preferences follow the override rule.

✔ Tip

■ The only instance where you should completely restrict access to the internal disks is if your client computers start up from a NetBoot server.

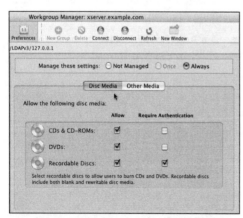

Figure 13.70 The Media Access managed preference lets you define controlled access to removable media on Mac OS X computers.

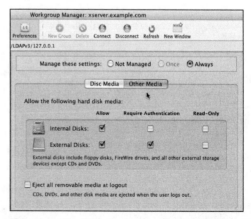

Figure 13.71 The Other Media tab offers additional options.

The Mobile Accounts managed preference

Before you read this section, be sure you're familiar with the concepts discussed in the task "To configure managed preferences," earlier in this chapter. The figures in this section show a variety of managed preference configurations. These are only examples, and they should not be interpreted as the most appropriate configuration for your needs.

A typical network user account requires that the client computer be always connected to the directory server and the home folder share point. On the other hand, mobile accounts are special network user accounts that don't require a persistent connection to your servers. The first time a mobile-account user logs in to a computer, a new home folder is created for this user on the client computer's local startup volume. The user's account information and managed preference settings are cached in the client computer's local user database.

A mobile-account user can disconnect from your network at any time, and all their account settings remain intact on the local client computer. Any time the computer is on your network and the user logs in, the account information and managed preference settings caches are updated. However, the user's home folder on the client computer's local startup volume is *not* synchronized with that user's home folder on your file servers.

The Mobile Account managed preference ![Mobile Accounts] lets you enable the mobile user account option on Mac OS X computers. More specifically, you can do the following (**Figure 13.72**):

- Enable the Mobile Account option
- Require administrator authentication to create the Mobile Account home folder on the local computer

The Mobile Account managed preference is available to user, workgroup, and computer list account types. You can't manage this preference just once, because it's either unmanaged or always managed. If there are conflicting account settings, all Mobile Account managed preferences follow the override rule.

✔ Tips

- The Mobile Account settings work only with Mac OS X 10.3 or later.
- Use a third-party tool, such as RsyncX, to synchronize home folders stored on the client computers with the home folders saved on your file servers. RsyncX is freely available at http://www.macosxlabs.org/rsyncx/.

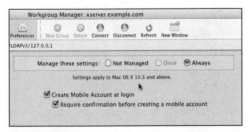

Figure 13.72 The Mobile Account managed preference lets you enable the mobile user account option on Mac OS X computers.

The Printing managed preference

Before you read this section, be sure you're familiar with the concepts discussed in the task "To configure managed preferences," earlier in this chapter. The figures in this section show a variety of managed preference configurations. These are only examples, and they should not be interpreted as the most appropriate configuration for your needs.

The Printing managed preference 🖨 Printing lets you define controlled access printers on Mac OS X computers. More specifically, in the Printer List tab, you can do the following (**Figure 13.73**):

◆ Specify the printers available in the Printer list

◆ Restrict the user from adding new printers to the local computer's Printer list

◆ Completely restrict access to directly connected local printers, or require administrator authentication

In the Access tab of the Printing managed preference, you can do the following (**Figure 13.74**):

◆ Specify the default printer

◆ Require administrator authentication on a per-printer basis

The Printing managed preference is available to user, workgroup, and computer list account types. You can't manage this preference just once, because it's either unmanaged or always managed. If there are conflicting account settings, the resulting Printer list is a combination of all the settings. Otherwise, all conflicting account settings for the Printing managed preferences follow the override rule.

✔ Tips

■ Workgroup Manager automatically finds printers in the Printer list on the computer it's running on.

■ When you're creating the Printer list, it's best to use Workgroup Manager from one of the clients you'll be managing.

■ Printer quotas are managed in each user's account settings. See Chapter 4, "User and Group Management," for more information.

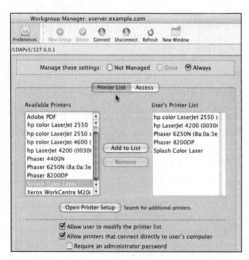

Figure 13.73 The Printing managed preference lets you define controlled access printers on Mac OS X computers.

Figure 13.74 The Access tab provides additional options.

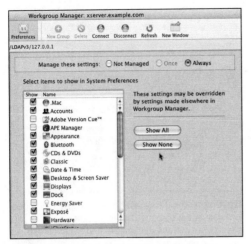

Figure 13.75 The System Preferences managed preference lets you restrict access to System Preferences panes on Mac OS X computers.

The System Preferences managed preference

Before you read this section, be sure you're familiar with the concepts discussed in the task "To configure managed preferences," earlier in this chapter. The figures in this section show a variety of managed preference configurations. These are only examples, and they should not be interpreted as the most appropriate configuration for your needs.

The System Preferences managed preference [System Preference] lets you restrict access to System Preferences panes on Mac OS X computers. More specifically, you can do the following (**Figure 13.75**):

◆ Specify a list of approved System Preferences panes

◆ Hide all other Preferences panes from the user

The System Preferences managed preference is available to user, workgroup, and computer list account types. You can't manage this preference just once, because it's either unmanaged or always managed. If there are conflicting account settings, the resulting System Preferences list is a combination of all the settings.

✔ Tip

■ If you restrict access to the System Preferences application using the Applications managed preference, then users won't be able to use any System Preference panes.

MANAGING PREFERENCES

The Universal Access managed preference

Before you read this section, be sure you're familiar with the concepts discussed in the task "To configure managed preferences," earlier in this chapter. The figures in this section show a variety of managed preference configurations. These are only examples, and they should not be interpreted as the most appropriate configuration for your needs.

The Universal Access managed preference Universal Access lets you define settings that help users who have physical limitations that impair their ability to use Mac OS X computers. More specifically, in the Seeing tab, you can do the following (**Figure 13.76**):

◆ Enable and specify screen zoom options that magnify the screen image

◆ Enable grayscale and inverted color options

In the Hearing tab of the Universal Access managed preference, you can do the following (**Figure 13.77**):

◆ Specify that the screen flash whenever the audible alert sounds

In the Keyboard tab of the Universal Access managed preference, you can do the following (**Figure 13.78**):

◆ Enable and specify Sticky Keys options that hold the modifier keys

◆ Enable and specify Slow Keys options that create a delay between when a key is pressed and when its input is selected

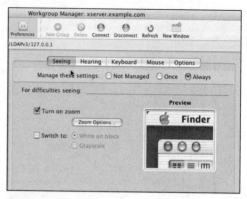

Figure 13.76 The Universal Access managed preference lets you define settings that help users who have physical limitations that impair their ability to use Mac OS X computers.

Figure 13.77 Additional options are available on the Hearing tab...

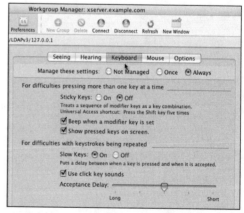

Figure 13.78 ...the Keyboard tab...

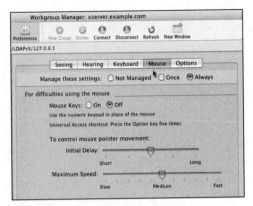

Figure 13.79 ...the Mouse tab...

Figure 13.80 ...and the Options tab.

In the Mouse tab of the Universal Access managed preference, you can do the following (**Figure 13.79**):

◆ Enable and specify Mouse Keys options that let you control the cursor using the number keypad

In the Options tab of the Universal Access managed preference, you can do the following (**Figure 13.80**):

◆ Enable the Universal Access keyboard shortcuts that let you toggle Universal Access features using various keyboard shortcuts

The Universal Access managed preference is available to user, workgroup, and computer list account types. In addition to leaving this preference unmanaged, you can manage it once or always. If there are conflicting account settings, all Universal Access managed preferences follow the override rule.

✔ Tip

■ Enabling Universal Access settings may drive a normal user completely insane if they aren't accustomed to them.

MANAGING PREFERENCES

Index

Safari BOOKS ONLINE
ENABLED

THIS BOOK IS SAFARI ENABLED

INCLUDES FREE 45-DAY ACCESS TO THE ONLINE EDITION

The Safari® Enabled icon on the cover of your favorite technology book means the book is available through Safari Bookshelf. When you buy this book, you get free access to the online edition for 45 days.

Safari Bookshelf is an electronic reference library that lets you easily search thousands of technical books, find code samples, download chapters, and access technical information whenever and wherever you need it.

TO GAIN 45-DAY SAFARI ENABLED ACCESS TO THIS BOOK:

● Go to **http://www.peachpit.com/safarienabled**

● Complete the brief registration form

● Enter the coupon code found in the front of this book before the Table of Contents

If you have difficulty registering on Safari Bookshelf or accessing the online edition, please e-mail customer-service@safaribooksonline.com.